COMPLETE

# AZ

## Media & Film Studies

HANDBOOK

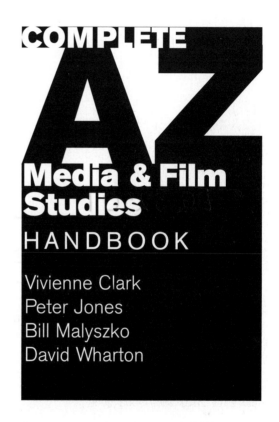

# COMPLETE
# AZ
## Media & Film
## Studies
# HANDBOOK

Vivienne Clark
Peter Jones
Bill Malyszko
David Wharton

A B C D E F G H I J K L M N O P Q R S T U V W X Y Z

# Hodder Arnold

A MEMBER OF THE HODDER HEADLINE GROUP

*British Library Cataloguing in Publication Data*
A catalogue record for this title is available from The British Library

ISBN 978 0 340 87265 9

First published 2007

Impression number 10 9 8 7 6 5 4 3 2 1
Year 2011 2010 2009 2008 2007

Cover photograph: Robert Daly/Stone/Getty Images.

Typeset by GreenGate Publishing Services, Tonbridge, Kent.
Printed and bound in Great Britain for Hodder Arnold, an imprint of Hodder Education and a member of the Hodder Headline Group, an Hachette Livre Company, 338 Euston Road, London NW1 3BH, by CPI Bath.

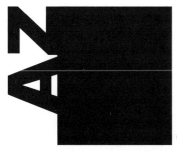

# CONTENTS

A
B
C
D
E
F
G
H
I
J
K
L
M
N
O
P
Q
R
S
T
U
V
W
X
Y
Z

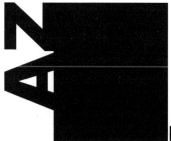

# FOREWORD

This dictionary, like any dictionary, is undoubtedly a labour of love on the part of its authors. To collect together every useful term and define each in turn for the media student is no mean feat. Their expertise has produced over 2000 entries spanning academic, technical and business terminology across the full range of media. The definitions are up to date and feature contemporary examples to aid explanation, as well as being fully grounded in historical context.

Coverage of the field is extensive and ranges across film, broadcasting, publishing, the internet and gaming, which is particularly welcome in such a volume. All the entries are elaborated with clear description and cross-referenced wherever possible to other terms. Key names are cited and key theories are explained succinctly. Technical terms are clearly defined as such, since the book is careful to differentiate between the language of academia and that of professionals. At the end of the book, summary lists are organised so that the reader preparing for exams has a structure for revising. There are useful tips for examinees, a select bibliography and a list of websites which should prove handy for students and teachers alike.

Examples cited are in most cases deliberately chosen so that the reader is drawn towards texts which are likely to be familiar, thus aiding digestion of what might sometimes appear to be quite obscure terms. That is the strength of this book – it makes the difficult simpler by making it clear and concrete wherever possible within the reader's frame of reference.

For any student at Advanced level, its equivalent, or beyond, this book is a handy addition to your media studies shelf. It will lead you to other texts, explain terms you come across in those texts and act as an excellent resource when it comes to revision.

I can confidently assert that this is the most comprehensive, most readable and indeed the best A to Z in this area which I have seen. A labour of love indeed by the authors for which readers can be grateful!

Pete Fraser, December 2006

# ACKNOWLEDGEMENTS

With grateful thanks to all our colleagues and students, past and present, for their enthusiasm, inspiration and creativity.

We should also like to thank our excellent team at Hodder Arnold for their guidance, support and efficiency, initially from Alexia Chan and latterly Anita Gaspar.

With apologies to our little Alexia for precious time missed together and with thanks to those who entertained her in our absence. Our thanks are also due to Tim Butterworth for his sterling help with the examination revision lists – Bill and Vivienne.

Cups of tea and other welcome distractions were provided by Bridget, Mr Twiggs and Spooky, for which much thanks – Peter.

Writing turns a person grumpy; writing definitions doubly so. Thanks, therefore, as ever, to Frances, Ben and Oscar for their tolerance – David.

## Publishing acknowledgements

The compilation of this A–Z list was a combination of our existing knowledge and additional research, from a wide variety of sources. We have listed the books in the Bibliography and the websites under A–Z of Websites and should like to acknowledge them all for their essential role in helping us to produce this book.

Vivienne Clark, Peter Jones, Bill Malyszko and David Wharton
November 2006

# HOW TO USE THIS BOOK

The *Complete A–Z Media & Film Studies Handbook* is an alphabetical reference book designed for ease of use which you can keep on your desk to check a term or concept quickly. Each entry begins with a one-sentence definition and most are followed by an example, where one would be helpful. You will also find lists in the Appendices that contain headings for most of the main topics you are likely to study – look up a topic, see the list of terms you can use, then find the definition in the main body of the book.

Our aim is to support your studies both in and outside the classroom and we hope that this reference book becomes your essential study companion, whether at A level or in the early years of degree-level study of film, media or cultural studies.

The greatest challenge of writing a book such as this is what to leave out. The subjects we now call film and media studies have evolved from many other subject disciplines, such as literary studies, linguistics, sociology, economics, politics, communication studies and psychology and, consequently, film and media studies could be described as multi-disciplinary subjects. Therefore there are many sources from which this list of terms could originate as these different subject disciplines are now a part of media and film studies. If we included them all, this book would be unwieldy and unhelpful, so we have chosen here to focus primarily on media-specific terms and key concepts and therefore some broader literary, cultural or business terms have been excluded.

Similarly, given the digitalisation of most contemporary media production processes, many terms that relate to ICT are now also used in film and media studies. However, we have not included some basic ICT terms (such as those referring to hardware components and specific software packages) as they can be sourced elsewhere or may already be part of our general knowledge. Also, neologisms such as 'vodcasting' or 'mobisode' may not survive and will have to prove their longevity before being included in subsequent editions (however, many of them are self-explanatory).

Some contextual terms from other subject disciplines have been left in where they are very closely associated with media analysis (for example '*chiaroscuro*', from fine art studies) because we felt that they would be useful in your studies.

It should also be stated here that the list that follows contains some terms used only *either* in media industries *or* in academic contexts. For example, film directors would never (unless they were lecturing on a film studies course), talk about '*mise en scène*' in US and UK film production, as it is a critical term used principally in academic and critical contexts (or in French film production). We have tried to include some basic up-to-date industry production process terms for all main media forms, but we considered that many are too specialist or not strictly necessary for you to know at this level of your studies.

You should bear in mind that there are some differences between production terms used in the USA and those current in the UK. Also, there are often several words for the same production process or feature, and different industries and companies have their own particular versions of terminology. However, we have tried to keep it simple for you, by using cross-references and giving alternative terminology where useful.

You will notice that we have not included film directors as individual entries, unless their name has become a term to describe a film style, technique or effect, such as 'Hitchcockian'. The omission is deliberate, as it is impossible to decide whom to include or exclude. Also, there are many quick and easy sources of information about film directors, actors and production personnel on the internet, so to reproduce them here would be superfluous. The same is true of other media personalities. We have, however, included references to specific individuals (whether directors, actors, producers or company owners) as examples within entries, where appropriate. The same is also true of most academics and theorists, who are included within the definition of a theoretical term rather than under separate entries.

We have provided some advice to help you improve your performance in exams. The book also contains lists of useful websites and books to support your studies, including independent research work.

Many of the terms and concepts listed have hotly debated definitions in academic circles; our aim has been to provide you with the most helpful definitions, with indications of areas of debate, rather than creating confusion and complication. We hope we have been successful.

The final list is the result of much discussion and debate and we are sure that it will generate just as much between your teachers! Our initial list was a much longer one, but we have tried to pick the terms most commonly used (or that could come up) in A level studies. We would be very pleased to receive any feedback about our selection of entries from both students and teachers, especially any essential terms that we have inadvertently omitted. If you are a media professional reading this book and would like to suggest a term or correction, please contact us via the publishers. We would love the next edition to be even better.

**For film and media teachers**: We hope that this book becomes a quick and useful reference source for you as well as for your students and we have provided lists of useful media education agencies in the Appendices, which we recommend.

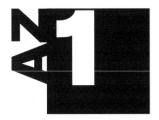

**3-D film:** a film process that creates the illusion of a three-dimensional reality on the two-dimensional surface of a cinema screen. It became one of the weapons used in the battle that cinema had with television for audiences in the 1950s in the USA. Examples of 3-D films include the *horror* film, *House of Wax* (André de Toth, USA, 1953) and Hitchcock's *thriller*, *Dial M for Murder* (USA, 1954). A 3-D film was produced as two films, shot with two cameras placed side by side, each to shoot a slightly different view. When watched with spectacles that have one green lens and one red lens, the effect of 3-D was produced. Many IMAX films are now produced in 3-D, the latest example being a 20-minute section of *Superman Returns* (Bryan Singer, USA, 2006).

**5 Ps (Price, Place, People, Promotion, Product):** when planning an advertising campaign, this is a succinct way of summarising the requirements. The essential elements the plan should contain are:

- Price – how much does the product cost?
- Place – where will it be advertised?
- People – who is involved in it?
- Promotion – how will the campaign raise awareness in order to sell the product?
- Product – how is the product featured/represented?

**5Ws and H:** useful for journalists writing a story, the essential questions to answer in any news article are:

- Who?
- What?
- When?
- Where?
- Why?
- How?

**8 mm/Super 8:** see *film*

**16 mm:** see *film*

**35 mm:** see *film*

**70 mm:** see *film*

**180-degree rule:** sometimes termed the '180-degree line', the '*line of action*' or simply 'the line', this refers to the basic film-making rule required by *continuity editing* in order to avoid confusing the audience. Objects/characters should always be shot so that their left/right relationship to each other (as if an imaginary line were drawn between them) is preserved if seen from one side of a 180-degree arc. Where this rule is not obeyed, either accidentally or deliberately (in order to disorientate the *spectator*), it is called 'crossing the line'.

**360-degree shot:** a camera shot that rotates around a character or an object that is at the centre of the audience's attention. This shot can be for an entire 360-degree revolve or for a considerable part of it, in order to place the character firmly in the middle of the *mise en scène*.

### What other subjects are you studying?

A–Zs cover a range of different subjects. See the inside back cover for a list of all the titles in the series and how to order.

**AA:** see *Advertising Association*

**A&R:** an abbreviation for 'artists and repertoire', A&R refers to someone in the music industry who scouts for new *talent* and coordinates the relationship between a record label and the artist(s).

**ABC:** see *Audit Bureau of Circulation*

**ABC1C2DE:** these grades are a way of categorising *audiences* by their socio-economic status in the UK, according to the occupation of the head of the household (presumed to be male). They were originally based on the Registrar General's six categories, indicated by Roman numerals (I–VI) but have been defined by the NRS (National Readership Survey) as above. While these have been replaced for government statistics and the Census, advertisers in particular still use these categories, as well as others, to identify and classify audiences. For example, the ABC1 male is the main target for many advertisers as he is presumed to have the highest level of disposable income, as well as the responsibility for major household purchases, therefore high-value products, such as financial services, cars and entertainment technology tend to be aimed at him. (See also *demographics, geodemographics.*)

**aberrant decoding:** also referred to as 'aberrant reading', this is the writer Umberto Eco's phrase for the process by which an audience member fails to recognise the meaning of a text as intended by its producer, and interprets it in a radically different way. The difference might be to do with the different values, experience or culture of the reader. (See also *active audience/reading, decoding, encoding, preferred meaning.*)

**aberrant reading:** see *aberrant decoding*

**above-the-line advertising:** conventional promotion of a product or service through newspaper and TV adverts, billboards etc. (See also *below-the-line advertising* and *through-the-line advertising.*)

**above-the-line costs:** the major expenses associated with the *budget* for any media production, mainly the salaries and expenses for the main creative and production personnel, such as for *rights* and permissions, writers, *producers, directors* and *talent*, as opposed to more minor, or *below-the-line costs.*

**absence:** a concept that is useful in *content analysis* and when analysing *representation* in media texts, namely that it is just as important to consider who or what is absent from a media text, as who or what is present. (See also *presence and absence.*)

**abstract film:** a type of *experimental film*, often linked to interpretation of music (and as such, abstract films could be considered as early examples of contemporary music videos) and following early twentieth-century developments in abstract painting and sculpture.

These features can be seen in the film work of Oskar Fischinger (1900–1960) and Len Lye (1901–1980), who often worked without a camera and scratched the surface of the emulsion on the film *stock* itself to create visual effects.

**Academy Awards:** awarded by *AMPAS* and more commonly known as 'the *Oscars*' (apparently after the resemblance of the award statuette to someone's Uncle Oscar). Created in *Hollywood* in 1929 to celebrate achievement in all areas of US domestic and international film production. They have become an important marketing tool: publicity attached to award winners has led to improved film sales or career profiles. However, some major names of the twentieth century were inexplicably overlooked, for example, Charlie Chaplin (1889–1977) and Alfred Hitchcock (1899–1980).

**Academy of Motion Picture Arts and Sciences (AMPAS):** created in 1927 to promote the professional image of all aspects of film-making in the USA. Today it is primarily involved in research and education and is responsible for the *Academy Awards*.

**Academy ratio:** sometimes referred to as 'Academy *aperture*' (the Academy being *AMPAS*), this is the ratio of 1:33, the full frame size used in 35 mm film production. (See also *aspect ratio*.)

**accelerated montage:** see *montage*

**accent:** (i) a difference in pronunciation of words due to regional or cultural differences. Received Pronunciation (RP), once the main accent used in broadcast media and still the preferred choice in some media contexts, has now largely been replaced by far more variety in accents in the media. The choice of a presenter may be based on their accent, as well as appearance, knowledge etc., in order to connect to the target *audience* or to create an image that is required by the programme makers. It is interesting to note that presenters of serious current affairs programmes tend have either RP or Scottish accents, whereas presenters of youth programmes tend to have so-called 'Estuary English' or Northern accents. There have been many studies researching the value of different accents in broadcasting and how different regions respond to presenters with regional or national accents. Much of this depends on long-standing stereotyping of people who come from particular regions or nations. (See also *dialect*.) (ii) can also be used to refer to an emphasis that might be used in the combination of music and moving images. A sound or instrument can provide dramatic emphasis to an action, movement or gesture. For example, Bernard Herrmann's legendary music *score* for *Psycho* (Alfred Hitchcock, USA, 1960) uses violins synchronised to the slashing movement of the killer's knife in the famous shower scene.

**access:** radio and television that is broadcast for non-commercial reasons. Known in the USA as *'public access'* broadcasting.

**accountability:** used in conjunction with debates about media freedom, responsibility, control and regulation, accountability refers to the degree to which the media are responsible for what they produce, and to whom. This is particularly relevant in news reporting in any medium, as it entails ethical considerations, such as legal, moral or social obligations to the truth.

**ACE:** see *American Cinema Editors*

**acquisitions:** a department in broadcasting that deals with acquiring the rights to air programmes purchased from other companies at home or abroad.

**action:** i) the recorded events that take place in front of a camera in a film or TV programme. ii) 'action!' is the call used to cue in actors in film and TV production after the camera starts rolling. iii) 'action' also refers to a broad film genre (also known in early *Hollywood* as an 'actioner'), which was characterised by its use of combat and conflict, usually conducted and edited at a fast pace.

**action/adventure films:** a combination (or hybrid) of action and adventure films, this is a film *category*, or *genre*, which now comprises a wide range of other film categories. It is characterised by the following *codes* and *conventions* (or *repertoire of elements*):

- *plots* involving an adventure into dangerous territory
- *archetypal characters* such as *hero*, *heroine*, villain
- exotic or exciting locations and *mise en scène*
- essential *props* such as weapons and vehicles
- set pieces where the hero is in *jeopardy*, featuring action such as chases and/or combat
- spectacular action *stunts*, *pyrotechnics*, *special effects*, frequently using *CGI*
- high *budgets*
- major *stars*
- *dominant ideologies* or *messages and values* that are usually unproblematic for a mainstream Western audience
- high-profile international *distribution* and *exhibition* strategies, whereby the film is advertised prominently and the theatrical run uses main cinemas in several territories at the same time.

It may also be referred to as '*action/spectacle* cinema'. This genre is now synonymous with *high-concept* film-making (and the films produced by Jerry Bruckheimer, in particular). It has developed from its earlier manifestations, with some variety, to accommodate mixed gender audiences, with the appearance of strong female characters, for example, *Lara Croft: Tomb Raider* (Simon West, USA/Ger/UK/Jap, 2001) and *Charlie's Angels* (Joseph McGinty Nichol, USA, 2000). Recently, there have been returns to earlier versions of the genre, with seafaring adventures such as *Master and Commander: the far side of the world* (Peter Weir, USA, 2003) and the *Pirates of the Caribbean* films (Gore Verbinski, USA, 2003, 2006 and 2007), based on the popular Disneyland ride, and *peplum* movies such as *Gladiator* (Ridley Scott, USA, 2000) and *Troy* (Wolfgang Petersen, UK/USA/Malta, 2004). It can also be seen in combination with other film genres to produce a generic hybrid or films in other genres which may contain elements of action/adventure, such as *science fiction*. For example, George Lucas' *Star Wars trilogy* (USA, 1977, 1980 and 1983) and its *prequels* (USA, 1999, 2002 and 2005) and *Spiderman 1, 2 & 3* (Sam Raimi, USA, 2002, 2004 and 2007). (See also *high-concept*.)

**action code:** an aspect of the semiological analysis of *texts*, also known as the *proairetic code*, as termed by writer Roland Barthes (1915–1980). Barthes identified five codes in the creation of a *narrative; action/proairetic*, semic (later called a semantic code), *enigma/hermeneutic*, *referential/cultural* and *symbolic codes*.

**actioner:** see *action*

**action/spectacle:** more recently, the *action/adventure* genre has been termed 'action/spectacle' (for example by José Arroyo, 1999), in order to link the on-screen content specifically with a distinct *spectator* response. In other words, the spectacle on screen is created expressly for its effects on the *spectator* (such as awe, wonder, excitement, thrills) over and above any involvement in the film's narrative or characters. Since the advent of the *multiplexes* in the 1980s, and the increasing use of *Dolby* and *THX* sound systems, together with increasingly impressive *CGI* effects, cinema audiences have enjoyed films which use these features for maximum effect. Their use can be said to have created conventions, which mean that we can define action/spectacle as a *genre*. (See also *high-concept*.)

**active audience/reading:** contrary to earlier thoughts about the power of the media to influence passive *consumers* (see also *hypodermic theory*), this is the theory that the *audience* is not passive but active in the process of making meaning.

**actor:** in film, television or theatre, this term is often now used interchangeably for both sexes.

**Actor's Studio:** established in New York in 1949, the actor, director and acting teacher, Lee Strasberg (1901–1982), became the Studio's artistic director and had a long career, influencing many past and current *Hollywood* 'greats', including Paul Newman, Marlon Brando, Robert De Niro and Al Pacino. His technique was known as 'the Method' or *method acting*, derived from the theories of Russian teacher Konstantin Stanislavski (1863–1938).

**actualisation:** see *Maslow's hierarchy of needs*

**actuality:** refers to film/TV footage and/or sound recorded of ordinary people and events, as they happen. It is therefore commonly associated with radio and TV documentary and current affairs programmes, for example, interviews or profiles of people in their own environment. The term can also be used to refer to footage that is recorded on location, rather than retrieved from a *library* or *archive*.

**AD:** see *assistant director*

**adaptation:** either literary, from a book, or from other sources, such as a previous film, TV programme, comic or cartoon, an adaptation is the revision of original story material for another purpose or medium. Literary sources are a very important, ready-made source of stories for an industry that desperately depends on new material, or the recycling of old, for its lifeblood, even more so as original writing is always a risk and texts that are familiar to an *audience* already have an advantage. This advantage can be lost, however, if the *producers* play too freely with the subject matter or characters from cherished stories, risking rejection at the box-office. Examples include J.K. Rowling's *Harry Potter* and the James Bond films, which are based on the novels of Ian Fleming.

**added value:** also referred to as 'additionality', this refers to the provision of extra features in any product, which can be considered as offering extra value for money for the consumer. Commonly used to describe the *special features* (or bonus features) on a *DVD*.

**additional photography:** additional scenes, or re-shoots, may sometimes be needed, in case of technical problems with some footage or poor reception to specific scenes from early audiences at test screenings. (See also *principal photography*.)

**address:** i) address to camera: in TV news reading, most of the communication is conducted by a direct address to camera. Also refers to the direct look of an actor at the camera. Originating from the world of the theatre, where the *audience* forms the *fourth wall* of a stage, the audience is rarely directly addressed, as this can break the *suspension of disbelief* that exists in theatre/film experiences. However, there are exceptions, for example, when a (usually) comic character turns to address the audience to share a joke or 'private' observation or a pantomime performer addresses the audience, to draw us in. Similarly, in a fictional TV programme or film, the camera is rarely addressed. Exceptions include when the intention is a comic one, where a joke is shared with the audience; or a dramatic, unexpected one that momentarily breaks the convention. For example, in *A Bout de Souffle* (Jean-Luc Godard, Fr, 1960) both Michel and Patrice look directly at the camera, which has the effect of drawing attention to the artifice of film *representation*. ii) *mode of address*.

**ad lib:** from the Latin ad libitum (at one's pleasure), this refers to an actor or TV/radio presenter departing from the written script at the time of the recording of a performance or presentation. For example, it might be necessary for a presenter/interviewer to ad lib in unscripted or unrehearsed situations, such as when speaking to members of the public or on *live* broadcasts, where there is extra time to *fill*.

**ADR (Automated Dialogue Recording/Replacement):** in film and TV, this is the recording, or *dubbing*, of dialogue in addition to that recorded on location, which is often recorded in front of a looped playback of the original scene, so that the sound and pictures can be synchronised. This may be necessary because the original sound recording is damaged, or when to have recorded it on location would have been impossible (for example, on board a ship in a storm sequence).

**ADSL (Asymmetrical Digital Subscriber Line):** a faster form of *internet* connection than via a modem.

**advance:** a payment made in advance of the provision of services. For example, a novelist will usually receive an advance on the *royalties* from the sale of their book before it is published, often paid at contract and delivery stage.

**adventure film** see *action/adventure films*

**advertisement:** the *promotion* of a product or service via a media product. An advertisement (more commonly 'ad' or 'advert') is the artefact itself (for example, a 30-second advert on TV, or a *billboard* poster).

**advertising:** the process of the promotion of products and the methods used to persuade us to buy products. Advertising is also the term for the career sector involved with creating promotion for clients in any media. Advertising media include: film, TV, print, web, direct mail, hoardings/*billboards*, Ad-Shels, LCD screens, buses and taxis. It has often been said that no one knows whether advertising actually works, but most major companies acknowledge that they cannot afford not to advertise, as the regular promotion of their product is essential in keeping their brand name in front of potential consumers.

**advertising agency:** a company that handles the advertising of products or services for a client. Examples of major UK/international advertising companies are: J Walter Thompson (JWT), Bartle, Bogle & Hegarty (BBH), WPP and M & C Saatchi.

**Advertising Association (AA):** a federation that represents the mutual interests of advertising organisations and trade bodies, and promotes the process of *self-regulation* (or voluntary regulation) in the industry.

**advertising revenue:** refers to the amount of income received by a media company that includes advertising as part of its service. So, for example, ITV earns advertising revenue from the sales of its advertising space between programmes (*commercial* breaks), which is its main source of income. Similarly, magazines and newspapers rely on advertising revenue rather than income generated by sales (charged as their *cover price*) in order to finance their production. One way of looking at *scheduling* for commercial TV and radio, for example, is that the function of the schedule is to deliver audiences to advertisers in order to maximise advertising revenue. One of the drawbacks of a *multi-channel environment* and increases in the number of magazine titles is that the amount of potential revenue rarely increases, but instead the competition for the same amount of revenue increases and so is split into smaller shares.

**Advertising Standards Authority (ASA):** organisation responsible for the *regulation* of all advertising. Produces a code of practice with which all advertisers have to comply. Members of the public can make complaints to the ASA if they find an advert offensive or misleading. The ASA's code states that advertisements should:

- not mislead
- not cause serious or widespread offence
- not cause harm
- be socially responsible
- have regard for the principles of fair competition.

(www.asa.org.uk/asa/adcampaign/rules.htm)

**advertorial:** technique whereby an *advertisement* in a magazine or newspaper is designed to look as if it is *editorial*. The aim is to give the piece a more convincing appearance than an obvious advert and so to influence people to read it carefully. Advertorials are often designed using a similar *typeface* and *layout* of *copy* and photos to the *next matter*, in order to blend in with the *house style*. However, because this approach could be misleading, there is a requirement that these pieces are labelled as advertising material, for example, with the words 'Advertising Feature' in a small but clear typeface at the top of the page.

**aesthetics:** the criteria used to measure the value, appeal or attractiveness of any visual design or artefact, in respect of use of colour, line, shape and composition etc.

**AFI:** see *American Film Institute*

**afilmic:** see *profilmic*

**AFM (assistant floor manager):** see *floor manager*

**agency:** an early concept in media education, this refers to the role that media *producers* play in controlling the production of meaning, linked to the key concepts of *audiences* and *institutions*, producers and audiences.

**agenda:** the hierarchical order of events and issues that are of prime interest in the media, often used in news and current affairs reporting.

**agenda-setting:** the media can be said to set the agenda for which topics are currently discussed in news and current affairs media, by deciding which issues are more worthy of coverage and debate than others at any one time. The media's dominance of agenda-setting means that it is very difficult for individuals and other social agencies to put their concerns onto the news agenda. (See also *gatekeeping*.)

**agent:** person responsible for representing *talent* in entertainment industries (e.g. a writer, artist, actor, musician, sportsperson) and arranging their work. In return, the agent receives a percentage of the client's fees. William Morris Agency (based in the USA) is the largest agency in the world. 'Swifty' Lazar (1907–1993) was a legendary *Hollywood* agent responsible for negotiating huge fees for his clients (such as Humphrey Bogart, who gave him his nickname). The role of agents today is a key factor in the escalating eight-figure salaries of many contemporary stars.

**agent of change:** when creating a *narrative structure* for a script, an agent of change is an essential type of character whose function is to have a dramatic effect on the *protagonist*, or *hero*. They provoke the protagonist into action/reaction that brings about a change in the plot. Sometimes referred to as *antagonist*.

**agony aunt/column:** see *problem page*

**AIDA:** a mnemonic sometimes used to remind *creative teams* of the important stages in the creation of any *advertisement*, that is to raise **A**wareness of a product and so create **I**nterest in it, then stimulate the potential customer's **D**esire for this product, which turns into **A**ction (when the customer buys the product). (See also *DRIP*.)

**air:** (i) the space available for broadcast media to be transmitted, relating to the air through which TV and radio waves travel in order to be transmitted. The verb, 'to air' is also used in the same way as 'to broadcast'. **air date**: the date on which a broadcast media programme is 'aired' or transmitted; **air play**: when music tracks are played on the radio, they receive air play, the frequency of air play of specific artists or tracks tends to depend on the *playlist* for a specific programme and its target *audience*; **air time**: what time in the *schedule* a programme is 'aired', or broadcast/transmitted; **dead air**: vacant space on radio or TV where no sound or images are broadcast, usually as a result of human error or technical fault. Dead air is usually quickly interrupted by an emergency transmission of a continuity announcement and (if on TV) an image or alternative footage. (See also *on air; off-air*.) (ii) **AIR** see *average issue readership*

**album:** in recorded music, a collection of songs or instrumental tracks, either on vinyl or CD.

**alienation:** (i) a concept from the writing of Karl Marx, in which the methods of mass production stole any part in the control of their own working life from workers, the term has also been used in relation to contemporary society, wherein the creation of a mass culture may threaten to deny and stifle individual creativity and difference. It has also been used to discuss the feelings experienced by those affected by the marginalisation of different social groups within a dominant culture, which may encourage extremism. (ii) **alienation effect** with reference to *acting*. (See also *Brechtian*.)

**allegory:** a literary technique which performs a function in any form of art or media, whereby the characters and events are used to illustrate a meaning that operates at a deeper level in the text, usually with the aim of educating or improving the reader/*spectator*. For example, the deeper meaning might be a political, moral or spiritual one. A well-known example from children's literature is C S Lewis' 1950 novel from the *Chronicles of Narnia*, *The Lion the Witch and the Wardrobe* (film version 2005, directed by Andrew Adamson, USA) in which the lion, Aslan, is an allegorical figure representing Jesus Christ, who, according to *The Bible*, dies in order to save others and who is resurrected from the dead. The film *Casablanca* (Michael Curtiz, USA, 1942) has been interpreted as a political allegory for the relationship between the USA and the Allies in the Second World War, as exemplified by the relationship between the US *anti-hero* Rick Blaine (Humphrey Bogart) and the French Chief of Police, Capt. Renault (Claude Rains) in a Casablanca occupied by Nazis. More recently, *Star Wars Episode III: Revenge of the Sith* (George Lucas, USA, 2005) has been discussed as a political allegory of US foreign policy in respect of Iraq; and *V for Vendetta* (James McTeigue, UK/USA/Ger, 2005) as an allegory on the nature of terrorism.

**'A' list:** a hierarchical list of *stars*, *producers*, *directors* and *celebrities* constructed by media industries. The 'A' list are those who are in the first division or top rank of fame, because of their international profile. Their place is not necessarily secure, however, as there are 'B', 'C' and 'D' lists, and people may be promoted and demoted (according to their levels of success, and/or their notoriety).

**alternative:** with reference to mainstream (or *dominant*) culture and the associated *ideology*, alternative culture is regarded as being opposite to the mainstream, with different ideas, values and beliefs. For example, mainstream (or dominant) ideology supports traditional ideas of sexuality, marriage and raising a family, whereas there are different, or alternative, ways of living and believing that challenge these traditional ideas. Over time, some aspects of dominant ideology can enter the mainstream. (For example, ecological concerns and recycling were once seen as unusual and pursued only by what the media tended to stereotype as zealots, whereas now, most local councils have a recycling programme and the need to take ecological issues seriously is on the international agenda in the context of global warming.) 'Alternative' can also refer to different means of media production, often associated with notions of *independence*, whereby a media product might be produced under different conditions, for example, self-publication such as for *fanzines*, or *community broadcasting*.

**AM:** amplitude modulation, an alternative band to *FM* for radio transmission.

**ambience:** an atmosphere or mood, often created by lighting or music and other sounds. For example, soft lighting and slow music are clichéd ways of creating a romantic ambience (in a film/TV text, or in a restaurant or sitting room); and traffic, aeroplanes or birdsong create an outdoor ambience in external film/sound recording. Ambience is important in any fiction or non-fiction media text to aid *suspension of disbelief*.

**ambient lighting:** the natural light in any scene or setting, which can either be recorded directly, also known as *available light*, or recreated using *lighting*.

**ambient music/noise/sound:** (i) *ambient music* describes a kind of background music (usually inane and characterless), often heard in US supermarkets (also known as 'elevator music'), which covers the possibility of embarrassed silences in public spaces. The term has also been used subsequently to describe a genre of contemporary instrumental music, related to 'trance'. (ii) **ambient noise or sound** is that which is natural to a setting. It can be recorded directly, at the same time as the action, or recreated afterwards, by separate recording of sound to be mixed in later. The separate recording is also known as the *buzz track* or *wild sound*/track. (See also *foley artist*.)

**American Cinema Editors (ACE):** the honorary organisation for US film and television editors founded in 1950, these initials can sometimes be seen after their names in the *credits*. Its existence highlights the importance of editors in the creative production of film-making, where they are required to collaborate very closely with the film director. Very few film directors have been allowed to edit their own work, as the process requires a particular set of creative and technical skills, as well as objectivity. For example, Thelma Schoonmacher-Powell has made a significant input to the films of Martin Scorsese as his regular editor and has so far received five Eddies (the ACE's equivalent of the *Oscar*), as well as many other awards. (See also film *editor*.)

**'American Dream', the:** a powerful myth underlying much American popular culture and therefore present in US literature, film and TV. The 'American Dream' comprises a set of ideas (originating from the US constitution) about equality of opportunity and the promise of prosperity based on merit (hence the US is a meritocracy) as opposed to status and inherited wealth. It is also responsible for the appeal of America for people from other countries, who, even now, see America as the 'land of opportunity'. Many US films of the late twentieth-century deal with the harsh realities which undermine this myth, e.g. the effects of wars and acute social problems on an increasingly large and diverse population.

**American Film Institute (AFI):** founded in 1967, the AFI is the US equivalent of the *British Film Institute* (BFI), namely, as a non-profit government-sponsored organisation, it works to foster knowledge and enjoyment of film and television, maintains a national film *archive* and produces education resources.

**American Society of Cinematographers (ASC):** honorary society for international *cinematographers* (or *DOPs/DPs*) who are granted the right to use these initials after their name. For example, the Oscar-winning cinematographers, Conrad L Hall (with Sam Mendes on *American Beauty*, 1999, and *Road to Perdition*, 2002 ) and Jack Cardiff (with Michael Powell and Emeric Pressburger on *Black Narcissus*, 1947, and *The Red Shoes*, 1948).

**American widescreen:** see *widescreen*

**'A' movie:** when cinema was the principal form of mass screen entertainment (from the 1930s to the 1950s), the 'A' movie was the main feature film (which usually had the most famous stars and biggest production budgets) in a *double-bill* programme which commonly also included a *newsreel* and a *'B' movie.*

**AMPAS:** see *Academy of Motion Picture Arts and Sciences*

**analogue:** the precursor to *digital* communication processes, whereby pictures and/or sound (for TV and radio) are transmitted by a *signal* that uses radio waves from *terrestrial* transmitters. This is a less stable signal than digital transmission, as radio waves can be affected by all manner of interference, for example atmospheric conditions or the presence of competing radio waves. In addition, the available 'slots' in the signal *spectrum* have been increasingly used up by the proliferation of more TV and radio stations, to the extent that more 'space' is needed to accommodate a *multi-channel environment.* In the UK, BBC's One and Two, ITV1, C4 and Five are (as at 2007) analogue TV channels (but also *simulcast* in digital for the increasing numbers of digital TV *subscribers*), whereas BBC's Three and Four are digital only.

**analogue switch-off:** as set out in the Broadcasting Act 2003, the regulator Ofcom is responsible for the regionally-phased discontinuation of broadcast transmission by analogue services (also known as the 'digital switch-over' or 'DSO'), which is planned to be completed by 2012.

**anamorphic lens:** used to shoot certain *widescreen* ratios. These lenses 'squeeze' the picture horizontally on to a standard 3:4 frame, and a special lens is required on the projector to 'unsqueeze' the image.

**anchor:** i) 'news anchor' is the term used in the USA for a main TV news presenter based in the studio, because of their role of holding a news programme together. The UK has used the terms newscaster or newsreader. ii) in *semiology*, an anchor is usually a word or sentence (but it could also be another image), such as in a caption for a photograph, that ties down the meaning of an otherwise ambiguous (or *polysemic*, having more than one meaning) image.

**anchorage:** in *semiology*, this is the process by which the meaning of a *sign*, or an image, is clarified, or tied down, by the addition of an *anchor* (either another image or words). For example, the reader can be led to the *preferred meaning* of an advertisement by the anchorage provided by words to the visuals.

**ancillary market/rights:** see *back end*

**angle:** (i) focus or slant used as an approach to a news story or documentary. For example, producers commonly talk of using the *human interest* angle to appeal to readers/viewers. (ii) camera angle, see *cinematography*

**animation:** the bringing to life of still images/drawings, puppets and models (and in the case of some *art film*, drawings on celluloid itself) which are filmed in a sequence to produce the illusion of movement (also known as cartoons). Animation in film has a long history (starting with Méliès, through Disney, to Pixar). Aardman is an important UK animation company, responsible for the film characters Wallace and Gromit; the hit film, *Chicken Run* (Peter Lord and Nick Park, UK, 2000); the Oscar-winning *Wallace and Gromit: The Curse of the Were Rabbit* (Steve Box and Nick Park, UK, 2005) and, with DreamWorks Animation, their first computer-animated feature, *Flushed Away* (David Bowers and Sam Fell, UK/USA, 2006). The animated feature film has usually been associated with children's films or with art film directors, such as the Czech film maker, Jan Svankmajer. However, the adult animation feature has seen a surge in recent years with the spectacular international critical success of *Spirited Away* (Hiyao Miyazaki, Jap, 2001) and *Belleville Rendezvous* (Sylvain Chomet, Fr/Can/Bel/UK, 2002). US director Tim Burton followed up his early hit, *The Nightmare Before Christmas* (USA, 1993) with *Corpse Bride* (USA/UK, 2005). *Team America: World Police* (Trey Parker, USA, 2004) is a controversial puppet animation feature film, which stars a team of puppets, heavily influenced in style (if not script) by Gerry Anderson's *Thunderbirds* puppet creations.

**animatic:** a very basic animation of single drawn/photo frames from a *storyboard*, sometimes used by creative teams in advertising in order to pitch their idea for a TV/film advertisement to their client, before full production.

**animatronics:** the use of technology/engineering to animate models (of humans, animals, monsters and aliens etc.) in film and TV production. Jim Henson's Creature Shop is the most famous company supplying this technique, as well as *prosthetics* and other *special effects*. Examples include the animals in *Babe* (Chris Noonan, Aus/USA, 1995) and in *Cats and Dogs* (Lawrence Guterman, USA, 2001). The technique is largely being overtaken by the arguably superior capabilities of *CGI*. One advantage that animatronics have is that they use 3-D objects and models, whereas CGI depends on the effect of recreating 3-D, and in some circumstances (for example, in a close-up) animatronics might be more convincing.

**anime:** short for *animation*, 'anime' is a term used in Japan for all kinds of animated film. It is also used outside Japan to identify a particular style of figure drawing in Japanese animation, or other animation influenced by this Japanese style. Some Japanese anime is influenced by Japanese *manga* comics. The most high profile creator of anime films recognised outside Japan is Hayao Miyazaki, who wrote and directed the feature, *Spirited Away* (Jap, 2001). The film was produced through his Studio Ghibli and won an Oscar for Best Animated Feature in 2003.

**antagonist:** usually the villain (of either *gender*), who is in opposition to the *hero*, otherwise known as the *protagonist*. The antagonist has an essential function in a *narrative* as his or her presence contributes to *conflict*.

**anthropomorphism:** where an animal or a usually inanimate object (such as a teapot or a car) is attributed with human physical features (and often human feelings) in order to engage and involve the *spectator*. This technique is commonly used in all types of *animation*, including feature-length films produced by Disney and Pixar.

**anti-hero:** a character who has flaws or who transgresses (for example by committing an unlawful act), an anti-hero is usually an ordinary man (as opposed to a 'professional' *hero*, such as a soldier) who is forced by circumstances to 'do the right thing'.

**anti-realism:** a rarely used mode of representation, this is the opposite of *realism* (that is, the projection of a shared and objective reality). Artists and film makers who were associated with *Surrealism* worked in anti-realist modes, for example by combining images and motifs that audiences do not expect to see juxtaposed in everyday life.

**anti-trust legislation:** (a US legal term; Europe uses 'competition law') this refers to any anti-competitive commercial situation where one company, or a collection of companies, dominate the market by holding a *monopoly* (or *duopoly* or *oligopoly*). Such a situation is bad for consumers, as competition tends to keep prices competitive, whereas any domination of a specific market means that the company can fix its own pricing. There have been several key moments where government has been asked to rule on this kind of situation and so creates anti-trust legislation, which means that such market dominance is illegal. In 1948, the outcome of the *Paramount Case* resulted in the protection of competition in the film and cinema industries in the USA. More recently, it applied to the computer industry in relation to Microsoft's use of software bundling.

**AOL Time Warner:** see *Time Warner*

**aperture:** an aperture is an adjustable opening in a camera lens which lets through light to expose *film* or capture an image digitally. If the light on the subject is bright, only a small aperture is needed to admit light; if it is dark, the aperture needs to be more open to allow more light in.

**Apple Computer Inc:** major company formed in 1976 in the USA. Apple has historically been the main rival to Bill Gates' Microsoft, but, since the late 1990s, Apple has pursued a high-profile marketing campaign of designer-led hardware, such as the various models of Mac; peripherals, such as the ubiquitous iPod; and, with iTunes, music software.

**arc:** (i) *ARC* – the Aspect Ratio Converter, which, in TV, converts pictures from one *aspect ratio* to another, for example from 4:3 to 16:9, in which case the *footage* is 'arc-ed'. (ii) a semi-circular upward curve that usually has a high point in the middle, this term is also used to discuss the trajectory of a *character*.

**archetype:** different from *stereotype*, this is the first version of a character in fiction, on which all others are based (for example the hero or villain) as in 'Errol Flynn was associated mainly with playing the role of an archetypal action *hero*.'

**archive:** like a *library*, an archive is responsible for the cataloguing and storage of all artefacts and data from TV/radio, newspapers, magazines, music, films etc. for future reference. A computer also archives its data.

**archive footage:** film or TV footage, especially of news events, is stored and catalogued (or archived) for further use in subsequent programmes, such as *documentaries* and *archive programmes.*

**archive programme:** a TV format that has grown in the past few years, especially on Channel 4 (for example, *The Top 50 Best Horror Films*). It intersperses clips from film and TV with interviews from celebrities and TV pundits who discuss the merits of the items on the list. Due to its nostalgia factor, the format is popular with audiences as an easy viewing experience. It is also relatively cheap to produce, as the main content of the programme is the use of brief clips from existing material; the interviews are *talking heads*, and the programmes can often occupy as much as three hours of evening viewing. The commercial benefits of the format are clear: high *audience* ratings attract potential advertisers and revenue.

**arc light:** a powerful electric lamp used in film and TV production.

**Aristotelian:** relating to the theories of the Greek philosopher Aristotle (384–322 BCE), a key figure in Western philosophy. His work on drama, *Poetics*, is one of the earliest forms of literary criticism. In it, he analyses dramatic structure, character motivation and the qualities of tragedies. Many of his ideas were subsequently developed by Shakespeare and others. They continue to be addressed today and are transferable to the analysis of cinematic narratives, especially with reference to the emotional effects of tragedy. (See also *catharsis*.)

**Arriflex**: a German brand (made by the company Arnold and Richter) of relatively lightweight and compact film camera, popular with French *new wave* film directors, *cinéma vérité* and *direct cinema*. This camera became associated with *documentary* film production because of its relative unobtrusiveness. The company still manufactures cameras today, with the term 'Arri' referring to their 16 mm film camera.

**art cinema/film:** is a kind of film-making that is not primarily concerned with financial profit. It tends to be more concerned with experimentation with ideas and the medium of film (similar to the ways in which an artist experiments with a variety of media), or as a personal statement by the film maker. The line between art and film can be blurred. Many artists, including Salvador Dali (1904–1989), Andy Warhol (1928–87), Damian Hirst (1965–) and Bill Viola (1951–), have experimented with film-making as an art form. The films of Derek Jarman are a good example of art cinema, notably, *Blue* (UK, 1993) and *Caravaggio* (UK, 1986).

**art department:** see *art director, production designer*

**art director:** known as *production designer* in film and TV, this is also a role in newspaper and magazine publishing. An art director determines the overall 'look' of a media product and is responsible for all aspects of design and realisation, from set design for films/TV programmes, to typeface and use of colour and photography for magazines and newspapers. The art director's job is to liaise with other key personnel such as the *director*, *producer*, *costume designer* and *set* construction or, in print media, *picture editors* and *graphic designers*. For example, Dean Tavoularis is an eminent production designer, responsible for such films as Coppola's *Godfather* trilogy (USA, 1972, 1974 and 1990).

**art editor:** person responsible for the selection and co-ordination of all artwork (original and sourced) for inclusion in a magazine or newspaper.

**art-house cinema:** an independent or small chain of cinemas that specialises in a varied film programme, usually, but not exclusively, with a bias towards non-commercial, *independent* or non-mainstream/*Hollywood* films. Currently, Screen and Oasis both own mini-chains of small, regional art-house cinemas in the UK. 'Art-house cinema' is also the collective term for art-house films. The term 'art-house film' can be used to identify films produced with this kind of market in mind (for example, the films of contemporary British directors such as Lynne Ramsay and Pawel Pawlikowski).

**artwork:** all forms of visual material to be included in a magazine or newspaper, such as photographs and graphics.

**artificial light:** the opposite of *available light*, this refers to any additional source(s) of light used in film and TV production, to produce optical clarity or specific lighting effects, such as to reproduce a time of day, kind of weather or mood (for example, soft lighting for a romantic scene; hard, blue lighting for an urban feel; red lighting for anger or violence or directional lighting for *horror* or crime thrillers).

**ASA (American Standard Association):** the speed of film *stock* used for *cinematography* and still photography, measured by the way in which film stock reacts to light. For example, lower-speed *film* (e.g. 50) produces less *grain* and more detail, requiring lots of light. Fast-speed film (200 or above) needs less light and so is useful for low lighting conditions and produces a grainy effect. Cinematographers/photographers can manipulate the look of a film/photograph by their choice of *film speed*, as well as in the developing stage.

**ASA:** see *Advertising Standards Authority*

**ASC:** see *American Society of Cinematographers*

**aspect ratio:** the shape and size of a screen, specifically the ratio of height to width of the dimensions of a TV screen or a projected film. For example:

- Standard TV ratio: 4:3 (width: 4 is longer than the height: 3)
- *Widescreen* TV ratio: 16:9 (i.e. for every 16 cm of screen width there are 9 cm of screen height)

Today, much of US and UK TV is shot in widescreen ratio.

**assemble editing:** in *analogue* video editing, a method where pictures and sounds are arranged in linear sequence along with the accompanying control track.

**assistant cameraman/operator:** see *camera operator*

**assistant director (AD):** also known as 'first assistant *director*' or 'first assistant', this person tends to have a more operational responsibility than creative input by arranging the logistics of a day's shoot. For large productions there may also be second and third assistant directors.

**assistant producer:** see *producer*

**associate producer:** see *producer*

**association:** the *cognitive* process by which we make meaning by connecting an idea, image or sound to a meaning, as in the processes of *signification* or *connotation*. So, when we see a red heart-shape we instantly link it with the concept of romantic love and its commercial manifestation, Valentine's Day. Some associations are shared and some are unique. This is because of the ways in which our individual brains and memories (each with their unique contextual programming) create connections between objects and so make different meanings. These cognitive processes of association are key ways in which we make sense of media products. Media producers use the associations we have with colours, shapes, sounds, words and so on to communicate with us.

**Asymmetrical Digital Subscriber Line (ADSL):** see *ADSL*

**asynchronous sound:** see *synchronous sound*

**atmos:** short for 'atmospherics', this refers to the recording of atmospheric sound (such as traffic, birdsong, background chatter etc.) on *location* in order to reproduce a realistic soundscape in film/TV/radio post-production or to cover continuity issues in editing. Sometimes called *buzz track* or *wild track*. (See also *ambient sound*.)

**audience:** the people who consume a media product. In film studies, there is a useful additional term, *spectator*, which refers to the individual person watching a film. Audience research and studies (for example by David Morley, Ien Eng and David Gauntlett) have long been an important aspect of media study and this key concept is often studied in conjunction with *institutions* and *industries* (also known as the concept of *producers*). Key related concepts are constituency, *mass*, *niche*, *mainstream* and *alternative*. For example, the main *target audience* for mainstream film products (especially *Hollywood* movies) is people aged 18–24. This age group remains an especially attractive market as it has a high disposable income and more free time. Therefore they are likely to go to the cinema more frequently and spend money in the food and drink concessions (from which film exhibitors make enormous profits that far exceed those generated by cinema seat tickets). This was especially so in the 1980s, when mainstream *Hollywood* focused mostly on male-oriented action films. However, through the 1990s to the present day, there has been significant growth in other cinema markets, namely for families and older adults. Also, the growth of *multiplex* cinemas has encouraged these more diverse audiences to go to the cinema. New media products and facilities, such as video games and web-based services (such as blogs and photo-sharing) offer opportunities to redefine this important key concept, as clearly the traditional top-down relationship between institution, text and audience is challenged.

**audience appreciation index:** used in broadcasting, this measures not how many people consume a particular product but what they think of it and the level of their appreciation. For example, a programme might be seen or heard by a large number of people, but might score a low audience appreciation index, which means that it was not as effective as hoped.

**audience expectations:** what the audience expects (in terms of emotions or information) from a particular media product, dependent on its genre. (See also *violation of expectation*.)

**audience fragmentation:** a consequence of a multi-channel broadcasting environment. As the number of channels for media output multiplies (and we can now elect to consume products at different times – see *scheduling* – via different media), the mass audience for any product fragments into smaller sections and (i) therefore the income derived from any one source is reduced. (ii) likewise, the audience for any broadcast is also fragmented. This reduces the number of people available to watch/listen to a programme at the same time and therefore the notion of a national role for broadcasting, whereby 'the nation' tunes in to watch/listen to something at the same time, is largely obsolete.

**audience measurement:** the number of people who are an audience/market for a particular media product. Several organisations deal with types of audience measurement, for example *BARB* and *NRS*.

**audience needs:** see *uses and gratifications theory/model*

**audience picture** refers to a very popular (or 'crowd-pleasing') film, which has a strong following.

**audience profiling:** see *consumer profile*

**audience research:** see *market research*

**audiences and institutions:** see *producers and audiences studies*

**audience share:** also known as *market share*, this is the percentage of the total available audience receiving a media product.

**audio:** any form of sound.

**audio clip/extract:** a short section taken from a longer sound recording, often used in radio, for promotional purposes, such as in a trailer for a forthcoming radio programme.

**audio description:** the description by recorded voice of any visual elements of a TV programme/film (for example, many DVDs have this facility as well as *subtitles*) for the benefit of people whose sight is impaired.

**audio mixer:** equipment, usually referred to as a mixer or mixing desk soundboard or console, that records different sound sources (instruments, voices, sound effects etc) onto any number of separate tracks. The tracks are subsequently combined ('mixed') using different levels and effects to produce a final *soundtrack*, either for a popular music track or for a film/TV/radio soundtrack.

**audio recording:** the recording and reproduction of sound.

**Audit Bureau of Circulation (ABC):** a UK organisation created (in 1931) to verify and make available the *circulation* figures for magazines and newspapers, which are of special interest to advertisers and *publishers*. The main circulation figures are also available to the public for research.

**auteur:** the French term for 'author', according to auteur theory, an auteur is a film maker with a distinct style or set of concerns that are evident from studying their films as a whole. This is a hotly contested debate in film studies as the opposite viewpoint is that, due to the collaborative nature of film-making, no one can be considered to be the 'author' of the text. (See also *politique des auteurs*.)

**auteurism:** see *politique des auteurs*

**auteur policy:** see *politique des auteurs*

**auteur theory:** see *politique des auteurs*

**author; authorship:** the person (or persons) responsible for the writing of a fictional text.

**Autocue:** the brand name for a TV prompting service; a computer with a screen built into a studio camera which displays a scrolling script (used for all kinds of TV presentation) from which a presenter reads. There are other brand names, such as Autoscript and Teleprompter but this term is now synonymous with the general process.

**Automated Dialogue Recording/Replacement (ADR):** see *ADR*

**available light:** literally, the light that is naturally available, without artificial help, on a particular location. It may be used in documentary filming or where a strong degree of *realism* is required. *Digital* film cameras have made the use of available light more effective.

**avant garde:** experimental, innovative, unconventional or challenging works of art, including film, which are considered to be ahead of their time, often using revolutionary formal features or promoting an ideology that challenges that used in *mainstream* art. Film directors associated with *avant garde* cinema include Luis Buñuel and Jean-Luc Godard.

**avatar:** a movable 3-D virtual character, which a gameplayer can assume as a substitute for her/his own, in order to participate in a *video game* or any other virtual environment.

**average issue readership (AIR):** the number of people who read an edition of a newspaper or magazine during the period in which is was issued, sometimes referred to as the 'readership'. The AIR figure is different from the smaller *circulation figure* (which is concerned with how many copies of a magazine or newspaper are printed and distributed) in that a single edition of one copy could be read by more than one person (for example, in libraries and cafes, or by several family members). The AIR figure is useful to companies when selling advertising space as evidence of the potential size of the market.

**avid:** a film *fan*(atic) or enthusiast who closely follows film news and collects all manner of film memorabilia (such as models, posters, books). Often associated with fans of a particular genre, such as *horror*, or of a particular film, such as *The Lord of The Rings* (Peter Jackson, NZ/US, 2001, 2002 and 2003) and the *Star Wars* series (George Lucas, US, 1999, 2002, 2005). Most avids go to the cinema frequently.

**Do you know we also have A–Zs for:**

- **ICT & Computing**
- **Psychology**
- **Sociology**
- **Travel & Leisure?**

Ask for them in your local bookshop or see the inside back cover for ordering details.

**baby legs:** a camera *tripod* with short legs, often used for very low angle, or *worm's eye*, shots.

**back catalogue:** the entire collection of a company or label's past production (of music, film, TV, radio and so on). For some organisations, for example, the *BBC*, it is a considerable financial asset. Income can be generated from releasing programmes as *repeats*, on DVD or in international sales.

**back end:** also known as points and ancillary rights, 'back end' is the term for the money from film *distribution* and *exhibition*. Film *stars* often get back-end points (a percentage of the box-office) as part of their deal. For example, Jack Nicholson made millions of dollars from his ancillary rights to *Batman* (Tim Burton, USA, 1988), although his fee from the film itself was low. The film was a considerable risk for Warner Bros as Burton was a relatively inexperienced director at that time. Nicholson's back-end deal meant he would earn money from every subsequent Batman film that Warner Bros produced. Alec Guinness's deal on *Star Wars* (George Lucas, 1977), in which he played the Jedi master, Ben Obi-Wan Kenobi, also proved lucrative.

**background:** contextual information on people, places and events, which a journalist/reporter researches when preparing a story or interviewing someone.

**background artist:** an artist (also referred to as a *matte*, or scenic, artist) who prepares any background artwork, for example of buildings or landscape. In the pre-digital era the artwork was painted on glass, and could be merged with the live action in a film to create a convincing sense of location.

**back lighting:** when a person or object is lit from behind, either by artificial light or by the sun. This produces a silhouette of the person/object and is useful in creating a sense of suspense or mystery.

**back lot:** *Hollywood* term for the large area behind a film studio that was used to construct and store large open-air sets. In some cases, standard, permanent sets were constructed (for example, for street scenes in Westerns or gangster films), which could be adapted and dressed for different films.

**back projection:** also known as rear projection, a special effect for film/TV used regularly from the 1930s to the 1970s (until *blue/green screen* technology took over) which placed live action on a set in front of a projected background film, in order to give the sense that the events are happening on location. This was commonly used to shoot dialogue inside a car, with a projection of a film of a moving road behind the car. Alfred Hitchcock regularly used back projection in his films (for example in *Vertigo*, USA, 1958 and *North by Northwest*, USA, 1959). It was also used when using a real location or stunt (such as model monsters

**19**

moving in front of a landscape or cityscape; or when combining models with live actors (as in Cooper and Schoedsack's *King Kong*, USA, 1933) would be especially difficult or expensive to recreate. However, it can look obvious and amateur today, when advances in camera and sound recording make it possible to film inside a car, or a complex backdrop can now be recreated using *CGI*.

**backstory:** used by writers to describe the events that occurred before the plot of a film/TV/radio programme. It often helps actors to know the backstory in order to understand their character's motivation.

**BAFTA:** see *British Academy of Film and Television Arts*

**bagging:** this refers to the common practice of wrapping a newspaper or magazine in a plastic covering in order to enclose supplements or free gifts, such as handbags, books or DVDs, safely.

**balance:** the reporting of facts on both/all sides of a story, in order to produce an unbiased view of a person or an event: balance is the opposite of *bias*.

**band/bandwidth:** see *spectrum*

**bankability:** term used in film production and distribution, an actor/*star*'s bankability is the degree to which they will attract an *audience* and create a profit for the film's *producer*.

**banner advert:** an advert on a website.

**banner headline:** a *headline* in a newspaper that goes right across the width and top of a page.

**BARB:** see *Broadcasters Audience Research Board*

**bar counting:** often used in the *gallery* during TV production, whereby a *production assistant* counts the beats and bars present in any music used in order to help the *camera operators* time their shots and the *director* and vision mixer edit between cameras in time to the music.

**barn doors:** the four, hinged metal flaps that can adjust the height/breadth of the beam, or spill, produced by an electric light used in theatre, film and TV production.

**Barthes, Roland:** see *connotation, narrative, poststructuralism*

**basic needs:** see *Maslow's hierarchy of needs*

**BBC:** see *British Broadcasting Corporation*

**BBFC:** see *British Board of Film Classification*

**beat:** (i) a feature of writing dialogue for the screen. A *script writer* usually tries to create a rhythm by their use of lines and silences (both known as beats, in much the same way as music has a beat), which can be explored by the director and actors. (ii) the scriptwriting guru Robert McKee refers to the beat as being 'a relationship between action and reaction'.

**behind-the-scenes:** any work that goes on off-camera or behind the scenes of an entertainment or media production. DVDs frequently now have a *special feature* which is a brief film showing what was happening while the film/programme was being made. This is an important part of many film and TV productions as it provides *added value* when the film is produced on DVD and it can also be used in promotional activities as a kind of *trailer*.

**below-the-line advertising:** promotion of a product or service through techniques such as *direct mail*, street representatives and e-mail. The latter is often referred to as *spam*. (See also *above-the-line advertising* and *through-the-line advertising*.)

**below-the-line costs:** the main practical day-to-day expenses associated with film and TV production, from transport to catering. Anything that is not factored into the *above-the-line costs*.

**Berlin/Berliner:** a newspaper size (315 x 470 mm) used by *The Guardian*, it is considered to be a more convenient smaller size for readers to carry about and read. Commonly used by European newspapers (which vary tremendously in size) for many years, it is called a 'Berliner' as Berlin was the base of the German Standards Committee, which set the standards for paper size as we now know it (A4, A3 etc.).

**Bertelsmann:** one of the *'Big Six'* international media *conglomerates*.

**best boy:** the assistant chief lighting electrician who works with the *gaffer*. (The name also applies when the person is female.)

**Betacam:** a professional video camera (developed in 1982 by Sony) which used the *Betamax* tape format, the term was also used to refer to the tape itself and to its video player. The tape is now available in a digital version called Digital Betacam tapes, or DigiBeta, to be used with *digital video* (*DV*) cameras.

**Betamax:** Sony's rival to *VHS* in the development of formats for video cassette recording and playback in 1975. A half-inch wide tape format for video recording, in many respects it was considered to be a far superior product, favoured by industry users. However, the battle for the domestic market was lost when the UK VCR market chose to manufacture video cassettes exclusively in the VHS format.

**BFI:** see *British Film Institute*

**bias:** a preferential emphasis, or slant, on some of the facts of a news story as opposed to others. It is also possible to demonstrate bias in other ways, for example, some commonly used language can indicate a *gender* bias, such as policeman, foreman etc. The UK political parties each monitor the amount of time devoted to their own party in news reporting in all media, in order that they receive coverage proportionate to their status. Due to numerous personal, institutional and cultural factors, no communication can be entirely free from bias.

**big close-up:** see *cinematography*

**'Big Five':** term for the five major film studios in Hollywood in the 1930s/40s:

- 20th Century Fox
- MGM (Metro Goldwyn Mayer)
- Paramount
- RKO (Radio Keith Orpheum)
- Warner Bros.

(See also *studio system*.)

**'Big Six':** six corporations own ninety per cent of the key US media companies (as at 2007), in what is called consolidation, which means that they can dominate specific areas of their markets and that their individual companies have the advantages of inter-'family' cooperation and the economies of scale available to the parent companies. The six companies are:

- Viacom (Sumner Redstone): Paramount, CBS, MTV Networks, and DreamWorks
- *Disney* (Robert Iger): ABC, Miramax, Pixar, Touchstone, Walt Disney Studios, Walt Disney Theatrical
- *Time Warner* (Richard Parsons): parent company of Warner Bros., HBO, half of the CW (co-owned with CBS Corp.), CNN, AOL
- General Electric (Jeffrey R Immelt): NBC Universal
- *Bertelsmann* (Carl Bertelsmann): Sony and BMG Music Publishing
- *News Corporation* (Rupert Murdoch): 20th Century Fox, Fox Broadcasting, MyNetworkTV, FX Networks, MySpace

Many UK and European media companies are also owned by these parent corporations. One of the key areas of investigation in media studies is the extent to which the concentration of ownership in such limited hands affects the choices of entertainment, and indeed *ideology* and *representations* of the world, that we have access to.

**billboard:** (i) surface used to display large adverts, usually in street and suburban settings, also called a 'hoarding'. The term can also be used to refer to the advert, or poster, itself. (ii) also the term for the board on which letters were used to spell out the name of a play, musical or film (and sometimes its stars) on the canopy above the entrance to a theatre or cinema.

***Billboard:*** the *trade paper* for the music industry in the USA (established in 1934), it was the first to publish a weekly chart (or 'hit parade' as it was then called). It still publishes data on the top 100 music artists, statistics that are based on number of *singles* sold, the amount of *air play* received, as well as internet music *downloads.*

**billing:** term that referred originally to the paper 'bill poster' that was stuck up outside a performance venue in the nineteenth century (such as a music hall or vaudeville theatre), which listed the performers in order of status, from top to bottom. The term now refers to the order of importance in which stars are listed on film posters and DVD covers. Double billing is where the film is led by two stars of equal status. Billing is often a hotly contested issue between the large egos of major film stars who are anxious to be accorded their rightful status as 'top of the bill'. The designs of many film posters show the ingenuity of film *producers* who try not to upset egos by making compromises, either by having the photos of stars in one order, reading from left to right (with the left being the most important) and the star names in another order.

**binary opposition:** Claude Lévi-Strauss (1908–) was a social anthropologist who studied the myths of tribal cultures and suggested that they all shared underlying themes, which he called 'binary oppositions', such as light/dark, good/evil etc. This aspect of his work has been adapted to the study of literature and art, including the narrative structures of film and TV and the functions of characters.

**Biograph Company:** an important film production studio in early Hollywood. The chief film maker associated with the company was the film pioneer D W Griffith, who directed the epics *Birth of a Nation* (USA, 1915) and *Intolerance: Love's Struggle Through the Ages* (USA, 1916).

**biopic:** films in this genre present a 'biographical picture' of the life of a famous person, historical or contemporary, typically monarchs or celebrities. For example: *The Aviator* (Martin Scorsese, USA/Ger, 2004) in which Leonardo di Caprio plays the reclusive 1940s millionaire aviator and film *producer*, Howard Hughes. Although the biographical nature of the story suggests a non-fiction film, most biopics use some degree of fiction to bring the figure to life.

**bird's-eye view shot:** see *overhead shot*

**Birtism:** (Sir) John Birt became the Director General of the *BBC* in 1992 and left in 2000. The term 'Birtism' was used to refer to a type of management (top-heavy, with production facilities significantly reduced) and economic policy which he used to (controversially) transform the BBC, which chiefly resulted in major job cuts and the loss of some long-standing and popular programme contracts in sports. However, he is now credited with making the BBC ready for the twenty-first century and the challenge of a *multi-channel* (and digital) *broadcasting environment*.

**bit part:** a very small and brief role, often an appearance in only one scene, often for inexperienced *actors*.

**black and white:** black and white photography and films pre-dated the invention and use of colour photography and is now considered synonymous with low-budget film-making or 'serious' (for example, *documentary*) or *art films*.

**black cinema/film:** films made by black film makers or with a predominantly black cast, usually in a US context. The history of the representation of black culture and peoples in cinema has developed from *early cinema*, where black characters were always minor and two-dimensional (commonly limited to such roles as slaves, servants and musicians/dancers) to the state of play where black actors and film makers are much more prominent in the USA, and other film industries, and in control of their own representation. Notable directors include Spike Lee, *Do The Right Thing* (USA, 1989); John Singleton, *Boyz n The Hood* (USA, 1991) and Mario van Peebles, *New Jack City* (USA, 1991). The UK has also had some respected black film makers (sometimes defined to include British Asians) from Horace Ové, *Pressure* (UK, 1976) to Gurinder Chadha, *Bend it Like Beckham* (UK/Ger/USA, 2002) and *Bride and Prejudice* (UK/USA, 2004). (See also *blaxploitation*.)

**black comedy:** a type of comic mode or genre whereby the *comedy* is derived from otherwise serious or dark (hence, black) subject matter, such as murder, war or crime. It may be used as part of a film or a whole film can be based on it, such as *Arsenic and Old Lace* (Frank Capra, USA, 1944), *Kind Hearts and Coronets* (Robert Hamer, UK, 1949), *Dr Strangelove or: How I Learned to Stop Worrying and Love the Bomb* (Stanley Kubrick, USA, 1964) and *How to Murder Your Wife* (Richard Quine, USA, 1965). More recently, black comedy has become a part of the *horror* and spoof horror genres, such as in *Scary Movie* (Keenen Ivory Wayans, USA, 2000) and its sequels. It has also mutated into so-called 'bad taste' comedy, as in the films produced by the Farrelly Brothers, such as *Stuck on You* (Bobby and Peter Farrelly, USA, 2003) and *The Ringer* (Barry W Blaustein, USA, 2005) in which the comedy evolves from situations involving mental and physical disability; or early Peter Jackson, which specialised in *gross-out comedy*, such as in *Bad Taste* (NZ, 1987), of which the theme was cannibalism, and in *Meet the Feebles* (NZ, 1989), which featured sexual deviance and drug-taking by animal puppets!

**blacklisting:** the creation of a list of people to be excluded either from employment or association with other workers due to their actions or their political views, as in the case of *Hollywood* in the 1950s, when many refused to cooperate with *HUAC* (House Un-American Activities Committee, chaired by Senator Joe McCarthy). *Guilty by Suspicion* (Irwin Winkler, Fr/USA, 1991) and George Clooney's *Good Night, and Good Luck* (USA, 2005) dramatised this period of Hollywood history.

**blaxploitation:** a loose category of films from the USA in the 1970s exemplified by Melvin Van Peebles' *Sweet Sweetback's Baadasssss Song* (USA, 1971), *Cleopatra Jones* (Jack Starett, USA, 1973) and *Shaft* (Gordon Parks, USA, 1971) which 'exploited' the need for black films for black audiences in the 1970s and the rise in Afrocentric culture. The style of films was very much of the moment, with the incorporation of 1970s music and fashion and made stars of its leads, for example Richard Roundtree and Pam Grier. However, from the point of view of the concept of representation, these films were problematic and caused controversy. They celebrated positive aspects of the Afro-American experience but at the same time perpetuated many negative black stereotypes, such as drug dealers and pimps.

**bleed:** (verb) a term used in newspaper, magazine and book publishing, whereby a photo is located on the page so that one or more sides of the photograph are printed up to or over the edge of the page; (noun) A 'bleed' or 'bleed-off' is the term for a page where this technique has been used.

**block-booking:** prior to the *Paramount Case* of 1948, this was the practice adopted by the *Hollywood* major studios whereby cinemas, also owned by the studio, had to book in blocks (several films) into their cinemas, which guaranteed *exhibition* for all of the studio's films and so reduced the risk of not making a profit. This was considered to be anti-competitive (as *independent* studios had very little opportunity to get their films shown in cinemas) and so was made illegal.

**blockbuster:** this term originates from the era of classic *Hollywood* (of the 1930s and 1940s) when the cinema was the main form of affordable popular entertainment. A block-buster was a film that was so popular it caused long queues of people around the 'block' (the US term for street) in the hope of buying a ticket at the *box-office*. Occasionally today, a film will generate a similar level of attention at the start of its *theatrical run* and be termed a blockbuster, such as the *Star Wars* prequels (George Lucas, USA, 1999, 2003, 2005) and *The Lord of the Rings* series (Peter Jackson, NZ/USA, 2001, 2002 and 2003). Commonly, according to IMDb (Internet Movie Database), a film that grosses more than $100m on its release can be considered a blockbuster. (See also *event movie.*)

**blocking:** the arrangement whereby a director decides where *actors* stand and move on a stage or set in relation to the location of the cameras and lights.

**blog:** (noun) a personal diary on a website (or 'web log', hence 'blog'), that allows space for photographs, video etc. For example, **www.blogger.com** is a website that publishes blogs. (verb) some A level students have used blogging as an interactive alternative to writing essays; and to conduct research, focus discussions or create production logs or reports for coursework projects.

**blonde:** a 2 kW lamp used for location shooting, which often has a yellow head at the back of the lamp, hence the name. (See also *redhead.*)

**blue-collar:** a term referring to *working-class* manual jobs.

**blue/green screen:** a process in film and TV whereby a subject/object is filmed against a blue or green background. The image is then digitally manipulated so that the original back-ground is invisible and can be replaced by another background image or graphics (also known as *Chromakey*). It has many uses, especially in film and TV special effects, but is commonly used for TV weather reports, where the weather reporter appears to be in front of a weather map. The same process is adapted for *CGI*, where an actor (such as Andy Surkiss, who played Gollum and King Kong in Peter Jackson's films) is filmed wearing a blue or green bodysuit connected to a computer to record movements. The CGI image is modelled on the recording, to make the movements as lifelike as possible.

**'B' movie:** a lower-budget film, with less well-known stars (which was cheaper for cinemas to buy in), which ran in support of the main or *'A' movie* in a *double bill* at a cinema. They first became common in the 1930s, when the US *studio system* meant that some films (commonly westerns and crime thrillers) could be made very cheaply and quickly and shown in a double bill to offer value for money for audiences during the Depression. Many of what we now recognise as classic *films noirs* from the 1940s and 1950s, such as *Detour* (Edward G Ulmer, USA, 1945), were considered to be 'B' movies when they were produced. The *Paramount Case* (1948) ended the practice.

**body copy/text:** refers to the words in the main body of a print article (as opposed to the *caption*, or other *copy*).

**body double:** an individual who stands in for an actor for specific scenes in a film or TV programme, either because the actor is not available; the appearance of a specific part of their body is considered unsuitable by the director; or because their contract forbids their participation in nude or sex scenes. Body doubles are usually filmed from the back or insert shots of specific body parts are used.

**body horror:** an effect used in some *horror* films that focuses on the transformation or disintegration of a body, or parts of a body, by use of *special effects* (such as *prosthetics*) in order to entertain/shock the audience by its gruesome and explicit nature. The term has also been used to identify a *subgenre* of the horror film.

**body language:** see *non-verbal communication*

**Bollywood:** the nickname for the centre of Indian popular cinema is the city of Mumbai (Bombay) which has become the Indian sub-continent's equivalent of the USA's Hollywood, in terms of the size of output (although Bollywood produces more films per year than Hollywood) as well as the dominance of the film industry in the city itself. Most films produced in Bollywood are in the Hindi language (hence are also called *Hindi film*), but some are made in other languages. Like Hollywood, Bollywood's film industry is heavily dependent on *genres*, *stars* and a studio production structure. Masala is an Indian mixture of spices and the term Masala movie is used to describe the dominant type of Hindi film, which is a mixture of several different genres, such as action, melodrama, comedy and musical/dance film. Examples include: *Dil Se* (From the Heart, Mani Ratnam, Ind, 1998), *Kuch Kuch Hota Hai* (Something is Happening, Karan Johar, Ind, 1998) and the English-language film, *Being Cyrus* (Homi Adajania, Ind, 2006).

**bonus features:** see *added value*

**boom:** a long pole extended above the actors, outside the camera frame, which holds a *microphone* to record dialogue and sound on location and sets. A boom can also be used to support overhead lighting. A **boom operator** is a member of the sound crew who has the job of holding the boom. Occasionally, the boom (or its shadow) accidentally appears in the top of a frame.

**bootlegs:** recordings made and/or distributed without the consent of the artist. Usually refers to tapes made by fans at live performances, or studio recordings that the artist did not wish to release. Some video/film recordings could be considered bootlegs. A famous example is the Paris Hilton sex video which was distributed over the internet without her consent.

**bounce board:** a white card or board that reflects light back onto the subject that is being photographed or filmed. Frequently used for location photography to maximise natural or electric light.

**box-office:** a place where theatre and cinema tickets are sold. Even though many tickets are now bought by telephone or through the internet rather than in person, the concept of the 'box-office' is used to measure the number of people buying seats for a film.

**BRAD (British Rate and Data):** a subscription service that collects data on all UK media and audiences. Used by advertisers to help them make media choices.

**brand extension:** taking a brand beyond its usual market into another one.

**brand image:** the personality of a brand as presented by the company who owns it, built on its reputation as well as its advertising (from logo to packaging).

**brand positioning:** how a brand performs in a market, in relation to other brands.

**'Brat pack':** (i) a group of young US film directors of the 1970s who were fresh from *film school* and took Hollywood by storm with their confidence and talent. It included: Steven Spielberg, Francis Ford Coppola, George Lucas and Peter Bogdanovich. (ii) a group of young US actors in the 1980s who featured in films concerning teenage angst and coming-of-age issues, characterised by *The Breakfast Club* (John Hughes, USA, 1985). The group included Matt Dillon, Rob Lowe, Emilio Estevez, Nicolas Cage, Molly Ringwald, Demi Moore and Ally Sheedy.

**break even:** to generate sufficient income to cover production costs, but not enough to make a profit.

**breaking news:** the occurrence of an important event just before or while a TV/radio news programme is *on-air*, which interrupts the programme. Such an event means that the programme's predetermined *running order* is abandoned and the presenters have to depend on their *talkback* connection to the programme *director* in the *gallery*, hard-copy scripts or computer screen for information.

**Brechtian:** used to describe a specific performance style and approach to stagecraft, named after the German political playwright, director and poet, Bertolt Brecht (1898–1956). The main feature of his influential theories on performance style is the verfremdungseffekt, translated as *alienation effect* or *distanciation*, in which the *actors* draw the *audience's* attention to the constructed nature of their experience of theatre by use of direct address to audience; placards; music; and the reading aloud of stage directions. His influence can be seen in the films of Jean-Luc Godard, Nagisa Oshima and Lars von Trier.

**bricolage:** a French term, which refers to improvising by putting together objects in a manner and for a purpose for which they were not designed, in order to create something new. Often used in *postmodern* analysis of communication and culture, whether of how language evolves, or the mixing, or recontextualisation, of different styles and ideas in fashion, music, art and media in order to create new meanings. Dada and *Surrealist* artists in the 1920s and 1930s were 'bricoleurs' who moved everyday objects (such as a telephone or a piano) out of their usual contexts, and juxtaposed them with surprising objects, such as a lobster (as in the ready-made *Telephone Homard*, Salvador Dali, 1936) and dead donkeys (as in the film *Un Chien Andalou*, Luis Buñuel, Fr, 1929). Contemporary *music videos* are excellent examples of bricolage, where the *director* is free to combine all manner of styles and motifs.

**bridging shot:** a shot which makes the transition from one shot to another more smooth, by indicating a change in location or time. (See also *sound bridge.*)

**brief:** a specification which a *producer* works to when making a media product. For example, a client seeking to employ an advertising agency will explain their requirements, which the creative team then prepare as a brief (sometimes referred to as a 'creative brief'): it states what is being advertised; the *target audience* and their profile; the ideas for the campaign and which media and strategies to use. It also provides a breakdown of the *budget*.

**British Academy of Film and Television Arts (BAFTA):** formed in 1947 (the UK equivalent of the US *AMPAS*, responsible for the annual *Oscar* awards), BAFTA has its own annual awards ceremonies for film and television.

**British Board of Film Classification (BBFC):** the body responsible for the classification of all films released at the cinema or in other formats, including DVD, as well as some *video games*.

**British Broadcasting Corporation (BBC):** the UK's main *public service broadcaster*, financed by the annual *licence fee*. The BBC has a Director General, who deals with operational issues; and a governing body, presided over by a Chair of Governors. The BBC was founded in 1936 and has a key role in UK broadcasting. The website gives a comprehensive history of the BBC, information about its structure and about how money is spent. The main area of debate for the BBC is whether it should continue to be financed by the *licence fee*.

**British Film Institute (BFI):** set up in 1933 to foster the preservation and enjoyment of the UK's film and TV cultural heritage, the BFI is now a registered charity established by Royal Charter. It is run by a board of governors (who are appointed by the board and ratified by the *UK Film Council*) and is headed by a chair (whose appointment has to be approved by the *DCMS*). The BFI has the largest film and TV *archive* in the world, the National Archive, and has a film restoration programme. It has a library of resources (including books, journals, magazines and posters) for anyone researching film and TV. Its main exhibition space is at the National Film Theatre (*NFT*) on the South Bank, London, as well as at the nearby BFI *IMAX*. Essentially due to the energetic role played by their former Head of Education Projects, Cary Bazalgette, the BFI has made key interventions to government education policy on the importance of media education at all key stages. The BFI also publishes DVDs, books and teaching resources, as well as the film magazine *Sight & Sound*. It also hosts the annual London Film Festival.

**British new wave:** similar to its French counterpart, the *nouvelle vague*, this was a brief but influential moment in British cinema history, from 1958–64, which coincided with a time of social and cultural change. This was chiefly to do with the international emergence of youth culture and associated political ideas, in which the younger generation challenged many of the ideas, values and beliefs (ideology) of the older generation and new styles of music, fashion and art/literature were produced. These influenced young playwrights of the time, such as John Osborne, whose seminal play, *Look Back in Anger*, was a rallying call to a young generation of playwrights, *actors* and film *directors* to experiment with old forms and new ideas. Directors associated with British New Wave include Karel Reisz, Tony Richardson and Lindsay Anderson. (See also *new wave.*)

**British Sky Broadcasting (BSkyB):** formed in 1990 from a merger of Rupert Murdoch's Sky TV and the late Robert Maxwell's BSB (British Satellite Broadcasting), this company (part-owned by Murdoch's parent company, *News Corporation*) now operates Sky Digital, which has the largest *audience* share of the *subscription* TV market in the UK.

**broadband:** a high-speed *internet* connection (transmitted over airwaves, copper wire or fibre wires) that facilitates the downloading of large files, such as films, games and music, to be transmitted far more efficiently than by dial-up connection. In 2006, *Ofcom's* annual Communications Market Report showed that broadband take-up had increased by 63 per cent from 2004 to 2005, with more than 9 million households now with broadband connection, far more than dial-up, and forecast considerable growth in the next few years. It also reported that, due to broadband, 'a new "networked generation" is turning away from television, radio and newspapers in favour of using online services (also referred to as "social networking"), including downloadable content – used on multiple devices such as iPods and mobile phones – and participation in online communities.' (Ofcom 2006)

**broadcast:** (i) (verb) to communicate to the widest possible audience. (See also *narrowcasting*.) (ii) (noun) transmission of a TV or radio communication.

**broadcaster:** a publicly-owned corporation (such as the *BBC*) or a privately-owned company (e.g. *Granada*) that is responsible for producing TV/radio programmes via a *digital* or *analogue* platform. (See also *publisher broadcaster*.)

**Broadcasters Audience Research Board (BARB)** is responsible for providing estimates of the number of people (categorised by their *demographics* and *geodemographics*) watching television (categorised by channel and programme) at any time of day. This is done by the selection of a number of households (as at 2006, just over 5,000) who are representative of the population. They agree to have a data box (*peoplemeter*) attached to their TV to record this information. BARB provides this essential television *audience* data to broadcasters and advertisers who pay to subscribe to their service.

**broadcast flow:** (i) the continuous output of TV and radio broadcasting (ii) situation in which the viewer/listener remains tuned to one station for as long as possible without changing channels – the central aim of all *scheduling* activities.

**broadcasting:** usually refers to the production and transmission of TV and radio.

**Broadcasting Acts:** several of these government Acts have had a significant affect on the UK broadcasting landscape. The two most significant in recent years were passed in 1990 and in 2003.

**broadsheet:** term used to describe the serious newspapers (for example, *The Guardian* and *The Times*), even though most of the broadsheets are now published in the smaller *compact* or *Berliner* size.

**BSkyB:** see *British Sky Broadcasting*

**BSC (Broadcasting Standards Commission):** see *Ofcom*

**buddy movie:** a film genre, especially popular in Hollywood cinema, which has at its centre a same-sex friendship between two characters (usually but not always male) who are often opposite personalities. It can tell the story of the friendship over several years, as in *Beaches* (Garry Marshall, USA, 1988); or follow the main characters through a series of dramatic events, as in *Butch Cassidy and the Sundance Kid* (George Roy Hill, USA, 1969) and *Thelma and Louise* (Ridley Scott, USA, 1991). There have also been *comedy* versions, such as *Dumb and Dumber* (Farrelly Bros, USA, 1994) and *The Wedding Crashers* (David Dobkin, USA, 2005). Its main common feature is that the characters ultimately support each other through all circumstances, even to the death of one or both characters. The 'buddy cop movie' is a *subgenre* of the buddy movie, where the pair are police officers, such as in *Bad Boys* (Michael Bay, USA, 1995) and *Miami Vice* (Michael Mann, USA, 2006). The genre is also seen on TV in the UK (*Rosemary and Thyme*) and in the USA (*Starsky and Hutch*, *Cagney and Lacey*, *Miami Vice*).

**budget:** the amount of money that has been calculated that a media product (in any medium) will cost to produce; or the limit that has been provided for its production (including *above-* and *below-the-line* costs). Film and TV directors are carefully monitored by *producer*s to ensure that their projects are made on budget and on schedule in order to minimise additional costs and so maximise the opportunity for profit.

**built-in obsolescence:** a feature of modern technology production practice, whereby a product is intrinsically designed to become outdated, obsolete, or broken, within a relatively short period of time, requiring the *consumer* to buy a replacement earlier than strictly necessary (often as a repair would be too costly and uneconomic). An aspect of a *consumer culture*, in which consumers are encouraged to regularly buy the very latest products on the market.

**bulks:** the many copies of national newspapers given away free (for example, in hotel foyers, at events, on first-class train carriages and aeroplanes) in order to boost *circulation* figures.

**bulletin:** a short news programme on television or radio. Can be regularly scheduled (for example, at lunchtime or early evening) or used to respond to events.

**bullet-time:** a technique whereby the speed of a film is manipulated in the production process so that it slows down a high-speed action, such as the passage of a flying bullet. The subject is recorded from several angles by cameras mounted in many positions, surrounding it. This technique creates the illusion that a camera has tracked around the speeding object. Previously seen in computer games and *anime*, such as *Akira* (Katsuhiro Ôtomo, Jap, 1988), it was used most notably in a mainstream feature-film context in *The Matrix* (Andy and Larry Wachowski, USA, 1999) and its sequels (the DVD special features provide a useful demonstration of how bullet-time is shot). The technique was parodied in *Scary Movie* (Keenen Ivory Wayans, USA, 2000) and *Shrek* (Adam Adamson and Vicky Jenson, USA, 2001).

**bump:** to move the position of a story or item in the running order of a broadcast *news* programme, or to change its location in a newspaper. For example, a more important breaking news story could bump another article off the front page to an inside one.

**business:** refers to the small gestures and minor actions of *body language* a film/TV *actor* can use to make their *performance* more convincing. It might affect how a character eats, carries or rearranges a *prop*, or how they behave when they are not delivering dialogue. Usually, this should be inconspicuous, but some actors are known for exaggerated and scene-stealing business in their performance style.

**buzz track:** location sound that is recorded separately from pictures, which can be used later in the editing process to cover any gaps or mistakes, as necessary. Also referred to as *wild sound* or track. (See also *atmos*, *ambient sound*.)

**byline:** a line of *copy* stating who an article in a magazine or newspaper is by: the name of the journalist. A picture byline includes a picture of the journalist or columnist.

**cable TV:** also known just as 'cable', this is a service which is received via a cable direct to a household which carries TV and other telecommunications facilities, such as telephone and internet connection, as opposed to that received via satellite or digitally. ntl: is currently the largest operator in the UK.

***Cahiers du Cinéma:*** influential French film magazine which challenged traditional ideas on film theory and criticism. Contributors included Francois Truffaut (1932–1984), Jean-Luc Godard (1930–), Eric Rohmer (1920–), Jacques Rivette (1928–) and Claude Chabrol (1930–), who all subsequently became influential film directors in their own right. Truffaut and Godard are especially worthy of interest in relation to their creation of the nouvelle vague (*French new wave* cinema) and the magazine was a powerful channel for promoting their ideas.

**call sheet:** a document which lists the personnel who are required for the daily schedule of a television or film shoot. It provides names and contact details of the actors and technicians, lists the scenes to be shot and identifies logistical issues such as transport, set requirements, etc.

**call-to-view:** the theme music played at the beginning of a radio or television programme that prompts us to pay attention, or even make us come running from another room.

**cameo:** a small television or film role taken by a leading *actor* or *star*. It is sometimes uncredited and even, on occasions, unpaid. It may be used as a publicity gimmick. The existence of such cameos makes the product much more likely to gain a larger *audience* and therefore enjoy greater *box-office* success. A cameo can be as brief as a few seconds, as when, for example, Robert Altman asked a number of stars to play themselves in *The Player* (USA, 1992) in order to create the right ambience of Hollywood as 'Tinseltown', as well as to add comic effect and a sense of realism.

**camera:** a piece of equipment that uses a glass lens to record still and moving images onto material that preserves them. The first camera was available to the public in the UK in 1839 and completely revolutionised our means of representation and communication. There have been many developments in camera technology, the latest and arguably the most significant being the replacement in all media production of the exposure of photo-sensitive material (known as film negatives) by *digital* photographic processes.

**camera obscura:** (meaning 'dark room') a dark chamber in which objects, scenes or events that are outside are projected inside via a small hole which acts as a lens and focuses the light rays to create an inverted image. The existence of such an invention is evident as far back as the tenth century. Several artists, including Leonardo da Vinci (1452–1519), used it as a drawing aid.

**camera operator:** non-gender specific term (unlike 'cameraman') for the person who controls a TV/film camera.

**camera script:** script given to the *camera operator* which states where a camera should move on a TV/film set and the types of shots to take.

**camp:** an aesthetic, or style of *acting*, or mode of self-expression which engages in elements such as excess, exaggeration, effeminacy, theatricality. Some have used the term in relation to self-reflexive, blurred gender identities and although it is frequently associated with the *stereotype* of a gay man, it does not always refer to that. For example: the *Batman* television series of the 1960s could be considered camp because of its tongue-in-cheek self-mockery; some older female characters in *soap operas* similarly so, such as Pat Butcher (*Eastenders*), who is notable for her huge, elaborate earrings. A camp aesthetic could be seen in the use of colour, retro costumes and interior design, props and acting style in some aspects of many of Pedro Almodovar's films, for example, *Women on the Verge of a Nervous Breakdown* (Sp, 1988) and *All About My Mother* (Sp/Fr, 1999).

**campaign:** a process or action-plan that aims to achieve a specific goal, as in the military. In a media context, the term is used to refer particularly to those activities that aim to influence people's behaviour or thinking, as in *advertising*, politics and humanitarian work.

***Campaign*:** a leading trade journal that specialises in *advertising*, *marketing*, media and *public relations.*

**Campaign for Press and Broadcasting Freedom:** a UK organisation founded in 1979 as a pressure group to make all aspects of the media in Britain more open and accountable. It is broad-based and non-political and aims to encourage diversity and accessibility, especially in journalism and the press.

**Canal + (or Canal Plus):** a French premium-pay television channel launched in November 1985, owned by Vivendi SA, which also has a high profile in international film production.

**canned laughter:** see *laughter track*

**Cannes Film Festival:** as its name suggests, a festival that celebrates the cinematic art form in the luxurious splendour of Cannes, on the south-coast of France on the Mediterranean. The festival was established in 1939 by the French Government, but was interrupted by events during the Second World War. It was relaunched in 1946 and quickly established itself as one of the most important (if not the most important), *film festivals* in the world. It is characterised by its keenness to represent European films and *art-house cinema* and it is an annual meeting place for 'wheeling and dealing'. It is an award-giving festival, with a jury of eminent professionals. The most prestigious award is the Palme d'Or (golden palm leaf), which is highly sought after by production companies as it boosts marketing and *box-office* performance, and by directors, as it greatly enhances reputations.

**canon:** a body of work, especially artistic.

**cans:** (slang) headphones/earphones in broadcast/film production.

**canted shot/frame:** a cinematic device where the camera is physically placed at an angle so that vertical and horizontal surfaces appear diagonal. This device was particularly enjoyed by directors of *German Expressionist* cinema, such as Wiene (*The Cabinet of Dr Caligari*, Ger, 1919) and Murnau (*Nosferatu*, Ger, 1922) and subsequently became a staple of the *genres* of *horror* and *film noir*, although it is now also quite common in *thrillers*, *action/adventure* films and *comic-book hero* films.

**caper film; crime caper:** also known as the *heist film*, a *subgenre* of the *crime thriller*, which is characterised particularly by a three part structure: 1. Lead *villain* (also sometimes seen as a *hero*) sets up a team of hand-picked specialist criminals and they train to complete a very difficult caper. 2. The caper is attempted and usually comes off because of the death-defying risks of the team and their specialist knowledge being put into operation – this often involves high-tech equipment, *pyrotechnics*, car/boat chases. 3. Because of some fault in the planning, or some flaw in a *character*, the authorities track them down and the precious item (e.g. money/jewels) is recovered or lost. Some notable examples of this genre are: *The Ladykillers* (Alexander Mackendrick, UK, 1955), *Heat* (Michael Mann, USA, 1995), *Ocean's Eleven* (Steven Soderberg, USA/Aus, 2001), *The Italian Job* (Peter Collinson, UK, 1969), *The Usual Suspects* (Brian Singer, USA/Ger, 1995), *Reservoir Dogs* (Quentin Tarantino, USA, 1992), *The Taking of Pelham 123* (Joseph Sargent, USA, 1974). We can see from this list alone how varied and robust this subgenre is and how it has maintained its popularity with its clever *plot* twists, unusual *characterisation* and gripping *cinematography*. Occasionally, in contemporary *postmodern* cinema, the criminals win (that is, they succeed in getting away with the money), which raises other moral and ethical questions.

**capitalism:** a social and economic system that is primarily driven by the motive for profit. It relies on the investment of the private sector to provide the means of production, distribution and exchange; it works essentially in a competitive free market and prefers the least interference from government regulation in property and the markets. An example of a capitalist state is the UK, although it is also described as a mixed economy, as there are both privately owned and state-owned enterprises and therefore in practice there is a combination of capitalism and socialism. From a *Marxist* point of view, much of contemporary media would be seen to be essentially upholding capitalist doctrines, for example, the *advertising* industry.

**caption:** words (or graphics) that appear on the screen. Captions are often used to inform us efficiently and unobtrusively of who is speaking in a *documentary* or *current affairs* programme.

**cardioid mic:** a hand-held *microphone*, often used in one-to-one interviews, which picks up the sound in a heart-shaped pattern.

**cartel:** a group of businessmen who share specific industry interests and who come together to protect their businesses or product viability by, for example, setting the price, controlling the *distribution* and fending off new competitors. The movie moguls of the 'golden age' of the *Hollywood studio system*, such as Darryl Zanuck, Sam Goldwyn, Jack Warner and Carl Laemmle, were seen by some commentators as a cartel because of their sharp and co-operative (at least among themselves) business practices.

**cast:** (verb) to give an actor a role to play as a *character* in a media production. The cast-list is the full list of people who are acting in the production. Casting is the process by which the actors are allocated roles, ranging from the *stars* right down to the *extras* required. All (bar the *stars*) is controlled in a major film or television production by the **casting director**.

**casting couch:** the offering of sexual favours by an aspiring *actor* to, for example, a *director* or *producer*, in return for a significant role in a film, or a break into the industry. It was thought to be prevalent in the classical *Hollywood* era and many apocryphal stories abound. Although in some actors' anecdotes it is spoken of quite casually, it is none the less an abuse of power.

**castration anxiety/theory:** Freud posited the idea that boys, during the phallic stage of their physical development, developed a deep-seated fear of castration, based on the misunderstanding that girls must have lost their penis at some stage, possibly because of misbehaviour. This complex and contested theory has been used in the *Freudian* analysis of some films and characters.

**catchphrase:** a phrase which is very closely, if not uniquely, associated with an individual television performer (as in, for example, a quiz-show host) or a *character* (or even actor) in, for example, a *sitcom* or *soap opera.* It is often used for humorous purposes but it is also a part of the identification and *celebrity* of the performer and helps to reinforce their longevity in the mind of the audience. Some performers can utilise such catchphrases for more or less their whole career, for example, Bruce Forsyth's 'Nice to see you, to see you, nice!' (The concept and practice was clearly being ridiculed in the BBC's *Extras* with the Ricky Gervais character overusing the line, 'Are you 'aving a laff? Is 'e 'aving a laff?')

**categorisation:** a key concept in media education, this is the arrangement of media texts and products into categories. The term 'category' is often used as well as or instead of *genre* to discuss texts, as it allows for more detailed groupings.

**catharsis:** (from Aristotle) literally a purgation or purification, referring to emotions within the *audience*; a cleansing of the soul; in Greek *tragedy*, the emotion felt by the audience at the end when the tragic *hero* nobly faces his punishment (death); the audience *pleasure* of experiencing pity and fear. This idea stems from Aristotle's reflection on why an audience, after seeing a tragedy, feels relieved and even elevated, rather than depressed. Put simply, why do we feel a lot better after a good cry (or laugh)? In what way does the act purify us? Such ideas carried forward through Shakespeare and into the twenty-first century. We can use this term similarly to refer to the emotional shock of tragic narratives in cinema. (See also *Aristotelian.*)

**cathode ray tube:** a vacuum tube into which electrons are directed towards a fluorescent screen; used in television sets before the flat screen, for example.

**causality/cause and effect:** the general principle that everything that happens must have a cause. This is important in *story* terms, certainly in traditional Hollywood *narratives*, as individual members of the *audience* are likely to raise *enigmas* during their viewing of the film and some of these will relate to their understanding of causality. If these cause-and-effect enigmas are not answered there is likely to be dissatisfaction with the film, to some degree. Also, the cause-and-effect relationship is an important part of the distinction between a *plot* and a story: when we watch a film we make sense of events as presented to us in the plot, by understanding the cause-and-effect relationships, and turn it into the whole story in our heads. This is an important part of understanding narratives in terms of *spectator* relationships.

**CCCS:** see *Centre for Contemporary Cultural Studies*

**CCTV (closed-circuit television):** television transmission that is restricted to a limited number of screens, usually directly linked by cable and not for open transmission. CCTV has been used since 1942 to monitor rocket launches. Its current use is widespread in a number of areas, such as the military or as part of security systems. It is more readily known as a surveillance technique within public places in contemporary society and its use is highly controversial (see also *surveillance society*). Some argue it is essential as a means of assisting law and enforcement officers in executing their duties; others argue it is an infringement of civil liberties, as we are not always aware that we are being filmed and have not given our consent. Evidence from CCTV is often used as part of the footage in news, current affairs, true crime and consumer programmes, and in *documentary* film-making.

**celebrity:** person (usually in an entertainment industry) who is famous in their lifetime. The concept encompasses a wide range of people, from megastars such as Madonna and Johnny Depp, to those who are well known for their brief appearance on reality television shows The latter group are often disparagingly referred to as 'Z-list celebrities'. Celebrities are essential for particular types of publishing, such as *Hello* magazine, and some television *genres* such as *chat shows*, *quiz shows*, cooking programmes; they are in fact becoming increasingly ubiquitous. The latter half of the twentieth century was partly characterised by the immense growth in celebrity cult status from Elvis and Marilyn onwards; the fact that a single name will suffice in identifying them tells you a lot. (See also *'A' list*.)

**celebrity endorsement:** in *advertising*, the use of a famous person to support a particular product by saying, for example, that they use it and recommend it. As a *marketing* ploy such endorsements can be both lucrative for the celebrity and profitable for the advertiser.

**cel, cell:** short for *celluloid.*

**cell animation:** a form of *animation* where individual transparent *cells*, usually made of cellulose acetate, are painted on and when overlaid give a sense of depth. They are flexible and efficient in construction as not everything needs to be repainted for each shot.

**celluloid:** the photographic film is used to record the images and then, after laboratory processing, played through a *projector.* The word is also used as a *metonym* for cinema itself (for example, the 'celluloid closet' refers to secretly gay actors during the 'Golden Age' of *Hollywood*).

**censorship:** the use of power by authority figures to control what individuals, groups or society can or cannot see, hear or read in media products, especially in *publishing*, film-making and *broadcasting.* It is a very contentious aspect of media production in many societies as the media are often seen as the main purveyor of *ideologies* and are powerful in persuading the *audience* towards particular views. Who controls what we can or cannot consume is central to this debate. In some societies, such as that in existence in the Soviet communist era or in contemporary China, censorship was and is seen as a way of protecting society from dangerous ideas from alternative foreign ideologies. Other aspects of censorship are seen as being more benign, such as parents' desires for stringent controls over products which may be seen to unduly influence, or even harm, their children.

**central casting:** a pool of *extras* for supply to film and television companies. There is a company in Burbank, California, which goes by the name of 'Central Casting', and specialises in this.

**Centre for Contemporary Cultural Studies (CCCS):** an academic research centre based at the University of Birmingham, founded by Richard Hoggart, who was its first director, in 1964. It was concerned with the new area of *cultural studies.* Many of the academics and theorists who worked at the Centre were responsible for influential research, including principally Stuart Hall and David Morley, who both contributed to the newly emerging interest in *media studies* in the 1970s.

**centre spread:** see *spread*

**certification:** the process by which a film is rated according to its 'suitability' for *audiences* of less than adult age. This also applies to material released on DVD, including video games. (See also *British Board of Film Classification*.)

**CGI (computer-generated imaging):** the use of *digital* technology to create complex and advanced artificial images which look realistic. CGI can be used for mere moments in films, or be the means by which the whole film is made. For example, although *Disney* held the film rights since the 1950s, the fantastical characters and settings of J R R Tolkein's *Lord of The Rings* remained unfilmed for many decades, (despite several aborted attempts by major *directors* and with the exception of an animated US version directed by Ralph Bakshi in 1978) and could only eventually be fully realised due to the immense capabilities of CGI.

**channel:** a route or means of communication. Channels can be technical, such as in broadcasting where the route is *analogue* or *digital*. They can also be seen as social, such as viewing the media itself as a channel for political *ideologies*.

**Channel 4:** the UK's fourth *terrestrial* channel, a publicly owned corporation whose board is appointed by *Ofcom*. It began in 1982, having been created by an Act of Parliament the previous year, to provide quality and alternative *programming* for commercial television and as such to compete directly with BBC2. As a *publisher broadcaster* it does not produce its own programmes, but commissions them from over 300 *independent* production companies across the UK. Since its beginnings it has been ground-breaking, innovative, controversial, highly popular and successful, attracting an *audience* that is varied in age, *gender*, race and social class.

**channel surfing/hopping:** with contemporary television technology, and the plethora of television stations now available, by adept use of the *remote control* an individual can jump between stations at the push of a button and in a split-second. This harmless pursuit is changing the way in which we use television: no longer are we restricted to three or four stations which we might stick to for hours on end; instead we can spend our time hopping from station to station and, in some senses, create our own entertainment.

**Chaplinesque:** used to describe an actor's performance that can be characterised by being similar to or imitating the great British actor Charles (Charlie) Chaplin. The term refers especially to the role created by Chaplin of the lonely, lovelorn, eternally optimistic tramp who battles against considerable opposition (from stock villains to snowstorms). It can also refer to the manner in which the actor moves/walks/looks and how they signify the elements described above. In some cases the term can be used in a much broader sense ideologically to refer to the type of film narrative where a minor character who is placed in a weak position overcomes great obstacles, or opposition from other characters, which may represent the evil in society.

**character; characterisation:** the roles created in a *narrative* and how they are developed. In virtually every fictional narrative there is a change in the leading character, or *protagonist*, as we get through the film or programme. The obstacles they face, and how they overcome them, in obtaining their object (desire) is an essential ingredient in the creation of the character. We refer to the journey that they take, and how they change on that journey, as the 'character arc'. Being visual media, film and television show us clearly what a character looks like, so the *mise en scène* is important:

- the clothes he or she wears are important signifiers to establish character

- also, the way they move, do things, use their faces and so on (the *performative*) is part of the mise en scène
- the places they inhabit (their homes, offices, etc) can reflect their character.

The dialogue they are given and the manner in which the lines are delivered (again, the performative) is also significant. There are different character types, sometimes dependent upon the *genre*. For example: in most action adventure films we can expect to see a *hero* and perhaps a villain; in *film noir* there are very particular character types such as the *femme fatale;* in crime thrillers there is an investigator. The work of Vladimir *Propp* is interesting in this area, especially at identifying character *archetypes* (such as the hero and villain), but it is only one way among many of approaching this concept. The establishment of character in a film can take merely seconds, and sometimes a lot longer. The opening of *North-by-Northwest* (Alfred Hitchcock, USA, 1959), for example, establishes the character of the protagonist, Roger Thornhill (played by Cary Grant) as a smart, fast-talking, womanising, Madison Avenue executive in a matter of seconds, as he dictates things to his secretary as they are on the move. By contrast, the opening 14 minutes of *Red Rock West* (John Dahl, USA, 1992) is all about establishing the likeability of the *victim hero*, Michael (played by Nicholas Cage), his moral rectitude and the precarious position in which he finds himself when we eventually get to the *inciting incident.*

**character actor:** an *actor* (but not necessarily a *star*) who specialises in playing strong character types or parts. They can be stars like Robert de Niro, who changes considerably in all the different roles that he plays, not just in the manner of his performance, but also in his appearance and the physicality he brings to the role, for example, his playing of Jake la Motta in *Raging Bull* (Martin Scorsese, USA, 1980). Less well known are actors such William H Macy, Steve Buscemi, Kevin Pollack, the late J T Walsh, Julie Kavner (now the voice of Marge Simpson), Miriam Margoyles and Kathy Najimy, who make considerable contributions to a film by creating interesting but crucial smaller roles. For example, in *A Few Good Men* (Rob Reiner, USA, 1992), the star who clearly hogs the limelight is Tom Cruise, but the foil he plays off against in most scenes is Kevin Pollack, whose presence in the smaller character role helps Cruise produce his impressive performance.

**character arc:** see *character*

**character type:** see *character*

**chat show:** a *genre* of television in which a host interviews various *celebrities* about their lives and current achievements/projects. The host may be, or become, a celebrity in their own right (for example, Michael Parkinson, Jonathan Ross, Graham Norton). The chat show is often an important element of a *marketing campaign*, especially for a film, book, album, theatrical/performance event or television programme and some shows have been criticised for the blandness of the interviews themselves. The chat show host is extremely unlikely to upset the guests (on the basis that you should not bite the hand that feeds you) although Ross and Norton have been known to be quite close to the edge on occasions. The chat show is a very good example of the way in which symbiosis works; in this case between the television *producer* and the *star*/performer/artist – they each need the other so they can work as effectively as they can.

**chiaroscuro:** the interplay of light and dark, or black and white, in the art design of a film. The term comes from art appreciation and refers to the use of light as an essential ingredient in the *construction* of a painting. Similar ideas have been applied to that which is in the *frame* of a film, or the *mise en scène*. Prime examples of chiaroscuro can be seen in *film noir*, where *directors* limit what the *spectator* can or cannot see by means of very carefully applied *lighting* techniques, often using *ambient light* as the only source.

**chick flick:** a film category that is aimed principally at female *audiences*, usually has female characters at the centre of the *narrative* and is concerned with a female perspective on life. The term tends to be used for marketing purposes rather than for film production or *genre* definition.

**Chomsky, Noam:** see *manufacture of consent*

**choreography:** the arrangement of moves in a dance or fight sequence, designed, controlled and directed by an expert in the field. Sometimes the choreographer is so important to the film that they are best placed to be the *director*, for example, Gene Kelly's *Singin' in the Rain* (Stanley Donen and Gene Kelly, USA, 1952) and Bob Fosse's *Cabaret* (USA, 1972) and *All That Jazz* (USA, 1979).

**Chromakey:** an effect used in moving image production where images are overlaid using *blue/green screen* technology, usually to place actors in different environments. It is a more sophisticated version of the technique of *back projection*. The use of this technique is to create more control of the *mise en scène* and to make the film-making efficient (and even, on occasions, cheaper).

**cineaste:** an enthusiast for cinema and film (such as the people who wrote this book).

**Cinecitta:** an Italian film studio in Rome, closely associated with the films of Federico Fellini (1920–1993).

**cineliteracy:** the ability to be able to 'read' a film; or to *decode* it, interpret it, understand it. From *semiology* we can see that individual *signs* have to be read, just as letters do in words, and words in sentences; hence *film grammar*. Although the concept is quite simple to understand, it suggests other aspects which are much more complex. Our cineliteracy may be dependent upon a number of things, for example: *schemata;* conditions of *reception;* narrative mode; *aberrant decoding;* and appropriation.

**cinema:** the *production*, *distribution* and *exhibition* of motion pictures. Refers to both film products themselves and the process associated with it, as well as other ideas such as that of national cinema. The term covers, therefore, the *aesthetic* and artistic aspects of film as well as the business and economics of the *industry*.

**cinema chain:** a series of cinemas that are owned by one organisation, for example, Odeon.

**cinema of excess:** often used to refer to film makers (*directors*, writer, designers, *actors*) who engage in a deliberately exaggerated mode of *performance* or *representation*. Examples include: in direction, Brian de Palma with *Scarface* (USA, 1983); in *screenplay*, Mike Werb and Michael Colleary for *Face/Off* (John Woo, USA, 1997); in design, Eiko Ishioka's costumes for *Bram Stoker's Dracula* (Francis Ford Coppola, USA, 1992); in acting, Al Pacino's performance as the devil in *The Devil's Advocate* (Taylor Hackford, USA/Ger, 1997).

**Cinemascope:** the trademark name for the process used to squeeze a wide frame image via *lenses* onto a smaller frame, and the reversal of this process in *projection* at the point of *exhibition*. The process was *copyrighted* by 20th Century Fox in 1953.

**cinematic/theatrical release:** the first showing of a film in a cinema. In contemporary *Hollywood* this is seen as very important for the viability of the product and so an immense amount of time and effort is put into such an event – so much so that *blockbusters* are described as *event movies*. Since *Toy Story 2* (John Lasseter and Ash Brannon, USA, 1999) the means exist to *produce*, *distribute* and *exhibit* a film entirely in its *digital* format. The implication of this is that in the near future it will be technically possible to open a film for its theatrical release worldwide on exactly the same day and time.

**cinematic new waves:** see *new wave*

**cinematographe:** the camera and projector system developed by the *Lumière brothers* and first demonstrated in 1895. It had the advantage of being smaller, lighter and more portable than similar machines being used in America and developed by *Edison.* With their ground-breaking equipment, the two Frenchmen were responsible for the first film exhibition in Paris on 28 December 1895, thereby inventing cinema as a fee-paying spectacle. Their first film showed people leaving their father's factory in Lyons.

**cinematographer:** commonly referred to as the director of photography (DP or DOP) or lighting cameraman, the cinematographer is a senior technician who takes overall responsibility for translating the screenplay into moving images. In close consultation with the *director*, the cinematographer organises the *lighting*, *framing* and *shooting* of the film. The DP does not usually operate the *camera* personally, but works closely with the *camera operator*, the *gaffer* and the *key grip.* The role is answerable directly to the director, but in practice it is often seen as a collaborative effort. Some DPs become associated with certain directors and form lasting partnerships: as director of *Citizen Kane* (USA, 1941), Orson Welles famously gave equal screen credit to his cinematographer Greg Tolland; Spike Lee's reputation was partially founded on the work of DP Ernest Dickerson, who worked with him on his first seven films; and the distinctive look of Wong Kar-wai's films is often ascribed to the work of DP Christopher Doyle.

**cinematography:** everything that pertains to the use of the *camera* in the creation of a moving image text, under the control of the *director* and/or *cinematographer.* There are many things we can do with a camera. We can:

- *pan* to the left or right
- *tilt* up or down
- *pivot* 360 degrees
- circle around an object through 360 degrees
- *zoom* in or zoom out
- *crab* to the left or right
- *track* a person or object
- put the camera on a *crane* and go up high
- put it in a helicopter and create an *aerial* shot
- look down from a *bird's-eye view*
- look up from a *worm's-eye view*
- attach it to a microscope
- use *steadicam* to attach it to the body of the camera operator so that he can run with it

- put the camera at an angle to create a *canted* shot

- put gauze over the lens to create a *diffused* shot.

The decision as to which *shot* a director will use lies mainly with the type of product being made or what the *mode* is. For example, it would be out of place and poor *cinematography* to use steadicam in *Eastenders* for a simple chat around the kitchen table, whereas it would be perfect for a chase sequence in an action adventure film, or if you wanted to create a POV (*point of view*) shot in a *horror* film – see the opening of *Halloween* (John Carpenter, USA, 1978). Another decision for a director to make is how close in or far out the shot has to be to its subject. The seven basic shot sizes are:

- *extreme long-shot (ELS)* or *wide shot (WS)*

- *long shot (LS)*

- *medium long-shot (MLS)*

- *medium shot (MS)*

- *medium close-up (MCU)*

- *close-up (CU)*

- *extreme close-up* (ECU) or *big close-up (BCU).*

**cinéma verité:** literally, 'film/camera truth', this refers to the mode of *documentary* film in which there is no attempt to hide or disguise the presence of the film maker, who may ask questions which provoke apparently spontaneous answers. It originates in the ideas of a Russian film maker called Dziga Vertov who referred to some of his work in the 1920s as 'kino pravda' ('cinema truth'). It did not really develop until the 1950s, when smaller, lightweight cameras were available, diegetic sound could be recorded as the film was being shot and, consequently, filming was less obtrusive. Contemporary exponents of this type of film-making include Albert and David Maysles and Richard Drew. (Should be compared to *direct cinema*, where such intrusions are not used but spontaneous responses are obtained by other means.)

**circular narrative:** a *plot* in which the end is reminiscent of, or returns us to, the beginning. For example, many *film noirs* begin near the end of the story and then unfold a plot which brings us back to the end point, at which closure takes place. Examples include *Double Indemnity* (Billy Wilder, USA, 1944) and *DOA* (Rudolph Maté, USA, 1950).

**circulation:** the number of people who buy a magazine or newspaper in a given sales period (for example, in the case of a daily newspaper, the number bought in one day). It is a way of measuring business performance.

**clapperboard:** a device used in film and video production which provides the names of the film/*director*/*camera operator*, the *shot* and *take* number and the date so that at the *editing* stage it is easier to keep track of which piece of film goes where. The board is in two parts, and is filmed and described aurally at the beginning of a take and then clapped together so that sound and vision can be synchronised later on.

**clapper/loader:** the person who holds the *clapperboard* in *shot* and also loads the film *magazines*; the second assistant *camera operator*.

**classic film:** a film regarded as excellent in almost every respect. For example, the film most often cited as a classic is *Citizen Kane* (Orson Welles, USA, 1941), which defined the limits of film achievement in its day, certainly on a technical and directorial level. The problem of using terms such as 'classic' is that it may lead to a hierarchical view of media texts, which can be misleading and debatable: a text that one person describes as a classic may be totally irrelevant for another.

**classical Hollywood (film):** see *classical style of narrative*

**classical style of narrative:** the style exemplified by *Hollywood* throughout its classical or 'Golden Age' from 1915, date of D W Griffith's *Birth of Nation*, until the 1960s. During this period the rule book was written, especially in relation to *continuity editing* and the so-called 'invisible' style, so named because it does everything it can to hide the artificiality of the construct. This style, in relation to both vision and sound, engages the audience in such a way that we temporarily forget where we are and seem to go into the world of the film – we engage in a *willing suspension of disbelief*. Because of the way the *studio system* operated, this style became uniform. Once the working practices of the studio system went into decline, starting with the *Paramount Case* in 1948, *independent producers* and *directors* began to emerge who had different ways of doing things, especially if they were influenced by European cinema, for example, the *French new wave* of the 1950s and 60s.

**classification:** see *British Board of Film Classification*

**classified advertising:** small advertisements consisting of just a few lines, used primarily by small businesses and individuals and usually placed towards the latter part of a newspaper or magazine. They are classified into sections such as 'items for sale', 'lonely hearts', etc.

**Claymation:** an *animation* method (used by Aardman Animation) which uses modelling material (but only rarely clay itself) in order to create characters and props.

**clearance:** see *rights*

**cliché:** an overused image or visual idea that has become cheap or predictable (in much the same way as it does in language).

**cliffhanger:** a *narrative* device whereby the *story*'s ending is dramatically or abruptly left open and the *audience* are left with a minor or major *enigma*, namely: what is going to happen next? It is often used at the end of an episode in a *drama* series or *soap opera*; the purpose being to lure you back to see the next thrilling episode. It can also happen in films, especially if there is a hint that a sequel may be on its way, and so can be seen as a marketing ploy, as in, for example, *The Empire Strikes Back* (Irvine Kershner, USA, 1980).

**climax:** (i) the emotional high point in a *narrative* sequence. (ii) approaching a turning point in the narrative, especially in a *mid-act climax*.

**closed set:** during film or video production, a *set* to which access is restricted to the minimum necessary cast and crew.

**closed sign/text:** in *semiology*, a *sign* in which the *signifier* in its context has only one *signified* (i.e. an image or sound with only one meaning). For example: 3 x 3 = 9; in this context, the sign 'x' clearly means 'multiplication'. With a visual image, the easiest way for it to become a closed sign is for it to have words (a caption) to be attached, as it *anchors* down the meaning. Often, we use *context* to establish the meaning of a visual image and thereby close down the sign.

**close-up (shot):** see *cinematography*

**closure:** in dramatic *narrative*, where all conflicts are resolved, all mysteries explained and the fate of all major *characters* revealed. Where this is not complete, there will only be a certain degree of closure.

**CMY:** see four-colour printing

**CNN:** Cable News Network, the US *cable* television network established in 1982 by Ted Turner and owned by the *conglomerate Time Warner*. It became prominent during the Gulf War (1990–91) for its use of *live broadcast* reports from location correspondents who were very close to the action, as opposed to commentating from a studio. In the competition for *audiences*, this has subsequently become the main style of international TV *news* coverage. It is debatable whether the news is any more reliable or noteworthy just because it is broadcast from a *correspondent* 'on the spot', but the producers' hope is that the sense of *actuality* for the audience is greater and therefore more visually appealing than *talking heads* in a studio.

**code:** in simple terms, a code is a system of letters, numbers and *symbols* that communicate ideas to a group or society. A simple example is *The Highway Code*: it is a set of rules that we must know and agree to, which is characterised primarily by a series of *signs*, which when decoded offer the exact information we need when we are driving or riding on the roads. In *semiology*, we can talk about *encoding* and *decoding* in relation to how images are put together (constructed) or read (deconstructed) in a media text, for example. In some ways, codes can be seen as a system of rules (as in *The Highway Code*), which must be learned by a group or society. In some cases, codes are understood by reading media texts and trying to make sense of them and they are established by practice; hence they also relate to *conventions*.

**codec:** an apparatus for *encoding* and *decoding signals*.

**'codes and conventions':** often used casually as a catch-all term to describe the things that we associate with a *text*; hence the phrase 'generic codes and conventions' to refer to the *signifiers* we can expect to see or hear in specific *genres*. (See also *code* and *convention*.)

**codes of practice:** agreed sets of rules, either voluntary or legislative, which determine professional practice, including in the media.

**cognition:** the processes by which our brain perceives and knows, as opposed to feels; the act or process of knowing; the mental process of acquiring knowledge. The cognitive process is responsible for how we make sense of the world.

**cognitive dissonance:** describes the discomfort we feel when holding two incompatible ideas at the same time (e.g. 'I am a nice person' and 'Sometimes I get so angry with people that I want to harm them.')

**cold light:** see *colour temperature*

**collaboration:** where two or more artists work together to create aspects or the whole of a media text. Examples include the effect the musical compositions of Ennio Morricone, or the *characterisations* created by Clint Eastwood, have on the films of the *director* Sergio Leone (e.g. *The Good, the Bad and the Ugly*, It, 1966); the importance of the work of the *cinematographer* Jack Cardiff on the films of Powell and Pressberger (e.g. *Black Narcissus*, UK, 1947).

**collectors' edition:** a version of a *DVD* that combines a wide number of extra features and is often unusually packaged. It is also a *marketing* tool for DVDs and exemplifies the *Hollywood* approach of: 'Why sell something once when you can sell it ten times?'

**Colorisation:** a patented process that changes *black and white* films into colour. Most film purists and *cineastes* are critical of this process, as it changes the original conception and intention of the film.

**colour:** all colours have associations for humans and these usually originate from a natural or empirical source. They are used in all aspects of visual design as instant communication.

**colour film:** early cinema experimented with the use of colour in film in the early 1900s. Two- and three-colour processes were used, with rotating coloured filters in front of the *camera lens*, as well as the colouring of specific sequences by hand, in order to convey particular information (for example, yellow was used for daylight and blue for night-time in *The Phantom of the Opera* (Rupert Julian, USA, 1925). The first use of colour in a major film was in the middle section of *The Wizard of Oz* (Victor Fleming, USA, 1939), where Dorothy goes to the Land of Oz. The first full-colour film (using the Technicolor process) was *Gone With the Wind* (Victor Fleming, USA, 1939). (See also *Colorisation, Technicolor.*)

**colour saturation:** in printing, the thickness of coloured ink on the page. In *digital* imaging and photography, the density of colour in the image or a selected section of it.

**colour separation:** see *four-colour printing*.

**colour TV:** first used regularly in the USA in 1954, colour TV was not introduced to the UK until 1967.

**colour temperature:** colour can be said to have a temperature. For example, red, yellow and orange are hot colours associated with warmth and heat (due to the colours of the flames of a fire) and blue and green are associated with cold (due to associations with water and ice). The temperature of a colour can be used in any visual design, including lighting for film and TV, with the use of filters or gels, which change the temperature of the lighting in order to create a particular atmosphere.

**Columbia:** see *Little Three*

**column:** a regular (daily, weekly or monthly) piece of writing for a newspaper by a prestigious journalist or writer (referred to as a 'columnist'). The writer can have an individual style of writing, may pontificate in a general way or may present an ideological stance that is understood by the readership. Successful columnists are important in keeping a readership loyal to the newspaper and sometimes they become celebrities in their own right.

**comedy:** a *genre* of which the main aim is to incite laughter. This is sometimes seen as a problematic definition, as it can be argued that comedy is not actually a genre but simply a *mode* that is in fact applied to other genres; e.g. *Young Frankenstein* (Mel Brooks, USA, 1974) happens to be a *horror* film in a comic mode. The idea of comedy as a genre is clearer when discussing the television category of *sitcom*, with its stock *characters*, limited *mise en scène* and very particular *acting* styles.

**comic/comic book/comic strip:** a *narrative* that is told in a series of drawings or pictures, either within another publication, such as a daily newspaper (comic strip) or as a whole publication (comic/comic book). They began in the late 1800s, but became especially popular in the USA in the 1930s. They were seen essentially as entertainment for young boys, but have since grown into a major *subgenre* of the magazine industry. Famous examples are *Batman, Superman, Spider-Man* and *The X-Men*. Since 1978, with *Superman* (Richard Donner, USA, 1978), *blockbusters* based on these have become a mini-industry in themselves. Marvel

Comics and DC Comics in the USA are the two most famous and successful comp
this production area.

**commercial:** *advertisement* placed between, or in slots during, radio and televisi
grammes.

**commercial broadcasting:** the production and transmission of television and radio programmes as a profit-making business, as opposed to *public service broadcasting* such as
the *BBC*. Revenue is normally earned by the interruption of programmes with *advertisements* (usually called *commercials*) and/or, if possible, the selling of products to other
providers, especially those abroad. Advertisers pay pro rata in relation to the size of the
*audience*. The Television Act of 1954 created *Independent Television* as a means of
competing with the BBC, with the intention of creating more diverse programmes and theo-
retically maintaining high standards. In the UK, since 2003, *Ofcom* has been responsible for
overseeing all commercial products. The success of commercial broadcasting, especially in
the last couple of decades following *deregulation*, has led to a proliferation of television
channels. This has, in turn, invited debate over whether 'more is less': that more choice has
led to many mediocre programmes being made simply to fill the airwaves, and that top
quality broadcasting is irrevocably in decline. It has also been criticised in providing too
much *air time* for advertisers. One other area of debate is *sponsorship*, where the advertiser
may attempt to control the content or *ideology* of the programme, although to date this
seems to be more of a concern in the USA.

**commission:** (i) a government agency or committee with a very specific brief, such as the
*Independent Television Commission* which oversaw the workings of *commercial broadcasting*
from 1991 to 2003. (ii) to employ someone to produce a media product for your organisation
(e.g. Channel 4 commissions independent specialist television companies to produce particular types of programmes for its broadcasting). (iii) a percentage payment paid for services
supplied (e.g. an actor will usually pay his *agent* a 10 per cent fee of the total earnings that
have been accrued through the agent's negotiations with media production companies).

**commissioner broadcaster:** see *publisher broadcaster*

**commissioning editor:** the main person responsible for buying or *commissioning* television programmes for a *broadcaster*.

**common sense:** any version of reality that is accepted by the majority. A 'common sense'
explanation for events is always favoured over alternative or minority viewpoints because it
most closely matches the world view of the *dominant ideology.*

**communication:** in simple terms, the exchange of information between people using a
common system of *signs*, be they visual or aural. Definitions of this term change quite considerably in different academic contexts. An early model offered by Harold Lasswell was,
'Who says what, in which channel, to whom, with what effect.' Other writers have dealt more
with the social or semiological aspects of this area. (See also *semiology.*)

**community broadcasting:** radio and television programmes made by the local community
for the local community. In the increasing diversity of media products, the rapid change in
access to specialist technology and the expansion of the *internet*, there are more people
who wish to communicate at a local level and it is now increasingly possible for them to do
so. It has been embraced enthusiastically in the USA. (See also *public access*.)

C D E F G H I J K L M N O P Q R S T U V W X Y Z

**commutation test:** in *semiology*, where one aspect (*signifier*) of a *media text* is hypothetically replaced by another to test the qualities of the original (or both). For example, it is often interesting to consider what would happen if the original *casting* of a film was changed. Imagine *Terminator 2* (James Cameron, USA, 1991) with Leonardo di Caprio as the Terminator and *William Shakespeare's Romeo+Juliet* (Baz Luhrmann, USA, 1996) with Arnold Schwarzenegger as Romeo; such a reflection would illuminate many issues to do with the *encoding* of *masculinity* and hence its *construction* in media texts.

**compact:** this is a small, convenient size of newspaper and magazine (also known as handbag-size) that has recently become popular because it can be carried easily in a pocket or bag. (See also *tabloid*.)

**complication:** a stage in a *narrative* (usually occurring in the first or second 'Act') whereby the initial *conflict* situation is further complicated by the occurrence of another event or the appearance of another *character*. This additional obstacle is useful in preventing the *audience* seeing the final outcome (or *closure*) of the narrative as being too predictable. It also makes the *hero/heroine* seem even stronger in the eyes of the audience if they can overcome the complication in addition to the original situation. Complication can also cause a dividing of the *protagonist's* loyalties and is used time and again, especially in *action/adventure* films, where, for example, a hero might be torn between saving his 'love interest' and saving the city/planet.

**composite shot:** a camera *shot* that is made, or composed, of elements from different sources, such as *live* footage with a *matte shot* of some spectacular scenery. Also refers to a scene in which an *actor* is seen on screen in two manifestations, for example, as when Eddie Murphy plays a whole family in *The Nutty Professor* (Tom Shadyac, USA, 1996).

**composition:** (i) see *news values.* (ii) the visual arrangement of elements within a *frame*/screen, or on a page.

**compositional modes:** see *documentary*

**computer-generated images:** see *CGI*

**concept:** (i) an idea for a media product. (ii) see also *key concepts*.

**conflict:** a clash between two or more persons, or between people and other entities (e.g. animals, weather, the supernatural), who have different objectives. Conflict is an essential ingredient in any fiction or non-fiction *narrative*. The source or type of conflict need not necessarily be major.

**conglomerate:** a large business organisation that comprises a number of different companies, often linked by area of interests or commodities, which when brought together have considerable strength and power. Six media conglomerates dominate the international media. Within a typical media conglomerate one could expect to see interests in news (both broadcasting and journalism), television, radio, magazine production, film production, popular music and dotcom companies, and of course in any technologies relating to these. (See also *Big Six*.)

**connotation:** an association that a *sign* may have. It is 'the second order of *meaning*', according to Roland Barthes (the first being *denotation* – the identification of the object or its surface meaning). When we consider that a sign could be a word, a sound, an image, a colour, a piece of music, *dialogue*, or something else, then it is clear that in a media product there are many connotations jostling against each other. Connotations are also read from the *text* and vary according to the reader. The concept raises all sorts of issues about the relationship between the reader and the text.

**consonance:** agreement, harmony. We may, for example, talk of consonance between the music and the images in a *text*.

**conspicuous consumption:** the spending habits of people who spend their money in a way that is obvious to others. The spending is less related to their needs and more indicative of their desire to display their wealth or status. Many of the objects that connect to conspicuous consumption are media products. This concept also relates to 'invidious consumption', which is motivated by creating envy in others.

**constituency:** see *audience*

**construct; construction:** something that has been built, put together. We use it in *media studies* to accentuate the fact that all *media products* are constructed, and can consequently be *deconstructed* as part of our study. More abstract aspects, such as *masculinity*, can also be seen as constructs.

**consumer:** person or organisation who buys a product or service.

**consumer-based television:** this refers to programmes that are based on the experience and opinions of consumers of various products and services, such as the *BBC* TV programmes, *Points of View* and *Watchdog*, and *ITV*'s *Holidays from Hell*.

**consumer culture:** a *culture* that is steeped in *consumerism*.

**consumerism:** a view in contemporary capitalist society that happiness is often achieved by how much we spend on material possessions. This relates quite powerfully to our study of the media, for example, in the following ways:

- Many material possessions are *media products* themselves, or provide the technology required to enjoy media products (e.g. television sets, DVD players, computers, iPods, mobile phones).

- The media in the West is often seen as an upholder of the capitalist doctrine and political economy.

- The media encourages consumerism – it sells the products and creates the demand.

**consumer magazine:** one which tests products that are on the market, available for consumption by the public (e.g. *Which?* magazine).

**consumer profile:** the details of lifestyle, income and so on of a potential type of *consumer* (rather than an individual) which is targeted in *advertising* campaigns or by a company *marketing* a specific *media product*. (See also *geodemographics*, *psychographics*.)

**consumer research:** see *market research*

**content analysis:** a method used in media analysis of print publications to look in detail at what is actually in the *text*. It is done by breaking the text down into sections and evaluating numerically how much space is given over to each area (e.g. *advertising*, regular *features*, competitions). Sometimes referred to as 'quantitative analysis'.

**context; contextualisation:** in print texts, the text surrounding a word or passage, or its relative position in relation to other aspects such as images. In moving-image texts, we can look at what surrounds a particular image and how it affects the *meaning* or *connotations* of the image.

**contiguity:** see *spatial and temporal contiguity*

**continuity:** the aspects of a *media text* that contribute to its continuous flow so that it is easier to consume.

**continuity editing:** the type of film *editing* exemplified by *classical Hollywood* in which every effort is made to make the film flow seamlessly, so that the *audience* does not notice its *construction* from many different *shots*. In most film-making today, the *continuity* is first worked out in pre-production, when the *art director* would prepare a *storyboard* under guidance, as a kind of blueprint for the *director* to work from. At this stage, the creative artists can choose and arrange exactly what the audience will see. When continuity is not achieved, this is called a 'continuity error'. For example, if a *character* in a scene wore clothes which kept changing colour from shot to shot (because two different shots were filmed on different days and then were edited together) this would be distracting for the audience and would be regarded as poor film-making.

**contrapuntal sound:** sounds that do not easily match the images they are accompanying, or even run against them. This can have quite a disorientating effect upon the *audience* and make them question what they are seeing. (An interesting demonstration of this effect is to choose music that the audience does not associate with a well-known film sequence and to apply it in place of the original *soundtrack*.)

**contra zoom:** very carefully tracking in and *zooming* out at the same time, ensuring that the object is in *focus*. This has quite a disorientating effect as the central object remains the same but the background changes quite dramatically. One of the early examples of this is in Spielberg's *Jaws* (USA, 1975), where the character of Police Chief Brody (played by Roy Schneider) is sitting on the beach watching the sea and the shark devours a little boy; the impact of the *shot* is quite breath-taking.

**controlling idea:** according to Robert McKee in his book *Story: Substance, Structure, Style and the Principles of Screenwriting* (1999), this 'may be expressed in a single sentence describing how and why life undergoes change from one condition of existence at the beginning to another at the end [of a *narrative*]'. It is a major *theme* that relates to function and structure and can be an overriding thrust for the whole narrative. McKee points out that it must have value and cause, and cites *Columbo*, the TV detective series, as one with a controlling idea of: 'Justice is restored because the *protagonist* is more clever than the criminal.'

**convention:** an established way of doing something. (See also 'codes and conventions'.)

**convergence:** the way in which businesses, or products, can converge (come together) to make a third entity. This concept can be applied at business level and product level. An example of convergence in new media technologies is the mobile phone, which is increasingly becoming a product way beyond its original *brief*; indeed some *advertising* relies on the fact that we cannot tell if the phone's function is primarily to be a mobile phone or a digital camera. Some theorists have argued that convergence is inevitable in a computer-driven age and it is this that is primarily leading to major changes in our society. How soon, for example, will it be before all of the functions in our home can be controlled from one central computer, which itself can be controlled from a distance?

**cool news:** *news* that has not just happened and therefore may not be given as high a profile in the news reporting process as *hot news*.

**co-producer:** see *producer*

**co-production:** see *international co-production*

**copy:** the written material (as opposed to images) for *newspapers* or *magazines*. It is edited by a *sub-editor* and then put into the right format and arrangement on the page.

**copy date:** the date by which all written material must be with the publisher.

**copy desk:** coordinated by the chief sub-copy editor and staffed by *sub-editors* (or 'subs') who work on writing *copy* for specific *news* item. Each section of a news publication or magazine has a different area, or 'desk' for specific types of news (e.g. entertainment, sport, fashion, health, politics, royal news). The copy editor liaises with the editor-in-chief for the production of each publication. Technically, the term 'copy writer' refers to anyone who writes copy for any purpose, but is specifically used to refer to someone who creates the words in an advert.

**copyright:** the legal ownership of intellectual property, such as that in publishing and the media. The copyright is often owned by the writer of a book, for example, but in *media products* the *rights* are often with the production company itself. In many media products there are a large number of subsidiary rights involved; for example, in the case of a film the *distribution* rights for the UK and those for the USA may be held by different people or companies.

**corporate identity/image:** the overall 'face' and 'personality' of a company, which is created as much by its self-representation through its name and logo design and all its media *representations*, as by what it actually produces. Designing the visual side of a corporate image (logo, website and stationery etc.) can be especially lucrative for an *advertising* company. Similarly, a TV *news* programme is an important flagship programme that proclaims its channel's corporate identity (such as the BBC, ITV and Channel 4 news programmes) and they are redesigned periodically with the aim of retaining and attracting *audiences*.

**correspondent:** in *journalism*, a specialist reporter who sends stories from overseas or works in a particular field, e.g. 'our health correspondent'. They are so called because in the past they sent correspondence (i.e. letters) back to inform *editors* about what was happening in far-flung areas of the world.

**costume:** the clothes worn by *characters* in a fictional text. The costumes are part of the *mise en scène* and as such are an important part of *signification* (for example, as a generic or period identifier).

**costume designer:** the person who is responsible for the design of the clothing worn by the characters in a fictional text. This is often a prestigious post and many leading designers have had considerable power and influence in film production (e.g. Edith Head, for many of the Hollywood films of the 1940s and 1950s). Major fashion designers have also been used in film costume design (e.g. Giorgio Armani for the production of *The Untouchables* (Brian de Palma, USA, 1987) and Jean-Paul Gaultier for Almodovar's *Bad Education* (Sp, 2004). Academics Stella Bruzzi and Pam Cook have written significant studies of the importance of costume design in creating meaning in film.

**costume drama:** a period piece involving lavish or spectacular *costumes* that are historically accurate (e.g., *Jane Eyre*, BBC 2006).

**counter cinema/film:** that which is in direct opposition to the *mainstream*, especially in terms of *ideology*, politics, *production* or social mores.

**counter-culture:** that which is in opposition to the dominant forces in society. For example, *youth culture*, in various periods, has often run counter to that of the *mainstream* (e.g. hippies in the 1960s and 1970s; punk in the 1970s and 1980s; goths since the 1980s and continuing).

**counterpoint:** in *music*, the term has a very specific meaning, namely, different melodies that come together, or melodies which provide a satisfying contrast. In *film*, counterpoint usually refers to the contrasts between *image* and music (See also *contrapuntal sound.*)

**coup de cinéma/théatre:** in narrative *closure*, an unexpected, dramatic and sudden twist; a dazzling and sensational revelation; a *narrative* device which excites the *audience* and ensures they leave with satisfaction (e.g. as in Bryan Singer's 1995 film *The Usual Suspects*).

**coverage (news):** the items that are included in a news production, and to what depth they are covered.

**coverage (film):** see *master shot*

**coverline:** a *caption* on a *magazine* cover; also called *sell lines.*

**cover mounts:** a selling device where a gift is stuck to the *magazine*'s cover.

**cover price:** the price printed on the outside of a *newspaper* or *magazine* front cover, usually with a bar code. It is a relatively minor source of income for its producers compared to its *advertising revenue.*

**cover shot:** (i) in print, a dominant *image* or photo on the front cover of a magazine. (ii) (in film and television) see *master shot*

**cover story:** the article or *story* in a newspaper or magazine that is showcased on the front cover, usually by an image and a *headline* or *splash.* The cover story is used to entice the readership into the magazine.

**crab dolly:** a device that moves the *camera* sideways, although in practice the dolly itself can often move in any direction.

**crab shot:** a *shot* made by using a *crab dolly* so that it moves sideways or in an angular direction; a particular type of *tracking shot.*

**crane:** a very large projecting arm on a trolley that has placed on one end a *camera* (and usually its operator too). It looks much like a small industrial crane.

**crane shot:** using a crane, this *shot* enables the *camera* to move up or down quickly, or to follow *characters* from a height. It can, if used quickly, give a very unusual effect, namely to make the *audience* feel quite dizzy. In many cases, the audience is hardly aware that the shot is being made on a crane as it is used so slowly and unobtrusively.

**creative:** in *advertising*, the term used for a person who is responsible for coming up with new ideas for advertising a product; usually a member of a creative team.

**credit sequence; credits:** a list of those who are responsible for the making of a film, and it can occur at the beginning, the end or both. Often, a film has a title sequence listing the leading players and the main creative/*production* team and then also a full, exhaustive credit roll at the end, which can go on for many minutes while the *audience* are invited to enjoy the *soundtrack* (and perhaps buy it later).

**crescendo:** the high point or climax of a sequence of *music* that is played increasingly loudly, or at speed, or both. It usually accompanies an equally high point in the *text* or *narrative.*

**crew:** the *production* team on the making of a film. Includes a very wide variety of craftsmen or technicians such as the electricians, lighting engineers, carpenters.

**crime film/thriller/series:** a *genre* in film and TV (either fictional or true crime). The piece may also be further categorised by referring to it as 'detective', 'gangster', 'police', 'murder-mystery' or 'whodunnit'.

**crisis:** in *narrative*, a decisive point in the *plot* when the *protagonist* faces a dilemma and must choose a course of action that may well be the turning point; the consequences of this point should lead to the resolution and ultimate *closure*.

**critic:** a person who is employed by a magazine or newspaper owner or a *broadcaster* to see or hear a *media text* and offer an opinion and a judgment on its worth so that the public may be better able to decide whether or not they want to experience it. *Copy* produced is referred to as 'criticism'. The body of critical opinion on the release of, say, a film is referred to as the 'critical reception' and this can on some occasions 'make or break' it commercially. Some texts are said to be critic proof, in the sense that they find an *audience* despite what the critics think. In recent years some producers have tried to hinder the power of the critics' reception by not inviting them to the official opening of a *film*, a ploy which carries its own risks. An interesting take on film criticism is the advent of websites which are offering the opinion of the everyday film-goer rather than an employed writer (e.g. *Ain't it Cool News*).

**crop:** to remove a section or sections of a *photograph*. This process can be ideologically motivated. For example, when cropping deletes aspects of an original photograph that the editor does not wish the readership to see, the *meaning* of the *image* is changed (and the presentation biased).

**cross-cutting:** in *editing* (especially a fictional narrative), jumping between two or more different scenes in order to create a link between them and subsequently to create a different, more powerful or dense sequence than that which would have been achieved by showing them in strict sequence. (It is, for example, a device much used by director Francis Ford Coppola.) When used for a dramatic and extensive sequence, it is referred to as '*parallel editing* of a parallel narrative'. Cross-cutting suggests to the audience that events are happening simultaneously.

**cross-fade:** quite a gentle way of *editing*, this is where one image is faded out as another is simultaneously faded in. It often signifies the passing of time or changing locations.

**cross-generic:** describes a *media text* that crosses more than one *genre* (for example, a TV programme such as the BBC's *The Office*, which is a cross between the genres of *documentary* and *sitcom*). Similar to generic hybrids, multi-generic hybrids.

**crosshead:** words used to break up *copy* and usually taken from the main text, presented in a larger font and in bold. Often cites original quotes from the text.

**crossing-the-line:** see *180-degree line*

**cross-media ownership:** the ownership of several companies that produce different media, also known as consolidation.

**crossover:** describes a *media text*, music artist or band that moves to another channel, medium, means of distribution or market because of popularity and/or initial success. Examples include: television programmes that begin on BBC2 but attract very large audiences and are therefore moved by the controller to BBC1; radio programmes that move to television (*Dead Ringers*, from Radio 4 to BBC2); and *comic book* characters that are originally created in print publications but become part of a major film franchise (e.g. *Batman*). Some music recording artists have also crossed over from their original market and widened their appeal.

**CU shot:** see *cinematography*

**cue:** a signal for speech or action to take place; it is most commonly used in relation to *actors* waiting for a line prompt from another actor in order to time their own line or action.

**cult film:** film that generates an enthusiastic following, often among young people. Sometimes a cult film can build up a reputation over a number of years, gradually gaining new audiences. A good example is *The Rocky Horror Picture Show* (Jim Sharman, UK, 1975), which began as a theatre production but which grew immensely in status once it became a film. There are now interactive showings of the film, where the *audience* can dress up and join in on stage, as well as throw significant objects around the auditorium. These events are sometimes referred to as *Sing-along-a-Rocky Horror Picture Show.*

**cultural artefacts:** the physical products of *culture*, such as a *media text.*

**cultural capital:** as proposed by Pierre Bourdieu, the knowledge, experiences, frames of reference, *values*, attitudes and *ideologies* that we possess individually, and that condition the way we read a *media text* or, indeed, create one. In terms of social status, cultural capital is often more important than financial capital (i.e. money and possessions). This concept is important in considering *spectatorship* and how we differ in our views about media texts. This idea of cultural capital also relates to issues of *social class* and the class identification of a product or audience. It raises questions about attitudes and values and how assumptions may be made by *producers* of media texts about the cultural capital that their *target audience* may or may not possess.

**cultural diversity:** refers to the variety of *cultures* available in a multicultural society (such as the UK) or to the existence of such diversity in the world as a whole. Study in this area includes, for example: the similarities and differences between cultures; the nature of different *cultural artefacts;* the effect of cultures on each other; the effects of *diaspora;* and *media products* as cultural artefacts representative of a society.

**cultural identity:** how individuals and groups recognise themselves and present a set of *codes and conventions* within society, especially through *cultural artefacts.*

**cultural imperialism:** the use of *cultural artefacts* to establish and maintain power or dominance over a subordinate group. This is best seen in the way a society may especially treat its own culture as being better or more important than others, invoking aspects of *ethnocentrism* and *hegemony*. For example, the history of *Hollywood* exemplifies this from 1917 onwards, when President Woodrow Wilson said, 'We need Hollywood to sell America', referring not just to products such as Coca-Cola, McDonalds or Levis, but also to the selling of its ethnocentric history, its cultural artefacts and its *ideologies* (e.g. the 'American Dream').

**cultural literacy:** the ability of individuals to understand their own *culture* and therefore their ability to function effectively within it.

**cultural studies:** the study of *culture* through a variety of disciplines, for example, history, sociology, anthropology and, of course, *media studies*. It also involves overtly political aspects of culture, such as *ideology*, and looks at representations such as age, *social class*, *gender* and *race*.

**culture:** (i) the outcome of human activity seen in areas such as the arts, media and sport. Deriving from the Latin for 'to cultivate', the term refers to the cultivation of the human mind. (ii) in a sociological sense, the set of practices and beliefs that makes one society or *subculture* different from another. For example, *mainstream* US culture is based around Christianity, capitalism and meritocracy, but there are many US subcultures (religious, political and youth) that signal their different values through dress, rituals and lifestyle.

**current affairs:** topical news items, often of a political or social nature. These are not just covered in broadcast or print news products, but can appear in a wide number of formats, ranging from *documentaries* to comedy *game show*s (e.g. the BBC's *Have I Got News for You*).

**cut:** the commonest form of *edit* in moving image texts, this is the instantaneous change from one *shot* to another in an edit (as opposed to, say, a *dissolve*). It is also the word a *director* calls when instructing a *camera operator* to stop filming.

**cutaway:** in *editing*, a shot that cuts to something outside the frame but in the vicinity of the previous shot. There are a number of different reasons why a cutaway might be included, for example, it can add variety, change the pace, or create suspense.

**cut-in shot:** in *editing*, a brief inserted *shot* that shows detail from the main shot or *character* (for example, a watch, the character's eyes.)

**cut scene:** many *video game*s are prefaced, before the *gameplay* starts, by a sequence which introduces the *setting*, the main *characters* and the *narrative*. It is commonly used in games derived from films where the *audience* is familiar with the *plot* and characters, or where the *game environment* is constructed with a high degree of *photo-realism*.

**cutting-room:** place where the film or television programme is *edited*; hence the phrase 'on the cutting-room floor', which refers to the discarding of film footage that is not used.

### Do you need revision help and advice?

Go to pages 251–292 for a range of revision appendices that include exam advice and tips.

**DAB:** see *digital audio broadcast*

**Daguerrotype:** invented by Louis Daguerre (1789–1851) in 1830, this was an early form of *photography* whereby images were exposed on metal coated with silver oxide.

**dailies:** see *newspaper*, *rushes*

**DAT:** digital audio tape.

**dateline:** the date a *newspaper* report was filed or published.

**daybook:** like a calendar, this is a source of information kept by all *news* producers, which records key events that are known to be happening on each day and whose reporting needs to be combined with that of unexpected events.

**day for night:** filming night-time sequences during the day, usually using filters, but more recently with *digital* technology. The advantage of this process is that the film-makers can see clearly what they are doing. An example of this can be seen in the night sequences in *Bridge on the River Kwai* (David Lean, USA/UK, 1957).

**dayparting:** see *scheduling*

**DBS:** see *direct broadcasting service*

**DCMS:** see *Department of Culture, Media and Sport*

**dead air:** see *air*

**debate:** to argue a case, or to consider something at length, from a variety of different angles. We use this term in *media* and *film studies* to refer to the issues that may pertain to a particular aspect of the media, and that can be discussed by students in their examination answers, backed up by practical and theoretical knowledge and reference points. It is also used to refer to discussions in the media itself, such as an ongoing *news* story.

**decisive moment:** in *photography*, the instantaneous moment when the photographer 'sees' the photograph and captures it by opening the lens shutter. French photographer Henri Cartier Bresson (1908–2004) had many useful things to says about this aspect of photography, including: 'There is nothing in this world that does not have a decisive moment,' 'To me, photography is the simultaneous recognition, in a fraction of a second, of the significance of an event as well as of a precise organisation of forms that give that event its proper expression,' and, 'Oop! The Moment! Once you miss it, it is gone forever.' This view stresses that the art of the photographer is quite different from that of the fine artist.

**decode; decoding:** just as we *encode* by putting *texts* together, much the same as we would put letters together to make words, we the receivers of a text must decode it to make sense of it. At some level we are therefore interpreting what we are seeing or hearing; or, put another way, we are reading the textual *signs*, just as we would read a textual passage in the English language. How we decode something depends very much on who we are and there is usually no absolute in the way in which someone interprets what they see. This leads to variant readings of the same text.

**deconstruct; deconstruction:** the process of studying *media texts* as *constructs*, using close textual analysis to investigate both micro and macro aspects. Many aspects of *semiology* are important tools for this type of study and should be referenced for the appropriate vocabulary.

**décor:** the style (of objects, props, drapes etc.) used to furnish a set or *mise en scène* of a film. The *art director* is usually responsible for this, in conjunction with the *director*.

**deep focus:** a *depth of field* where everything is in *focus*, both near and far.

**de-focus:** where a *camera operator* causes some, or all, images on screen to go out of *focus*.

**de Havilland decision:** in February 1945 the glamorous *Hollywood* star Olivia de Havilland won her court case against *Warner Bros*, effectively limiting the powers of major studios from punishing *actors* who refused a role during their seven-year contract. (This preceded the *Paramount Case* of 1948, after which Hollywood studios had to sell off their cinemas.) The decline of the powers of the major studios began here.

**demographic profile:** a set of data relating to the population of a group, such as an *audience* for a *media text*.

**demographics:** study of populations, especially size, growth, density, distribution, and the interpretations relating to these statistics.

**denotation:** see *connotation*

**dénouement:** the part of narrative *closure* that entails all mysteries being explained and everything being made clear to the *audience*. For example, this happens in the final scene of a *Poirot* story, when the Belgian detective explains everything to the *characters* within the *diegesis* of the film (or television programme) and to us, the audience. In conventional narratives it is important that we feel a sense of audience satisfaction and that we do not leave the cinema with too many questions unanswered.

**Department of Culture, Media and Sport (DCMS):** government department with the brief to oversee all media production (and media literacy) in the UK.

**depth of field:** in *photography* and *cinematography*, the entire area which is in *focus*, both in front of the object and behind it. The depth of field will change depending on things such as: the focal length of the *lens*; the f-stop of the *camera* (how narrow the aperture is); the *lighting*; the space used. In moving-image texts, the depth of field gives the *director* and *cinematographer* many visual aspects to play with and to choose from. They must decide what the *audience* looks at. One simple device that controls what the audience sees would be to have a figure in the foreground that is in focus, but not have the background in focus, and then to switch this around. This change will then allow the audience to see the figure as the central object within the frame. The opposite of this would be a widescreen action film that uses *deep focus*, where everything is in focus in a long shot. This would allow the audience to look at whatever they like within the *mise en scène*.

**deregulation:** with reference to public services, the ending of regulation by government authority, usually leading to greater competition. Although the rules, orders or restrictions on these services may have been seen as a hindrance, the absence of them puts more responsibility on the service provider and takes away some element of protection. A good example is the *Broadcasting Act* of 1990, which transformed the organisation and management of future providers of broadcasting *channels* and stations and increased their number. This has increased competition immensely. Some have argued that this deregulation, although in tune with the fast-changing world, has been detrimental to the quality of output and is not necessarily what many sectors of the British public wanted, especially those who support *Reithian* views.

**desensitisation:** in the discussion of *effects theory*, the idea that the more the public are exposed to media images of violence and various forms of antisocial or deviant behaviour, the more likely they are to be unconcerned by such aspects of conduct either onscreen or in real life.

**desktop publishing:** a software package (for example Quark Express or Creative Suite) with which all the *copy* and *images* for print media are prepared on the desktop of a computer, ready for printing. This process replaced the former compositing processes of *hot metal*. *Today* newspaper (1986–1995) was the first UK daily newspaper to use this process and, while the paper did not survive long, the process revolutionised UK newspaper and magazine production.

**detective film:** a *narrative* that involves the investigation of a crime, normally by a police officer or private detective, and ends with a solution, usually with the criminals being punished in some way (arrest or death). With some *subgenres*, the evident clues can engage the *audience* much like an amateur sleuth (e.g. stories involving Sherlock Holmes, Hercule Poirot, Miss Marple, Maigret). In some incarnations the detective has taken a particularly strong and controversial moral stance (e.g. in Don Siegal's *Dirty Harry* films starring Clint Eastwood), leaving the audience with an ambivalent attitude towards the investigative *hero*. More recently, there has been further blurring of moral standpoints between detectives and criminals, such as in *Heat* (Michael Mann, USA, 1995), *LA Confidential* (Curtis Hanson, USA, 1997) and *The Departed* (Martin Scorsese, USA, 2006).

**deus ex machina:** (from Greek tragedy) 'a god from a machine' (literally, from above in a crane) arrives on the stage to bring about *closure* of a play, which often involves the god passing some form of judgment. We may use this term when referring to the *closure* of a *narrative* of a complicated *plot*, especially when the *dénouement* is particularly contrived or the difficulty of the plot cannot be resolved easily or to complete satisfaction. It can also refer to a the arrival of new *character* at the end bringing about the narrative closure.

**development; development hell:** the period in the creation of a *film* when the writer and/or *producer* have successfully sold their pitch to a studio or executives, and so have been given the green light, but are now enduring the pre-production stage where things can go well or disastrously. Sometimes the reasons involve a change of personnel at some part of the process and the incoming executive has quite different ideas about how the project should develop. Many films get as far as this development stage but no further, with the key personnel sometimes being cited as having 'creative difficulties'. The project may subsequently be shelved indefinitely, depending upon who has ownership of the *rights* and for how long. Examples of films, television series and video games that endured 'development hell' include: *Basic Instinct 2* (Michael Caton-Jones, Ger/UK/US, 2006), which took over ten years and involved Sharon Stone taking legal action against the producers to force an out-of-court settlement; *Blake's 7: a Legacy Reborn* (the project came to a standstill in 2002 despite having the original Avon, Paul Darrow, as executive producer); *Prey* (2005) – this video game took eleven years to get to its audience.

**deviancy:** behaviour that is deemed by society to be sharply different from the norm and therefore unacceptable within the social community. This, of course, is highly dependent on what a society at any given time considers to be the norm. For example, there have been periods of our history when men have conformed to the norm of wearing short hair, and in the 1960s when *youth culture* became more powerful and long hair became more common among males, many older people referred to the young as 'long-haired deviants'. The media have been well placed to represent groups in particular ways and so be an agent of social change, including having an effect on what the dominant society deems to be the consensus view.

**diachronic:** from linguistics and *semiology*, meaning 'historically' or 'through time'. The term refers to seeing a film text as a linear *narrative* that we see develop from point to point through a period of time, as opposed to seeing it as *synchronic*, which means seeing the film as a whole entity, at a specific moment in time. We can see film holistically from a diachronic perspective, which sees it as an evolving language and art form; or from a synchronic perspective, which sees it within its context and with its own internal features.

**dialect:** regional language that is characterised by its vocabulary, pronunciation and idiomatic expression. Other more complex aspects of this involve identification by *social class* and/or race. For example, in the past British society saw regional dialects as inferior to standard English; this indicates a highly hierarchical society where one particular aspect of dialect, the *accent* (the pronunciation), was an instant *signifier* of social class and status. In order to achieve upward social mobility a person had to be prepared to change his or her accent and dialect. When BBC1 began in 1955, all the presenters spoke with the same 'received pronunciation' (educated English). During the 1960s this began to change, as it became fashionable to have a regional accent (e.g. Liverpudlian, because of the Beatles; or Cockney, because of the emergence of working-class Londoners in fashion, photography and media). Today, UK television presenters often speak with a distinct regional accent but avoid dialect words.

**dialogue:** the conversation that occurs between *characters* in a work of fiction, or the lines spoken by *actors*. In moving-image texts it is important that the speech of the actor is synchronous with the *images* (except in the case of voice-overs). In many situations, the sound recording of the dialogue is added after shooting, especially if the quality cannot be guaranteed on location itself. Some media forms (e.g. radio) rely heavily on dialogue, others much less so (e.g. silent cinema). In 1927, sound recording for *film* arrived and changed film forever. *Singin' in the Rain* (Stanley Donen and Gene Kelly, USA, 1952) provides an entertaining look at the complications of making sound pictures, in a very famous mid-act sequence. Since then, dialogue has been an important part of most *narratives* (Hollywood genres in particular).

**dialogue overlap:** see *overlapping sound*

**diary (news):** the daily list of major events that are known in advance so that *editors*, reporters and their *news* teams can be prepared to cover them. For example: the state opening of Parliament; all major sporting events; Royal engagements; celebrity weddings; the arrival of foreign dignitaries, including Heads of State. It is the job of many *publicists* to get their clients into the news diaries. What gets into, and is taken out of, the news diary is under the control of individual *gatekeepers*, especially the editors. Over 80 per cent of news stories are known about in advance.

**diaspora:** the migration of an ethnic group from its traditional homeland and its consequent dispersal around the world. It usually applies to groups who have been encouraged or forced to leave their native soil by war, the natural elements or economic necessity. Once a group have moved elsewhere their continuing identity and development can often be seen in the new location as the refugees establish (and sometimes change) their *culture*. We can see many aspects of this diasporic *cultural identity* in media forms, especially cinema: for example, films that examine black identity in Britain since the 1950s.

**diction:** enunciation and expression in speech or singing, including pronunciation; choice of words and manner; appropriate *register.* These all contribute to the impression that a person or actor presents. Diction is an important part of *non-verbal communication.*

**diegesis:** in a fiction film *narrative*, anything that is part of the story-bound, cinematic world of the *characters*, whether we see it on screen or not (although usually, we do). The diegesis is the world that the characters inhabit; if they can see, hear or experience it then it is part of that world. If only the *audience* can see or hear something, then it is not part of the diegesis. The diegesis obviously includes things like: the *mise en scène;* the *dialogue* between characters; music playing in that world (e.g. from a radio that one of the characters switches on, or someone playing a guitar); the ambient sound of things we can see ( e.g. cars passing by). On a more complex level, the diegesis also includes things like: sound which is part of the fictional world of the film but which we cannot actually see on the screen (e.g. crickets chirping in the bush); events which we never actually see but are referred to by the characters as having happened; characters who are being referred to, but whom we do not see (at that moment, or at any time). *Non-diegetic* elements include the music soundtrack of the film; the titles and intertitles; voice-overs and credit sequences. An interesting example of diegesis is in the film *The Truman Show* (Peter Weir, USA, 1998) where the audience initially believes in the diegesis that Truman inhabits, but realises (before Truman does) that the real diegesis is much bigger than Truman's world, which is a town created for a TV show.

**diegetic:** that which can be seen and heard by the characters in the world of the film. (See also *diegesis* and *non-diegetic.*)

**diffused/soft lighting:** the process of softening the lighting in a shot by placing a diffuser (e.g. gauze, netting) in front of the camera, or around the edges. In *classical Hollywood* this technique was commonly used to film female stars (especially in their later years); or romantic sex scenes. (See also *soft light.*)

**Digi-beta:** see *Betacam* and *Betamax*

**digital audio broadcast (DAB):** from its invention in the 1920s, radio has been broadcast in *analogue* formats (such as *AM*, MW, LW and *FM*). However, since the 1980s, developments in digital technology have enabled radio to be broadcast digitally. The advantages of this are similar to those of digital television, including greater signal stability, more channels and the provision of *interactive* services.

**digital camera/camcorder/video camera:** camera that uses digital methods of transmitting/recording still and moving images.

**digital decoder:** see *set-top box*

**digital image manipulation:** altering, enhancing or editing any images and photographs using an appropriate software package (e.g. Adobe Photoshop), which has a wide variety of cropping, line, airbrush and colour tools. This process is now used for almost every image seen in professional print, photographic and moving-image media.

**digitalisation:** the use of computer technology to store information digitally, using zeros and noughts (or bits). Digital technology now exists in all forms of mass and personal media communication. Its advantages include:

- a more stable signal than *analogue*
- a greater profusion of channels than analogue.

**digital video:** see *DV*

**diminuendo:** in music, the dying away of the sound; the opposite of a *crescendo*.

**direct address (to camera):** see *address*

**direct broadcasting satellite/service (DBS):** since the mid-1990s, the broadcast of many television services has been achieved using *satellite* technology, which bounces signals off a satellite directly to individual homes via compact receiver dishes.

**direct cinema:** see *fly-on-the-wall*

**directional:** this refers to *microphones* that can pick up sound in different zones for specific purposes, whether transmitting one or more sources of sound.

**direct mail:** unsolicited advertising sent directly to a person's address by post, also known as 'junk mail', due to its likely destination. Many companies maintain a database of their customers' contact details and sell this information to other companies, which they can then use to send direct mail.

**director, film:** the creative individual responsible for making and putting together a film or television programme, especially in relation to artistic, visual and aural aspects. The director is usually with the project through pre-production, production and post-production, and in some cases is involved in marketing, especially if they are well known in their own right. The director has control of the daily life of the film-making process and makes most of the creative decisions on set and elsewhere, in collaboration with other members of the creative team, including actors, writers, cinematographers, editors and composers. It can be argued that some directors are the true authors of their films (see *politique des auteurs*). Despite their power, directors are still answerable to the *producer* and may be removed from a project.

**director's commentary:** on a DVD, an extra that involves adding a soundtrack in which the director of the film talks about the making of the film and various topics they think would be of interest to the general public, or to a *cineaste* audience. Some directors' commentaries can be very illuminating and are of immense use to film students; others are not so, especially when they become too anecdotal or if the director merely chats amiably with one of the actors.

**director's cut:** the *edit* of a film that the *director* chooses; this is not necessarily the cut that an *audience* sees on *theatrical release*. A notable example was the studio's cut of *Blade Runner* (Ridley Scott, USA, 1982), which included a voice-over from the character of Deckard to elucidate a number of points that made it easier for a mainstream audience to understand (at least, that was the defence of the studio). Ten years later, Scott was allowed to bring out his cut (minus the voice-over), which transformed the film into a much more ambiguous and enigmatic narrative and was popular in both cinemas and on VHS/DVD, especially with film fans. Like a *collector's edition* of a DVD, however, a director's cut can also be seen as a marketing ploy by the production company to entice people to buy the same product more than once.

**director of photography (DP or DOP):** see *cinematographer*

**direct sound:** that which is recorded directly and simultaneously from its source.

**disaster film:** a film in which the narrative is of an impending disaster. Examples include *Airport* (George Seaton, USA, 1969); *Twister* (Michael Almereyda, USA, 1990); *The Poseidon Adventure* (Ronald Neame, USA, 1972); *The Day After Tomorrow* (Roland Emmerich, USA, 2004) and *Armageddon* (Michael Bay, USA, 1998). The genre is quite varied in terms of the nature of the disaster but what is central to all successful films of this type is the way the *audience* becomes closely involved in individual stories. *Titanic* (James Cameron, USA, 1997), for example, is a film where everybody knows the outcome (plot spoiler: the ship sinks!) is based on a true story. However, the cleverness of the narrative is that it centres on a love story between two people whom we care about and like, and we do not know the outcome of their story, so the tension and suspense is maintained. Disaster films can also be quite ideological in tone as they frequently carry a message. Examples include *The Towering Inferno* (John Guillermin, USA, 1974), in which the Chief Fire Officer, played by Steve McQueen, delivers a speech at the end warning of the dangers of buildings being too tall; and *WarGames* (John Badham, USA, 1983), which went with the tagline 'Where the only winning move is not to play,' referring to the existence of MAD (mutually assured destruction, between two warring nuclear-powered nations). Disaster films can also be comedies, such as *Dr Strangelove: or How I Stopped Worrying and Learnt to Love the Bomb* (Stanley Kubrick, UK, 1964), or *Airplane* (Jim Abrahams, David Zucker, Jerry Zucker, USA, 1980).

**disc jockey:** more commonly known as a DJ today, this is someone who plays (and mixes) music tracks on the radio or in clubs.

**discontinuity:** a sudden jump or break in the *continuity* of a narrative or edit: the *jump cut* is a good example. There are several reasons why a director would choose to do this: for example, to disconcert the audience; to bring attention to the artifice of film; or to parallel objects or events to create deeper meanings. (See also *cross-cutting*.)

**discourse:** speech, language, conversation, discussion. This straightforward definition is merely the starting point, as discourse in our field would also include discussions about:

- the control of what is discussed in the media (e.g. Who are the *gatekeepers* in news production?)
- how it is discussed (e.g. What kind of *representations* are associated with it?)
- the kind of language that is used
- contexts of discussion (e.g. *mise en scène*, dress codes)
- social aspects
- *non-verbal communication* attached to the discussion
- power relationships
- *ideology.*

**disequilibrium:** see *narrative*

**Disney; disneyfication:** Walt Disney (1901–1966) was a *producer* of animated cartoons and films and consequently the founder of the Disney studio and the Disneyland theme parks. The most famous of his character creations (and there were many) is probably Mickey Mouse. The company also made live action films, especially for children, and provided so-called wholesome fare for all the family, and, as Disney MGM, continue to do this. The term 'disneyfication' is sometimes used negatively to refer to the proliferation of this type of product, which is seen by some to be sentimental and cheap, but which appeals to a mainstream American audience.

**display advertising:** that which uses images, photographs, logos etc., in magazines and on billboards, as opposed to, for example, *classified ads*, which essentially use words only.

**dissolve:** in *editing, a cross-fade* between two shots: one fades out as another fades in.

**dissonance:** a discordant combination of sounds or music that clash against each other and disturb the audience. (See also *cognitive dissonance*.)

**distanciation:** see *Brechtian*

**distribution:** the circulation of a film for cinema *exhibition*; originally this meant the transportation of the film around cinemas and negotiation of *rentals*. Now it is much more complex, involving DVD releases, TV rights and in some cases internet downloads as well as the original theatrical release.

**diversification:** in industry, a production company that moves into a different (but usually related) area. This may lead to, for example, increased profits and efficiency, because of shared resources or risk limitation. For example, Sony, an electronics specialist that produces CD players, moved into music production to make the CDs themselves.

**docudrama:** a dramatised version of real historical events. Sometimes includes documentary footage as well as the 'fictional' sections.

**documentary:** a non-fiction film that deals with facts and real events as opposed to fiction, and is concerned with real people, places and events. Documentary film began with the invention of film-making itself: the first film made by the Lumière Brothers in 1895 was of workers leaving a factory. In fact, for some time many people thought that the only valid purpose of film was to record real events and capture historical moments. There are a few different documentary modes or movements, such as *cinéma vérité* and *direct cinema.* Documentary film-making is not just limited to cinema; it has also been a very important part of British television.

**documentary realism:** a style of film-making associated with documentary film and television production, in which visual and emotional realism are the key features. This style of film-making is often used for fiction film-making, as well as for non-fiction, in order to create greater realism, which convinces the spectator as to the truth of the film/television programme by constructing an unmediated effect. Many of the films of British directors Mike Leigh and Ken Loach (who uses realistic lighting and *mise en scène*, and develops scripts and performances during rehearsals) are good examples of documentary realism.

**docu-soap:** a weekly *reality television* programme, combining elements of documentary and TV soap-opera.

**Dogme 95:** in Copenhagen in 1995, the directors Lars von Trier (1956–) and Thomas Vinterberg (1969–) composed a set of rules called 'The Vow of Chastity' pertaining to their

A B C D E F G H I J K L M N O P Q R S T U V W X Y Z

future film-making. They wished to challenge conventional notions of film-making and the direction in which it was going, much like *new wave* film makers have done. Indeed, their announcement is in a long line of film manifestos going as far back as Dziga Vertov (1896–1954) in the 1920s. Their timing coincided with the centenary of the birth of film. Their first three films were *The Celebration* (Den, 1998), *The Idiots* (Den, 1998), *Mifune* (Den/Swe, 1999). The rules of Dogme 95 can be summarised as follows:

- Shooting must be done on location.
- The sound must never be apart from the images.
- The camera must be hand-held.
- The film must be in colour.
- Optical work and filters are forbidden.
- The film must not contain superficial action.
- Temporal and geographical alienation are forbidden.
- Genre movies are not acceptable.
- It must be 35 mm.
- The director must not be credited.

Interestingly, the last point appears to refute the notion of the director as *auteur*, one that became prevalent with the French *nouvelle vague* in the late 1950s.

**Dolby sound:** noise reduction system used in both cinema and domestic sound equipment. Originally developed by Ray Dolby in the mid-1960s to reduce the effect of analogue tape hiss in music recording, Dolby sound was introduced into cinemas in the early 1970s. Dolby Digital now delivers a six-channel 'surroundsound' mix in cinemas, as well as being a standard feature of all DVD technology.

**dolly:** a small, wheeled platform used to move a film or video camera during the course of a shot. As well as creating freer and more dynamic moving images, it also has the advantage of creating a sense of depth in a shot – something that a zoom shot does not. A dolly can be used on floors or mounted on rails, known as dolly track. Some are fitted with a hydraulic arm for raising and lowering the camera. A dolly shot is more commonly known as a *tracking shot*.

**domestic box-office:** a term used in the film industry to describe the exhibition (i.e. cinema) end of the business in the country of production. It can also refer to the amount of money paid by audiences to see a film on the big screen; in this context, domestic box-office often refers to the money taken in its country of production, as opposed to its worldwide box-office take or any subsequent *back end* income.

**dominant cinema:** a term for conventional Hollywood or Hollywood-style films. It is used by film theorists to identify these films, which are made for entertainment and whose primary purpose is commercial, in order to differentiate them from two different modes of cinema: the art film (also known as 'second cinema') and the politically committed or radical '*third cinema*'. Under this system of classification, commercial or dominant cinema films are known as 'first cinema'.

**dominant discourse:** any form of communication within a culture that embodies all the assumptions, ideas and attitudes of the ruling class. All of these communications are 'coded', (i.e. contain buried messages), but since the codes are unrecognised they remain unquestioned by those using them. The dominant discourse therefore becomes accepted as the only true and valid way of interpreting the world. This acceptance is essential for the ruling class in order to justify and maintain its power and authority (also known as the 'status quo'). In media and cultural studies, the term is used to show how alternative discourses (i.e. other ways of interpreting the world) are denigrated or become marginalised. (See also *hegemony*.)

**dominant hegemonic:** where audiences 'read' (i.e. interpret) a media text from a culturally conventional standpoint, accepting all its encoded assumptions, regarding them as '*common sense*'. (See also *hegemony*.)

**dominant ideology:** a set of the most widespread and generally accepted ideas in any given *culture*. For example, in the developed world, and beyond, the dominant ideology currently favours free market capitalism, individualism and a particular model of representative democracy. Elsewhere, or at other times, the dominant ideology takes different forms (e.g. communism or Islamism).

**dominant reading:** the concept of the dominant (or *dominant hegemonic*) 'reading' of a media text was used by the sociologist Stuart Hall to differentiate between two other possible readings – the *negotiated* and the *oppositional*.

**doorstepping:** in journalism, the practice of visiting the homes of newsworthy people in order to speak to them, and waiting outside until the source either arrives or appears from inside. This technique is normally used with people who are reluctant to speak to the media.

**double:** actor who resembles the star of a drama and can stand in for him in certain shots if necessary. (See also *body double* and *stand-in*.)

**double bill:** also known as a double feature, this is a cinema programme in which audiences may watch two films for the price of one. The double bill was common in mainstream cinemas up until the early 1970s, when low-budget 'second features' or *B-movies* were routinely screened prior to the main feature to add value to the price of a ticket.

**double exposure:** a feature of traditional chemical-based *photography* or *cinematography* in which the film negative is exposed twice in order to create a second image that combines with the first. (This may also happen accidentally.) Double exposure allows the photographer to create a wide range of special effects which, in digital photography, are achieved through the use of computer software such as Adobe Photoshop.

**double-page spread (DPS):** a newspaper or magazine layout in which a story or feature appears as a coherent whole across both a left- and a right-hand page. Also called a *spread*.

**dougal:** fleecy cover on a *rifle mic*, a highly directional *microphone*, used to cut down on wind noise.

**downlink:** the reception of a satellite communications signal by a ground station. (See also *uplink*.)

**download:** to select text, images or sound files from the internet and electronically transfer them to one's own computer. *Video on demand* may also involve downloading programme material from a supplier, such as a cable TV provider.

**downmarket:** a media product that caters for a less serious or well-educated audience, sometimes identified as the 'C2DE' sector of the population. Examples of downmarket products might include the *News of the World* newspaper and most television game shows. Occasionally, a media product will be deliberately moved downmarket in order to reach a new audience: this was seen by many as the strategy adopted by *ITV News* after it ceased to be *News at Ten* in 1999.

**downtime:** periods during which equipment is not being used. Film makers who want to reduce the costs of film or video editing, for example, may be able to negotiate a lower fee for the hire of specialist computer equipment during downtime, since the hire company or facility would not normally be earning any income from the machines at such times.

**DP/DOP (director of photography):** see *cinematographer*

**DPS:** see *double-page spread*

**drama:** a story performed by actors for the benefit of an audience, whether on stage, on radio, in film, television or video. Ancient Greek in origin, the term first applied to theatre, and was subsequently used in film, radio and television. Drama relies principally on staging various forms of conflict arising from social and personal tensions. This allows the *audience* both to explore the issues raised and to share the characters' resulting emotions. Many originally Greek dramatic terms, such as hubris, nemesis, pathos, bathos and catharsis, continue to be used today in a range of contexts. The most common icon of drama, two Greek masks – one smiling, one frowning – represent the original dramatic genres of comedy and tragedy. However, in the modern era, as these genres have fragmented into numerous subgenres, the difference between them is regarded as less important than that between drama and documentary.

*Drama masks*

**drama-documentary:** a type of documentary in which dramatic techniques are used. One example is the imaginative restaging of actual events with the aid of as much factual content as possible, e.g. in TV's *Crimewatch UK* or in history documentaries; another is the use of court transcripts, for example, Channel 4's 1997 restaging of the *McLibel* trial.

**dramatic device:** any technique used in drama to produce an effect. In the literary sense, Shakespeare uses such dramatic devices as characters going about in disguise, or receiving a letter, or committing suicide; another is the play-within-a-play. In film and television drama, *editing* and other post-production techniques can often be used as dramatic devices (e.g. fast cutting to heighten excitement, or different kinds of music to enhance mood).

**dramatic irony:** term used to describe when an audience knows more about a character's situation than the character does. This creates a pleasing sensation of *omniscience* in the *spectator*. Although dramatic irony dates back at least as far as Sophocles, it is also common in film. Alfred Hitchcock (1899–1980) frequently used it to create suspense, causing characters to do things out of ignorance that are not in their best interests. For example, in *Psycho* (USA, 1960), as the audience watches detective Arbogast walking up the stairs in the old house, it knows that a crazed killer (presumably Mrs Bates) is lurking somewhere nearby because, unlike Arbogast, it has just witnessed the bloody murder of Marion Crane in the shower.

**dramatic tension:** the use of dramatic devices to heighten audience anxiety and thereby increase the sense of involvement in the story. This is often achieved through the techniques of suspense, but also through emotional and physical confrontations between characters, particularly where the outcome is uncertain.

**dream factory:** term used to describe *Hollywood*, it refers to the illusory, escapist nature of much of mainstream commercial cinema, but also to the way in which the materially privileged lives and complete freedom of many film characters appeal to audience members' personal aspirations.

**DRIP:** According to the *Advertising Standards Authority*, this is a commonly used acronym to describe the purpose of advertisements: **D** – differentiate a company's products from those of their competitors. **R** – reassure and remind consumers of the benefits of the products or services. **I** – inform people about an advertiser's products, services or cause. **P** – persuade people that they should believe what they see in the advert and to take action in light of it, by purchasing the product.

**drive-by shot:** a crabbing (i.e. sideways) moving camera shot, often achieved by shooting from the side of a vehicle.

**drive-in cinema/movie:** an open-air cinema in which the audience watches the film while seated in the car they arrived in. Drive-ins became popular in late-1940s America, and reached a peak of around 4,000 theatres in 1960. They became the prime exhibition space for *low-budget* and exploitation films, but gradually declined in popularity for a variety of reasons, including the construction of multiplexes in the 1980s.

**DRM (digital rights management):** see *piracy*

**dub; dubbing:** the recording or re-recording of film sound at the *post-production* stage, prior to its inclusion in the completed soundtrack. Dubbing (also known as looping or post-synching) often takes place where *dialogue* recorded on a set or on location was not of suitable quality and needs to be re-recorded under studio conditions by the original actor; it is also used in foreign language versions of films, where an approximate match is made between dialogue translated into a different language and the character's original mouth movements. Music or sound effects may also be dubbed on to an existing soundtrack as part of the overall sound mix.

**dub editing:** a form of editing in which sound is added to the master track without erasing what has been previously recorded. In analogue video, dub editing is more commonly known as insert editing (as opposed to assemble editing). This is where material is inserted into a master tape on which other materials, including a control track, have already been recorded.

**dumb-down:** an accusation made in cases where media products appear to have moved *downmarket*. The broadcast news media are frequently accused of dumbing down, usually on the assumption that they are more concerned with *audience* ratings than with providing a public service, because only a small cultural elite is supposedly interested in intelligent coverage. Dumbed-down news coverage relies more on human interest and celebrity than on serious political debates about policy.

**duopoly:** where ownership and control of an industry is split between two organisations. For example, before the launch of Channel 4 Television in 1982, television broadcasting was a duopoly shared between the BBC and ITV.

**duration (shot):** the length of time that a shot remains on the screen.

**Dutch angle:** where the camera is turned in order to frame a shot 'off-kilter', so that the usual perpendicular sides and flat horizon become diagonals. It is used to convey shock, extreme danger and other highly dramatic situations or subjective states of mind. *The Third Man* (Carol Reed, UK, 1949) is an example of a film in which Dutch angles abound. Also known as a *canted shot.*

**DV/digital video:** the modern form of video which has largely replaced analogue. Digital video has numerous advantages over analogue: while the hardware is equally inexpensive, it enables users to record significantly higher quality sound and images; to edit on computer without the need for specialist equipment; to edit very precisely, frame by frame; to add special effects very quickly and easily; to edit and copy material repeatedly without loss of quality; and to eliminate or avoid altogether unwanted sound (e.g. tape hiss). The steady improvements in quality (i.e. greater richness and detail in the sounds and images) have meant that DV is now challenging traditional celluloid film to the point where an increasing number of feature films (e.g. *Collateral*, Michael Mann, USA, 2004), are being shot on high-end DV, which is then processed to resemble traditional film.

**DVD/digital versatile disc:** digital storage disc has largely replaced analogue videotape. The result has been higher quality without the physical deterioration that tape suffers over time. A DVD can hold audio and computer data as well as video, and has greater storage capacity than a CD. This is partly because it uses a shorter wavelength laser, and partly because better focusing optics allow tracks to be closer together and to contain smaller pits. Commercially recorded DVDs, (e.g. for feature films) are encoded according to region, the original intention being to allow Hollywood studios to control global release dates. However, many DVD players are now multi-region.

**dynamics (narrative):** the pacing of a story. To maintain audience interest, a drama (or documentary) needs to vary in intensity from scene to scene and from sequence to sequence. Too many dialogue scenes in succession can be boring; similarly, the excitement generated by action scenes can wane if they are not varied by quieter, more reflective moments. Scripts use the techniques of narrative dynamics to build up to the story's climax.

**dynamics (sound):** the difference between the loudest and quietest audible sounds in any given situation. Thus the dynamic range of a microphone is a measure of its ability to pick up sounds of greatly varying intensity.

**dystopia:** the opposite of *utopia*. A vision of a future world that has gone badly wrong, perhaps due to a nuclear or biological war, alien invasion, ecological disaster, the abuse of new technology, or the concentration of political power. Urban dystopia is a common setting for science fiction narratives such as *Blade Runner* (Ridley Scott, USA, 1982) and *28 Days Later* (Danny Boyle, UK, 2002).

**Eady Levy:** a former tax on cinema tickets, intended to encourage British film production in the face of competition from Hollywood. Proceeds were divided between exhibitors and producers. Established in 1957, the Eady Levy was also used to fund the National Film and Television School. It was abolished in 1985.

**Ealing Studios:** a West London production company most often associated with a gentle and eccentric style of British comedy film. These include *Hue and Cry* (Charles Crichton, UK, 1947), *Whisky Galore!* (Alexander Mackendrick, UK, 1948), *Passport to Pimlico* (Henry Cornelius, UK, 1949), *Kind Hearts and Coronets* (Robert Hamer, UK, 1949), *The Lavender Hill Mob* (Charles Crichton, UK, 1951), *The Man in the White Suit* (Alexander Mackendrick, UK, 1951), *The Titfield Thunderbolt* (Charles Crichton, UK, 1953) and *The Ladykillers* (Alexander Mackendrick, UK, 1955). The company was founded in 1931 on the site of a late-nineteenth-century studio, and despite several changes of ownership there are still studios on the site today. However, the era of Ealing comedy, under the leadership of *producer* Michael Balcon, lasted only from 1947 to 1955. As well as comedies, Ealing was responsible for historical adventure films, notably *Scott of the Antarctic* (Charles Frend, UK, 1948), wartime films such as *Went the Day Well?* (Alberto Cavalcanti, UK, 1942) and *The Cruel Sea* (Charles Frend, UK, 1953), and social dramas like *Pool of London* (Basil Dearden, UK, 1951) and *I Believe in You* (Basil Dearden/Michael Relph, UK, 1952).

**early adopter:** person who acquires new forms of consumer technology as soon as they come on to the market, i.e. before their likely usefulness has been generally appreciated and when the price is still high.

**early cinema:** generally considered to be the period between the projection of the first film by the *Lumière Brothers* in Paris in 1895, and the first full-length features, beginning with D W Griffith's silent classic *The Birth of a Nation* (USA, 1915). However, the term can also be interpreted more broadly to include nineteenth-century developments towards cinema, such as Henry Fox Talbot's improvements to still photography in the 1830s, various optical toys that created the illusion of movement such as the *zoetrope* and the *praxinoscope*, the photographic sequences of Eadweard Muybridge, and the inventions of Thomas *Edison* and W K L Dickson. The post-1895 period includes the pioneering work not only of the Lumières but also of such film makers as Georges Méliès, R W Paul, George Smith, Cecil Hepworth and Edwin S Porter. Whereas the Lumière brothers filmed apparently unstaged events, and are thus considered the inventors of the modern documentary, Méliès constructed elaborate *fantasies* full of special effects. His 531 films (some only a minute long) included the famous *A Trip to the Moon* (Fr, 1902) and *The Impossible Voyage* (Fr, 1904). Most of them were subsequently melted down by the French Army to make boot heels. D W Griffith (1875–1948) dominated the silent era and established the long-format feature film at a time when companies such as *Biograph* preferred to make shorts. Griffith perfected many elements of *film grammar* and continuity that audiences now take for granted, particularly the use of *cross-cutting* to suggest simultaneous action in different locations. He also became a master of the dramatic *close-up*, the *tracking shot* and rhythmic editing. While he did not invent the majority of these techniques, he developed them effectively in such films as the three-hour epic *The Birth of a Nation* (USA, 1915), which caused nationwide controversy over its portrayal of black people. This was followed by *Intolerance* (USA, 1916), *Broken Blossoms* (USA, 1919) and *Way Down East* (USA, 1920). He was a co-founder of *United Artists.*

**Easter egg:** hidden feature on a DVD.

**echo:** where a television *audience* remains watching at the end of a programme and can be targeted by the broadcaster running a *trailer* for a subsequent programme during the *credit sequence.*

**economies of scale:** the ability of larger-scale enterprises to make products more cheaply and efficiently than smaller-scale enterprises.

**ECU:** acronym of extreme close-up, this is the term for a type of camera shot. In such a shot the subject may be a person's eyes, mouth or hand, or the detail of an object, such as the handle on a door. Normally used for emphasis or for shock effect.

**Edison, Thomas:** American inventor and developer of much fundamental technology that we today take for granted in our everyday lives, including the electric light, the telephone, the movie camera and the phonograph (a precursor of the hi-fi). (See also *Kinetograph* and *Kinetoscope.*)

**edit decision list:** see *EDL*

**editing:** the third part of the media production process following preparation (pre-production) and production. Also known as post-production, editing takes place in all forms of media, and is necessary to finalise the media product by assembling and shaping the production elements into a coherent whole. In print media, editing involves cutting, extending, correcting and/or rewriting copy submitted by journalists, and writing headlines (sub-editing) and making decisions about the use of photographs (picture editing). In time-based media, an *editor* is a post-production specialist, an assembler and shaper of sounds and images. In some cases they may also add special effects and/or titles and credits. Now that it usually takes place on a computer rather than at a Steenbeck or Moviola machine (film) or analogue video edit suite, this kind of editing has become a faster and cheaper process.

**edition:** a complete version of a media text. In book publishing, a first edition may be followed by any number of subsequent editions, which can be corrected, extended and updated from the original where necessary. In daily newspapers, several editions are produced in a single day as older stories give way to fresh news. In film, as in many other products, the term 'special edition' has come to mean a version containing previously unavailable extras.

**editor:** the post of editor is the most senior on a publication. It embraces the whole process of long-term publication strategy, chairing planning meetings, commissioning copy and pictures, deciding what material to use and what should be *spiked*, and approving page layouts. In addition the editor has managerial functions such as hiring, promoting and firing staff, and external functions such as representing the publication in public. In broadcast journalism, the editor is responsible for the content of a programme while the *producer* is in charge of its technical production. (See also *editing.*)

**editorial:** (i) the areas of a publication prepared by journalists, as opposed to those which are the responsibility of the advertising department. (ii) the 'comment' page or columns of a publication, representing its 'voice' (e.g. '*The Sun* Says'). In this meaning, it is more commonly known as a *leader.* (See also *editor.*)

**EDL:** an abbreviation of edit decision list, this is a sequential list of the film or video edits to be used in any given television or video programme, film or sequence. In digital editing systems, an EDL is automatically generated by the software. It identifies the electronic location of every clip that will form a part of the final version, or edit. An EDL can also be a hand-written plan made in preparation for the edit itself.

**effects (film and TV):** see *special effects*

**effects model/theory:** a model of *audience* reception that suggests that human behaviour is directly affected by media consumption. It was first proposed by the *Frankfurt School* of Social Researchers in the 1920s, who saw confirmation of their ideas in the enthusiastic response of the German public to Nazi *propaganda.* In the USA, where the Frankfurt School's members subsequently took refuge, the theory was used to explain *consumer culture:* the American public were seen to make unnecessary purchases in response to advertising. The effects model is also known as the '*hypodermic model*', in that the media's effects supposedly act on us like a drug. Today, children and young people are regarded as more vulnerable to the media's negative effects than adults, and the effects model remains popular in the news media as the driving force behind *moral panics.* However, it fell out of favour among academics long ago, who tend to see the issue as more complex and problematic, especially in a media-saturated environment in which it is impossible to isolate the supposedly influential factors. Rival theories, which suggest that the media are far less influential, include the *two-step flow theory* and the *uses and gratifications theory.*

**elaborated code:** a relatively complex form of speech used by the educated *middle classes*. The term was first used by sociolinguist Basil Bernstein to distinguish it from the 'restricted code' used by *working-class* people. His argument was that, among other things, knowledge of the elaborated code allows middle-class individuals to obtain better education and career opportunities. (See also *social class.*)

**electronic press kit (EPK):** a publicity pack distributed in the form of a CD or DVD. EPKs are delivered to journalists or handed out by public relations staff at product launches. Typically, they contain press releases, biographical and other background information, still photographs and video footage that often includes interviews.

**electronic programme guide (EPG):** a television screen display allowing viewers to see the programmes that are due to be broadcast in order to plan their viewing and recording. Information provided includes the relevant channel, programme title, description of content, genre and start and finish time. Often offers the option of accessing additional details such as a list of cast members, a brief synopsis and the year of production.

**elite:** the small, privileged upper layer of any group or community. Individuals may join an elite through personal wealth, via election (e.g. political), by appointment (e.g. to a government quango) through birth (e.g. social class), past achievements (e.g. sport or the arts) or through media attention (e.g. *celebrities*). The privileges accorded to a member of a social elite place them in a more favourable position than a non-member: they enjoy a higher standard of living, their views are listened to with more respect, they wield greater personal power, and may maintain a higher public profile. Anyone's right to belong to an elite is therefore often highly contested. An example in the world of the media is the group known as 'celebrities', in whom there is so much public interest that even their most mundane activities are photographed, filmed and discussed. The presence or involvement of an elite person makes any event more newsworthy. Elite nations perform a similar function on the world stage (for example, any action taken by the American government is more likely to be reported than one taken by the government of Burkina Faso). An elitist is a person prejudiced in favour of those who belong to elites, and is likely to be a member of one.

**ellipsis:** a gap in a story. For a *narrative* to hold the attention of its *audience*, it must include only what is essential and leave out what is not. For example, if a film narrative requires the protagonist to drive 200 miles by car, we are unlikely to see the entire journey, but the film may show us its beginning and end. The concept of ellipsis helps to illustrate the difference between *plot* (syuzhet) and *story* (fabula), the former being (among other things) an elliptical version of the latter. Ellipsis can also be used as a narrative technique, through which audience interest focuses on what has been deliberately left out, and tries to fill in the gaps (e.g. a murder mystery, in which the audience adopts the point of view of the detective as he seeks to establish 'whodunnit', their motive, means and opportunity). Highly elliptical narratives are those that provide the audience with few clues about what is going on (e.g. Peter Greenaway's *The Draughtsman's Contract*, UK, 1982; or the science-fiction film *Primer* (Shane Carruth, USA, 2004). Such films may be termed *avant-garde*, due to the absence of conventional story information. Small-scale ellipses are often used by editors to hurry the story along from scene to scene and from shot to shot.

**ELS:** abbreviation of extreme long shot. In such a shot the subject is a relatively long distance from the camera. Not to be confused with a *wide shot* (WS) or general view (GV).

**emblematic shot:** one that highlights something of particular importance in a film, usually by symbolising visually its overall themes and preoccupations. Examples include the famous shot in *Lawrence of Arabia* (David Lean, UK, 1962) where the figure of Sherif Ali (Omar Sharif) on the back of a camel slowly materialises through the shimmering desert heat haze. Another, from *Silence of the Lambs* (Ridley Scott, USA, 1991) is of Hannibal Lecter strapped to a trolley and wearing a muzzle. A well-chosen still selected for use on the film's poster might well be one that is emblematic.

**emergency drama/series:** one with an emergency services setting, such as a hospital, fire station or police station. *Casualty*, *London's Burning* and *The Bill* are examples.

**emoticon:** an icon used in email and other forms of digital communication to indicate a simple emotion. Used by a sender to encourage the receiver to interpret the accompanying words in the spirit intended.

*Examples of emoticons*

**empathy:** emotion felt by an *audience* when shared with that of a dramatic character or real person, particularly when the audience has experienced similar circumstances.

**encode:** to communicate meaning through the use of *signs*. The study of *semiology* during the twentieth century began from the premise that no communication can be neutral, or uncoded. In other words, communication is never a simple matter of sending a message to a receiver as if delivering a parcel, but involves active interpretation by the receiver. This is because in order to work effectively, *codes* depend on a shared view of the world, and therefore have to be learned in order for encoded messages to appear 'natural'. The sociologist Stuart Hall has argued that media messages can be interpreted in a range of possible ways, depending on the cultural background and experience of the receiver. Broadly, these interpretations can be categorised as *dominant*, *negotiated* or *oppositional*. The philosopher and novelist Umberto Eco (1932–) added a fourth – the *aberrant decoding*. He also distinguished between *open* and *closed texts*, the latter being those that are encoded to encourage a particular interpretation.

**encryption:** to hide a message using a secret *code* so that unauthorised parties are unable to access it. Subscription satellite and cable television channels are electronically encrypted in order to ensure that only paying subscribers can receive them.

**enigma code:** according to Roland Barthes, a type of *narrative* code in which the *audience* is presented with a mystery. Their curiosity is stimulated in trying to explain it, or in watching the characters trying to, and this helps to retain their interest in the narrative. One example is the discovery of a corpse at the beginning of a detective drama. Another might be a strange remark made by a soap character at the end of an episode, which is explained in a subsequent episode. Also known as a hermeneutic code.

**ensemble:** where the role of the *protagonist* in a dramatic narrative is divided among several leading characters. For example, in the film *10 Things I Hate About You* (Gil Junger, USA, 1999) there are four protagonists of equal importance to the story and in the TV sitcom *Friends* there is an ensemble cast of six characters.

**enunciation:** the degree of clarity with which words are spoken. (Has nothing to do with accent.)

**EPG:** see *electronic programme guide*

**epic film:** one encompassing a large, ambitious sweep of time, space and/or theme. Derived from long literary works such as Homer's *Odyssey* or Tolstoy's *War and Peace*, films often described as epic include the original *Star Wars* trilogy (George Lucas, USA, 1977–83), *Titanic* (James Cameron, USA, 1997), and older 'sword and sandal' films such as *The Ten Commandments* (Cecil B DeMille, USA, 1956), *Ben Hur* (William Wyler, USA, 1959) and *Spartacus* (Stanley Kubrick, USA, 1960).

**episode:** (i) one programme in a drama serial that forms part of a longer *narrative*, although the term can also apply to a series. (ii) a complete event within a narrative sequence. For example, most prison movies contain an escape attempt episode.

**episodic narrative:** one in which cause and effect do not drive the plot. Instead, scenes follow each other without any clear connection apart from featuring roughly the same group of characters. Sometimes seen as a looser, more *naturalistic* method of storytelling than conventional narratives. Favoured by European *modernist* and *neo-realist* film directors such as Ermanno Olmi and Michaelangelo Antonioni, who used it in films like *The Passenger*

(It/Fr/Sp/USA, 1975) to subvert traditional storytelling. Here, rather than pursuing a familiar set of goals and encountering equally familiar problems on the way, characters seem to be adrift in the world and at the mercy of fate.

**EPK:** see *electronic press kit*

**equilibrium:** a *narrative* term to describe the state of play as the *plot* begins, in which its elements are in balance. Derived from the work of Tzvetan Todorov, it is part of a simple model of storytelling whereby equilibrium is followed by disruption, which in turn is resolved at the end into a new and different equilibrium.

**Equity:** in the UK, the trade union representing *actors* and other performers. In order to work in film or television, actors need to join the union to obtain their 'Equity card'. This is to their advantage since the union negotiates terms and conditions with producers to ensure minimum rates of pay.

**erotic thriller:** a thriller with a sexual theme e.g. *Body Heat* (Lawrence Kasdan, USA, 1981) and *Basic Instinct* (Paul Verhoeven, USA, 1992).

**escapism:** any form of *narrative* entertainment designed to help the *audience* temporarily forget (i.e. escape from) the reality of their everyday lives. This involves various forms of fantasy, romance and adventure, frequently set in attractive, exotic locations. Escapist novels, television dramas and films are common. Typical film examples are *Romancing the Stone* (Robert Zemeckis, USA, 1984); *Independence Day* (Roland Emmerich, USA, 1996); and the early *Bond* films, such as *Goldfinger* (Guy Hamilton, UK, 1964).

**essay film:** a *documentary* film with clearly defined subject matter and a strong authorial voice. Three examples: Dziga Vertov's *Man with a Movie Camera* (USSR, 1929) is an *avant-garde* celebration of communism, city life, and of the '*kino eye*'; Orson Welles's *F for Fake* (Fr/Ir/W Ger, 1974) is a highly 'unreliable' film essay on the theme of trickery and fraud; Errol Morris's *The Fog Of War* (USA, 2003) features the musings of former US Defence Secretary Robert McNamara.

**establishing shot:** the opening shot in a dramatic scene that establishes the disposition of people and objects in the *mise en scène*. As such it is usually a *wide shot*, and is likely to be followed by a succession of closer shots.

**establishment, the:** those who wield real power and influence in any society. The nature of the establishment changes over time. Up until the 1960s the establishment was solidly upper and upper-middle class: people who had held the reins of government and the Civil Service for hundreds of years. However, as class hierarchy gave way to meritocracy, a new establishment arose, consisting of those who had achieved status through their own efforts, and often reflecting the growing importance of celebrities and the media (e.g. newspaper editors).

**ethics:** a set of moral principles based on agreed notions of good and right behaviour. Often used in the professions to establish codes of conduct, particularly in medicine, where new scientific developments frequently trigger debate about what is right and wrong. In the media, journalistic ethics are enshrined in the *Press Complaints Commission*'s Code of Practice, voluntarily maintained by a committee of newspaper editors, and dealing with issues relating to invasions of privacy, the identification of children, clandestine recordings and payments to witnesses.

**ethnicity:** a person's cultural, religious and linguistic origins. Ethnicity is not synonymous with *race*, since that term suggests that there is a biological difference between human beings.

**ethnic minority:** any social group whose origins are different from those who form the majority in their country of residence, and who form a minority of the population as a whole. Often taken to mean those who look different (e.g. darker-skinned in a largely white society) but also likely to include cultural differences – in dress, language and religion. Many ethnic minorities believe that they suffer discrimination and rejection by the majority. In extreme cases 'ethnic cleansing' takes place – a euphemism for mass murder and forced deportation of the minorities. The Nazi Holocaust against the Jews of middle and eastern Europe is the most notorious example, but there have been many others, including the 1994 massacres of the Tutsis by the Hutus in Rwanda.

**ethnocentrism:** the belief that one's own cultural experience and perspective is superior to all others. This is of significance when studying world cinema, due to the obstacle that the ethnocentricity of American and European audiences causes to the appreciation of, for example, Japanese film. Similarly, Hollywood cinema is intrinsically ethnocentric.

**ethnographic film:** one that focuses on tribal communities, for example Robert Flaherty's *Nanook of the North* (USA, 1921) and *Moana* (USA, 1926), set among the Inuit and Samoan peoples respectively.

**European cinema:** a varied set of filmic traditions and styles used in European film production. When used to differentiate it from Hollywood, the term suggests *art-house* or *auteur* cinema, a *high culture* entity compared with the sort of low-culture industry of America, in other words less commercially driven, audience-pleasing or generic in nature. Although the film industry developed simultaneously in Europe and America in the early twentieth century, Hollywood's global dominance has led European cinema to be termed 'second cinema'.

**event movie:** a film that gains publicity beyond the usual confines of the arts and entertainment media and becomes 'news'. Event movies are keenly anticipated film releases which a larger audience than usual goes to see, sometimes because they have already proved highly popular elsewhere, usually in America, e.g. *Titanic* (James Cameron, USA, 1997).

**excess:** (i) the tendency of *mainstream* media texts to provide too much exposition or explanation, on the assumption that without it the audience will not understand what is going on; (ii) an exaggerated, overblown quality in art or entertainment, and hence a feature of *camp.*

**exclusive:** a much-abused term for media *news* stories or interviews that have not yet appeared in any rival media. Also known as a *scoop*, an exclusive is traditionally the preserve of the print media. Literally speaking, when a newspaper has an exclusive, its rivals have been 'excluded'. In practice, exclusives are not always what they are claimed to be, and several newspapers will claim them simultaneously. In other cases, on learning of an 'exclusive interview', a rival publication will endeavour to publish a *spoiler.*

**executive producer:** (i) in television, one who supervises a team of *producers* on any programme, particularly when it is part of a *strand* or *series*; (ii) in film, someone who handles business and legal issues but has no involvement in any of the technical aspects of film-making. However, the term can often be used almost as a courtesy title for people with a broad range of functions: in television, an executive producer may be the person responsible for the original series concept, or a key scriptwriter; in film, he may be one of the financiers, the author of the original book, or the studio representative for the film.

**exegesis:** detailed critical interpretation, explanation or analysis of a text.

**exhibition:** the sector of the film industry that shows films to the public; in most cases this will be a cinema. Exhibition is the third stage in the overall life of a film after *production* and *distribution*, and the one at which its ultimate commercial fate will be determined. A film that is successful at the *box-office* (i.e. at least recoups its production and distribution costs) is likely to make a profit overall once overseas and *back-end* sales are taken into account. However, many films, particularly independent productions made without pre-sales to distributors, do not reach the exhibition stage, and sit 'on the shelf' after production, or are released straight to video (this includes films that are released in their home country but not deemed commercially viable elsewhere). Since cinemas are expensive to run, the management's first priority is to achieve the weekly 'house *nut*'. For this reason, exhibitors usually retain 60 per cent of each film's box-office take, the remainder being divided between its distributor and *producer*. Contrary to popular belief, cinemas make their real profits not from exhibiting films but from selling drinks and snacks.

**exhibitionist:** an attention-seeking person who gains pleasure from displaying him or herself in public, sometimes through extreme behaviour. *Big Brother* contestants are one example of this tendency. There is often a sexual element to exhibitionism: in western culture women are traditionally considered to be 'on display', and are encouraged to show themselves off and be admired, to arouse desire in men, and to compete with other females for this attention.

**exhibitor:** the person ultimately responsible for showing any film, which they rent from its distributor. In the case of *independent* cinemas, the cinema manager decides what films to exhibit; in the case of *multiplexes* and other chains, a film booker takes that decision, while the manager is responsible for supervising the day-to-day running of the cinema.

**existential hero:** a dramatic *protagonist* who embodies the central ideas of existential writers and philosophers such as Kierkegaard, Nietzsche and Sartre. Although there are many varieties of existentialism, many begin from the premise that since there is no God, life has no meaning or purpose other than what individual human beings decide to make of it. The existential hero is therefore very often someone seeking meaning, failing to find it, and falling prey to anger and despair. Examples in film include numerous *film noir* protagonists, such as the central character of Bobby Dupea (Jack Nicholson) in *Five Easy Pieces* (Bob Rafelson, USA, 1970) or the nameless narrator (Edward Norton) of *Fight Club* (David Fincher, USA, 1999).

**expectations:** *audiences* have pre-existing ideas about media products based on their previous experience, their ability to decode media messages, and their understanding of *genre*. For example, if we are told about a new television series featuring John Pilger, experience tells us that he is a campaigning journalist, and that the genre is likely to be a particular style of documentary. We therefore have a fairly clear idea of what to expect even before we see any of the programmes. Expectations can also be deliberately subverted, particularly in comedy: *The Day Today* (1992) depended for its effect on the audience's knowledge of the news genre, and worked by exaggerating its more absurd and pompous *codes and conventions*.

**experimental film:** any film whose structure, content or methodology consciously and radically breaks with convention. It is also known as *avant-garde* cinema, and more concerned with artistic self-expression than with commerce. Examples include Fernand Léger's abstract Dadaist film *Ballet Mécanique* (Fr, 1924), David Lynch's surreal, nightmarish drama *Eraserhead*

(USA, 1977), and Godfrey Reggio's impressionist documentary *Koyaanisqatsi* (USA, 1983). All films are risk-taking ventures, but experimental films are far riskier than most, since at the time they are conceived and produced, the film makers have no expectation of commercial rewards. On the rare occasions that an experimental film succeeds in these terms, it can be highly influential (e.g. Reggio's innovative use of time-lapse photography).

**explicit meaning:** that which is obvious to the vast majority of the audience, since it is the *dominant*, or intended, meaning of the text. Explicit meaning is to be considered alongside less obvious *implicit meanings*.

**exploitation film:** any film which depends on *voyeuristic* displays of sex, violence, gory horror, and other varieties of sensational content for its appeal. Also known as 'trash cinema', exploitation films have existed in some form since the early days of cinema (e.g. Tod Browning's 1932 movie *Freaks*). All the major Hollywood studios once had *'B' picture* units that made low-budget westerns and detective dramas, but with the end of the studio system in the early 1950s came cheap horror, science fiction, teenage, biker and other exploitation films, made by *independent* companies like Samuel Arkoff's AIP and Roger Corman's New World Pictures.

**exposé:** in journalism, a *news* story that uncovers or 'exposes' some shocking, and hitherto unknown, scandal.

**exposition:** the part of any narrative – usually at the start – that establishes the time and place and initial situation, and introduces the protagonist and other important characters. Further exposition can also be provided at other points of the story.

**expository documentary:** one whose style and structure resembles a written essay or report (i.e. it argues a case). According to film scholar Bill Nichols, an expository documentary should proceed by means of a linear, chronological flow of image and argument. Examples include wildlife documentaries (e.g. *Big Cat Diary*), which follow a year in the life of a group of animals.

**expository text:** exposition presented through words (rather than sound or pictures) appearing on the screen.

**exposure:** (i) what stars and would-be stars in the entertainment industry achieve through photographs and interviews in the media in order to become well known to the public. (ii) photographic term for what occurs when light passes through a camera lens to create an image on film.

**expressionism; expressionistic:** in film, a distorted, emotionally heightened style in which the depiction of *objective* reality takes second place to the often tortured sensibility of a character. The best-known examples are found in the films of the *German expressionist* movement, but certain modern films have also adopted an expressionist approach, for example *Taxi Driver* (Martin Scorsese, USA, 1976), in which the unusual camerawork and framing, low-key lighting, garish colours, jarring music and choppy editing combine to create the impression of Travis Bickle's *subjective* world.

**exterior:** a scene in film or TV drama that takes place in the open air. Abbreviated in scripts as 'EXT'.

**extra:** (i) someone who appears, uncredited, in a film or television drama to provide visual background or as part of a crowd scene. (ii) additional material to the main feature provided on a *DVD*.

**extreme close-up:** see *ECU*; *cinematography*

**extreme long shot:** see *ELS*; *cinematography*

**eye-level shot:** one in which the camera is level with the subject's eyes.

**eyeline match:** a visual code used in filming interaction between characters so that they appear to be looking at each other, even when only one of them is on the screen in any given shot. This is particularly important in a *shot/reverse shot* sequence: if in shot A, character 1 is looking offscreen to the left and in an upward direction, then in shot B, character 2 must be looking downward and to the right. This ensures that the *audience* does not get confused about who is addressing whom, and from what physical placement in the scene.

**eyeline shot:** a camera shot showing something that a person was looking at in the previous shot. In other words, their *point of view.*

### What other subjects are you studying?

A–Zs cover a range of different subjects. See the inside back cover for a list of all the titles in the series and how to order.

**fabula:** in dramatic narrative, a term for the background story, as opposed to the *plot* (syuzhet) presented on the screen. The term, first used by Russian formalist critics in the 1920s, refers to all the possible story information we have, or infer, that contributes to the plot of the film. For example, in *Walk the Line* (James Mangold, USA, 2005), the first half of Johnny Cash's life, everything that led up to it and everything we surmise about it (the fabula), has been condensed into the 136 minutes of the film (the syuzhet).

**faction:** a portmanteau word for a fictional narrative based on factual events. Dramatic techniques are used to tell the story. *United 93* (Paul Greengrass, Fr/UK/USA, 2006) is one example, where the screen drama uses all the known facts, only introducing fictional elements where the actual details are unverifiable. Similar in meaning to '*docudrama*'. (Not to be confused with its other meaning: a grouping or body of opinion.)

**factual programming:** TV and radio programmes such as documentaries, for example on art, history, geography and wildlife.

**fade-in/out:** an *editing* technique in which a shot gradually and smoothly appears on or disappears from the screen. Typically, this is a fade to or from black, although sometimes white is used (in a fade-out, the latter is also called a bleach-out). A fade-out followed by a fade-in traditionally signals to the audience that there has been a fairly substantial *ellipsis* in the narrative.

**fan; fandom:** an enthusiast for a certain *star*, media product or genre. Film fans were important to the *Hollywood* film industry during the Hollywood studio era for the creation of stars, but the demise of the studio system in the early 1950s, quickly followed by the arrival of television and rock music, split fans into different factions. Today the *internet* is an important tool for fans and fandom (as the phenomenon is known), and to some extent has led to their revival.

**fantasy film:** one in which anything can happen, including magic and other manifestations of the impossible. Very often a complete fantasy world is created, as in *The Lord of the Rings* trilogy (Peter Jackson, New Zealand/USA, 2001–3) or the *Harry Potter* films (Chris Columbus/Alfonso Cuaron/Mike Newell, UK/USA, 2001 onwards). In other cases, the fantasy is localised in a particular character or group, as in *Bewitched* (Nora Ephron, USA, 2005).

**fanzine:** an unofficial magazine produced by fans. Popular in football and pop music.

**fashion:** cultural trends that come and go according to variations in public taste.

**feature:** (i) see *feature film.* (ii) in journalism, an article that explores a topic at greater length and in more depth than a news story. (iii) in advertising, a promotional article that visually resembles editorial coverage but has been paid for, and is designed to sell a product or service. Also known as an *advertorial.*

**feature film:** any modern film running roughly between 90 minutes and two hours, although many are longer and some are a little shorter. The term originated in the days when cinema programmes included newsreels, cartoons, serials and 'second features' (often only an hour long or less), as well as trailers and advertisements. The feature film was the main attraction.

**female gaze, the:** a psychoanalytical term for the ways in which women, as opposed to men, might watch the screen. Invented by critic E Ann Kaplan in response to film scholar Laura Mulvey's influential essay *Visual Pleasure and Narrative Cinema*. (See also *male gaze*.)

**femininity:** the traditional attributes of the female, particularly as approved by men. These include sexual attractiveness, playfulness, the occasional tantrum, passivity and deference towards men, physical weakness, difficulty with anything mechanical, and a preference for appearances over substance, emotion over reason and indirectness over confrontation. However, the distinction between culturally determined femininity and biologically determined femaleness is difficult to define, since women are also often considered to be better communicators, and more sensitive and concerned about interpersonal relationships, than men. An example of femininity is the character of Cher in the film *Clueless* (Amy Heckerling, USA, 1995).

**feminism:** an *ideology* drawn from a wide range of concerns affecting women, but broadly insisting on equal rights for women to those enjoyed by men. Feminists believe that women's biological function as childbearers and traditional subservience to men should not dictate the course of their lives. The campaign for equal rights in the modern era began with the suffragette movement in the early twentieth century and revived in the 1970s with the publication of such popular and influential books as Germaine Greer's *The Female Eunuch* (1970). (See also *postfeminism*.)

**feminist film:** one illustrating or advocating a feminist point of view. Feminist films such as Peter Wollen and Laura Mulvey's experimental *Riddles of the Sphinx* (UK, 1977) and Sally Potter's *Thriller* (UK, 1979), have often adopted *avant-garde* or *counter-cinema* strategies. More realist and commercial films that have stimulated interest among feminist critics include Gillian Armstrong's *My Brilliant Career* (Aus, 1979), Jon Avnet's *Fried Green Tomatoes* (USA, 1991), Jane Campion's *The Piano* (Aus/NZ/Fr, 1993), P J Hogan's *Muriel's Wedding* (Aus/Fr, 1994) and Marleen Gorris's *Antonia's Line* (Holl/Belg/UK, 1995).

**feminist film theory:** ways of critiquing and explaining film from a feminist perspective. Feminist film theory first emerged in the early 1970s, when writers such as Claire Johnston examined the portrayal of women in *Hollywood* films, suggesting that female characters are the result of ideological myth-making, and defined not as women but as 'not-men'. Laura Mulvey, in her influential essay *Visual Pleasure and Narrative Cinema* (1975), worked from a psychoanalytical basis: she suggested that all viewers, male and female, are positioned to see screen events from a male point of view (the '*male gaze*'). Female characters, who are usually passive and peripheral to the main action, become the object of desire for male characters and *spectators* alike, while the latter are also encouraged to identify with the more active and centrally important male characters. More recently (1992) Carol Clover has taken a less pessimistic view in her study of modern horror/slasher films in which the '*final girl*' succeeds in dispatching the monster; in adopting a traditionally heroic and masculine role, she thus 'feminises' the audience. Other notable writers include bell hooks (sic) and Lola Young, who have combined issues of ethnicity with feminist film theory.

**femme fatale:** the main female character in many *film noirs*. Beneath her mask of *femininity*, this 'fatal woman' is usually deadlier than the male *protagonist*, and lures him into danger for her own nefarious purposes. The archetypal femme fatale is the character of Phyllis Dietrichson (Barbara Stanwyck) in *Double Indemnity* (USA, 1944), who persuades insurance salesman Walter Neff (Fred MacMurray) to kill her husband. In some modern films such as *The Last Seduction* (John Dahl, USA, 1994), the mask of femininity has dropped, and the femme fatale has become an avenging fury.

**fiction:** a form of *narrative* that invents *characters* who do not exist in the real world (i.e. outside the narrative) and relates a sequence of imaginary events involving them.

**field research:** that carried out in the 'real world' as opposed to the artificial conditions of a laboratory. Field research into *audience* behaviour (e.g. carried out in people's homes) has consistently produced different results to those produced in the laboratory.

**fight arranger/choreographer:** the person who plans every detail of the fights that take place in drama (not including those behind the scenes). As well as concern for realism, the fight choreographer must consider both health and safety issues and camera positions.

**fill:** a term used in *radio* to indicate a period of airtime between one scheduled item and another. For example, there may be 30 seconds to fill between the end of a piece of music and an advertising break.

**filler story:** a *newspaper* article of small importance that can be used to fill space when necessary.

**fill light:** in *three-point lighting*, the diffused light that 'fills' the areas left unlit by the key light by softening or eliminating shadows.

**film:** (i) a photographic medium in which silver halides are embedded in a light-sensitive emulsion within a thin, flexible, transparent plastic strip. When exposed to light, film undergoes a chemical change, thus imprinting a negative image of the subject. A positive then needs to be developed in a laboratory. Different types of film are used for still cameras and movie cameras, and may be either monochrome or colour. Movie film is viewed by projecting the images in rapid succession (24 frames per second), illuminated by a powerful lamp, on to a screen. This creates the illusion of movement. The most common film gauge or width is 35 mm, but 16 mm stock is also common for movie cameras, and some movies are shot on 70 mm. 8 mm was a popular domestic format before the availability of video camcorders in the early 1980s. (ii) any kind of movie, whether it was created using chemical-based film or digital video. (iii) to create a moving image.

**film buff:** an enthusiast who has detailed knowledge of films and film makers.

**film commission:** an organisation set up to encourage and assist film-making in any city, region or country. This will usually include giving film makers local advice or permission about shooting, providing information on suitable locations, crew members, actors, weather conditions, legal matters and accommodation. In the case of larger organisations, funding or tax breaks (i.e. exemptions) are also available.

**film culture:** one that has grown up around film-making and viewing. This includes *fandom*, film criticism, education, and connections with other modes of production in the arts and entertainment, including literature and painting. A strong film culture will not only provide screen entertainment but also reflect current social debates and political trends.

**film festival:** an event at which any number of films are shown. Film festivals vary greatly in size, function and content, from major international occasions such as those held annually in *Cannes* or Venice, to small local festivals. Some are competitive (e.g. Cannes, Venice, Berlin), with prizes awarded in certain categories, and some are not (e.g. London). Many festivals double as markets, where film options and distribution rights are bought and sold (e.g. Sundance in the USA). Others showcase films of a particular genre (e.g. shorts, documentaries, animation, fantasy and science fiction, wildlife) or the films of a particular country or region. Festivals are often visited by the producers, directors and stars of the selected films.

**film form:** a term used to distinguish structure from content in film analysis. It usually refers to the elements of *genre, narrative, mise en scène, cinematography*, sound and *editing*. Analysis of film form helps students to be objective about the construction of films and the ways in which they achieve their effects.

**Film Four:** originally Film on Four, an important film production body set up in 1982 by the newly established Channel 4 television in order to commission and finance *low-budget* British films at a time when the industry was at a particularly low ebb. Notably successful productions in the 1980s included *The Draughtman's Contract* (Peter Greenaway, UK, 1982), *My Beautiful Laundrette* (Stephen Frears, UK, 1984), *A Room with a View* (James Ivory, UK, 1985), and *Hope and Glory* (John Boorman, UK, 1987). Film Four is now a *free-to-air* television channel specialising in films.

**film grammar:** the complete set of techniques available to film makers, and how these combine to create meaning for the audience. When we understand the 'rules' of film grammar, as with spoken and written grammar, we can understand clearly what is being communicated and how, through camerawork, graphics, editing (including the manipulation of time), lighting and sound. For example, in *The Blair Witch Project* (Daniel Myrick/Eduardo Sanchez, USA, 1999), the character of Heather addresses her hand-held video camera in a state of terror one night after the crew have become hopelessly lost in the woods. The camera partially frames her face in a shaky, low-angle, *extreme close-up;* the lighting is harsh; there is no music – the sound consists of the terrified young woman struggling to speak through her sobs; the shot duration is long. Each of these elements communicates a sense of fear to the audience, through a mixture of documentary-style realism and unsparing intensity.

**filmic:** (i) having the quality of film as a medium. For example, visually oriented novels are sometimes described as filmic. At the same time, modern high resolution digital video has also been called filmic in its ability to capture the subtleties of colour and light in a similar degree to film. (ii) techniques associated with film (e.g. scriptwriting, lighting).

**film industry:** usually refers to the *producers, distributors* and *exhibitors* of films. Others working full- or part-time in the industry include writers, actors and stunt performers, technical crew, drivers, talent agents, sales agents, publicists, designers and equipment and facilities hire companies.

**film language:** see *film grammar*

**film look:** the visible attributes of film, which can be simulated by video software (e.g. making it look more grainy, adding hairs in the gate, de-interlacing).

**film maker:** one who makes films, usually referring to a *producer* or *director*.

**film noir:** a highly influential style of crime or detective film popular in the 1940s and 1950s, and revived frequently since. *The Maltese Falcon* (John Huston, USA, 1941) is generally considered to be the first, and *Touch of Evil* (Orson Welles, USA, 1958) the last of the 'classic' period. Stylistic features include minimal, high-contrast lighting, 'hard-boiled' dialogue, dramatic orchestral music, sadistic violence, and a downbeat plot with an unhappy ending. Stock characters include the tough, trenchcoat-clad male protagonist, who is often an *anti-hero*, and the seemingly innocent *femme fatale* with a shady past. *Chinatown* (Roman Polanski, USA, 1973), *The Long Goodbye* (Robert Altman, USA, 1974), *The Usual Suspects* (Bryan Singer, USA, 1995) and *Sin City* (Frank Miller/Robert Rodriguez/Quentin Tarantino, USA, 2005) are more recent examples, sometimes known as *neo-noir*.

**filmography:** a list of films, sometimes pertaining to a particular film maker, referred to in an article, piece of research or academic writing. Analogous to a bibliography.

**film school:** where people can go to learn about film production and the film industry. In the UK, the best-known example is the *National Film and Television School* in Beaconsfield.

**film speed:** (i) the sensitivity of film *stock* to light. Fast film (i.e. any with an ISO/ASA rating of 500 or above) is more sensitive; slow film (125 or below) less so. Hence the stronger the light available while photography takes place, the slower the film that is needed. (ii) more accurately known as 'film running speed', the rate at which movie film passes through a camera or projector. If film is '*undercranked*', i.e. images are captured at a slower rate than the standard 24 frames per second, action in the resulting footage will appear in fast motion; if 'overcranked', a slow-motion effect will be produced.

**film stock:** see *stock*

**film studies:** the academic study of all aspects of film. These include not only film theory but the history of film, the techniques of film analysis and criticism, its genres and international varieties, the inner workings of the film industry, the work of individual directors and stars, and the social and political implications of film.

**film style:** the cumulative effect of every production technique used in any particular film to create its overall manner of presentation. This is most easily observed in films of certain *genres*: for example, *horror* films will often employ a range of stylistic techniques including very low lighting, shock editing, hand-held or canted camerawork, gruesome special effects and sudden bursts of loud, dramatic music. Individual *directors* may work in a variety of film styles across a variety of genres, but those acknowledged as *auteurs* have usually developed a unique individual style, in which it is possible to detect *motifs*, or repeated stylistic features.

**filter:** (i) a transparent gel used with a camera lens to boost or suppress certain types or colours of light, or to create certain photographic effects. For example, if *motion blur* is the desired effect, a neutral density filter can produce this by reducing the intensity of light, allowing a slower shutter speed or wider aperture. (ii) a sound-recording device with a similar function, in that it cuts out or reduces certain unwanted audio frequencies.

**final cut:** the version of a film seen by the public. Even while a film is being shot, the *editor* will begin to assemble a rough cut, usually very long and without music or titles, which will gradually be refined into a fine cut, and lastly the final cut. The issue of who has the final cut (i.e. who decides exactly what will be in the completed film and what will not) has often led to confrontations between *directors* and studios. This has led in turn to the phenomenon of the *director's cut* – notably Ridley Scott's version of *Blade Runner* (USA, 1992 – the original version was released in 1982), in which the director omitted Harrison Ford's voiceover and added other material that allowed for drastic re-interpretation of the plot.

**final girl:** a classic convention of *horror/slasher* movies, the 'final girl' is the only person left to confront the killers after the characters around her are murdered one by one. For example, the character of Sydney in *Scream* (Wes Craven, USA, 1996). (See also *feminist film theory*.)

**fine cut:** an edited version of a film just prior to its *final cut*.

**Firewire:** a cable (also known as a '1394 cable') that connects a DV camera or data storage device to a computer, allowing shot footage to be downloaded and then edited.

**first-person narrative:** a story told from the point of view of a character (uses 'I' and 'me' rather than 's/he' and 'him/her').

**first run:** a film's initial cinema *release*, during which it will generate its main box-office return. A film may have its first run in very few cinemas and gradually 'go wide' across the country afterwards, or open with a wide release.

**fish-eye lens:** an extremely wide-angle lens with a field of view of up to 180 degrees, and a focal length of between 8 and 16 mm. It distorts the image, giving a convex appearance to the shot as if it were projected on to a sphere. Fish-eye lenses are useful for creating dreamlike or hallucinogenic images.

**fishpole:** in sound recording, a length of wood or metal held by a *boom* operator to position a *microphone* as close as possible to the source of the sound without being visible to the camera.

**fixed camera/fixed lens/fixed focus:** a fixed, or 'locked off', camera is one that does not move during the shot; a fixed lens is one that cannot be zoomed or refocussed, as used on cheap cameras; a fixed focus lens is one that cannot zoom. Also known as a 'prime lens'.

**flashback/flashforward:** *narrative* techniques in which the chronological sequence of the story is disrupted to show the *audience* what took place in the past, or what will happen in the future. Certain films are 'told in flashback', i.e. the beginning and the end are set in 'the present', while the main body of the film tells the story of how events have reached this point. One example is *Sunset Boulevard* (Billy Wilder, USA, 1950), in which a corpse narrates how it came to be floating face down in a swimming pool. Flashbacks are far more common than flashforwards.

**flat plan:** one which shows graphically the intended contents of a *magazine* at the beginning of the pre-production stage. A flat plan indicates which pages will be allocated to advertising and which to editorial, but there is usually no detail beyond the titles of certain regular items and special features.

**Fleet Street:** *metonymic* term for the UK national press, which until the 1980s was based in and around this central London street. The newspapers moved out as *hot metal* printing technology was replaced by computers.

**floor manager:** in television, the representative of the *director* on the studio floor, who relays the latter's instructions to cast members and camera crew. This is necessary because the director is likely to be seated in the *gallery*, or control room, during recording, and communicates with the floor manager using *talkback* (i.e. through an earpiece).

**floor runner:** junior member of a film or television studio crew who fetches and carries items and messages.

**flow:** the way in which television delivers itself to the *audience* – not as a discrete artefact like a film, but as a long, continuous sequence of images, including programmes, idents, advertisements and trailers. Flow is an idea first proposed by cultural critic Raymond Williams in the early 1970s.

**flying cam:** a remote-controlled camera suspended from a wire to enable swooping shots (e.g. over the heads of a studio audience).

**fly-on-the-wall:** a type of *observational documentary* technique in which participants appear not to be conscious of the camera. Extensively used in such *'reality'* television formats as *Big Brother*, fly-on-the-wall was first used in films like D A Pennebaker's *Don't Look Back* (USA, 1965) and Frederick Wiseman's *High School* (USA, 1968). These films employed no *voice-over* narration or music, and featured no interaction between film makers and subjects, in order to create an impression of unmediated reality.

**FM:** short for frequency modulation, FM is the part of the *analogue* broadcast radio spectrum between 87 and 108 Mhz. It provides higher fidelity sound than can be obtained from medium- or long-wave transmission. (See also *AM.*)

**focus:** the degree of sharpness and definition of an image, achieved at the point where light rays from the subject of the shot converge behind the camera lens (i.e. on the film). **Focal length** is the distance between the lens and the film, and is measured in millimetres. **Sharp focus** refers to maximum sharpness and definition; **soft focus** means that the image is slightly blurred. **Deep focus** occurs where everything in the frame is in focus, however close to or far from the lens. A **focus puller** is the member of a camera crew responsible for adjusting the focal length during a shot, as the camera and the subject move closer together or further apart. Sometimes he will also **follow focus**, i.e. continually adjust the focus during a moving shot to keep the subject sharp.

**focus group:** a selected group of people whose opinions and reactions are monitored for the purposes of research and *marketing*.

**fog index:** a readability test of a piece of writing. The fog index tells us how many years of education the reader needs in order to understand it easily, by taking into account both the length of sentences and the number of words of three or more syllables. Calculating a fog index is an interesting exercise when applied to newspapers, since it enables us to determine the educational level of the *target audience*.

**foley artist:** the member of a film crew who creates post-production *sound effects* (e.g. footsteps, doors opening and closing). Traditional methods include using gloves to simulate the flapping of a bird's wings, and stabbing a cabbage for a knife in the ribs.

**font:** see *typeface*

**footage:** an amount of film shot or used.

**Fordian:** relates to the work of John Ford (1895–1973), an important American film director, whose career lasted from 1917 to 1973. Although he made films in other genres, notably war, he was primarily famous for his *Westerns*, particularly those starring actor John

Wayne, including *Stagecoach* (USA, 1939) and *The Searchers* (USA, 1956). Ford both defined the Western genre and contributed to its eventual downfall: while his early films celebrated the *heroism* of those who settled the 'Old West', and represented the native American Indians as faceless savages, his later ones (e.g. *Cheyenne Autumn*, USA, 1964) were concerned with their destruction. Hence the term 'Fordian' refers to films which foreground the bravery and heroism of the indomitable American hero, as embodied by his regular lead John Wayne, defending the US flag, whether at war with native Americans or twentieth-century adversaries such as the Germans, Koreans, Japanese and Vietnamese.

**Fordism:** the model of industrial mass production by which films were made in *Hollywood* during the Hollywood studio era. Named after car manufacturer Henry Ford, Fordism is an assembly-line system in which raw materials are combined into a finished product. Specialised craftsmen participate at different stages of the manufacturing process; beginning with writers, then directors and other production crew, then editors, and so on.

**format:** (i) a technological configuration standard such as *VHS* or Hi-8, PAL or SECAM. **Format wars** break out when incompatible rival systems are launched, as in the early years of video when the VHS format battled it out with *Betamax* and V2000 for public acceptance. (ii) a template for a television programme which, if successful in its original country, can be reproduced by broadcasters elsewhere (e.g. the format of the quiz show *Who Wants to be a Millionaire?* has been exported to dozens of countries, from Argentina to Vietnam).

**foreshadow/ing:** a *narrative* event that in some way reflects an important future event in the story, thus suggesting the workings of fate. For example, in Hitchcock's *Vertigo* (USA, 1958), the death of a police officer by falling from a building in the opening scene foreshadows the manner of Mrs Esler's death towards the end of the film.

**form/formalism:** formal elements are those which give a media product its overall structure and character (e.g. genre, narrative, soundtrack). Formalism is therefore the type of analysis or criticism, particularly in film, that emphasises the significance of these formal elements, as distinct from the content. For example, the frequent use of fluid tracking shots in the films of Max Ophuls. (See also *film form*).

**formula film:** a film that closely follows the *conventions* of an established *genre* without contributing anything new or unusual to it.

**found footage/images:** footage or images incorporated into a film that were not created by the film maker. Derived from the modern art term objet trouvé (found object).

**four-colour printing:** the process used in *magazines*, *newspapers* and *posters* whereby a full-colour image is reproduced for publication by separating it into its cyan (blue), magenta (red), yellow and black components. Full colour is then recreated by printing these separations on top of each other.

**fourth estate:** the *press*, and by extension, the *news* media in general. So called because of the power they wield in the political life of the country. The three original 'estates' were the church, the nobility and the common citizens.

**fourth wall:** in stage drama, that part of the traditional proscenium set that allows the *audience* to see the action, since only three of the four walls are present. This invisible 'fourth wall' is also what separates the audience from the *characters*, until of course a character addresses the audience directly.

**fragmentation:** the postmodern tendency for numerous *niche audiences* to develop, as opposed to the *mass audiences* of the past, and the ways in which the media industry has responded to this. Although hundreds of television channels are now available in the UK, until 1964 there were only two – *BBC* and *ITV*. Fragmentation has had implications for social cohesion, since the once unifying experience of discussing last night's TV programme is no longer possible in a world in which everyone has been watching something different. The production process has also fragmented, with a large proportion of programmes made by independent producers rather than *in-house*.

**frame:** (i) to position a camera so as to include some elements of a scene (sometimes known as the 'profilmic') and exclude others; hence framing a shot is analogous to framing a painted picture. (ii) the shot as bounded by its edges, hence 'in the frame' or 'out of frame'. (iii) the smallest unit of a moving image, each second of which, in the case of film, is made up of 24 individual still frames.

**frame rate:** (i) the speed at which film or video tape runs through the camera, i.e. 24 frames per second (fps) in modern films; 18 fps in older films of the silent era. (ii) the fps at which images arrive on screen during a television transmission. (iii) the fps captured when transferring footage from a digital video camera to a computer for editing or playback.

**franchise:** in business, the authorisation by a parent company (or franchise holder) for a smaller company to sell goods or services under its name. Also refers to a long-running series of films with different directors. The *James Bond* film franchise is the most obvious example: the key elements of the original film remain the same, in terms of back story and characters, but successive directors may introduce different stylistic or ideological interpretations.

**Frankfurt School:** a group of neo-Marxist philosophers and cultural critics best known for developing the *hypodermic* or *effects model* of media consumption in the 1930s. The Institute for Social Research was part of the University of Frankfurt; its members, which included Theodor Adorno, Walter Benjamin and Herbert Marcuse, pioneered the study of mass media, particularly in relation to the perceived audience effects of Nazi *propaganda* and, later, the American *advertising* industry.

**Free Cinema:** a movement in 1950s British film that sought to break away from the established film industry and make *low-budget* documentaries about the working and leisure lives of ordinary people. A precursor to the better-known *British new wave*, Free Cinema was founded by Lindsay Anderson, Karel Reisz, Tony Richardson and Lorenza Mazzetti.

**freelance:** self-employed and hired to work for different companies on particular assignments. In modern film and television, and to a large extent print journalism, working freelance is the norm. It has the advantage of allowing media practitioners to work on any number of projects simultaneously, hence increasing earnings potential, but the disadvantage of lacking any job security.

**free market:** see *market*

**free press:** a press industry that is autonomous. A free press is able to report independently without *censorship* or pressure from its owners, governments or private industry to 'tone down' criticism or 'bury' stories, and to toe the 'official line'. Journalists with press organisations that are not free often work under threat of imprisonment, torture or even death.

**freesheet:** a newspaper financed entirely from *advertising* and distributed free of charge. This dependence on advertisers may compromise its editorial independence (see *free press*). Many local newspapers in the UK are freesheets. *The Metro* is a national freesheet.

**free-to-air:** broadcast media that can be received without paying a subscription or *pay per view* fee (i.e. in the UK, all BBC services, all radio stations, ITV, Channel 4 and Five, and all *Freeview* channels). However, in the UK all TV viewers must pay an annual *licence fee* for the BBC's services.

**Freeview:** a consortium that broadcasts *free-to-air* digital terrestrial television and radio channels and interactive services, received via a set-top decoder or built-in digital tuner.

**freeze frame:** a still image selected from a moving image sequence and 'held' in order to capture a single important moment in the story (e.g. the moment at the end of *Thelma and Louise* (Ridley Scott, USA, 1991) where the women plunge to their deaths.)

**French new wave:** a radical cinema movement of the 1950s and 1960s founded by young critics of *Cahiers du Cinéma* magazine. Exponents included Claude Chabrol (*Le Beau Serge*, 1959), François Truffaut (*The 400 Blows*, 1959), Jean-Luc Godard (*Breathless*, 1960), Eric Rohmer (*My Night at Maud's*, 1969) and Jacques Rivette (*Paris Belongs To Us*, 1960). They rejected the bourgeois 'cinéma du papa' that had dominated French cinema since the Second World War and made *low-budget* films that deliberately broke with narrative and stylistic convention through the use of improvised dialogue, location shooting, long tracking-shots and jump-cuts, and a spontaneous, informal manner. The French new wave, or 'nouvelle vague', influenced many key *Hollywood* directors, notably Arthur Penn, Robert Altman and Quentin Tarantino.

**frequency:** (i) in practice, a term to describe whatever part of the broadcast spectrum is allocated to a particular service (e.g. BBC Radio One's frequency is in a band between 97.6 and 99.8 MHz). Frequency is in inverse ratio to wavelength i.e. the higher the frequency, the shorter the wavelength. (ii) the number of times an activity is perceived to occur in a film sequence. For example, in *Wedding Crashers* (David Dobkin, USA, 2005), the film cuts rapidly between several weddings attended by John and Jeremy, and the audience understands that these represent many more such occasions. (iii) how often a publication is produced (e.g. the *Mail on Sunday* is weekly, while *Private Eye* is fortnightly). (iv) a *news value* – according to Galtung and Ruge, events unfolding gradually or at times that are not convenient for a news organisation's production cycle are less likely to be reported than those which are sudden and take place during office hours. (v) in *advertising*, the number of times an *audience* member is exposed to an advertisement. (See also *opportunities to see*.)

**Freudian:** any term derived from the work of Sigmund Freud, known as 'the father of psychoanalysis'. Freud's theories concerned the human unconscious and its hidden and unrecognised effects, particularly sexual and aggressive, on our conscious lives. Among his many ideas were those of childhood sexuality and development, *narcissism*, the existence of the Id, the Ego and the Superego, and the frequent use of defence mechanisms to protect ourselves from unpalatable truths. Cultural critics have adopted Freud's ideas to reveal symbolism in media texts, and to analyse character motivation, *narrative* structure and *audience* reactions. The films of Alfred Hitchcock are a goldmine for such interpretations, especially where they deal with themes of sexual obsession (*Vertigo*, USA, 1958), imputations of guilt (*North by Northwest*, USA, 1959), scopophilia, or the pleasure of looking (*Rear Window*, USA, 1954) and the desire to kill close relatives (*Strangers on a Train*, USA,

1951). Followers of Freud, particularly Jacques Lacan, have been adopted by feminist critics such as Laura Mulvey to explain aspects of *spectatorship*.

**front cover:** the most important element of any magazine, since it is the means by which the magazine attracts its readers, through careful use of images, colours, written text and cover mounts, or giveaways. For this reason, the cover's written descriptions of the magazine's contents are known as *sell-lines.*

**frontier film:** usually a *Western*, although many elements of the frontier film have been appropriated by the *science fiction* genre, when it concerns the exploration of unknown worlds. The theme of the frontier film is often the conflict between nature (or savagery) and civilisation (or culture), as in the films of *John Ford.*

**f-stop:** the measurement of the opening of a camera's lens aperture. The f-stop number varies according to the aperture: larger apertures are expressed as smaller f-stop numbers, and vice-versa.

**full shot:** see *long shot.*

**future-noir:** a hybrid of *science fiction* and *film noir*, *Blade Runner* (Ridley Scott, USA, 1982) being the best-known example. In future-noir, the *dystopian* future of science fiction combines with the bleak, hard-boiled *existentialism* of the noir *anti-hero.*

**future-proofing:** the attempt to minimise the negative effects of rapid technological change by anticipating it and including it in product design. This is particularly the case with computer data, which is at risk from becoming inaccessible due to changes in format (i.e. certain file types being superceded by newer and better formats).

**futurism:** an art movement prominent in Italy and Russia in the early twentieth century. It rejected all links with and values of the past, embraced technology (especially the car) and later became linked with Fascism. Subsequent ideas about the futuristic 'man-machine' emerged in the music of Kraftwerk and Gary Numan. 'Future shock' is a phrase coined by writer Alvin Toffler and used as the title of his book; it examines the consequences of too much change taking place in too short a period of time, such as stress, disorientation and information overload.

**FX:** shorthand for 'effects', whether *special effects* (SFX) or *sound effects.*

**Do you know we also have A–Zs for:**

- **ICT & Computing**
- **Psychology**
- **Sociology**
- **Travel & Leisure?**

Ask for them in your local bookshop or see the inside back cover for ordering details.

**gaffer:** chief electrician on a film set. The gaffer works closely with the *cinematographer* (the DP) on the selection, placement, balance and level of the *lighting*, and is responsible for its care and maintenance.

**gallery:** the control room for a TV studio. It may be on a different floor of the building from the studio, and links to it are therefore provided through *talkback* and television monitors. The director, production assistant, sound and vision mixers are among the personnel who work in the gallery rather than on the studio floor.

**galley proof:** see *proof*

**Galtung and Ruge model:** see *news values*

**game:** when used in the context of new media technologies, game means *video game*. Sophisticated modern 3-D games are one of the few genuinely *interactive* media forms, in that almost everything that takes place depends on the actions of the player. The range of important game *genres* includes:

- **First-Person Shooters**, in which the player looks through the eyes of a gun-carrying character and tries to kill as many opponents as possible. Many *James Bond* games adopt this format.

- **Adventure Games**: these are usually from a third person perspective. The player controls an *avatar* who is aiming to complete an adventure. This requires the completion of various challenges. Frequently, as in Nintendo's *Mario* and *Zelda* games, this will require a combination of puzzle-solving and skill with the *games controller*.

- **Fighting Games**: also known as 'beat 'em ups' (where the avatars are fist fighting) or 'slash 'em ups' (where swords are used). Examples include *Soulcalibur*.

- **Sports Games**: almost every sport has a videogame equivalent. *Tiger Woods Golf*, *Tony Hawks Pro Skater* and *FIFA Soccer* are just three examples from hundreds.

- **Skill Games** require the player to learn precise and often complex movements of the game controller in order to achieve increasingly difficult tasks. The classic skill game is *Tetris.*

- *Sims*: games in which some element of reality is simulated.

There is, however, much crossover between game genres. For example, *Metroid Prime* is an adventure game combined with a first-person shooter.

**game environment:** the 3-D space in which a *video game* takes place. In some games *genres*, this is merely a realistic representation of the type of place where such activities would occur. For example, in a snowboarding game, the game environment, or **game world** consists of a selection of simulated mountain slopes. Production of these is a highly complex process, requiring sophisticated animation techniques. In other genres, the game environment needs to obey a detailed set of logical rules, and to create a sense of *spatial and temporal contiguity*. For example, the classic adventure game, *The Legend of Zelda: Ocarina of Time*, requires the hero to travel around a very large geographical area completing tasks in many different locations. While he is doing so, time passes repeatedly from day to night. He is also able to switch between his childhood and adult selves. Of course, his actions in childhood often have direct effects on the world as seen by his older self. The complexities and logical problems involved in designing this sort of game environment are enormous.

**gameplay:** a term used when discussing *video games* to describe the overall experience. Good gameplay is achieved through a combination of factors, such as well-designed animation, precise response to the *games controller* and an interesting idea. Some would say that simplicity is the essence of good gameplay, and many *gamers* maintain that the most sophisticated 3-D games actually offer poorer gameplay than an old-fashioned 2-D *platformer* such as *Donkey Kong.*

**gamer:** a player of *video games.* The term suggests a high level of commitment and skill. Some high level gamers play professionally in tournaments; some are employed by games developers to test new products.

**games console:** a small personal computer designed solely for playing games. Most consoles operate *proprietorial formats*, meaning that they will only run games made (or licensed) by the console manufacturer.

**games controller:** the hand-held *interface* used by the player of a *video game*. Manufacturers of *games consoles* aim to construct the most distinctive controllers possible.

**game show:** long-running TV *genre* in which contestants compete to win prizes. *Codes and conventions* of the game show include brash theme music, a noisy studio audience, a colourful, brightly-lit set which resembles a fairground stall, a former comedian as host, a glamorous female assistant, and some sort of elimination format through which one contestant emerges triumphant at the end. Examples include *The Generation Game* and *The Price is Right.* Not to be confused with *quiz show.*

**gangster film:** enduringly popular film *genre* almost as old as cinema itself (e.g. D W Griffith's *Musketeers of Pig Alley*, USA, 1912), in which criminal gangs slug it out with the police and each other. Often seen as a useful metaphor for the workings of American business and professional life as a whole. The biggest early star of the gangster film was James Cagney (e.g. *The Public Enemy*, USA, 1931; *Angels with Dirty Faces*, USA, 1938). More recent gangster specialists have included actors Robert de Niro, Al Pacino and Joe Pesci, and directors Martin Scorsese (*Goodfellas*, USA, 1990; *Casino*, US, 1995) and Francis Ford Coppola (*The Godfather* trilogy, USA, 1972–1990).

**gate:** the aperture of a *camera*, the point at which the film is exposed. On set, the *director* cannot be sure that a shot has been successfully completed until the *camera operator* has checked to ensure that there is no 'hair in the gate' (i.e. a human hair over the aperture), which can ruin the shot.

**gatekeeper; gatekeeping:** gatekeepers are media professionals who decide what appears in the media and what does not. For example, news stories coming into newspaper offices from outside the organisation (e.g. from news agencies and freelance journalists) are filtered by a copytaster, whose job it is to sort the suitable stories from the unsuitable. The term was invented by social psychologist Kurt Lewin in 1947. Editors, commissioning editors, TV producers and researchers, and radio station bosses are further examples of gatekeepers. In 2003, records by leading country music act The Dixie Chicks were banned from airplay by American programme directors after one of them criticised President George W Bush.

**gauge:** the width of film *stock* measured in millimetres (i.e. 16 mm, 35 mm or 70 mm).

**gauze shot:** a soft-focus camera shot achieved by placing a flimsy transparent material in front of the lens. Frequently used to photograph female stars during the *Hollywood* studio era, this effect creates a romantic image, e.g. Ingrid Bergman in *Casablanca* (Michael Curtiz, USA, 1942).

**gay and lesbian film:** the cinema of homosexuality. Characters in films may be explicitly gay and the plotline may reflect this, e.g. *La Cage aux Folles* (Edouard Molinaro, Fr/It, 1978), *Desert Hearts* (Donna Deitch, USA, 1985), *Brokeback Mountain* (Ang Lee, USA, 2005). In other cases – particularly older films – an implicit suggestion or subtext of homosexuality may be present that may have gone unnoticed by 'straight' audiences on original release, but that modern audiences are able to 'read', for example, the character of Mrs Danvers in *Rebecca* (Alfred Hitchcock, USA, 1940). Certain directors (e.g. Douglas Sirk) and genres (especially the musical) have also found favour with gay audiences. Not to be confused with *camp*. (See also *queer theory*.)

**gaze:** see *female gaze, male gaze, object of the gaze*

**gel(atine):** on stage, in film or television, a gel is a transparent coloured sheet of plastic placed in front of a light. In colouring the light that falls upon the scene, the gel helps to create a certain mood. For example, blue gels were frequently used in 1980s TV police show *Miami Vice*, perhaps to create a feeling of 'cool'.

**gender; gendered reading/viewing:** gender refers to our cultural ideas about *masculinity* and *femininity*. As such, it is not synonymous with 'sex', a term used simply to define either 'male' or 'female'. For example, wearing one's hair long, or wearing the colour pink, is traditionally coded as feminine. There are also cultural notions of gender roles, e.g. men are often regarded as more aggressive and risk-taking by nature than women, this being ascribed to the effect of the male hormone testosterone; yet a counter-argument would be that these characteristics are conditioned in boys from birth, suggesting that they are due to the social environment rather than nature. We can examine these contradictions in media texts through 'gendered' readings or viewings of texts. Since the 1970s this has usually involved looking at texts in an *oppositional* way to highlight a perceived cultural *bias* against women; a gendered reading might point out how images of women are demeaning and disempowering because they are sexualised or rendered marginal or inferior to those of men. However, more recent gendered readings have also examined the representation of men in such films as *Fight Club* (David Fincher, USA, 1999), where the crisis in masculinity becomes an issue. (See also *female gaze* and *male gaze*.)

**genre:** a genre is a loose category or classification of media product (e.g. tabloid newspaper, soap opera, science fiction film). Classification into one genre or another is governed by *codes and conventions*, and each has its own more or less obvious *iconography*. The codes and conventions of a genre refer both to the cultural signals contained in the text and to the ways in which the text's content is presented. For instance, although a *tabloid* newspaper is strictly speaking one of compact size, compared with a broadsheet or quality newspaper, it is also likely to contain more sensationalised stories, bigger headlines, more photographs and simpler language, and to present opinion as fact. Similarly, the term '*soap opera*' classifies a text which exists in television, features a large cast located in domestic and 'local' settings, is narratively in the serial format and has multi-stranded storylines and unresolved endings. However, because every media product is unique in one way or another, not all generic elements will invariably be present in every example of a genre. Genre acts as useful shorthand for *producers*, for whom it helps to generate profit, and for *audiences*, to whom it provides pleasure. It helps audiences know in advance what to expect of the product, and many become fans of certain genres; for producers, genre helps to make clear what is being proposed when they are pitching ideas for new products. Conversely, a media product that does not fall into a clear genre, and is therefore more challenging to describe, may be less successful than one that does. Genres can die out or mutate over time: the *Western* is an example of an important film genre which has almost disappeared, while since the 1950s the *horror movie* has often combined with science fiction, e.g. *The Thing* (John Carpenter, USA, 1982). This is an example of a generic hybrid (which involves genre-bending or genre-surfing) – a mixture of two or more genres.

**geodemographics:** the way sociologists, marketeers and statisticians arrange the population into social classes by analysing where people live and how they live. This has largely superceded the old *ABC1C2DE* classifications: since neighbourhoods generally contain people of similar lifestyle and spending habits, a person's postcode is now seen as a more reliable indicator of his social class.

**Gerbner model:** a model of the interpersonal communication process that emphasises the importance of form and context in the way messages are delivered and received. For example, the sentence 'I love you' has a radically different meaning when said as a routine way of finishing a phone call than it does over a candlelit dinner for two. Named after communications theorist George Gerbner.

**German expressionism:** a European art movement in which reality is distorted and exaggerated in order to express the inner torment of a character or characters. It began in painting in the late nineteenth century (Munch's *The Scream* being the most famous example) and became a feature of German cinema, with such films as *The Cabinet of Dr Caligari* (Robert Weine, 1920), *Nosferatu* (F W Murnau, 1922) and *Metropolis* (Fritz Lang, 1927).

**gesture:** in dramatic performance, a means of expressing the thoughts, feelings, desires and intentions of a character without using words. Gesture, or body language, is known to be a more powerful means of communication than words in the real world, where it is also known as *non-verbal communication* (NVC).

**ghost film:** popular genre, particularly in Japanese and *Hollywood* cinema of the 1990s and early twenty-first century. Although it can create sensations of *horror*, and hence overlaps with the horror film, the main convention of the ghost film is in suggesting that the dead can communicate with the living and affect events in the real world. Hollywood has remade a number of Japanese ghost films, including *The Ring* (Hideo Nakata, Japan, 1998 and Gore Verbinski, USA, 2002) and *Dark Water* (Hideo Nakata, Japan, 2002 and Walter Salles, USA, 2005). Other examples of the genre include *The Shining* (Stanley Kubrick, USA, 1980), *The Sixth Sense* (M Night Shyamalan, USA, 1999) and *The Others* (Alejandro Amenabar, Sp/Fr/USA, 2001).

**ghosting:** a feature of poor analogue *terrestrial television* reception, in which the picture displays a second image – faint and slightly displaced – along with the first. This is usually caused by an additional signal being received that has been reflected off a nearby building or hill.

**global village:** the idea that because international communications are now instantaneous, we can communicate as quickly and easily with someone on the far side of the world as we once could with people who lived in our own village. Hence we are now living in a 'global village'. The concept was first suggested by Marshall McLuhan in 1964, and has since been accelerated by the invention of the *internet*.

**globalisation:** the complex process by which countries around the world are becoming more closely intertwined economically, politically and environmentally. This can be interpreted from both a positive and a negative standpoint: on the one hand, globalisation can be seen as spreading the benefits of rich countries – consumer goods, employment, democracy, communications – to poorer countries; on the other, it can appear to destroy indigenous cultures, spread pollution, increase global warming, lay poor countries open to exploitation by giant corporations based in the developed world, and cause the export of jobs from the developed world, thus creating unemployment.

**gonzo journalism:** a style of journalism in which objectivity, balance and even facts are considered less important than the journalist's personal response to the story and the adventures and mishaps involved in obtaining it. Invented by American writer Hunter S Thompson in the 1970s, a good example of the gonzo style is his book *Fear and Loathing in Las Vegas* (1971).

**gothic:** a romantic style in the arts, originally inspired by literary ideas about medieval times. Gothic fiction tends to be set in crumbling castles full of secret passageways and imprisoned mad women, and surrounded by a population of fearful peasants practising barbaric forms of ancient religion. Gothic *horror*, as in the work of nineteenth-century American novelist and poet Edgar Allen Poe, and the films produced in the 1950s and 1960s in England by *Hammer* Studios, pursues the themes of obsession, decay and death. In more recent times gothic style has continued to influence films (e.g. *Bram Stoker's Dracula*, Francis Ford Coppola, USA, 1992; *The Crow*, Alex Proyas, USA, 1994), music – particularly heavy metal bands – and fashion, with the persistence of the goth cult among *middle-class* teenagers. Suburban gothic focuses on the darkness lurking beneath the bland surfaces of modern life (*Blue Velvet*, David Lynch, USA, 1986; *American Beauty*, Sam Mendes, USA, 1999), while the new gothic embraces many modern forms of self-expression, from retro-styling of consumer goods to computer games and the internet.

**grain:** the imperfect visual texture of film, particularly when viewed on a big screen, or blown up from 16 mm to 35 mm. The characteristic grainy look is a result of tiny imperfections caused by the tendency of silver halide grains in the film's emulsion to clump together.

**Gramsci, Antonio (1891–1937):** see *hegemony*

**Grand Guignol:** a style of dramatic production featuring blood, *horror* and vengeance. The original Grand Guignol was a small theatre in Paris where gruesome plays were enacted in the first half of the twentieth century. The term is often applied to gory horror films like *Saw* (James Wan, USA, 2004).

**graphic design:** the way in which ideas are given visual form, through the use of page layout, typography, illustration and photography.

**graphic lines** are used as borders or dividers and as such are another tool at the designer's disposal.

**graphic match:** a compositional device on screen, whereby objects with common charac-teristics of shape or colour are used in successive shots. For example, in *Psycho* (Alfred Hitchcock, USA, 1960), after Marion has been murdered, there is a graphic match between a shot of the plughole and the next – a big close-up of her dead, staring eye.

**graphic novel:** a novel in which the story is told in pictures, as in a comic strip. Graphic novels differ from comic books in their greater length and more adult content and themes.

**graphics:** are drawn illustrations for use in any visual medium.

**greenlight:** a term used in *Hollywood* to indicate that a film project has received approval to go into production (e.g. 'I hear they greenlighted Police Academy 9.')

**green screen:** a *chromakey* technique. Green is more commonly used today than blue because it works better with digital cameras and requires less light. (See also *blue screen*.)

**grip:** a film crew member who moves camera and lighting equipment around the set, erects scaffolding for lights, lays down *dolly* track for the camera, moves props and scenery and maintains equipment. There are usually several grips working on any film, headed by the key grip, whose assistant is the *best boy*.

**gross:** the amount of money received at the *box-office* from cinema patrons for viewing a film. Gross does not represent pure profit for film producers, since most of the money is deducted by the *exhibitor* and *distributor* before it reaches the *producer*.

**gross-out:** a type of comedy or horror film whose effect depends upon arousing some element of disgust in the audience, for example by focusing on bodily functions of various kinds or particularly unpleasant special effects. In comedy, examples include the infamous apple-pie scene in *American Pie* (Paul Weitz, USA 1999); in horror films, cannibalism, entrails, wounds and projectile vomit all have a contribution to make (e.g. *The Exorcist*, William Friedkin, USA, 1973).

**group shot:** a camera shot featuring more than three people.

**guerrilla film:** *low-budget* productions on which there is no money to pay for the use of certain locations and that are therefore made 'on the run' without seeking permission. Actors are also unlikely to be paid.

**gun mic:** a highly directional *microphone*, often clad in a '*dougal*' or fleecy cover to cut down on wind noise, and attached to the end of a *fishpole*.

**gutter:** in print or web media, the space that separates two columns of text.

**gutter press:** a disparaging term for the kind of print media that specialises in gossip and scandal.

A B C D E F G H I J K L M N O P Q R S T U V W X Y Z

**halftone:** the way in which pictures are printed in newspapers and magazines, by which shades between solid colour (e.g. black) and white are made up of tiny dots, creating the illusion of continuous tone (e.g. grey).

**Hammer horror:** British horror films made by Hammer Film Productions at Hammer Studios, near Bray, on the River Thames in Berkshire. Hammer produced a large number of successful low-budget *gothic horror* movies from the mid-1950s to the 1970s, such as *The Curse of Frankenstein* (1957), *The Brides of Dracula* (1960) and *Lust for a Vampire* (1971). Shot in lurid *Technicolor*, they made stars of such actors as Peter Cushing, Christopher Lee, Oliver Reed, Ingrid Pitt and Vincent Price.

**hammocking:** a television *scheduling* technique whereby a channel protects (i.e. retains an *audience* for) a weak (i.e. relatively unpopular) programme is by positioning it between two strong ones. The theory is that audiences will be too lazy to switch channels in the interim. However, in the modern *channel-surfing* climate, the power of hammocking appears diminished.

**hand-held shot:** one in which the camera is not mounted (i.e. on a *tripod*, *dolly*, *jib* or *crane*). In *drama*, hand-held shots are often used to create a sensation of human movement (e.g. in *POV shots*). They are also common in *documentaries*, (for example those of Nick Broomfield) where the spontaneity and speed of events precludes the use of cumbersome equipment.

**hard copy:** version of a written text printed on paper rather than stored electronically.

**hard lighting:** lighting without diffusion that produces clearly-defined shadows, thereby creating both strongly-lit and completely unlit areas, as by the sun on a cloudless day. Also known as high-contrast lighting.

**hard news:** 'pure' news, as opposed to features, opinion or gossip.

**hard sell:** aggressive sales techniques designed to pressurise customers into buying a product. In *advertising*, this often takes the form of an excited, fast-talking voice-over and loud, dynamic music.

**Hays Code:** also known as the Production Code, an elaborate set of rules that *Hollywood* film makers had to abide by in the portrayal of sex and violence and use of bad language. Named after Will Hays, its first head, the Code was in force in the USA between 1934 and 1967, and was voluntarily adhered to by the Hollywood studios, who were anxious to avoid the danger of legislation in response to complaints by the Catholic League of Decency.

**HDTV (high definition television):** television displaying pictures of higher screen resolution than, for example, the traditional 625 lines used in the UK, where HDTV became nationally available in 2006. The *BBC*'s HDTV broadcasts use 1080 lines. HDTV is designed for use in semi-widescreen format, although there are variations from country to country.

**headline:** the main title running above any story in the print medium, and also by extension in broadcast *news*. A headline attempts to sum up the story in as few words as possible: *The Sun*'s notorious headline on the sinking of the Argentine warship Belgrano during the Falklands War (1982), was 'Gotcha' – a sentiment that effectively summed up not only the story but the popular patriotic Conservative *zeitgeist*.

**headroom:** the small space above a subject's head in a camera shot. This is to avoid the impression that the head is touching or 'scraping' the top of the frame. Conversely, allowing too much headroom can make the subject look weak.

**hegemony:** crudely, the power one social group wields over all the rest. However, hegemony is a more elusive and complex concept than this, involving not only the exercise of naked military and cultural power, but also the acceptance of this domination by the less powerful groups. History is full of examples, but in the modern era, the very fact that the USA is routinely referred to as the world's only superpower, despite the existence of China, serves to illustrate the stranglehold that the idea of supreme American power has on the popular imagination. One example of American hegemony is the cinema industry: *Hollywood*'s ownership and control over distribution and exhibition in most countries of the world has resulted in films made in southern California being regarded as the *norm* by audiences worldwide, although the lifestyles and attitudes on show in these films are very often radically different to local experience and tradition. Antonio Gramsci put forward the best-known explanation of hegemony, arguing that the ruling elite always makes great efforts to persuade the rest of the population that maintaining the status quo is '*common sense*'. This involves convincing them that supporting the interests of the elite is in their own interests.

**heightened realism:** where the elements of traditional realism are present, but in a dense, intensified form that approaches *expressionism.* For example, the films of Wong Kar-wai (e.g. *Chungking Express*, Hong Kong, 1994; *In the Mood for Love*, Hong Kong/Fr, 2000) often contain little 'action' in the *Hollywood* sense, and could therefore be seen as more realistic. Yet by combining the use of saturated colour and stylised though understated performances, the sense of heightened realism is achieved.

**heist film:** the heist (robbery) film or *caper film* is a *subgenre* of the *crime film*. Examples include *Reservoir Dogs* (Quentin Tarantino, USA, 1992) and *Inside Man* (Spike Lee, USA, 2005).

**heritage cinema/film:** a feature of British cinema in the 1980s, heritage films adopt a visually attractive, nostalgic and selective view of England, rooting it firmly in its past, even if the film is set in the present day. Implicitly suggesting that life was both simpler and better then, heritage cinema seems to regret the demise of the class system, in which everyone 'knew their place'. The lavish and commercially successful Merchant Ivory Productions *A Room with a View* (UK, 1985) and *Howard's End* (UK/Japan, 1992) are examples, both based on literary sources and set in the Edwardian era. Examples set in the modern era include *Four Weddings and a Funeral* (UK, 1994), the story of a wealthy, upper-*middle-class*, all-white group of friends, plus one *token*, *working-class* character.

**hermeneutic code:** see *enigma code*

**hero/heroine:** a hero or heroine is the embodiment of a culture's values, whether in mythology, literature or fact. For this reason, different types of hero have emerged in different eras: in classical Greek and Roman mythology and literature, the hero was noble in spirit and interacted with gods (e.g. Odysseus), although he was often cursed with a tragic flaw (e.g. Oedipus). As western literature developed, the type of the hero began to change, becoming an aristocrat (King Arthur, Sir Galahad) and eventually an ordinary man (Henry Fielding's novel hero *Tom Jones*, 1749). In the post-war era the hero began to diminish in favour of the *anti-hero* (Holden Caulfield in the novel *Catcher in the Rye*, 1951; Renton in the film *Trainspotting*, Danny Boyle, UK, 1996). Today, the notion of a hero has become limited to that of any *protagonist* in a work of fiction, or else a real-life person who performs an act of courage (the crimefighting 'have-a-go hero' beloved of *tabloid* newspapers). The heroine is simply the female version of a hero. However, what we consider to be heroic qualities are those of the original classical hero – courage, strength, fortitude, selflessness, generosity, leadership, imagination, honesty. (See also *existential hero*, *victim-hero*.)

**heterogeneity:** being made up of varied parts. A common use of the term is to describe a diversity of origins and cultures in any given population. The opposite of heterogeneity is *homogeneity.*

**heterosexual:** sexual orientation towards the opposite sex. Also known as 'straight'.

**hidden agenda:** where the true reasons for doing things are different from those openly stated. Politicians and other powerful figures are often accused of having a hidden agenda, e.g. intervening in the affairs of a Third World country: the stated concern may be to bring about democracy, but this may disguise an attempt to appropriate the country's natural resources.

**hierarchy of discourse:** where certain forms of knowledge are more highly valued than others. The hierarchy of discourse is a reflection of where power resides in any society. Hence the discourse of law enforcement is favoured above the discourse of criminality, that of the medical profession above that of faith healers, and that of business interests over that of environmentalism. One function of the media is to make the hierarchy of discourse part of its overall ideological work in manufacturing consent to the status quo. *Common sense* is thus part of the equation. (See also *hegemony.*)

**hierarchy of needs:** see *Maslow's hierarchy of needs*

**high-angle shot:** abbreviated as H/A, this is a camera shot taken from a higher level than the subject, and angled down towards them. This shot can have the effect of diminishing the authority of the subject, making them look weak. (See also *low-angle shot.*)

**highbrow:** a derogatory term for *high culture* products and audiences, as in, for example: 'I can't stand all that highbrow arty stuff.'

**high-concept:** films of this type have one simple idea that can be explained in a few words. Characters are straightforward rather than complex, and there is little in the way of *sub-plot*. As an approach to film-making, the high-concept film first appeared in the mid-1970s with Steven Spielberg's *Jaws* (USA, 1975). Typically, these films have a large budget, an emphasis on special effects, and a storyline featuring such topics as alien invasion or dinosaurs e.g. *Independence Day* (Roland Emmerich, USA, 1996) and *Jurassic Park* (Steven Spielberg, USA, 1993).

**high-contrast lighting:** see *hard lighting*

**high culture:** that area of the arts that cannot easily be appreciated without specialist knowledge and education. Often considered *elitist* compared with *popular culture*, high culture includes opera, ballet, the theatre, classical music, literature, painting, sculpture and art-house cinema, as well as broader social behaviour such as etiquette and the enjoyment of haute cuisine.

**high-definition television:** see *HDTV*

**high-key lighting:** very bright film or television lighting that pervades every area of the set, leaving no shadows. Often seen in television *sitcoms* and *game shows.*

**high-school movie:** *genre* of film overlapping with the *teen picture*, in which the action revolves around a school. Examples include *10 Things I Hate About You* (Gil Junger, USA, 1999) and *Mean Girls* (Mark Waters, USA 2004).

**Hindi cinema:** see *Bollywood*

**historical film:** see *costume drama*

**Hitchcockian:** relating to the work of Alfred Hitchcock, London-born film director known as the 'Master of Suspense', who became perhaps the best-known film director of all time. The term Hitchcockian denotes not only the genre of psychological thriller that he single-handedly created, but the techniques of audience manipulation in which he excelled. Hitchcock was considered by the influential *Cahiers du Cinema* critics as one of cinema's greatest *auteurs*. In a career stretching from 1922 to 1976, his films included *The Lodger* (UK, 1927), *The 39 Steps* (UK, 1935), *Rebecca* (USA, 1940), *Rear Window* (USA, 1954), *Vertigo* (USA, 1958), *North by Northwest* (USA, 1959), *Psycho* (USA, 1960) and *The Birds* (USA, 1963). A common theme is that of an innocent man being mistaken for a guilty one. Most of his films include cameo appearances by himself, and many feature blonde women with names beginning with M (Madaleine, Marnie, Marion, Miriam) – staircases and the number 13 also recur frequently. Films described as Hitchcockian are those that use similar techniques to attempt to emulate the master's work.

**Hollywood:** *metonymic* term for the Los Angeles-based American film industry. The director *D W Griffith* was the first to discover Hollywood, a village in southern California. He shot a film there in 1910. Cheap land prices, good weather that allowed shooting all the year round, and the desire to put as much space as possible between themselves and Thomas Edison's patent lawyers caused the whole industry to relocate in Hollywood from New York over the next few years.

**Hollywood studio system:** see *studio system*

**Hollywood Ten, the:** the screenwriters and directors, including Dalton Trumbo, Ring Lardner and Edward Dmytryk, who were given prison sentences for refusing to testify to *HUAC*. They were also blacklisted (i.e. banned by Hollywood from working in the industry), along with up to 500 others, several of whom left the USA to live and work in Europe. Charlie Chaplin, Orson Welles, Joseph Losey, Paul Robeson, Cy Endfield and Marsha Hunt were among them.

**homage:** pronounced '*om-ahj*' in the French style, homage is a tribute made by one artist to another by consciously making some stylistic reference to the latter's work. For example, Todd Haynes's *Far From Heaven* (USA, 2002) is a feature-length homage to the work of 1950s director Douglas Sirk, particularly his 1955 film *All That Heaven Allows.*

**Home Box Office (HBO):** innovative American *cable* television network launched in 1972. Viewers subscribe to receive sport, films and original drama, uninterrupted by commercials. This has allowed HBO to take more risks than the traditional *networks* in portraying sex, violence and strong language, with such productions as *Sex and the City*, *Six Feet Under* and *The Sopranos*. Other original drama productions have been made in partnership with the *BBC*, including *Rome* and *Band of Brothers.*

A B C D E F G H I J K L M N O P Q R S T U V W X Y Z

**home cinema:** a combination and extension of the television set, the projector, the hi-fi system and the DVD player that, with its wide screen and *surround-sound* speaker system, attempts to simulate the experience of cinema viewing in a domestic setting.

**home video:** a revolution in television that for the first time enabled viewers not only to rent films to watch at home, but to record programmes *off-air*. Beginning in the late 1970s, home video broke the home entertainment *monopoly* of broadcasters and eventually developed into an industry larger than the traditional *Hollywood* business of cinema. In giving films a second life beyond their *theatrical release*, home video is the cornerstone of the *back end*, making it more likely that the film will recoup its production costs and perhaps go into profit. (See also *time shifting; VHS*.)

**homogeneity:** a close similarity of origins and culture in any given population. The opposite is *heterogeneity.*

**homosexual:** sexual orientation towards members of one's own sex.

**horizontal integration:** where a media company owns several businesses in the same sector of the industry, e.g. Trinity Mirror Newspapers own both the *Sunday Mirror* and *The People.*

**horror film:** like the *western* and the *gangster film*, a perennially popular film *genre*. Its intention is to create a sensation of fear and/or disgust in the audience. Almost anything can inspire horror, but typical subjects are sadism, insanity, cannibalism, the supernatural and every form of evil. Horror films began to appear almost at the birth of cinema: Georges Méliès made the two-minute *Devil's Castle* in 1896. Later examples include the influential *German expressionist* films *The Cabinet of Dr Caligari* (Robert Weine, Ger, 1919), *The Golem* (Henrick Galeen/Paul Wegener, Ger, 1915) and *Nosferatu* (F W Murnau, Ger, 1922). These were followed by such Universal Pictures productions as *The Phantom of the Opera* (Rupert Julian, USA, 1925) and *Dracula* (Tod Browning, USA, 1931). There has always been an overlap between horror and *science fiction*, *Frankenstein* (James Whale, USA, 1931) being the classic example. The 1950s saw numerous *low-budget* American horror and also the first *Hammer horror* productions from the UK. Wet horror, also known as the *splatter movie*, involves blood and gore, whereas dry horror tends more towards the psychological. Examples, respectively, include *Evil Dead* (Sam Raimi, USA, 1981) and *The Blair Witch Project* (Daniel Myrick/Eduardo Sanchez, USA, 1999). In recent years the *conventions* of the horror genre have been parodied in the series *Scream* (Wes Craven, USA, 1996–2000) and *Scary Movie* (Keenen Ivory Wayans/David Zucker, USA, 2000–2006).

**hospital drama:** enduring television *genre* in a hospital setting. Among the *codes and conventions* of the hospital drama are the passing of knowledge and wisdom from senior to junior doctors, the challenges to idealism posed by ethical dilemmas, and romances between doctors and nurses. Many hospital dramas feature an *ensemble cast* (no single protagonist). Recently there has been a growing tendency to depict operations, wounds and other medical situations in highly realistic (and often disgusting) detail. In its early days (e.g. *Dr Kildare, Dr Finlay's Casebook*) the doctor was a competent and reassuring figure. More recently the hospital has become a battleground dominated by financial cutbacks and heartless senior administrators (*ER, St Elsewhere*).

**hot metal:** technology used in the print industry prior to the emergence of desktop publishing in the late 1980s. For 350 years since the invention of printing, type had been set by hand, one letter at a time, by a compositor or typesetter. By the late nineteenth century, compositors working at either a Monotype or Linotype machine were able to produce text much faster, but this still involved retyping copy submitted by journalists and authors. Hot metal was so called because once each letter or line of type had been produced, it automatically became part of a matrix, which was then surrounded by a mould. Molten metal was pumped into the mould to create a cast impression of the type, which would then be used for printing.

**hot news:** what gets reported as opposed to what does not. The existence of *news values* dictates that certain *stories* are always hot news, i.e. anything involving *celebrities* and other *elite* persons, or anything with obvious visual potential. On the other hand, some important stories are not pursued, particularly when they are complicated to explain or concern long-running issues that remain unresolved.

**house ad:** one which is produced 'in-house' (e.g. those produced internally by the BBC).

**house nut:** see *nut*

**house style:** style *conventions* that all journalists and other writers need to learn when producing *copy* for any particular publication. For example, whether writing for *The Sun* or *The Guardian*, journalists need to take into account the educational level of their readers by using either simple or complex language. Similarly, a journalist for *Kerrang!*, a weekly magazine devoted to heavy metal music, must write in a different house style (i.e. youthful, informal, enthusiastic, fashion-conscious, specialist) from that used by a writer for *The Tablet*, a Catholic weekly newspaper (i.e. religious, formal, serious, general interest).

**HUAC (House Un-American Activities Committee):** notorious US House of Representatives committee that launched an anti-communist witch-hunt against certain *Hollywood* writers and *directors* in 1947. (See also *blacklisting*; *Hollywood Ten*.)

**human interest story:** *news* story that focuses on individuals in order to highlight a particular case that may have wider social implications. A human interest *angle* is more likely to help readers understand an issue than one that merely outlines the situation (e.g. a factory closure). In such a case, a human interest story might focus on the effects of the closure (e.g. unemployment, family breakdown) on one particular family.

**Hutton report:** the official investigation into the death of scientist Dr David Kelly that led to the resignations of both the *BBC*'s chairman Gavyn Davies and its director-general Greg Dyke in 2004. The BBC claimed that the government, in an official report later dubbed 'the dodgy dossier', had exaggerated Iraq's military capabilities in order to justify invading the country the previous year. Dr Kelly, a weapons expert, allegedly committed suicide after being exposed as the BBC's source for the story. Many, particularly those working in the media, found the case worrying: as a sign that journalists were coming under political pressure to conform to a higher standard of proof than the government itself; and as a reminder that the BBC's independence from government is always compromised by the fact that it is the government who determine the level of the *licence fee.*

**hype:** an abbreviation of hyperbole, or exaggeration. Most commonly used in connection with intensive publicity campaigns, in which the virtues of, for example, a new recording artist or film are exaggerated by both publicists and journalists.

**hyperreality:** a *postmodern* condition in which the distinction between reality and illusion have disappeared. For example, in *Big Brother*, there is no longer any distinction between reality and entertainment, due to the artificiality and pointlessness of the housemates' situation. Other examples are Disneyworld and Las Vegas, where everything that can be seen is a copy of something else, an impossibly perfect simulation of some forgotten original. Key theorisers of hyperreality include Jean Baudrillard and Umberto Eco.

**hypodermic model/theory:** the idea that media products have an immediate, negative effect on the behaviour of specators, so called because the effect on the *audience* is thought to resemble that of a drug. (See also *effects model.*)

**Do you need revision help and advice?**

Go to pages 251–292 for a range of revision appendices that include exam advice and tips.

**IBA:** see *Independent Broadcasting Authority*

**IBC:** abbreviation of inside back cover, usually of a magazine.

**icon:** (i) a person – living or dead – seen to embody certain ideal qualities. For example, Nelson Mandela is widely regarded as an icon of nobility, courage, wisdom and principle. At different times certain celebrities have become fashion icons, e.g. Madonna, David Beckham. (ii) in Charles Peirce's work on *semiology*, a type of signifier that physically resembles what it refers to. Examples of an iconic *sign* include any representation such as a photograph or drawing (e.g. the road sign with the image of a man with a shovel, indicating roadworks). In its original meaning, in the Greek Orthodox religion, an icon is a wooden tablet bearing the image of a saint.

**iconography:** a set of visual *representations* in a media text that, taken together, indicate its *genre*. For instance, you may switch on a television and see two well-dressed adults holding a conversation. If they are in a brightly-lit set, one sitting behind a desk and the other on a sofa, within a few seconds you will be certain that you are watching a *chat show* – even if the sound is switched off. This is because the iconography of the chat show is instantly recognisable.

**ident:** an identifier, or moving image logo, for a television channel. Examples include BBC1's red-clad dancers and tai chi practitioners, or Channel 4's variety of landscapes into which the figure 4 is digitally interweaved.

**identification:** a process whereby we *empathise* with the experiences and/or personality of a certain character in fiction or fact, to the extent that we may temporarily imagine being that character. An important element of *spectatorship* in the cinema, and related to the concepts of *scopophilia* and *suture.*

**identity:** the ways in which people define themselves as belonging to certain social groups, whether racial, national, religious, or connected with disability or sexual orientation.

**identity politics:** the beliefs and activities of minority *identity* groups (and their supporters) who consider themselves to be oppressed, ignored or discriminated against, and who form organisations in order to campaign for improved rights.

**ideolect:** each individual's unique way of speaking. For example, while we may all consider ourselves to be English speakers, we each habitually use certain words, phrases and grammatical constructions selected from all those available.

**ideological state apparatus (ISA):** a phrase coined by Louis Althusser, ISA refers to the social institutions that continually, but unconsciously, reinforce the values and practices of an *ideology* through *propaganda*: the family, schools and universities, and the media. (See also *repressive state apparatus.*)

**ideology:** any system of ideas and values concerning the nature of the world, most of which end with -ism (e.g. conservatism, environmentalism, Islamism, Nazism). The ability to 'read' the ideological message *encoded* in every media text is important in studying the media, since it enables us to uncover meanings that may not be immediately apparent. Every society has a dominant ideology that is shared unthinkingly by the majority of its members, who are encouraged to regard the values of the ideology as 'natural'. Until recent years, political parties embodied the struggle between conflicting ideologies (e.g. socialism versus *capitalism*), but today all the major parties in the developed world are capitalist. Some believe that the current lack of ideological choice explains the steady decline in voting across the developed world. (See also *hegemony*.)

**idiot board:** a large white card used in television to cue presenters. Held just off-camera by a crew member, the idiot board may contain script prompts or tell the presenter how much time remains before a commercial break.

**IFC:** abbreviation of inside front cover, usually of a magazine.

**i-link:** see *Firewire*

**ILM:** see *Industrial Light & Magic*

**image:** (i) normally a visual representation, although there is also such a thing as *sound image*. An image may be a photograph, film or video sequence, drawn or painted illustration, cartoon or logo. In studying the media, we are concerned with the range of possible meanings *encoded* within images, since they are not free-standing and absolute in their meaning but *signs* that carry both denotations and *connotations*, and are part of the wider *code* systems that are central to our culture. We uncover these meanings through image analysis, in which we break images down into their component parts to examine what they convey by their colour, texture, size, arrangement, lighting and so on. In the media, images are considered more powerful in their effect on the *audience* than words: for example, news *footage* of a train disaster will communicate the horror far more effectively than a purely verbal description; in cinema, directors normally prefer to tell the story in images rather than through dialogue. An image bank is a large collection of images available to media professionals for a fee. (ii) an idealised notion of what a person or organisation is like. The maintenance of image in this sense requires consistency: professionals in the field are known as *public relations* consultants, whose job is to persuade the public that the image they have created is an accurate reflection of the reality.

**image system:** in the construction of film, the way the *director* (with *cinematographer* and production designer) will use recurring visual motifs in the *cinematography* and *mise en scène* which are connected to *themes*, *genre* and even structural aspects. For example, in the mise en scène of the *film noir* genre, we often see Venetian blinds, frames and mirrors, and the lines, reflections and shadows these make (which therefore constitute an image system) relate to thematic ideas such as imprisonment, entrapment and claustrophobia.

**IMAX:** a film format that projects a much larger image than those found in any conventional cinema. First appearing in the early 1970s, IMAX film *stock* is 70 x 48.5mm, and the screen usually 22 x 16 m. From the *spectator*'s point of view, the size of the screen results in the experience of total *immersion* in the film, since it fills his entire field of vision. Although most IMAX cinemas show features specially shot using the format, some IMAX versions of popular feature films have been released, including *Star Wars Episode II: Attack of the Clones*

(George Lucas, USA, 2002), *The Matrix Reloaded* and *The Matrix Revolutions* (Wachowski Brothers, USA, both 2003).

**immediacy:** one of Galtung and Ruge's *news values*, suggesting that a story is more likely to appear if the events in question have occurred very recently.

**immersion:** what happens when the *audience* temporarily forget their real lives in order to experience maximum emotional impact and *identification* with the events and characters of a media experience. With all fictional *narratives*, since the *spectator* knows that the experience is not real, he must *willingly suspend his disbelief*. Immersion can only work in the kind of sensory environment where there are no distractions (e.g. in an *IMAX* cinema). (See also *suture.*)

**impartiality:** the quality of even-handedness, particularly in news and current affairs. Impartiality is necessary to avoid *propaganda*, *misrepresentation* and unfairly one-sided reporting. In practice, this means that statements made by politicians are usually 'balanced' by opposing statements from politicians of other parties, or at least tested by probing questions from an interviewer. UK broadcasters are required to be impartial under the terms of successive broadcasting and communications Acts. The same does not apply to newspapers.

**imperfect cinema:** a style of film-making that prioritises the social and political message of the film above glossy production values and other commercial, crowd-pleasing strategies. First proposed by Cuban director Julio Garcia Espinosa in the late 1960s, imperfect cinema is a concept allied to *third cinema.*

**implicit meaning:** one which is unstated (i.e. not *explicit*) in a media text, but nonetheless present. Implicit meaning can be created through the style of verbal language, the selection of images, or the *editing*. For example, in *The Godfather* (Francis Ford Coppola, USA, 1972), Michael's Corleone's hypocrisy is shown implicitly through the editing: the film *cross-cuts* between the scene of his nephew's christening, at which Michael solemnly agrees to renounce Satan, and a succession of brutal killings that he has ordered.

**improvisation:** spontaneous *creativity*. Improvisation in acting is often used as a way of capturing authenticity. Film and theatre director Mike Leigh creates his productions by encouraging the actors to improvise their characters as well as the dialogue. However, Leigh does not use improvisation on camera: just before shooting begins he writes a script based on the improvised work already done. In jazz, although each tune's performance begins and ends with a statement of the melody, the solos are always improvised around the tune's chord sequence.

**in-camera:** editing in-camera means filming in sequence, with the shots beginning and ending as they will appear in the final film. In-camera effects are simply those achieved by using whatever technology is supplied with the camera. The disadvantage of using an in-camera effect is that because it is part of the original shot, it cannot subsequently be removed from the *footage*.

**incentives:** an encouragement to film investors, whereby there may be tax-breaks in return for their investment in film, this has been a topic of contention between the British government and the UK film industry. Other national cinemas, such as the French, have received assistance for the financing of indigenous film production. Consequently, the French film industry has historically been seen as more healthy and capable of rivaling US exports than that of the UK.

**inciting incident:** one which initially provokes the action of a *narrative*. The inciting incident takes place near the beginning and upsets the balance of the *protagonist*'s life. An example is *Glengarry Glen Ross* (James Foley, USA, 1992), in which the working lives of four real-estate salesmen are turned upside down by Blake from head office, who arrives with the message that those who come third and fourth in next month's sales drive will be fired. The importance of the inciting incident is discussed by scriptwriting guru Robert McKee in his book *Story: substance, structure, style and the principles of screenwriting* (1999).

**indent:** to shift the left-hand alignment of a section of printed text rightwards from the main body of the text.

**independent:** media *production*, *distribution* or *exhibition* that is not owned or controlled by a large organisation. The idea of independent (or 'indie') media is an attractive one, suggesting freedom from interference by big business or the state, and a certain fearless, original, buccaneering style. *Private Eye* magazine is a good example of independence in the print medium. However, true independence is hard to achieve in most media apart from the internet: for example, due to their sheer cost, films are invariably subject to the influence of financiers, distributors, censors or exhibitors, whose price for becoming involved in a project is to retain a degree of control and often to demand changes. Therefore even 'independent production companies' are forced to compromise before their films reach the public. Sometimes the term 'independent' is merely used to distinguish any organisation from some other more dominant force in its particular industry (e.g. any film that is not a product of *Hollywood*). In the UK, any broadcast organisation that is not part of the *BBC* is described as independent.

**Independent Broadcasting Authority (IBA):** regulator of UK commercial television from 1972 to 1990, when it was replaced by the *Indepenent Television Commission (ITC)*.

**Independent Televison (ITV):** major *terrestrial broadcaster* that first went on air in 1955, becoming only the second UK television channel after the *BBC*. Financed by *advertising*, but subject to *Public Service Broadcasting* rules, ITV was set up to create competition for the BBC, which had until then enjoyed a *monopoly* in both television and radio. Initially available only in London, the Midlands and the North, by 1962 ITV was a network of 15 regional companies across the UK. It was Britain's most popular channel, regularly gaining a larger *audience* share than its rival BBC (later BBC1). The gradual erosion of this audience began in 1990 with the launch of BSkyB. The regional nature of ITV then began to erode in a wave of takeovers and mergers, until by 2004 it had become a single company. With the explosion of digital channels in the early twenty-first century, the original ITV became ITV1, and further channels were added. By this time, however, numerous competitors were eating into ITV1's audience, which by 2006 was falling sharply.

**Independent Television Commission (ITC):** regulatory body set up in 1991 to replace the *Independent Broadcasting Authority (IBA)* in overseeing *ITV* and Channel 4. The ITC administered the auction of ITV broadcast licences and dealt with complaints. It was itself replaced in 2003 by *Ofcom*.

**Independent Television News (ITN):** a television and radio news organisation. Set up at the same time as ITV to provide its news coverage, ITN also produces *Channel 4 News*, and supplies commercial radio with news bulletins through its radio service Independent Radio News (IRN). After being criticised for going *downmarket* during the 1990s, ITN was caught up in further controversy in 1999: its flagship ITV programme *News at Ten* was moved to a later time slot to allow films to be broadcast without interruption from the news. The *BBC* then moved its main evening news from 9 pm to 10 pm. The effect of both moves was to reduce ITN's audience.

**index:** in Charles Peirce's work on *semiology*, a type of *signifier* that acts as a form of evidence for the signified. While not physically resembling the signified, the indexical sign carries connotations of it; for example, the Christian cross is an indexical sign for the religion because of its part in the Christian story. Other examples are: clocks, which are indexical signs for the time of day; smoke, which indicates fire; a footprint, which indicates the recent presence of a person.

**Index on Censorship:** a magazine that monitors and promotes free speech and expression in the media and public life around the world. Founded in 1972, it also presents annual awards to journalists and film makers who have taken a stand against *censorship*.

**indigenous film industry/production:** that which is based in a particular country or region, as opposed to production originating elsewhere, such as *Hollywood.*

**Industrial Light & Magic (ILM):** company founded by *Star Wars* director George Lucas in 1975 to create special effects for the cinema. ILM pioneered the use of computers in this field, particularly for the generation or partial generation of screen characters (e.g. *Terminator 2*, James Cameron, USA, 1991), but also in the development of such techniques as *morphing.*

**industry:** the creative and business organisations and individuals who work in particular areas of the media, e.g. newspapers or radio. Because it creates and distributes *media products*, industry forms one corner of the *media triangle*, along with *text* and *audience*, and is therefore a key concept for both film and media studies. When studying a media industry, one basic idea to bear in mind is the relationship of *producer* to *audience*. In general it can be said that producers give *pleasure* to audiences in exchange for money. Industry must therefore target its products at specific audiences in order to be successful. This process determines the character of the products, which we can study as 'texts'. With the partial exception of *public service* organisations such as the *BBC*, the media industry is a business that exists to make profits. In common with all businesses, media organisations need capital to invest in equipment and infrastructure, and revenue to pay costs of production and overheads, including staff salaries. What makes the media industry different from, for example, food manufacturing, is that although its products are to a large extent predictable and made to a formula, they all contain cultural ideas and show significant individual variations. The *ownership and control* of media is therefore a key issue, since the industry is constantly creating representations of our society, whose meanings and implications are always being contested in ways that other products (like baked beans or washing machines) are not.

**infomercial:** a television commercial in the guise of a programme. Developed in the USA, infomercials are often around 30 minutes long and mimic such formats as talk shows and panel games. They can provide television channels with cheap programming, for example 'the making of' certain new film releases: these, while resembling real behind-the-scenes documentaries, are made by the production companies themselves in order to promote their films.

**information superhighway:** the internet.

**infotainment:** media content that is motivated by the need to entertain as much as by the need to explain or provide information. This is an important element of the *tabloid* press, which critics argue is dominated by gossipy stories about entertainment and *celebrity* culture, at the expense of 'real' stories, i.e. those in the public interest.

**inheritance factor:** in television *scheduling*, where the *audience* for a particular programme that has just finished waits to see whether the next one on the same channel is also worth watching. The next one therefore benefits to some extent from the inheritance factor. An example is the BBC's *Question Time*, which follows the *Ten O'Clock News.*

**in-house:** 'within an organisation', as opposed to 'from outside'. In the media, many *freelance* workers and independent organisations provide product or contribute services of various kinds. However, in certain cases a television channel may decide to produce a programme in-house rather than commission it from outside. Similarly, an organisation may employ an in-house lawyer, or publish an in-house magazine.

**in medias res:** Latin term meaning 'into the middle of things' – used for a *narrative* that begins with the action of the story already under way, and with little or no *exposition*. Films have to be scripted tightly due to the limited time available for telling the story; jumping straight in medias res is therefore helpful, since explanations can be woven into the dialogue. An example is *The Terminator* (James Cameron, USA, 1984), which begins as the war between men and machines is already taking place, and further exposition is provided later.

**inoculation effect/theory:** a way of 'protecting' people from the influence of *alternative ideologies.* The theory suggests that those who have difficulty in thinking for themselves are easy prey for cults and ideologies that actively recruit members through argument and persuasion. For example, during the Korean War, captured American soldiers were allegedly 'brainwashed' – a process that often consisted of nothing more sinister than verbal attacks on their beliefs. It turned out that although most of the soldiers were in favour of 'democracy', they did not know why. Inoculation training was later introduced to prepare them for such attacks by getting them to defend what they believed through argument. We also see 'inoculation' taking place through the media, when politicians 'prepare' the public for controversial measures such as warfare, not only by putting forward persuasive arguments in favour of it, but also by anticipating what the opposition's arguments will be, and pre-emptively 'inoculating' the *audience* against them.

**insert:** an *advertising* leaflet distributed with newspapers or magazines. Inserts help advertisers reach their target market more effectively than random door-to-door delivery, since products and services can be matched to specific readerships.

**insert editing:** a now almost redundant form of analogue video editing in which images or sounds are added to a video tape on which a control track has already been recorded. This allows for smooth playback.

**insert shot:** in *continuity* shooting and editing, a *shot* that gives the audience a close-up of something that was only a detail of the previous shot. For example, if the first shot shows a footballer walking to the penalty spot and placing the ball on it, the insert shot that follows might be a close-up of the ball being kicked. Also known as a 'cut-in'.

**Institute of Practitioners in Advertising (IPA):** A professional body representing the interests of advertising, media and marketing communications companies. Like the *Press*

*Complaints Commission*, the IPA is a voluntary organisation that encourages its unregulated industry members to maintain a professional code of conduct.

**institution:** any organisation operating in the media. This may refer to official bodies such as the *British Board of Film Classification* or *Ofcom*, or to commercial organisations like Associated Newspapers, or public bodies like the *BBC*. The importance of media institutions is that they supply the context within which media products are produced. For example, News International is a powerful, *multinational* business organisation founded and controlled by the enormously wealthy *media magnate* Rupert Murdoch. Given this institutional context, it is logical that it produces right-wing newspapers like *The Times* and *The Sun*. Similarly, *The Guardian* and *The Observer* are owned by the British-based Scott Trust, whose left-wing, liberal tradition is reflected in these newspapers.

**institutional practices:** the ways in which any given institution goes about its business. In the media these might include *news-gathering* and production methods, as well as the way decisions are made within the organisation, how money is allocated, and how employees are treated.

**Integrated Services Digital Network:** see *ISDN*

**interactive documentary:** one in which the film maker is seen to be personally involved in dealings with participants such as eyewitnesses. Any Nick Broomfield film is a good example of this: Broomfield appears frequently on camera with his trademark *boom* microphone as he pursues his often reluctant interviewees and engages in arguments with them.

**interactive media:** that which actively promotes and involves the participation of the *audience*. In the modern media world, interactivity has superseded earlier models of the producer/audience relationship. Previously, the audience were seen as passive receivers of media output. The digital television environment, the *internet* and mobile phones have been major contributors to greater interaction: the existence of digital channels has enabled the audience to make more decisions about what to watch (i.e. using 'the red button') while the internet is a medium that can only work when its audience is actively visiting sites. Other forms of interactivity include competitions and voting phone-lines in television and the print media, and radio phone-ins.

**intercutting:** see *cross-cutting*

**interface:** the point of communication between any media technology and its user. (See also *user interface*.)

**interior:** in film and television scripts, a scene that takes place inside a building, car, etc. In scripts, interior is always abbreviated as INT. (See also *exterior*.)

**interior monologue:** in film or television drama, an interior or internal monologue is a *voice-over* in the form of a stream-of-consciousness (what a character is thinking). *Film noir* frequently uses this device.

**international co-production:** a film or television production financed by organisations in more than one country. Outside America, international co-productions are the norm in the modern film industry due to the high costs involved. For example, Mike Leigh's film *Vera Drake* (2004) was a co-production between the UK, France and New Zealand.

**internet, the:** the global communications network that today links most of the world's computers via telephone lines and wireless connections. In its modern form, the internet was invented by Tim Berners-Lee and first became available for general use in 1991. Alongside the existing media – newspapers, magazines, radio, film and television – the internet quickly evolved into a medium in its own right, with its own workforce of practitioners, its own genres and audiences. The internet also has the unique ability to incorporate the other media, the phenomenon of *convergence*.

**interpellation:** the way in which we are addressed or 'hailed' by the media. First proposed by Louis Althusser, interpellation is a complex idea that suggests that the media encourage us as *audience* members to identity ourselves with the sort of imaginary people they want us to be. For example, if we are watching a TV advertisement there may well be a *voice-over* that addresses the audience directly by using 'you' (e.g. 'You should try this great new shampoo.') What is happening in this process is that by interpellating us in this way, the media are incorporating us into their *ideology*, constructing us as the consumers of whatever they are trying to sell us. We can either accept or resist interpellation.

**interpersonal communication:** communication between two or more people (but not many more), which may be verbal or non-verbal. It need not be face-to-face, although this is the most common form: interpersonal communication can also take place electronically, e.g. by telephone or email. It operates in different ways from mass communication or intrapersonal communication.

**intertextuality:** where a *media text* contains references to another media text or texts, with the expectation that the *audience* will be able to recognise and appreciate its significance. The modern media-saturated environment is a fertile breeding ground for intertextuality, since we all absorb so many media messages every day, and have a broadly shared set of reference points. An example is *The Simpsons*, many of whose jokes depend on the audience's knowledge of other media, particularly films and television programmes.

**intertitle:** in *silent film*, screen text that, in the absence of sound, appears between shots to explain what is going on or to indicate dialogue.

**intervalometer:** a time-lapse *camera*, i.e. one designed to photograph frames at widely-spaced intervals, thus producing a massively speeded-up effect. Often used to demonstrate the growth pattern of plants, compressing into a few seconds what actually took place over several days or weeks.

**interview:** a structured conversation whose direction is usually controlled by the interviewer with the object of gaining information about the interviewee(s). An interview may be conducted electronically or in person. Media interviews are intended to establish or clarify the interviewee's opinions or knowledge of a subject, or the details of an activity in which they have been involved. An interview may not necessarily have a journalistic or current affairs purpose. For example, *celebrity* interviews are often arranged for the sole purpose of generating publicity for some product or other commercial enterprise, e.g. a new film or line of perfume.

**intro:** the first paragraph of any *news* story, which aims to explain what it is about in the fewest possible words. For example, 'A man has been arrested in connection with missing schoolgirl Jane Smith.' More details will then follow.

**introductory cue:** in radio or television, a short tune or other sound that signals some significant item in a programme (e.g. the week's star prize).

**invasion of privacy:** where a person's right to *privacy* has not been respected by the press or other media. *Celebrities* are the most likely to complain about invasion of privacy, which may take the form of intrusive *doorstepping*, long-lens *paparazzi* photography, or even the illegal interception of e-mail or mobile phone messages. The existence of numerous publications that depend on celebrity stories puts pressure on individual journalists and photographers to come up with 'unofficial' photographs and gossip. This in turn has increased the number of complaints about invasion of privacy. However, the *Press Complaints Commission* code of practice states that 'everyone is entitled to respect for his or her private and family life, home, health and correspondence… The use of long lens photography to take pictures of people in private places without their consent is unacceptable.'

**inverted pyramid:** the way in which a *news* story is written, with the main facts presented first, and with increasingly greater detail as it continues. The purpose is both to supply the gist of a story quickly to readers who have limited time, and to make it easier for the story to be cut by a sub-editor where there is pressure on space.

**investigative journalism:** that in which journalists devote weeks or months to complex stories that often involve allegations of wrong-doing. Investigative journalism methods may include going 'undercover' to discover the truth, using hidden cameras, trawling through large amounts of official records and other paperwork, and conducting interviews – sometimes with 'whistleblowers' who are reluctant to be identified. Examples of investigative journalism include the Watergate scandal of the early 1970s, later dramatised in the 1976 film *All The President's Men* (Alan J Pakula, USA).

**invisible editing/style:** see *classical style of narrative*, *continuity*

**IPA:** see *Institute of Practitioners of Advertising*

**iris:** the adjustable aperture of a *camera*, analogous to the iris in a human eye, which controls the amount of light entering the *lens*, and hence the exposure setting. For example, the lower the light in any location, the more the iris needs to be opened, although this also has the effect of decreasing the *focus* and *depth of field.* The iris setting is expressed as an *f-stop* number. An **iris shot** is one associated with the silent era of cinema, when scenes sometimes began or ended with an iris-in (gradual opening of the iris) or iris-out respectively. Occasionally a partial iris-out was used within a scene in order to highlight a particular character or action.

**irony:** any communication whose denotation differs markedly from its *connotation*, i.e. it has a double meaning – one on the surface and another apparent to those in the know. Irony is used in a wide variety of situations, often as a source of dark or dry humour. In narrative, dramatic irony exists when the audience know more about a character's fate than the character does.

**ISA:** see *ideological state apparatus*

**ISBA:** the Incorporated Society of British Advertisers, a representative body for advertisers in the UK.

**ISDN:** acronym of Integrated Services Digital Network, a digital telephone network. Because digital information is made up of purely numeric data, cables are able to send far more messages, of higher quality, far faster than previous analogue systems. An ISDN connection can send and receive voice messages from telephones and data of various kinds via modems, and allow video-conferencing to take place.

**issue:** a specific weekly, fortnightly, or monthly edition of a publication, usually a magazine (e.g. 'the October issue').

**issue-led drama:** that which serves to illustrate a particular social or political concern (homelessness, unemployment, racism, the environment, cloning, IVF and so on). One example is the film *Erin Brockovich* (Steven Soderbergh, USA, 2000), based on a true story, in which a working-class single mother leads a battle against industrial polluters.

**ISP:** abbreviation of internet service provider – any organisation that provides access to the internet, usually for a monthly fee.

**Italian neo-realism:** an influential film-making movement that developed in Rome at the end of the Second World War. Italian neo-realism was a conscious attempt to divert the course of Italian cinema away from the bourgeois 'white telephone' movies of the fascist-dominated 1930s and 1940s, towards films that focused on the plight of poor, working-class people. Neorealist directors like Roberto Rosselini (*Rome Open City*, 1945; *Paisà*, 1946), Vittorio de Sica (*Bicycle Thieves*, 1948; *Umberto D*, 1952) and Luchino Visconti (*La Terra Trema*, 1948) shot their films in real locations using non-professional actors. Ermmano Olmi's 1979 film *The Tree of Wooden Clogs*, about a year in the life of three peasant families around 1900, is a notable more recent example. Italian neo-realism was a major influence on the *French new wave*, and continues to influence the style of *national cinemas* throughout the world.

**ITC:** see *Independent Television Commission*

**ITV:** see *Independent Television*

### What other subjects are you studying?

A–Zs cover a range of different subjects. See the inside back cover for a list of all the titles in the series and how to order.

**jeopardy:** in narrative *drama*, particularly in the *action-adventure genre*, the physical danger that characters face, from which they must either escape or have to be rescued. For example, in *The River Wild* (Curtis Hanson, USA, 1994) a family on a river rafting trip face the twin dangers of a group of villains and a deadly stretch of river known as 'The Gauntlet'. This film subverts the jeopardy tradition, in which women have to be rescued by men, by having a woman (played by Meryl Streep) as the dominant character in the family.

**jib:** an inexpensive alternative to a camera crane. A jib is a *boom* device with the *camera* placed at one end and a counterweight and camera controls at the other. It can be mounted on a *tripod* or *dolly* to create a variety of motion and high-angle effects.

**JICREG:** acronym of the Joint Industry Committee of Regional Newspapers, an organisation that supplies readership data for most UK regional and local newspapers. This information is important for advertisers and *advertising agencies* because it allows them to calculate the cost-effectiveness of placing *advertising* in these publications.

**journalism:** the activity of researching and gathering factual material with some contemporary relevance, and producing a report or review of it for the benefit of a readership or *audience*, in print or other media. Sometimes referred to as 'the first draft of history' (Philip Graham, publisher of the influential US newspaper, *The Washington Post*, from 1946–1963) journalism takes many forms: for example, editors and sub-editors, photographers ('photojournalists') and production staff are all journalists even if they do not necessarily do any reporting. Most journalists work not in the national press but on one of the hundreds of local newspapers, trade journals and specialist magazines. The foundation of journalism is *news*, the reporting of which requires ability not just in writing but in self-motivation, along with the skills of research and analysis, and an understanding of the importance of certain ethical procedures: the verification (and sometimes the protection) of sources; *objectivity*, balance and fairness; and knowing and following *ethical guidelines* drawn up by such organisations as the *Press Complaints Commission*. A successful journalist needs to gain a degree of trust from the audience, even if not working in news. Feature writers, for example, need to develop a reputation for 'readability' or humour. Reviewers must take into account not just their personal opinions but those likely to be adopted by the audience. (See also *new journalism* and *gonzo journalism*.)

**JPEG:** the commonest format of digital image. JPEGs are lower resolution versions of original photographs, compressed for ease or storage and internet transmission. Acronym of Joint Photographic Experts Group.

**jump cut:** in moving-image media, a transition from one shot to another, in the course of which the image appears to jump. This effect – usually accidental and unwanted – is created by editing together shots that are too similar to each other. Jump cuts can be avoided by adhering to the rules of *continuity editing*. However, many *directors* have deliberately exploited the jarring potential of jump cuts, most famously Jean-Luc Godard in *Breathless* (Fr, 1959).

**junket:** see *press junket*

**justification:** written text aligned with a left- or right-hand margin, or both. Where text is 'justified left', as is usual, the right-hand edge is often left 'ragged'.

**juxtaposition:** where one thing is placed next to another. This is an important concept in image analysis, where the juxtaposition of objects can be significant, particularly if we would not normally expect to see them together. Juxtaposition affects our interpretation of an image. For example, a picture of an old man holding a paint spray can would become significant – and striking – if he was also standing next to a wall full of graffiti. Juxtaposition is also an effect of film and video editing, where one shot follows another in time. (See also *Kuleshov effect.*)

**Do you know we also have A–Zs for:**

- ICT & Computing
- Psychology
- Sociology
- Travel & Leisure?

Ask for them in your local bookshop or see the inside back cover for ordering details.

**kerning:** in typography, the expansion or contraction of the space between letters on a page to improve the appearance of the text. Kerning is used with proportional fonts such as Times New Roman and Arial, but is not necessary with monospaced fonts (e.g. Courier).

**key concepts:** in *film* and *media studies*, the key concepts are the main ideas that are used to analyse and discuss the study of the media and which are defined in this book (e.g. *representation*, *narrative*, *genre*, *mise en scène*, *ideology.*) However, both film and media studies (in which the content overlaps) have borrowed extensively from other, longer-established disciplines such as psychology and sociology, literary theory and the fine arts.

**key drawings:** in animated cartoons, the drawings done by the chief animator in a team, usually one for every five frames of a sequence. Those in between are drawn by assistants.

**key grip:** see *grip*

**key light:** the main light used by a photographer or cinematographer to illuminate the subject. A key light is a hard source, or undiffused, and placed at an angle to the subject.

**kill:** a *news* or *feature* story is said to be 'killed' when the editor decides not to run it. A kill fee is usually paid to the author of the piece if it was originally commissioned (i.e. specifically ordered by the publication). (See also *spike*.)

**Kinetograph:** an early version of the movie camera developed by Thomas *Edison*. The Kinetograph was used to capture brief moving images for the *Kinetoscope*.

**Kinetoscope:** an early peep-hole motion picture viewer invented around 1890 by Thomas *Edison* and William Dickson, and a forerunner of the modern film projector. It had a window at the top through which the viewer could watch a continuous loop of film; however it was this 'single-user' aspect that limited its commercial viability.

**kino eye:** a term coined by Russian film maker Dziga Vertov to suggest all the new ways in which a movie camera could be used, transcending the human eye. The kino eye would, he believed, give humanity a fresh perception of the world, much as communism had in the recently established USSR, in the aftermath of the 1917 Russian Revolution. 'I am kino-eye,' Vertov wrote. 'I am mechanical eye. I, a machine, show you the world as only I can see it.' He experimented with these ideas in his ground-breaking *avant-garde* film *Man with a Movie Camera* (USSR, 1929).

**kiss-and-tell story:** prurient *newspaper* story, usually told in exchange for money, by those who have had sexual relationships with celebrities.

**Kuleshov effect:** the power of *editing*, as demonstrated in a famous experiment by Russian film director Lev Kuleshov. He alternated a repeated shot of an actor's expressionless face with shots of a bowl of soup, a baby, a dead woman, and so on. The audience was convinced that the actor looked accordingly hungry, sentimental, or grief-stricken. In this way Kuleshov proved that, in the absence of an *establishing shot*, audiences would draw their own conclusions about the meaning of a sequence because they were more influenced by the *juxtaposition* (i.e. editing together) of images than by their individual effect.

**kung-fu film:** a *genre* of *martial arts films* popularised by the Hong Kong cinema industry. Kung fu became popular in the west with films like *Enter the Dragon* (Robert Clouse, Hong Kong/USA, 1973) starring Bruce Lee. Modern exponents of the genre include Jackie Chan and Jet Li.

### Do you need revision help and advice?

Go to pages 251–292 for a range of revision appendices that include exam advice and tips.

**label/record label:** the business organisation, large or small, responsible for the production and marketing of recorded music. A record label may be independent, but is more likely to be owned by a *conglomerate* such as EMI, Universal, Sony-BMG, and Time Warner, an *oligopoly* who between them control around three-quarters of the global music market.

**lad mag:** UK magazine *genre* targeted at young men. The first of its type, launched in 1994, was *Loaded*, soon followed by *FHM* and *Maxim* and, in 2004, by *Nuts* and *Zoo*. The arrival of the lad-mag genre marked a radical shift away from the older and more upmarket readership of such long-established titles as *GQ*, *Esquire* and *Arena*. Lad culture, as defined by these magazines, is primarily concerned with provocative photographs of attractive starlets, and articles on fashion and gadgets.

**language:** in media and film studies, this term often refers to the *style* of language used when addressing a particular *audience*, largely depending on its age and educational level; for example, the language used in *The Sun* is more simple and colloquial than that used in *The Daily Telegraph*. *Film language* refers not to words but to images, sounds and *editing*: certain shots and editing *conventions* are so familiar to audiences that they function exactly like a verbal language; for example, a *dissolve* is normally interpreted by the audience as indicating a brief *ellipsis* in the narrative. In *semiology*, anything can be a language because anything can send a message (e.g. clothing).

**languages and categories:** see *genre; language*

**langue:** in *semiology*, a total language system, in the sense of a pool of all the many thousands of possible words and sentences that we may call upon in order to communicate. Ferdinand de Saussure and his followers made a distinction between langue and *parole* – individual expression.

**lap dissolve:** (abbreviation of overlap dissolve) see *dissolve*

**laughter track:** in television, *audience* laughter added to the soundtrack of a *sitcom* or other genre. (Laughter tracks are not used in film comedy.) Television producers have frequently used a laughter track in order to cue the audience at home when a joke or funny situation has supposedly occurred. The laughter may be real (as in the case of most sitcoms, which are normally recorded in front of a live audience) or 'canned' (i.e. fake), as in the case of many animated cartoons. In recent years there has been a trend for TV comedies such as *The Office*, *The Royle Family* and *Curb Your Enthusiasm* to dispense with a laughter track altogether.

**layout:** the way words, images and graphic elements are arranged on any printed or web page. These elements may be split between *typography*, consisting of headlines, sub-headings, straplines, cross-heads, captions, quote boxes and body text; and *graphics*, consisting of photographs, drawings, lines and borders. Effective layout takes account of the way we scan the page: in the western world, our eyes move from top to bottom and from left to right; good layout is both 'clean' (i.e. uncluttered) and clear, making it easy for readers to follow what they are looking at on the page and to make sense of it.

**lead actor:** in *drama*, the person who plays the *protagonist*. 'Lead actor' is a different concept from *star:* For example, he could be unknown at the time of the production, although he could later become a star.

**lead character:** see *protagonist*.

**leader:** see *editorial* (ii). A *leader column* is the regular spot or location in a newspaper where the leader can be found.

**lead-in:** introduction to a media item. In broadcasting, the lead-in could be an announcement or *voice-over*, perhaps combined with music. In journalism, a lead-in could be a paragraph in large or bold type that introduces the rest of the news story or article.

**leading:** pronounced 'ledding', the amount of space between lines of text on a page. This is because in the *hot metal* era – the days before digital typesetting – strips of lead were placed in the printing press between the lines to keep them apart. The purpose of leading is to combine legibility with efficient use of the available space: the more leading, the more legible the text but the more space is taken up. The converse is also true.

**leading caps:** how stories often begin in newspapers, with the first word or words in capital letters.

**lead story:** in *news*, the main story of the day, which in newspapers is the largest story on the front page. In broadcasting it is the first story covered in detail after the initial *headlines*.

**left-wing:** a term describing those *ideologies* such as socialism and communism that insist on greater equality between people, and which regard the community as more important than any one member of it. A left-wing (or 'progressive') person tends to interpret history and politics in terms of *social class*, seeing it as a struggle between rich and poor, in which the poor are constantly exploited and attacked by the forces of *capitalism*. In the UK the Labour Party was until the 1990s more left-wing than the Conservatives; today the differences between them are less clear-cut. Most British national newspapers are right-wing, supporting the Conservatives, while broadcasters are required to maintain a balance between left- and right-wing views. (See also *Marxism* and *political spectrum*.)

**legend:** (i) a *narrative* that has become part of a culture's tradition. The concept overlaps with that of *mythology*. Legends tend to contain fewer supernatural elements than myths and usually have more basis in historical fact. (ii) used in film journalism to describe a Hollywood *star* of long-standing fame, e.g. 'screen legend Marilyn Monroe'.

**legislation:** a law or set of laws passed by parliament.

**leitmotif:** in *music*, a repeated phrase or theme used to suggest an idea or character in a story. (See also *motif* and *theme music*.)

**lens:** a transparent glass disc in a *camera* that *focuses* light rays on to the film or digital videotape behind it to form an image. Different lenses have different focal lengths, measured by the distance between lens and film: a *wide-angle* lens is one with a focal length of less than 40 mm; long-focus or *telephoto* lenses are those whose focal length is greater than 50 mm.

**letterer:** in comics, the artist who writes out the dialogue that appears in word balloons, as well as sound effects ('Squelch!') and exclamations ('Eeeek!') and any other words appearing in a frame.

**letterboxing:** the attempt to present feature films on television by replicating their original cinema *aspect ratio* (usually 1.85:1 or 2.35:1 – roughly letterbox-shaped). Achieved by leaving the top and bottom of the screen blank, letterboxing was necessary before the advent of wide-screen TV, when television screens were squarer than cinema screens.

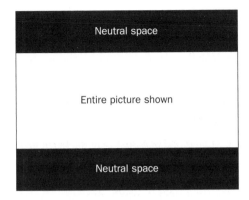

Neutral space

Entire picture shown

Neutral space

*Letterboxed film*

**Lévi-Strauss, Claude (1908–):** see *binary opposition*

**libel:** a crime involving the publication or broadcast of untrue and defamatory statements about individuals. Libel is something that *journalists* and *producers* have to be extremely careful about, particularly in *news, current affairs* and *documentary*, and even more particularly in those programmes or news stories that allege wrongdoing. People in the public eye have been awarded large sums of money in court after suing newspapers for libel: in 2004, *The Daily Telegraph* was obliged to pay MP George Galloway £150,000, and print an apology, for falsely accusing him of being in the pay of former Iraqi dictator Saddam Hussein. In 2006, the newspaper also lost its appeal against paying Galloway's legal costs of £1.2 million. The British courts have a reputation for punishing libel more harshly than those in other countries.

**liberal:** in politics, one who sees the need for reform rather than wholesale or revolutionary change. As such, a liberal is traditionally positioned somewhere between the left and the right. Confusingly, the term economic liberal refers to any fervent admirer of the free market, i.e. a right-winger. (See also *political spectrum.*)

**library:** in the professional media, collections of films, photographic images, *sound effects* or music. Where the library is the *copyright* owner, these collections may continue to earn money for many years, since they are available for use on payment of a fee.

**licence:** in broadcasting, all commercial (i.e. non-BBC) *television* and *radio* stations are required to pay for a licence to broadcast from *Ofcom*, the industry regulator. There is con-siderable variation in the way licences are awarded, and for how many years, depending on whether the service is for television or radio, whether for a local, national or restricted service audience, and whether the broadcaster is digital or analogue. Some licences are simply awarded to the highest bidder who meets the criteria for a specific licence.

**licence fee:** payable in order to finance the *BBC* by all UK households with a television set. The amount of the licence fee is decided by the government.

**licence to print money:** a phrase coined in the 1950s by Roy Thomson, then owner of Scottish Television, to describe the huge profitability of the business, and since applied to

A B C D E F G H I J K **L** M N O P Q R S T U V W X Y Z

**115**

any media venture deemed an infallible means of generating income with minimal risk. The *ITV* franchises were indeed like licences to print money until competition arrived with *multi-channel* television in 1989, when the ITV *audience* began to dwindle.

**licensing:** where it is agreed that new versions of a *media product*, or spin-offs from it, may be produced for a fee for the rights to do so. A common example is the *DVD* release of a film or television series, where the original product is licensed for production and distribution in a new format by a separate *producer*. Similarly, the use of logos, *copyrighted* music or cartoon characters in any format must first be licensed by the copyright owner. Unauthorised (i.e. unlicensed) use of such sounds or images leads to legal action.

**lifestyle advertising:** that which associates a product with a way of life, such as health, glamour, fun, travel, family, sports or outdoor activity. The intention is to suggest that purchasing the product or service in question will bring with it the benefits of the chosen lifestyle (e.g. if you buy a certain brand of muesli, you will become the sort of healthy person who goes skiing).

**lifestyle magazine:** a loose term for magazines promoting a particular culture shared by a particular audience. By this definition, most magazines could be defined as lifestyle magazines, since the media today often target audiences by lifestyle rather than social class. Hence there are magazines for gay men, young Asian women, stay-at-home mothers and so on.

**lifestyle programming:** television programmes about the way people live or aspire to live. These include programmes with such themes as buying or improving property, gardening, clothes and fashion, cookery, and collecting antiques. They cover similar ground to numerous well-established printed magazines. Lifestyle programming has been part of the boom in *reality TV* (i.e. factual programmes featuring 'ordinary' people).

**light box:** a simple apparatus used by photographers, picture editors and production designers that enables the easy viewing of photographic *transparencies*. A light box is a shallow box with a large translucent top, through which light shines from below. The light is diffused to produce even illumination of transparencies when they are laid out on the top.

**light entertainment:** a broad swathe of television programming catering for a *mass audience*, and incorporating *genres* as diverse as comedy, talent shows, quiz and game shows, chat and variety shows. Light entertainment consists of popular, undemanding television, often studio-based and with a comedy element. It excludes drama (such as soap opera), sport, factual programmes (such as news, current affairs and documentary).

**lighting:** in photography, film and television, the artificial illumination directed at and around the subject of the shot. Lighting is perhaps the single most important factor in establishing mood. It is possible to rely entirely on available light – daylight, or whatever lights there are in the room already – and this can give the shot quite a naturalistic or documentary tone, but the photographer or *cinematographer* has more control when lighting is used. Arranging the lighting set-ups for film and television drama is a complex and time-consuming process. It accounts for most of the time spent on a film set, since lights usually have to be reset for every individual shot. The variables in lighting are as follows:

- **quality** – generally defines the intensity or otherwise. *'Hard' lighting*, as on a sunny day, is relatively intense, and creates distinct shadows; *'soft' lighting*, as on a cloudy day, is diffused, and creates little or no shadow. *Diffusion* can be created artificially by placing gauze or paper in front of a light.

- **direction** – different effects can be produced depending whether light shines from above (toplighting), from the front (frontal lighting), from the side (sidelighting), from behind (backlighting) or from below (underlighting). In the latter case, most children are familiar with the 'spooky' effect of shining a torch on one's face from below. Toplighting appears quite naturalistic because the commonest source of both natural and artificial light is from above. Frontal lighting, when used alone, can flatten the features, reducing definition, whereas sidelighting can have the effect of 'modelling' the features in a striking way. Backlighting creates silhouettes, but also has the effect of outlining the subject with light, giving a 'halo' effect.

- **source** – in *three-* or *four-point lighting*, the source is usually defined as a *key light, fill light, back light* and often a background light too, although other kinds of light are also used.

- **colour** – usually white, but coloured *filters* are also used (e.g. yellow or orange to suggest a setting sun, blue to suggest moonlight).

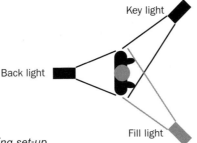

*Standard three-point lighting set-up*

**lighting cameraman:** see *cinematographer*

**lineage:** the rate at which *classified advertisements* are paid for (i.e. by the line).

**linear narrative:** in drama, one which does not contain *flashbacks*, although it may contain *ellipses*. In other words, events in the narrative are shown chronologically.

**line of action:** in conventional film or television drama, an imaginary line that must not be physically crossed by the camera between shots, since to do so would destroy visual *continuity* from one shot to the next. Crossing the line can disorientate the *audience*, who become uncertain about the positioning of characters within the *mise en scène*, about who is talking to whom, and about the direction in which characters are moving or facing. Also known as the *180-degree line.*

*Camera 1 films two-shot: woman on left, man on right. Camera 2 shoots close-up of man over woman's shoulder. Camera 3 shoots close-up of woman over man's shoulder. Camera 4 crosses axis and films over wrong shoulder of man, thus transposing players: man is now on left and woman on right*

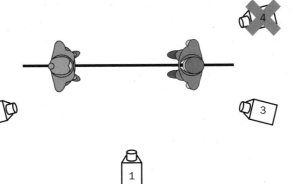

**line producer:** the producer's representative on the set of a film or television drama. The line producer manages the budget during the shoot, and may also hire crew members and devise the initial production schedule (i.e. the order of scenes to be shot day by day).

**lip-synch:** the technique of matching lip movements with a voice from a different source. Pop singers frequently 'lip synch' (i.e. mime to the playback of a pre-recorded song) to make it appear that they are actually singing in music videos or occasionally even in 'live' performance. In film and television, lip-synching is the technique required for re-recording dialogue during post-production to improve its technical quality. It is also used to approximate the mouth movements of characters on screen when *dubbing* dialogue into other languages, and when providing voices for animated cartoon characters.

**literary adaptation:** film or television version of a book, short story or play. Literary adaptations are common in the film industry, partly because a well-known and popular book will to some extent guarantee an *audience* for the film. Selling the film *rights* to a novel or short story can therefore be lucrative for writers, who can expect high fees when the book has been a best-seller. Some of the most successful films of all time have been literary adaptations, including both the *Lord of the Rings* series (Peter Jackson, NZ/USA, 2001–3) and the *Harry Potter* films (Chris Columbus/Alfonso Cuaron/Mike Newell, UK/US, 2001 onwards). Considerable skill is required in adapting a book or play into a script. The most immediate problem is to reduce the length, typically dispensing with at least 90 per cent of the original material, while retaining the story's key elements with a sufficient degree of narrative coherence to keep the audience interested.

**Little Three:** Universal and Columbia Studios, and United Artists, during the era of the *Hollywood studio system.* The Little Three were so called because they were not *vertically integrated* as businesses in the same way as the *Big Five* (or *majors*): Universal and Columbia *produced* and *distributed* films but had no theatres of their own in which to exhibit them; United Artists only distributed films made by independent *producers.*

**live:** an event that is transmitted to a *radio, television* or internet *audience* as it takes place. In the early days of television, before the use of videotape became widespread, every type of broadcast was live, including drama. Today the majority of television programming is pre-recorded, with the exception of news programmes and major sporting events. Until the late 1960s, television news reports from overseas were shot on film, then flown to London and edited; now they are transmitted live by satellite from the most remote corners of the world. In radio, live programmes have always been the norm.

**live action:** a term used to differentiate filmed performances using *actors* from animated *footage* of cartoon characters. Films such as *Song of the South* (Harve Foster/Wilfred Jackson, USA, 1946), *Mary Poppins* (Robert Stevenson, USA, 1964) and *Who Framed Roger Rabbit?* (Robert Zemeckis, USA, 1988) have combined cartoon *animation* with live action. Richard Linklater's *Waking Life* (USA, 2001) and *A Scanner Darkly* (USA, 2006) also mix animation and live action, using digital *rotoscoping* to overlay live action digital footage with painted figures and backgrounds.

**live feed:** sound, television or web *footage* transmitted continuously from a location or event. Originally available only to a limited number of professional subscribers such as news organisations, live feeds first became generally available when *Big Brother* was put out as continuous *streaming video* on the *internet*, and subsequently 'almost live' on the digital television channel E4. Live feed material can be monitored and used either live or edited.

**location:** a 'real' place, as opposed to a studio, in which something is filmed or otherwise recorded. A location might be a New York City street or a desert. *John Ford*'s favourite location for *Westerns*, including *She Wore a Yellow Ribbon* (USA, 1949) and *The Searchers* (USA, 1956), was the remote Monument Valley on the border of Utah and Arizona in south-western USA. A film shot largely on location may benefit from an enhanced sense of visual authenticity compared to one shot on studio *sets* and lots.

**location manager/scout:** the film crew member who travels to locations in advance of shooting to establish their suitability with regard to logistics and appearance, and who organises permits and compensation for the various inconveniences and disruptions caused by the presence of a film crew.

**logging:** writing up a list of camera *takes* previously recorded. The importance of logging is not only to keep track of what has been shot – and thus what still remains to be shot – but in what order, so that *footage* can easily be found by the *editor*. Takes are logged with a brief description of the contents, and the running time of each. If the recording has been made on video, an automatically generated *timecode* enables the editor to locate material with complete precision.

**logo:** a simple visual symbol designed to provide instant recognition of an organisation or other entity. A logo may consist partly or entirely of a graphic image, such as the face of Colonel Sanders or the Nike 'swoosh'; or it may consist of words set out in a particular *font*, such as the elaborate script style used by Coca-Cola. Famous logos have frequently been subverted, or spoofed (e.g. t-shirts reading Enjoy Cocaine, printed in the same font as that used by Coca-Cola).

**long shot (LS):** see *cinematography*

**long take:** not to be confused with a *long shot*, a long take is a shot of comparatively long duration. A long take involving complex movement is known as a *sequence* shot. Examples include the seven-minute opening shot of *The Player* (Robert Altman, USA, 1992); the opening of Orson Welles's *Touch Of Evil* (USA, 1958); and the whole of Alfred Hitchcock's *Rope* (USA, 1948), which consists of eight ten-minute takes – ten minutes being the full length of a reel of film. Long takes often involve complex camera movement and 'flyaway' sets that allow the camera to pass over or through such impediments as furniture and windows. Due to the greater length of digital tape cassettes, long takes can be far longer in digital movies than those shot on film: *Russian Ark* (Aleksandr Sokurov, Rus/Ger, 2002) consists of a single take lasting 96 minutes. *Timecode* (Mike Figgis, USA, 2000) takes this a step further by using four digital cameras running continuously and simultaneously for 93 minutes.

**looking room/space:** in camera *framing*, the empty space on the screen into which the subject looks. In conventional framing, where the subject is looking at someone or something off-camera, he/she is framed off-centre, allowing more space in the direction of the look than on the other side.

**looping:** see *dubbing*

**lowbrow:** a derogatory term for *downmarket* media products and audiences, e.g. *The Daily Sport* newspaper and its readers.

**low budget:** a cheap film production. The term 'low budget' also connotes a particular ethos that does not rely on stars, 'name' directors or special effects – the most expensive elements of *mainstream* (big budget) *Hollywood* production – to make an impact. Originality is more likely to be the selling point. However, 'low budget' is a relative term: a British film considered expensive in the UK would still cost less than one-tenth of an average 'low-budget' Hollywood film.

**low-angle shot (L/A shot):** see *cinematography*

**lower case:** in the early days of printing, when type (letters) was set in individual wood and then metal letters, the capital letters were kept in an *upper case* and the small letters were kept in a lower case, so the compositor could find them easily when constructing words and sentences. Even though this kind of printing is almost obsolete, the terms lower and upper case still persist.

**low-key lighting:** lighting used to create a clear contrast between dark and light areas of the set, producing a *chiaroscuro* effect by using little or no *fill light*, thus allowing the *key light* to create shadows. This style may be frequently seen in *film noir.*

**ludology:** the recently-established academic study of computer and *video games*. Ludology investigates the social significance of games from the perspective of their rules and interface, and the idea of play itself.

**Lumière Brothers:** French cinema pioneers who held the world's first performance of projected films to paying customers in Paris in December 1895. Numerous other pioneers were working towards the invention of film at around the same time in France, England and the USA, including some who invented methods of making and showing films before the Lumières. However, the brothers are usually considered to be the first to combine the main elements of projection and exhibition in its modern form. They are also frequently cited as the founding fathers of *documentary*, since all their subjects were factual. At the 1895 screening, their patrons watched ten short silent films made by the brothers, each lasting less than a minute, beginning with the 46-second *Workers leaving the Lumière factory at Lyon.*

**lure:** also known as a *cover mount*, a free gift attached to a magazine or other print product to add value and attract customers. Sachets of shampoo and CDs are popular lures.

**What other subjects are you studying?**

A–Zs cover a range of different subjects. See the inside back cover for a list of all the titles in the series and how to order.

**MacGuffin:** an object of great interest to *characters* in a *drama*, but of no interest to the *audience* (e.g. secret plans, stolen jewellery, buried treasure). The MacGuffin, a term popularised by Hitchcock, is hence merely a dramatic device designed to animate the action and send the characters on an urgent quest. A typical example of a MacGuffin, in *Desperately Seeking Susan* (Susan Seidelman, USA, 1985), is a stolen pair of priceless Ancient Egyptian earrings.

**McDonaldisation:** the process by which society increasingly shares the values and attributes of a fast-food restaurant. These attributes are efficiency, calculability (data and statistics being valued more highly than any individual notions of quality), predictability (standardisation) and control (i.e. over employees). The term was first suggested by sociologist George Ritzer in his 1993 book *The McDonaldization of Society*.

**McLuhan, Marshall (1911–1980):** see *global village*, *medium is the message*

**McQuail, Blumler and Brown model:** see *uses and gratifications*

**macro analysis:** specific to the wording of the WJEC Film Studies specification (but not in wider use), this is an analysis that examines the elements of *genre* and *narrative*, and thus the overall pattern and type of the film – in other words *film form*. (See also *micro analysis*.)

**macro lens:** a long-barrelled lens used for photographing small objects such as insects, bringing them into sharp focus. The effect of using a macro lens is to create an image that is the same size as the subject, or larger.

**made-for-TV:** usually refers to a *drama* with most of the hallmarks (e.g. *running time*) of a feature film but whose intended medium is television. Made-for-TV movies usually feature actors best known for their work in television; are likely to focus on the relatively small-scale and domestic, or familiar, cheap-to-produce *genres* such as crime; and are unlikely to feature expensive special effects.

**magazine:** (i) a publication, also known as a periodical, most commonly appearing weekly, fortnightly or monthly, and usually financed by a mixture of cover price and advertising, although many are distributed 'free' with newspapers. Others are produced *in-house* by organisations as a communications tool with the workforce. While a newspaper is primarily concerned with news and current affairs, the contents of magazines vary enormously. They fall into two broad categories: *consumer* and *trade*. Consumer magazines are available to the public in retail outlets; trade magazines can often be obtained by subscription only (e.g. *Meat Trades Journal*, *Lighting Equipment News*). (ii) the detachable light-proof chamber used with movie cameras to hold the film *stock* and take up it again after it has been exposed.

**magazine format:** a *genre* of television programme that resembles a printed magazine in structure, having an overall subject or specific *target audience*, and featuring both regular items and special features. Examples are motoring, consumer and children's programmes (e.g. the BBC's *Top Gear*, *Watchdog* and *Blue Peter*).

**magic lantern:** precursor of the modern slide projector. The magic lantern consisted of a light source (usually an oil lamp), a set of lenses and a collection of glass plates on which images were painted; these were projected onto a wall or screen.

**magnetic sound:** a method of recording or reproducing sound on film in the pre-digital era. An iron oxide strip containing the sound runs alongside the other elements of the film strip – the images and the sprocket holes. For exhibition purposes, magnetic sound was only used on 70 mm and special 35 mm prints, but in some cases 16 mm film was used which recorded simultaneous picture and magnetic sound.

**mainstream audience:** consumers of mass-produced media products such as *blockbuster Hollywood* movies, *tabloid* newspapers, *celebrity* magazines and pop radio stations. The tastes of the mainstream change over time: for example, extreme violence and swearing are more acceptable in films today than they were to the mainstream audience of the 1960s. Similarly, newspapers today print more lurid sexual detail than previously, because of changes in mainstream acceptability. For the same reason, overt racism on television has become a thing of the past (although it can still be found in mainstream *right-wing* newspapers). Media audiences outside the mainstream include those for *art-house*/foreign-language cinema, classical music, and enthusiasts for specific *subgenres* such as slasher horror films.

**mainstream media:** mass-produced media products and their producers. (See also *mainstream audience*.)

**major key:** in music, a scale in any key whose intervals correspond with a scale starting with C and played only on the white notes of a piano keyboard. The pattern of intervals from the first to the last note in an octave is therefore tone, tone, semitone, tone, tone, tone, semitone. In mood, the major scale 'feels' positive and upbeat compared with the minor scale.

**major plot reversal:** a twist in the plot of a dramatic *narrative*, where events which had previously been unfolding in one way suddenly change direction. This might take the form of a drastic alteration in the power relationship between two characters, as the previously dominant one is suddenly at the mercy of the other. An example is the film *Hard Candy* (David Slade, USA, 2005), in which a 14-year-old girl turns the tables on a predatory 32-year-old man.

**majors:** see *major studio* and *Big Five*.

**major studio:** the modern equivalents of the majors of the *Hollywood studio* era, (i.e. the mainstream, largely American financiers, *producers*, distributors and/or exhibitors of films). In the early twenty-first century, the major studios are Columbia-Tristar, Lionsgate Films, MGM, New Line, Paramount, 20th Century Fox, Universal, Walt Disney/Buena Vista, Warner Bros, and The Weinstein Company. As a result of successive mergers and takeovers, the business entities considered to be major studios have come and gone over the years. For example, The Weinstein Company was founded in 2005 by Bob and Harvey Weinstein some years after they sold the Miramax company (which they founded) to Disney. Their departure has meant that Miramax is no longer considered a major studio. Dreamworks, founded in 1994 by Steven Spielberg, David Geffen and Jeffrey Katzenberg, was considered a major studio until it was sold in 2006 to Viacom, which also owns Paramount.

**make-up:** cosmetics used to change the appearance of a performer. This may be something as basic as a little powder applied to the face of a TV interviewee in order to remove the 'shine' effect of bright studio lighting. In film and television drama, make-up is an element of the *mise en scène*, since it is applied to actors in order to make them appear more like the characters they are portraying. On most occasions, make-up aims to improve an actor's appearance by covering up skin blemishes. At other times the make-up artist is required to create such blemishes (e.g. acne, age lines, wounds and bruises). The make-up artist's role is most prominent in *horror* films, where it can overlap with the work of the *special effects* designer, e.g. in transformation scenes such as the change from man to wolf in *An American Werewolf in London* (John Landis, USA/UK, 1981).

**male gaze, the:** a concept first suggested by critic Laura Mulvey in her famous essay *Visual Pleasure and Narrative Cinema* (1975). It proposes that, as a result of male domination of the film industry, 'the camera is male'. According to Mulvey, this has resulted in the *audience* being *voyeuristically* encouraged to view women as sex objects while *narcissistically* identifying with the male protagonist. Certain critics have subsequently rejected or modified the idea of the male gaze. (See also *female gaze; feminist film theory.*)

**manga:** the distinctive style of modern Japanese comic books. As well as being extremely popular in Japan, manga has also developed a major cult following in the West in recent years. In its animated form, manga is known as *anime.* Influenced by *Disney* animation, manga was originally the brainchild of Osamu Tezuka, who developed the style soon after the Second World War. *Characters* are drawn with big round eyes, small noses and mouths, and flat faces. The drawings feature a complex set of non-western style codes and conventions for the representation of dialogue; a range of different emotions; action sequences and background effects.

**manipulation:** (i) the alteration of media images and sounds in post-production. This process highlights the difference between realism and reality: in the *digital* era a high degree of realism can be achieved in representing the impossible through manipulation of still and moving images. Hollywood *special effects* are an obvious example: in *Forrest Gump* (Robert Zemeckis, USA, 1994), the protagonist is seen meeting President Kennedy in footage that has obviously been manipulated because it could not have happened in real life, yet it looks entirely realistic. Still photographs can also be manipulated. Kate Winslet is one of many actresses and models whose bodies have been digitally manipulated for magazine *cover shots*: she claimed that in their February 2003 issue GQ magazine had made her legs appear slimmer than they really were. Others have complained that images of themselves have been assembled from three or more different photographs. The result of manipulation of this sort has been to increase *audience* scepticism about the authenticity of what they see and hear in the media. (ii) manipulation of audience emotions – often to produce feelings of sympathy for screen characters – is achieved by film makers through a range of techniques, including big, lingering close-ups, slow zoom-ins and surging music.

**manual focus:** a photographer or *camera operator*'s adjustment of the camera focus, as opposed to an automatic focus setting calculated by the camera itself. Manual focus is generally preferred to autofocus since it gives the photographer more control over the image.

**manufacture of consent:** the tendency of the *mass media* to disseminate *propaganda* in favour of the social and political *status quo*. The term was popularised by Edward S Herman and Noam Chomsky in their 1988 book *Manufacturing Consent: The Political Economy of the*

*Mass Media.* Their argument is that since the mass media are owned by giant business corporations, it is inevitable that their output will reflect the relatively narrow interests of business, rather than the broader and more pressing concerns of society as a whole. Therefore the media tend to represent favourably those institutions that create a climate favourable to the accumulation of profit (e.g. the American version of democracy), while undermining those which appear to threaten or question it (e.g. the United Nations).

**market:** a system in which suppliers sell goods and services to customers in competition with other suppliers, and customers exercise choice over which supplier to use. Like other forms of business, the media operate in a competitive market, and specialist international events such as AFM (American Film Market) are held annually for the buying and selling of media products. In the wider world, the term 'market' became highly *ideological* in the 1980s, when large state-owned utilities previously considered to exist purely as public services – the telephone network, water, gas, electricity, transport – began to be converted into businesses. Right-wing economic theory argues that exposing the workplace to market forces of competition, profits and shareholder influence increases efficiency. This is achieved through privatisation – the selling off of public *monopolies* to the private sector. During the 1980s and 1990s the utilities duly became subject to the same market conditions as any other commercial company, facing competition for customers for the first time. This process began in the UK in 1984 when British Telecom (later BT) became the first utility to be privatised, and has continued ever since under both Conservative and New Labour governments. In the media, the publicly owned *BBC* has so far resisted any suggestions that it too should be privatised, on the grounds that it is already operating in a highly competitive market (for audiences), with numerous rivals in the commercial sector.

**market economy:** one in which the state does not (in theory) intervene in the operations of the market, on the grounds that the market is constantly adapting itself to the conditions of the real world, and does so much faster and more efficiently than would be possible under state control. A market economy is also known as laissez-faire – or free market – *capitalism*.

**marketing:** the effort made to create a climate of success for a product by ensuring that it is researched, designed, promoted and sold effectively to its customers. Hence marketing is in operation at each stage of a product's life. In the film industry, marketing is most commonly considered to be part of the *distribution* process, where it is divided into *above-the-line* (advertising) and *below-the-line* (PR). A marketing plan is one which sets out the specific strategy which will be used to market a product. In the film industry, the marketing budget of a film is typically as high as its production budget, and often higher.

**market penetration:** the degree to which any company manages to capture a share of the market when it introduces new products or services, or rebrands existing ones for a new market.

**market research:** that which assesses the likely success of any new commercial venture by investigating its potential demand from customers, and compiling the results in the form of data. An essential preliminary to the launch of any new product or service, and in monitoring the performance of existing ones, market research takes a variety of forms including street and telephone interviews, *focus groups* and *questionnaires* – all of which are designed to find out what customers want or expect.

**market share:** the proportion of a market captured by a product or service. For example, in April 2005, when the end of the popular ITV series *Ant and Dec's Saturday Night Takeaway* coincided with the BBC's relaunched *Doctor Who*, ITV's share of the market – the viewing *audience* – fell to 18 per cent of the total.

**martial arts film:** an action *genre* that developed in Hong Kong and later became popular throughout the world in the early 1970s, when *kung-fu* movies starring Bruce Lee became international *box-office* hits. American-born Lee, who died at 32, became the iconic figure of the martial arts movie with *The Big Boss* (Wei Lo, Hong Kong, 1971), *Fist of Fury* (Wei Lo, Hong Kong, 1972), *Way of the Dragon* (Bruce Lee, Hong Kong, 1972) and *Enter the Dragon* (Robert Clouse, Hong Kong/USA, 1973). His mantle has passed to Jackie Chan, whose films combine martial arts with comedy. The martial arts film originated in the popular wuxia Chinese novels, analogous to western sword-and-sorcery novels, which featured tales of timeless heroic warriors, with a strong dash of mysticism and fantasy. The 1990s films of John Woo, such as *Hard Boiled* (Hong Kong, 1992) and *Face/Off* (USA, 1997) indicated that the public appetite for the genre remained undimmed, as did the enormous success of *Crouching Tiger, Hidden Dragon* (Ang Lee, Taiwan/Hong Kong/US/China, 2000), featuring Jet Li. Its influence on other genres is evident in the combat sequences in *The Matrix* series (Wachowski Brothers, USA, 1999–2003).

**Marxism:** a profoundly influential system of thought, which originated in the writings of German philosopher, economist and revolutionary Karl Marx, and was developed by his followers. Although Marx claimed that he was not himself a Marxist, his ideas led directly to the creation of the *left-wing* Communist and socialist *ideologies*, the foundation of the Labour Party in the UK, and the Russian Revolution of 1917, which resulted in the world's first Communist government, under Lenin. China also fell under Communist rule under Mao Zedung in 1949 after a 22-year civil war. Marx's most well-known works are *Das Kapital* (1867) and *The Communist Manifesto*, the latter co-authored by his friend Friedrich Engels, and published in 1848. In this they analysed history as a struggle between *social classes* of which, in the industrialised nineteenth century, there were two: the bourgeousie and the proletariat. They defined the economic and political system as *capitalist* (i.e. a society controlled by the bourgeoisie, the wealthy class, who owned the factories and workshops). The proletariat, or workers, actually produced this wealth through their labours, but gained nothing from it. The misery and poverty arising from this unfair distribution of wealth meant that the class system had to be abolished, and the only way to achieve that was revolution. Although Marxist thought is currently unfashionable throughout the world, following the final collapse of Communism in Europe in 1989, Marx's analysis of social class continues to be influential in explaining the underlying conflicts in modern society. For media students, his work is central to the understanding of social class and *ideology*. (See also *political spectrum*.)

**Masala movie:** see *Bollywood*

**masculinity:** the traditional attributes of a man, including physical strength, courage and leadership. Other masculine traits include a goal-oriented approach to all situations, poor communication, lack of empathy, and an inability to carry out more than one task at a time. As with *femininity*, the distinction between culturally determined masculinity and biologically determined maleness is difficult to define. Some believe that the increasing social equality of women since the twentieth century has brought about a crisis in masculinity among those men who feel deprived of their traditional role – see for example the character of Travis Bickle in *Taxi Driver* (Martin Scorsese, USA, 1976). Examples of traditional masculinity are the characters played by Arnold Schwarzenegger in his action films of the 1980s and 1990s (e.g. James Cameron's *True Lies*, USA, 1994).

**Maslow's hierarchy of needs:** a psychological theory first proposed by Abraham Maslow in 1954. Maslow suggested that the needs of human beings exist in a particular order of precedence, each level of which must be satisfied before higher-level needs can be addressed. This hierarchy is usually expressed in the form of a pyramid, with the base consisting of physiological needs (e.g. for food, sleep and comfort). The second level is the need for safety and security. The third level contains love and a sense of belonging; the fourth, self-esteem and the esteem of others. In the fifth, at the top, is what Maslow called 'self-actualisation', or the need to reach one's full creative and moral potential. In order to understand how the hierarchy works in practice, bear in mind that the need to use the bathroom – a level-one need – is always more urgent than the need to carry on a conversation with friends – a level-three need. Knowledge of Maslow's hierarchy is useful when studying the *uses and gratifications theory* of *audience* behaviour, and when analysing the different strategies used by the advertising industry.

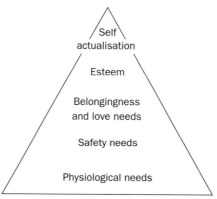

*Maslow's heirarchy of human needs*

**mass audience:** (i) the concept of audiences that positions them as *homogenous* in their response to and use of the media. The *hypodermic model* assumes that all audience members behave in the same way – as a mass, not as individuals. The idea of the mass audience fell out of favour after *field research* into film and television viewing revealed that audiences actually respond in a wide variety of ways that have more to do with individual lifestyles and *sub-cultures*, and that broad general theories failed to reflect this. (ii) extremely large numbers of media users, as targeted by the *mass media*.

**mass communication:** that which is directed at social groups rather than individuals. Mass communication is carried out by the media through a range of methods, from junk mail (and junk email and text messages) to poster advertisements, *blogs*, *podcasts*, television and radio broadcasts, film, website, newspaper and magazine production, and recorded music. It differs from individual or person-to-person methods such as telephone calls and individual email or text messages.

**mass media:** those which communicate to a mass *audience* rather than to individuals.

**master genre:** one defined by its tone, narrative and the expectations of the *audience* rather than any typical setting. Master genre therefore refers to comedy, tragedy, romance and satire rather than, for example, science fiction or detective stories.

**master shot:** in film and television *drama*, a camera shot that shows the *audience* the whole scene in a wide shot. For any scene, a director will nearly always film a master shot, then re-shoot the scene from different angles and closer positions. This gives the *editor* choices about which shots to use at any particular point in the scene. A master shot can also function as a safety shot, which can always be used if other shots are unusable.

**masthead:** the title of a *magazine* or *newspaper* as it appears on the front cover. Confusingly, the term is also sometimes used for a newspaper's list of senior personnel and contact information, usually found on the *editorial* or *leader* page.

**match cut:** see *graphic match*

**match on action:** in *continuity* film or television production, two shots in which an action begun in the first is completed in the second, thus disguising the fact that there has been a cut. For example, in a shop scene, shot A might be a medium shot of the assistant taking coins from the till, holding out his hand and giving them to the customer; shot B might be a close-up of the customer's open hand receiving the coins. The match on action only works when the action is continuous from shot A to shot B, with no chronological time either added or subtracted from the sequence.

**materialism:** (i) an *ideology* that values money and material possessions above other priorities such as quality of life, family, moral or religious belief. (ii) dialectical materialism is a term from *Marxist* philosophy for the struggle between bourgeois and proletarian thought. What mattered to Marx was the day-to-day hardship suffered by the poor due to their physical, or material, condition. Arguments over the existence of God or other abstractions were irrelevant and would change nothing in the real (i.e. material) world.

**matte:** a range of techniques for combining images in film or television – for example, adding a painted background to a shot of an actor. At one time this was a complicated process of painting glass or board with black paint in order to leave areas of the film negative unexposed for the second image to be added later. Today, however, images are usually combined using digital *blue or green screen* technology.

**MCU (medium close-up):** see *cinematography*

**meaning:** the underlying *messages and values* of any representation or narrative. The goal of most textual analysis is to uncover these meanings, which may be *implicit* or *explicit*, or a combination of the two. Since texts are *polysemic*, and hence likely to be interpreted in a range of different ways by different audiences and individuals, meanings may be discovered which were not intended by the *producer*. The sociologist Stuart Hall argues that because no text has any fixed meaning, *audiences* may take up *preferred*, *negotiated* or *oppositional* positions (i.e. interpretations) regarding its meaning. (See also *encoding*.)

**meaning systems:** the ideas and *values* through which we interpret the world around us. In *Class Inequality and Political Order* (1972), Frank Parkin suggested that there are three dominant meaning systems in any society:

- the **dominant** value system, derived from the ruling elite, which promotes the idea that social inequality is natural and right;
- the **subordinate** value system, held by those who have adjusted to the reality of inequality and the low status that goes with it;
- the **radical** value system, which is opposed to inequality and seeks to end it through political action.

**meaningfulness:** a *news value*, according to Galtung and Ruge, that makes a story more newsworthy when the *audience* is able to identify with the situation or the people involved. As such, what constitutes meaningfulness varies according to the local or national *culture*.

**media/medium:** in its modern sense, 'the media' refers to the *mass media*, i.e. methods of communicating with a large audience, including books, newspapers, advertising bill-boards, magazines, cinema, radio, television, the internet, computer games, CDs, DVDs, and more recent technologies such as *blogging* and *podcasting*. Each of these is a 'medium' of communication. Systems originally designed for person-to-person use, such as telephones, were not until recently thought of as mass media. However, since email and text messages began to be sent to large numbers of people, the distinction between person-to-person communication and *mass communication* has become blurred. In addition, the digital era has brought together media which were once considered separate.

**media education/studies:** the academic discipline that attempts to understand the workings of *media texts*, *industries* and *audiences*, and their relationships with society and each other. *Media studies* began in the early 1930s, soon after the establishment of radio, notably at the Institute for Social Research in Frankfurt (more commonly known as the *Frankfurt School*). Since it became a *mainstream* academic subject in the UK, media studies has often received hostile *coverage* from the media themselves, with frequent ref-erences to it as a 'Mickey Mouse' subject, compared to more 'serious' and traditional subjects such as history, geography or physics. 'Media education', as a concept, generally receives less criticism than media studies as a subject.

**media effects:** see *effects model*

**media imperialism:** the idea that modern empires are built not through military conquest but through the *globalised* media industry. Every empire in history has been created in order to increase the power and influence of a *culture* or *ideology*, and to increase trade and profit. Alexander the Great, Julius Caesar, Napoleon and Hitler all created empires by sending armies into other countries, crushing local power and indige-nous culture, and imposing Greek, Roman, French or German culture. The British Empire did the same in North America, India, Africa, Australasia and the Caribbean. Today, this is an unnecessary way to establish an empire, since the same effect can be achieved through the media. In practice, media imperialism usually refers to the spread of American culture across the globe. This process began with the international dominance established by *Hollywood* in the 1920s, and increased greatly with the spread of global cable and satellite channels *MTV* and *CNN* in the 1980s. This notably affected India, which had previously remained relatively free from American cultural influence due to its thriving *Bollywood* film industry.

**media literacy:** the ability to 'read' (i.e. interpret) *media texts* and hence *decode* their *messages and values*.

**media magnate:** a powerful media businessman, one who owns and controls large areas of the media industry. For example, Silvio Berlusconi, former Prime Minister of Italy and the country's richest man, owns three national television channels through his company Mediaset, as well as Arnoldo Mondadori, the largest magazine publishing company in Italy, and the major advertising agency Publitalia. His other media activities include film and video distribution. Members of his family also own right-wing newspapers, which supported him throughout his political career.

**media pack:** a set of *press releases*, photographs and other *publicity* materials distributed by organisations to members of the media by *public relations* representatives. Media packs are used for a variety of purposes, but particularly when commercial organisations launch new products and attempt to influence the media coverage of them. A magazine or newspaper media pack will usually contain an advertising *rate card.*

**media plan:** a strategy, usually drawn up by an *advertising agency*, for the placement of *advertisements* during a campaign. A media plan seeks to maximise the impact of the client's sales message on its *target audience*, within the constraints of the available budget; thus it will determine the duration of the campaign, the type of media to be used (e.g. television and magazines), and the specific media outlets (e.g. Channel 4, *GQ* magazine).

**media product:** any artefact created for the purposes of distribution through the *mass media*.

**media production:** the act of creating *media texts*, whether by professionals, amateurs or media students.

**media research:** that which measures media *audiences* for newspapers, radio and television. As well as determining its size, media research breaks an audience down into various categories such as age, sex, socio-economic class and geographical region. Once these facts have been established, the information is provided to advertisers in order to persuade them to buy airtime or other forms of *advertising* space.

**media sales:** an organisation, or department within a media organisation, that is responsible for selling *advertising*.

**media schedule:** a diary of forthcoming *advertising* and *publicity* events.

**media studies:** a combination of academic disciplines (including linguistics, literary and fine art studies, communication studies, sociology, economics, history and politics, philosophy and psychology) which has the processes and products of the media as its objects of study. The study of the subject at HE level emerged in the late 1970s and media-related degrees are very popular and often over-subscribed. The number of students taking GCSE and A level Media Studies has increased significantly since 2000, which fuels concerns (usually unhelpfully expressed when exam results are published in the summer) of the *dumbing-down* of secondary and higher education, regularly proclaimed by the right-wing media (such as the *Daily Mail* newspaper and pundits such as the MP Boris Johnson, on the one hand, and sceptics in the left-wing media, such as *The Guardian* (ironically the obvious choice of reading for media studies teachers and lecturers) on the other. (See also *media education.*)

**media technology:** any technological equipment that is used in the *production* or *consumption* of *media products*. This may include cameras, lights, microphones and all the other equipment needed for moving image production, as well as film projectors and DVD players needed to view them. In the days before the digital era and media *convergence*, media technology was often larger and more cumbersome (e.g. printing presses, analogue video editing suites, typewriters).

**media text:** a media product that is the object of study and analysis (e.g. a newspaper front page, film sequence or advertisement).

**mediation:** the process by which the media select, alter, interpret, edit or invent aspects of the world before presenting it to the *audience* in the form of *representations*. There is an important difference between mediated experience and one's direct personal experience. As a society we sometimes have more faith in the reality of mediated experience than in our own (e.g. the fascination with *celebrities* or the phenomenon of *moral panics*). According to the *tabloid press*, Britain is in imminent danger from ever-increasing levels of crime and terrorism, and from rapidly growing numbers of illegal immigrants and paedophiles. However, these concerns tend to reflect the media's ceaseless quest for news rather than the personal experience of most people.

**media triangle:** a reference to the three major areas of *media study*: *texts*, *audiences* and contexts (i.e. *producers* and societies). The media triangle is a useful way for students to remember the importance of all three when studying any individual topic.

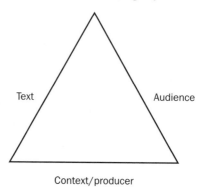

*The media triangle*

**Mediawatch-UK:** a pressure group that campaigns against violence, strong language, blasphemy, homosexuality and pornography in the media. Originally known as the *National Viewers and Listeners Association (NVLA)*.

**medium is the message, the:** the idea that the lives of human beings are influenced more by the very existence of a medium than by its content. 'The medium is the message' is a saying coined by pioneering media scholar Marshall McLuhan in his 1964 book *Understanding Media: the Extensions of Man.* McLuhan believed that the content of the media was of minimal importance compared with the impact of the media themselves. The *audience*'s experience of a medium varied depending on its form: hence film is a 'hot' medium because it expands the audience's vision, whereas television is a 'cool' medium because the picture is of lower resolution and therefore makes more demands on the audience to 'fill in the gaps'. However, this distinction has become less clear-cut with the universal practice of watching films at home on *DVD*, and the advent of *home cinema* and *wide-screen* television. Since the digital era has created a large measure of *convergence* between media, the differences between all of them have become less clear-cut.

**medium close-up:** see *cinematography*

**medium shot:** see *cinematography*

**medium long-shot:** see *cinematography*

**melodrama:** a film *genre* featuring straightforward conflicts between good and evil charac-ters, in which the good invariably triumph. Usually told from the female *protagonist*'s perspective, the *plot* and heightened emotional appeal, or *excess*, of melodrama take prece-dence over character and motivation. Derived from the Victorian theatre, melodrama was ideal for the *silent* era of cinema, with its *expressionist* acting style and simple plots (e.g. a moustache-twirling villain ties a fainting virgin to the railway track as the *hero* rides to the rescue on horseback).

**merchandising:** in the media, the practice of generating additional profits by *licensing* film or television characters for use in other media or in general product manufacturing, such as children's toys. One example is the *Disney* film *The Incredibles* (Brad Bird, US, 2004), which spawned an entire industry of products including books, CDs, posters, hats, boots, bags, 'bathtime playsets', video games, character models, cake decorations, sweets, backpacks, pillows, clocks, t-shirts and toothbrushes.

**merger:** the result of two or more companies combining. Mergers and takeovers are a feature of the business world in general, where they tend – in a lightly regulated environment – to forms large clumps, or *oligopolies*. This is the case in the modern music industry, which is controlled by four giant *multinational conglomerates*. In the early days of cinema, the '*majors*' were created through numerous mergers and takeovers of previously independent businesses. For example, *Warner Bros* merged with First National in 1929, thus acquiring its lucrative chain of theatres. In 1989, Warner Communications, as it had then become, merged with Time Inc to create *Time Warner*. Mergers have been criticised for reducing competition and consumer choice, and for creating the conditions for price-fixing.

**message:** an *ideological* conclusion, whether implicit or explicit, that producers expect audiences to draw from a *media text*, providing they accept its *dominant reading* (e.g. drugs destroy lives, racism is wrong, love is more important than money, all power corrupts). All media texts contain messages of one sort or another. More or less explicit messages are also known as *propaganda*. Implicit messages are less obvious and may escape many audience members altogether. Producer Sam Goldwyn famously criticised films with clear social messages: 'If you want to send a message, call Western Union.'

**messages and values:** *values* are the cultural *norms*, moral principles and priorities which every individual has learned, which give a personal and social context to the *messages*. Both messages and values are *ideological* in nature, and are encoded in all *media products* because media products are made by human beings. The combination of messages and values in a media text give it its *meanings*, which can be revealed through the process of textual analysis.

**metalanguage:** a language about language, for example, grammatical terms such as 'verb', 'noun' and 'adjective' or linguistic terms such as 'sign', 'index' and 'referent'. The terms of *film grammar*, such as 'cut', 'pan', 'track' and 'focus' are also metalinguistic, since they describe elements of the language of the moving image.

**metaphor:** a poetic device, a way of illustrating a concept by suggesting that it is the same as another concept. The nature of metaphor is more easily understood through examples: evangelical Christians describe themselves as 'born again', whereas in fact they were only born once. What they mean is that their conversion to Christianity was so radical and life-changing that it was *as if* they had been born again. Metaphor is frequently used in media texts, and may be visual as well as verbal. For example, a television commercial for shampoo might be set by a mountain stream in a beautiful woodland setting. This is a visual metaphor for the idea that the product is equally 'clean' and 'natural'.

**method acting:** an approach to acting in which the *actor* immerses himself in the role and seeks to 'become' that character rather than simply behave like him. For example, Daniel Day-Lewis prepared mentally and physically for the role of Christy Brown in his Oscar-winning performance in the film *My Left Foot* (Jim Sheridan, Ire/UK, 1989) by living in a wheelchair for the duration of filming and refusing to do anything for himself. Introduced by Lee Strasberg at the *Actors Studio* in New York, method acting, or 'The Method', describes a range of techniques designed to bring a lived sense of realism and authenticity to a role. Marlon Brando, Marilyn Monroe, Rod Steiger, Al Pacino and Robert de Niro are all well-known exponents of 'The Method', which was originally derived from the work of theatre director Konstantin Stanislavski in Moscow.

**metonym:** the use of a part of the whole to describe something bigger and more complex. For example, in news reports the Prime Minister and his many advisers are often described as 'Number 10', a metonymic reference to the Prime Minister's residence at 10 Downing Street in London. Similarly, '*Hollywood*', geographically a small part of Los Angeles, is a metonym for the whole corporate film and television entertainment industry based there. (See also *synecdoche*.)

**metrocentric:** a city-dweller's view of life that regards the interests of rural or suburban people as of secondary importance. The media are often accused of being metrocentric in outlook, for the simple reason that they are almost invariably based in cities.

**Metro Goldwyn Mayer:** see *MGM*

**metropolitan bias:** that held by a *metrocentric* person or organisation.

**metteur-en-scène:** dismissive term for a film *director* who does a professional job of making films, but whose work is neither consistently stylish nor personal enough to make him worthy of the term *auteur*. The French *Cahiers du Cinéma* critics divided directors into these two camps (e.g. 'Michael Curtiz is a mere metteur-en-scène.')

**MF/MFL:** abbreviation used by newspaper *sub-editors* at the bottom of a page of *copy* to indicate that there is 'more to follow' on subsequent pages (i.e. the article does not finish at that point).

**MGM:** Metro Goldwyn Mayer, one of the *major studios* of the *Hollywood studio* system era and still distributing and, to some extent, producing films today. At its height, MGM held some of the biggest stars in Hollywood under contract, including Greta Garbo, Clark Gable, Judy Garland and Fred Astaire. As America struggled to pull out of the Great Depression, followed by the Second World War, the studio developed a reputation for *escapist* glamour and fantasy in its films. Today, after numerous upheavals, MGM is owned by Sony. The company's value is partly based on its legendary name, but more particularly on its enormous *library* of films, said to be the world's largest.

**Mickey-Mousing:** in film, a term for the precise matching of *soundtrack* music to on-screen action. It derives from *Disney* animations, in which every movement of a cartoon character was exactly followed by the music.

**micro analysis:** a term specifically used in the WJEC Film Studies specification (but not in wider use), this is an analysis that examines the elements of *mise en scène*, *performance*, *cinematography*, sound and/or *editing*. The word 'micro' suggests that these elements can be observed and analysed in very short sections of a film. (See also *macro analysis*.)

**micro budget:** funds needed for media production when using modern digital technology, which enables every stage of the process – including *distribution* and *exhibition* via the *internet* – to be done at extremely low cost. The term most commonly refers to independent digital film productions.

**microphone:** a device for turning sound into an electrical signal. Sound, often from a voice, causes the microphone's diaphragm or ribbon to vibrate, and the resulting signal is sent down a cable. At the other end of the process it is reconverted into sound and emerges from a loudspeaker, sometimes greatly amplified. Microphones have a range of uses, one of the earliest being the telephone, and there are therefore of several different types with different pick-up or response patterns. These can be summarised as omni-directional, bi-directional and uni-directional:

- **omni-directional** microphones pick up sound from any direction, as the name suggests, and are useful for recording ambient sound

- **bi-directional**, or 'figure 8', microphones are generally of the ribbon type, and are able to pick up sound from both front and back simultaneously

- **uni-directional** microphones may be of a 'cardioid', 'hyper-cardioid' or 'shotgun' type, and have much tighter response patterns (i.e. they only pick up sound from the direction required). Shotgun mics are the most directional, and are thus used extensively used in film and television (often in conjunction with a *boom*), where it is important to record only the sound from a particular subject, and to exclude all others as far as possible.

Other types include lavalier or 'tie-clip' microphones (frequently used in TV studios, and wireless or radio microphones) which operate as transmitters and thus allow the voice to be recorded from a distance without the need for cables or a boom. (See also *cardioid mic.*)

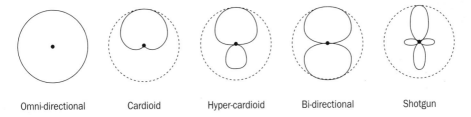

| Omni-directional | Cardioid | Hyper-cardioid | Bi-directional | Shotgun |

*Common polar patterns for microphones (microphone facing up in diagram)*

**Microsoft:** developers and owners of the Windows operating system used in the majority of the world's computers, and of the Office suite of software programmes which are also used internationally. Founded in 1975, has Microsoft made its founder Bill Gates the world's richest man. The company is important for the study of the media due to its involvement in the development of the *internet*, and its central role in the technology of media *convergence*. Microsoft has frequently been attacked for its business and employment practices, and for alleged abuse of its almost total monopoly in the market, which raises issues of *ownership and control*.

**mid-act climax:** the turning point in the second act of a *narrative*, a structural ingredient used in writing for the screen.

**middlebrow:** a description of mass market audiences and media which are neither *highbrow* (high culture) nor *lowbrow* (crass popular culture). Middlebrow products include newspapers like the *Mail on Sunday*, musicals by Andrew Lloyd Webber and British *heritage* films like *Four Weddings and a Funeral* (Mike Newell, UK, 1994). The term is sometimes used in a negative way by highbrow critics, to describe a product designed for a lower-middle-class *audience* which lacks real taste and sophistication.

**middle class:** the large, middle tier of modern society (the highest tier being traditionally the aristocracy, a powerful but single-figure percentage of the UK population), consisting of people who are relatively well-educated and work in 'white-collar' occupations. Traditionally, middle-class people are more likely to be financially well-off and own their own homes than those from the *working classes*. However, this definition is highly problematic in contemporary contexts. (See also *social class*.)

**mid-market:** often used to describe the market position adopted by newspapers like the *Daily Mail and Mail on Sunday*, and the *Daily* and *Sunday Express*. A more neutral term than '*middlebrow*'.

**minority:** any social group that sees itself outnumbered by a majority who are unlike them in significant ways. Minorities include the disabled, homosexuals, people from various ethnic communities and speakers of minority languages.

**minor key:** in music, a scale in any key whose intervals correspond with one starting with A and played only on the white notes of a piano keyboard. The pattern of intervals from the first to the last note in an octave is therefore tone, semitone, tone, tone, semitone, tone, tone. In mood, the minor scale 'feels' sad and downbeat compared with the major scale.

**Miramax:** a film production and distribution company now owned by the *Disney* corporation. It was founded in 1979 by Bob and Harvey Weinstein, brothers who specialised in spotting *crossover* potential and applying mainstream promotional techniques to *independent* and *low-budget* films which might otherwise have been confined to *art-house* cinemas. This often produced unexpected hits with such films as *Reservoir Dogs* (Quentin Tarantino, US, 1992), *Clerks* (Kevin Smith, US, 1994), *Muriel's Wedding* (P J Hogan, Aus/Fr, 1995) and *The English Patient* (Anthony Minghella, USA, 1996).

**mise en scène:** the look of a film, derived from its use of sets and settings, lighting, colour, costumes, hair and make-up, props, actor movement and the overall placement and visual composition of these elements by the director. Mise en scène is a critical term, and is not used by industry professionals except in France.

**misrepresentation:** a printed or broadcast interview or report that fails to convey accurately what someone has said, or gives a distorted, one-sided or false impression of an event.

**mix:** (i) in television, an *edit* transition in which one shot fades out as another fades in, overlapping with it. In film this technique is known as a *dissolve*. (ii) a sound mix is the result of editing together sound material – dialogue, music, sound effects and ambient sound – so as to achieve the desired overall balance of volume levels and tones.

**MLS (medium long shot):** see *cinematography*

**mockumentary:** a piece of filmed fiction – usually comedy – in the guise of a *documentary*. One example is *Best in Show* (Christopher Guest, USA, 2000), the story of a Philadelphia dog show, told using such documentary techniques as interviews and behind-the-scenes footage, but performed by actors and largely scripted.

**modality/multi-modality:** many *new media* products are considered multi-modal in that they use modes from several different media and change the user–*text* relationship significantly, in order to create *meaning*. Andrew Burn and David Parker (2003) discuss this in their analysis of digital formats, including video/computer game *narrative*, which uses modes from several different media forms (web, book and moving image language) and requires the player to be a participant in the creation of the text's meaning, due to interactivity/role-play, as well as the more conventional *consumer*/spectator role.

**mode:** a particular manner or style used in moving-image production, where the word *genre* is too definite. Mode refers to the borrowing of a genre or *narrative* style (e.g. a thriller might be made in the *film noir* mode – with *low-key lighting* and hard-boiled *dialogue* – without actually being a full-blown noir itself).

**models of communication:** those which use diagrams in order to explain how people communicate. Since the late 1940s there have been numerous attempts, one of the simplest being Harold Lasswell's formula of 'who says what to whom in what channel with what effect'. Shannon and Weaver's influential model introduced a further element, that of '*noise*' (i.e. anything that somehow distorts or otherwise changes the message before it reaches the receiver). All these are 'transmission' models, based on the concept of communication as a one-way process, with an active sender and a passive receiver. In 1975 this was challenged by James Carey, who suggested that most communication is not carried out as a means of sending information, but is a matter of ritual, of exchanging shared values and beliefs. More recent theorists, particularly Denis McQuail, have cast doubt on the validity of these models in the light of technological developments such as the internationalisation of communication and the *convergence* of media resulting from the digital revolution.

**mode of address:** the manner, or 'tone of voice', in which the media 'speak' to their *audience*. The mode of address adopted by any individual media outlet is based on a mixture of knowledge and assumptions about the nature of the audience. For example, journalists on *The Sun* may imagine themselves addressing the typical driver of a white van (at one time the newspaper actually ran a regular column headed 'White Van Man'). It would be assumed that this person was *working class*, possibly self-employed, with a set of right-wing opinions. The mode of address of BBC 3's '60 Seconds' news bulletin is youthful and informal compared with that of Channel Four News, which adopts a more serious, 'concerned' tone.

**modernism:** a broad artistic and cultural tendency that rejects historical tradition and concentrates instead on simplicity of form and the importance of function over decoration. Modernism came about in art as a response to advances in science and technology, and the work of such revolutionary thinkers as Darwin, *Marx* and *Freud*, all of whom radically altered mankind's view of itself.

**mogul, movie:** a person at the head of any major film production organisation who has the power to decide which films get made and which do not. The moguls of the *Hollywood studio system* were domineering, autocratic men, such as Jack Warner at Warner Bros, Harry Cohn at Columbia, and the powerful independent David O Selznick.

**monitor:** a TV screen that allows the director and other crew members to see the image being recorded by a camera. In *multi-camera* environments such as a TV studio, a bank of monitors is used to help the vision mixer judge when to cut between cameras.

**monochrome:** in *photography* or *cinematography*, pictures shot in black and white, as opposed to colour. This includes black and white images that have been tinted with a single colour (as were many *silent* films).

**monomyth:** the idea that all the world's myths have the same fundamental structure. Developed by the scholar Joseph Campbell in his book *The Hero with a Thousand Faces* (1949) and adapted by screenwriting guru Christopher Vogler in *The Writer's Journey* (1992).

**monopoly:** dominance over a market by a single organisation. For example, until the arrival of *ITV* in 1955, the *BBC* had a monopoly over television broadcasting in the UK. Its radio monopoly was always threatened by *pirate* broadcasters (such as Radio Caroline) or those transmitting from overseas (particularly Radio Luxembourg), but officially it lasted until 1973, when the first commercial stations came on air.

**monster movie:** a *subgenre* of the *horror* film, in which the focus of interest is the threat posed either by a creature of vast size and power, as in *Godzilla* (Roland Emmerich, USA, 1998) or *King Kong* (Peter Jackson, USA, 2005), or a human being who has undergone some grotesque and catastrophic transformation, as in *The Fly* (David Cronenberg, UK/Can/USA, 1986).

**montage:** an approach to moving image *editing* in which images are not designed to flow seamlessly together as in the continuity system, but simply follow one another. Montage is the normal editing method in *documentary* and *advertising*. It was the style favoured by the Russian film makers of the 1920s, notably Sergei Eisenstein (1898–1948), whose idea of montage was to produce visual clashes. Eisenstein was the central figure in the development of the *Soviet montage* movement of the 1920s. As an openly propagandist film maker, Eisenstein's chief concern was to promote socialism to a largely illiterate Russian audience. In such films as *Strike* (USSR, 1925), *October* (USSR, 1927) and *Battleship Potemkin* (USSR, 1925), Eisenstein rejected the *continuity* techniques that had become established in the production of *Hollywood* and Hollywood-style films only a decade earlier. Instead, he based his style on 'intellectual *montage*', the jarring approach to editing in which shots do not slide harmoniously together, but create a series of visual clashes in order to force the audience to take a more active part in the creation of *meaning*. Ironically, the montage style is most frequently used today in advertising, a quintessentially capitalist form of *propaganda*. Eisenstein explored his theories of film in two books – *The Film Form* and *The Film Sense*.

**montage sequence:** one consisting of a series of *ellipses*, often using *dissolves* as shot *transitions*, with the object of compressing time. One example is the brief sequence in *Psycho* (Alfred Hitchcock, USA, 1960) where detective Arbogast goes from motel to motel in search of Marion.

**moral panic:** an overreaction on the part of the media – often the *tabloid* press – to some new or previously unknown social phenomenon which appears to pose a threat to the established order. Children and teenagers, particularly when they embrace some new form of media and/or technology (*video nasties*, *video games*, mobile phones), are most frequently seen as both the problem and its victims. Other recent examples of moral panics have included press campaigns against paedophiles and asylum seekers. They were first identified by the sociologist Stanley Cohen in his book *Folk Devils and Moral Panics* (1972). Cohen outlined the typical stages of a moral panic as follows:

- A condition, episode, person, or group of people emerge to become defined as a threat to social values or interests.

- Its nature is presented in a stylised and stereotypical fashion by the media.
- The behaviour is condemned by editors, religious figures or politicians; experts offer explanations and solutions.
- Ways of coping are evolved, and the condition disappears, submerges or deteriorates and becomes more visible.

**morphing:** an image manipulation technique in which shots are digitally combined to produce a visual transformation, often from one person into another. This was originally achieved by *cross-fading* two images, but today is done by computer software that calculates the corresponding features in each image, calculates the changes needed for one image to become another, and creates all the stages in between.

**morphology:** see *narrative* and *Propp, Vladimir*

**motif:** in film, this refers to any element in sound or vision that is repeated often enough to suggest an underlying thematic significance. For example, in Wong Kar-wai's *2046* (China/Fr/Ger/Hong Kong, 2004) the motif of Christmas Eve appears several times, perhaps suggesting feelings of anticipation.

**motion blur:** in *photography*, a lack of focus due to the movement of the subject. This can create a dynamic impression in an otherwise static photograph (e.g. of a racing car speeding around the track).

**motion control:** in film, the techniques used to create perfectly controlled moving image shots that are difficult for a manual operator to achieve, often when the *camera* and the subject are in close proximity. Motion control may involve the use of programmable computer settings to ensure that a camera can take difficult shots repeatedly in identical fashion. In some cases it may involve moving the subject, rather than the camera.

**motion picture:** an American term for *feature film*.

**MPAA:** the Motion Picture Association of America, an organisation formed by the major studios in order to represent them, and also to manage the voluntary American film rating system.

**MPPC:** the Motion Picture Patent Company, a short-lived (1908–1917) forerunner to the *oligopoly* of the *Big Five* and *Little Three*. It consisted of the leading production companies, main distributor and leading supplier of film *stock*.

**motivation:** (i) the reason for the presence of any element in a film, including costume, *lighting*, camerawork and *editing*. In editing, 'motivating the cut' means that there was a specific reason for switching from one shot to another during a scene (e.g. from a wide shot to a close-up in order to show an object in more detail). In the same way if a character is lit from the side, there must be a motivation in the form of a visible light source from that direction (e.g. a window or table lamp). (ii) *character* motivation refers to the reasons why a character behaves in a certain way. An *actor* may ask the director 'What is my motivation in this scene?' in order to enact it more convincingly (e.g. pacing up and down because the character is waiting for an important phone call).

**movies:** now used in the same sense as *films* or *feature films*, the term movies was originally coined in the early days of *Hollywood* to differentiate them from still photographs.

**moving image, the:** film, television or any other technology that enables pictures to move.

**MPEG:** file formats used for digital video and audio that allow for compression. The most common are MPEG-1 (used in MP3 audio) MPEG-2 (used for digital television and DVD) and MPEG-4 (used for web streaming of video, compressing the quality of a DVD on to a CD, or making phone calls over the internet). MPEG is the acronym of the industry body Moving Picture Experts Group, which agrees the standards to be adopted.

**MS:** *medium shot*, in which the subject is depicted from the waist upwards.

**MTV:** influential *cable* television channel launched in 1981 to show pop music videos, although today it has largely moved into the *reality TV* market. An abbreviation of Music Television, MTV not only provided pop stars and record companies with a new shop window for their products, but caused them to consider visual presentation as an even more central part of their marketing effort than before. The non-stop nature of MTV led it to become a by-word for low *audience* attention span. Attempts to counter this with ever-faster editing in MTV's music videos influenced television and film editing generally, causing the average duration of shots on the screen to become greatly reduced. Numerous film *directors* (e.g. David Fincher, Spike Jonze) gained their first experience directing music videos for MTV. In later years the channel became notable for innovative *animation* (e.g. *Beavis and Butthead*) and for reality shows such as *The Osbournes.*

**mugging:** an overly self-conscious style of screen acting – particularly on television – in which the *actor* is too aware of the camera and tends to overact as a result.

**multi-channel environment:** that of modern television in the UK, in which an ever-growing number of channels competes for an ever-diminishing share of the viewing audience. (A similar process has taken place in radio.) The multi-channel environment emerged gradually, the *BBC*'s broadcast *monopoly* first being breached in 1955 with the launch of *ITV*. BBC2 followed in 1964, and Channel 4 in 1982. By the time Five, the newest of the *terrestrial* general interest channels, arrived in 1997, the environment was already changing rapidly: in 1989 Sky Television (now BSkyB) was launched, providing the UK's first broadcasting by *satellite* and its first subscription TV network. Today, the popularity of the digital *Freeview* platform has greatly increased the number of multi-channel households. Superficially multi-channel television has the advantage of providing audiences with greater choice, particularly with the arrival of *niche* channels devoted to specialist interests (e.g. comedy, children's programmes or science fiction). However, some critics have argued that more channels simply means more of the same.

**multi-camera production:** in television, programmes made using more than one camera at a time, particularly studio-based programmes and coverage of sporting events. Films are still primarily made using a single camera, although complex scenes and expensive special effects are likely to involve the use of several cameras.

**multi-media:** art or media that draws on a mixture of disciplines (e.g. written text, animation, photography, sound). The *internet* is essentially a multi-media environment due to the digital *convergence* of media that were once separate.

**multinational:** an organisation which is not contained within a single country, but operates globally and has headquarters around the world (e.g. Wal-Mart, *Microsoft*, General Motors). In the media, the major *Hollywood* studios are subsidiaries of multinational corporations (e.g. News Corporation owns 20<sup>th</sup> Century Fox as well as hundreds of newspapers and magazines around the world). There is widespread concern about the enormous wealth and power of the multinationals, many of which are now economically larger than some countries, but are not subject to the same scrutiny and accountability as elected governments.

**multi-stranded narrative:** one in which there is either no central *story*, or in which apparently separate strands eventually come together to form a central story. *Soap operas* are the commonest example of multi-stranded narrative, since it is a convention of the genre that several stories are being told in the course of any given episode. There are also examples in film, e.g. *Crash* (Paul Haggis, USA/Ger, 2004) or *Short Cuts* (Robert Altman, USA, 1993), where the characters' individual stories all turn out to be linked.

**multiplex cinema:** the modern standard for the *exhibition* of commercial films. The first multiplex in the UK was The Point at Milton Keynes, a 10-screen cinema that opened in 1985. Significantly, the previous year had been an historic low point in cinema-going, with only 54 million tickets sold nationwide. From this point on, more multiplexes were built and audiences began to rise, reaching 167 million in 2003. Multiplexes have several advantages over traditional town-centre cinemas, most of which were built in the 1920s and 30s: they offer a larger choice of films, with staggered screening times; they provide other sources of amusement such as restaurants and bowling alleys; and they feature good-quality seating, projection and sound.

**multi-skilling:** an individual's ability to deploy several skills in a job, thus increasing his versatility. For example, in the 1990s *BBC* reporters were expected to learn how to shoot and edit as well as report. The move was viewed with suspicion by the trade unions, who regarded it as a way of reducing the workforce by getting rid of specialists.

**multitrack:** sound recording technology that combines several sources to create the finished work. Most sound recording today is multitrack. Tracks can be recorded simultaneously or built up in layers of overdubs. For example, a rock band might play a tune together and be recorded simultaneously onto several tracks via a set of microphones and direct injection (DI) inputs. The band may then add vocal harmonies or instrumental overdubs, which are placed on additional tracks. Film sound is also built up in layers using multitrack techniques to ensure the correct *mix* of dialogue, music and sound effects.

**Mulvey, Laura (1941–):** see *male gaze, visual pleasure*

**murder mystery:** an enduringly popular dramatic *genre*, also known as a 'whodunnit', in which the focus of interest is a detective's quest to establish the identity of a murderer by discovering his motive, means and opportunity to commit the crime.

**music:** a form of art and/or entertainment consisting of sounds, usually punctuated by silences of varying duration. The exact definition of what constitutes music varies from culture to culture, and is often hotly disputed. In the western tradition, music is made up of rhythm, melody and harmony.

**musical:** a stage and film *genre* in which dramatic action and song alternate. As such, musicals are traditionally lacking in *realism*, on the grounds that people rarely burst into song with full orchestral backing in real life. Notable musicals of the past include *Singin' in the Rain* (Stanley Donen/Gene Kelly, USA, 1952), *West Side Story* (Jerome Robbins/Robert Wise, USA, 1961), *My Fair Lady* (George Cukor, USA, 1964), *The Sound of Music* (Robert Wise, USA, 1965) and *Grease* (Randal Kleiser, USA, 1978). Musicals are notoriously expensive to produce, and the advent of *music video* in the 1980s made them less attractive as commercial projects. However, their popularity on stage has resulted in a comeback for the film genre in recent years, with such productions as *Evita* (Alan Parker, USA, 1996), *Chicago* (Rob Marshall, USA, 2002) and *The Producers* (Susan Stroman, USA, 2005).

**music cue sheet:** documentation that must be completed by any radio, television, video or film production organisation when using *copyrighted* music. This is a legal requirement to ensure that writers, performers, producers and record labels receive payment for the use of their work.

**music video/promo:** a visual rendition of a piece of music, usually consisting of a single song, made as a means of promoting it to the public. As such, music videos are a *subgenre* of the TV advertisement, and hence a very cheap form of programming, since royalties do not have to be paid. Music videos became widespread in the 1980s around the birth of *MTV*, but there had been several forerunners, notably the jazz 'soundies' of the 1940s. (These were short 16 mm films made for playing on a special jukebox, and featured such artists as Nat King Cole, Louis Armstrong and Fats Waller.) The modern era of music video began with Queen's *Bohemian Rhapsody* (1975) and the Buggles' *Video Killed the Radio Star*, the first song to feature on MTV at its launch in 1981.

**myth:** (i) a story from ancient sources that narrates the adventures of gods, *heroes* and monsters from some distant or non-historical era (e.g. the myths of King Arthur and the Knights of the Round Table). (ii) a widely believed idea or story with no basis in fact (e.g. a falling cat will always land on its feet). (iii) a set of beliefs whose potency is derived from their perceived underlying truth. Myth in this sense is linked to *ideology*. For example, the myth that black people were lower on the evolutionary scale than whites supported the institution of slavery in the eighteenth and nineteenth centuries. Today's urban myths are also beliefs unconnected with facts, but they often reflect a wider paranoia about conspiracies between governments and the media to hide or distort the truth.

**NAG:** (acronym of 'news at a glance') short news summaries that give the main points of each story.

**Napster:** iconic MP3 file-sharing website operating between 1999 and 2002. Its service, which allowed music fans to *download* music free of charge, became the subjects of lawsuits by recording artists and record companies on the grounds that it violated *copyright* law. However, others have claimed that the promotional value of Napster and similar services can actually stimulate sales. The company was sold and now sells music, although other free file-sharing services such as Kazaa and Limewire continue to operate.

**narcissism:** *Freudian* term for self-love. In her explanation of the *male gaze*, Laura Mulvey argued that the *pleasure* experienced by film *spectators* when they identify with the male *hero* is narcissistic.

**narrative:** a story, whether factual or fictional. Narrative is a *macro* element in any film, which can only be understood by looking at the film as a whole. The term 'narrative structure' describes the way a story is told, and during the twentieth century numerous theorists constructed various models of the process:

- Vladimir Propp studied Russian folk tales, and detected in them an underlying narrative structure consisting of eight character roles, or 'spheres of action' and 31 possible story events or 'functions'. His 1928 book *The Morphology of the Folk Tale* was later appropriated by film scholars to analyse story structure in films.

- Claude Lévi-Strauss is an eminent anthropologist who studied tribal *myths* and argued that they contained sets of *binary oppositions* that revealed the deep structure of the myths and hence their relevance to a society's innermost beliefs.

- Roland Barthes identified different narrative devices or *codes* in film and television drama, such as the *action code*, suggesting to the audience that an action is about to take place, and the *enigma code*, planting a mystery in the story.

- Tzvetan Todorov (who coined the term 'narratology' for the study of narrative) suggested that all narratives begin in a state of *equilibrium*, or balance, which is then upset by some event, and the story continues until a new and different equilibrium is established.

- David Bordwell and Kristin Thompson have described such aspects of narrative as range and depth – respectively the amount of information available to the audience at any given point, and how much of a character's point of view the audience shares.

- In his 1997 book *Story*, Robert McKee examined film narrative from the point of view of the screenwriter, insisting that all effective films have a three-act structure, and that action is always more important than dialogue.

- Christopher Vogler, another screenwriting 'guru', also emphasised the importance of story structure in *The Writer's Journey* (1999), arguing the enduring power of traditional myths, and seeing in them underlying structures reminiscent of Propp.

By convention, different *genres* adopt different narrative structures: those of a *soap opera*, for example, are *multi-stranded* and *open-ended*, whereas films usually achieve narrative *closure*.

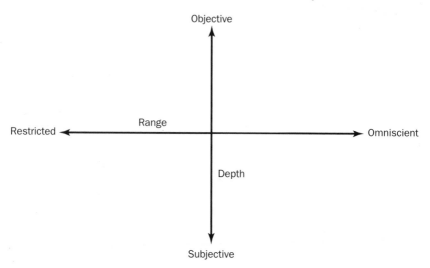

*Narrative range and depth*

**narrative film:** a term used to refer to fictional cinema as opposed to *documentary*.

**narrative trajectory:** the overall shape of a story and its characters, also known as the *story arc*.

**narrator:** the person whose *voice-over*, or narration, we hear on the soundtrack of a screen *drama* or *documentary*, adding thoughts and interpretations. In drama, the narrator may not always be trustworthy, but it will be his story that we see and hear. Sometimes several narrators are present, as in *Election* (Alexander Payne, USA, 1999).

**narrowcasting:** the idea that in today's *multi-channel environment*, *audiences* actively choose to receive certain *niche* television channels and programmes, which means that producers target them rather than the *mass audience* suggested by the term *broadcasting*.

**national cinema:** that which reflects the concerns, culture and history of a particular nation, as opposed to cinema that is designed to appeal to a broad international *audience*. British cinema has often veered between these two approaches.

**National Film and Television Archive:** a huge collection of nearly 800,000 largely British films and television programmes held at Berkhamsted, Hertfordshire, by the *British Film Institute*, including film classics, rare silent films, and a wide range of TV material such as advertisements and soap operas.

**National Film Theatre (NFT):** cinema complex near London's Waterloo station, operated by the *British Film Institute* and housing three screens. It shows a wide variety of films and other moving image material, often grouped into 'seasons' featuring particular *directors* or *stars*; and hosts many educational events, talks and interviews. The NFT allows *audiences* to watch archive films and other rarities unavailable elsewhere.

**National Union of Journalists (NUJ):** a trade union representing journalists in both print and broadcast journalism.

**National Viewers and Listeners Association (NVLA):** a campaigning organisation active from the 1960s to the 1980s, whose mission was to put a stop to sex, violence and swearing on television. Among its successes was a campaign against *video nasties*, which resulted in the *Video Recordings Act* of 1984, regulating the content of videos for the first time. The NVLA was renamed *Mediawatch-UK* in 2001.

**naturalism:** a style of artistic presentation that reflects everyday reality, e.g. in the way characters talk and the appearance of their living conditions. By contrast, some cinematic or televisual styles adopt a deliberately artificial style, e.g. *German Expressionist* cinema or the romantic glamorous style of an *MGM* musical.

**NBC:** acronym of the National Broadcasting Company, one of the three traditional *free-to-air* television and radio networks in the USA (the others being CBS and ABC). NBC was founded in 1926 as a radio broadcaster.

**NCTJ:** acronym of the National Council for the Training of Journalists, an industry organisation that provides and accredits training courses for journalists on local and regional newspapers in Britain. National newspaper journalists will usually have achieved the NCTJ qualification at an earlier stage in their career. It consists of a preliminary exam, followed by further one taken within two years of starting work on a newspaper.

**negative:** the raw film *stock* loaded into a camera and exposed in the making of still photographs or moving *film* images. The negative is a valuable commodity, since any damage to it will affect every print. In order to create film prints for screening, the negative must be developed in a laboratory and an 'interpositive' print struck from it. *Exhibition* prints are then struck from an 'internegative' struck from the interpositive. This process protects the original negative.

**negative cutter:** the member of a film crew whose job is to physically cut and splice sections of the original camera negative in accordance with the *editor*'s instructions.

**negativity:** a *news value* that reflects the news media's preference for bad news over good news. In other words, when things go according to plan there is no excitement and hence no story.

**negotiated reading:** according to the sociologist Stuart Hall, an interpretation that *audiences* make of *media texts* in which the *preferred* or *dominant* reading is recognised and broadly accepted, but with reservations and modifications reflecting personal circumstances and experience.

**neo-noir:** modern *film noir*, i.e. films made since the 'classic' noir period, which is usually considered to have ended with Orson Welles's *Touch of Evil* (USA, 1958). Neo-noirs often omit or modify certain generic conventions, e.g. *Chinatown* (Roman Polanski, USA, 1974) does not feature typical noir lighting, and in *The Last Seduction* (John Dahl, USA, 1994) the *femme fatale* has become the *protagonist*.

**neo-realism:** a film style first developed in Italy in the second half of the Second World War, emphasising the lived social conditions of the time – see *Italian neo-realism*. Neo-realism was and continues to be highly influential on such modern directors as Ken Loach (*My Name is Joe*, Sp/Ital/Fr/UK/Ger, 1998; *Sweet Sixteen*, UK/Ger/Sp, 2002) and South American directors like Walter Salles (*Central Station*, Braz/Fr, 1998) and Fernando Meirelles (*City of God*, Braz/Fr/US, 2002).

**network:** a distribution system for television programming in which the content is produced centrally (i.e. in a major city) and fed out to a system of geographically widespread stations. Examples include the *BBC* in the UK, CBS in the USA and ABC in Australia.

**New American Cinema:** an idealistic film movement launched in New York in 1962 with the object of making experimental, *low-budget* films free from the constraints of producers, financiers and studios. Film makers such as John Cassavetes were influenced by *Italian neo-realism*, the *French new wave*, the English *Free Cinema* movement and other European ideas, including those of the *avant garde*.

**New German cinema:** a renaissance in German film-making which lasted from the late 1960s to the early 1980s. Films made during the period include *The Goalkeeper's Fear of the Penalty* (Wim Wenders, West Ger/Aust, 1972), *The Bitter Tears of Petra von Kant* (Rainer Werner Fassbinder, West Ger, 1972), *The Lost Honour of Katharina Blum* (Volker Schlöndorff/Margarethe von Trotta, West Ger, 1975), a remake of *Nosferatu* (Werner Herzog, West Ger/Fr, 1979), *The Marriage of Maria Braun* (Fassbinder, West Ger, 1979), *The Tin Drum* (Volker Schlöndorff, West Ger/Fr/Poland/Yugoslavia, 1979) and *Fitzcarraldo* (Herzog, Peru/West Ger, 1982).

**New Hollywood, The:** young film makers hired by the Hollywood studios between the late 1960s and mid-1970s to recapture its dwindling youth market. Directors who emerged at this time included Mike Nichols (*The Graduate*, USA, 1967), Dennis Hopper (*Easy Rider*, USA, 1969), Bob Rafelson (*Five Easy Pieces*, USA, 1970), John Schlesinger (*Midnight Cowboy*, USA, 1969), Martin Scorsese (*Taxi Driver*, USA, 1976), as well as some who had already established a reputation, including Arthur Penn (*Bonnie and Clyde*, USA, 1967) and Sidney Lumet (*Dog Day Afternoon*, USA, 1975).

**new journalism:** style of journalism originating in the 1960s, involving a more personal, *subjective* style of reporting than was conventional at the time, and borrowing techniques from literary fiction. Among the exponents of the new journalism were Tom Wolfe, Norman Mailer, Truman Capote and Joan Didion.

**new media:** media that first appeared in the digital era, including web pages, email, *podcasts* and *blogs*.

**new wave:** any group of artists who appear to challenge the established way of doing things, whether in the form of a conscious 'movement' or as a collection of individuals who come to public notice at around the same time. In addition to the French *new wave* in film, there were notable new waves in Czechoslovakia and Brazil in the 1960s, and more recently in Hong Kong, Taiwan and South Korea.

**news:** information about recently occurring events, reported through a variety of means, whether by word-of-mouth or through the media. What constitutes news – the *news agenda* – is always a matter for debate, since the inclusion or exclusion of a topic is subject to a variety of factors, principally the target audience, the *producer*, and the existence of *news values*. News is also open to accusations of *bias* due to the effects of *ideology*, political *spin* and commercial manipulation. In the UK, bias in reporting is permitted in the print media and the *internet* but not in the broadcast media, which are required to abide by the rules laid down by *Ofcom* regarding fairness and balance.

**news agency:** an organisation, also known as a 'wire service', which supplies news stories to its subscribers in the print, *internet* and broadcast news media. Among the best known are Reuters, Associated Press and UPI.

**news agenda:** what is considered to be news at any given moment. The question of who controls the news agenda is key to the political life of any country, since it governs which issues are talked about and which are not. The news agenda is therefore often a battle-ground between politicians and the *editors* and proprietors of newspapers.

**news anchor:** a television or radio presenter who reads the news, conducts interviews with newsworthy people and discusses stories with correspondents (journalists) in the field.

**news copy:** the text of stories written by journalists.

**News Corporation:** a *multinational* media *conglomerate* with assets in newspapers, magazines, television, film and book publishing. Its founder and chief executive is Australian-born Rupert Murdoch. In the UK, News Corporation owns *The Sun*, *The News of the World*, *The Times* and *Sunday Times*, book publishers HarperCollins, and 38 per cent of BSkyB. In the US, it owns *20$^{th}$ Century Fox* film studios and the Fox television network, and in Australia, at least 22 newspapers. In Asia it owns the Star satellite television network, with reportedly 300 million viewers in 53 countries.

**newsgathering:** the *pre-production* process of obtaining news prior to writing it up. Sources include news agencies, telephone calls and interviews, press releases and field reporting.

**newspaper:** printed medium whose main focus is news, but which also includes some pro-portion of opinion, entertainment and advertising. Newspapers may be local, regional or national, *tabloid* or *broadsheet* (or *Berliner*, in the case of *The Guardian*), daily or weekly, paid for or *freesheets*. The first newspapers in the UK appeared at the end of the seven-teenth century, but they only gained large circulations as literacy became widespread in the nineteenth century. The newspaper industry is self-regulating under the supervision of the *Press Complaints Commission*, which deals with complaints from the public and operates a voluntary code of conduct. This includes guidance on such matters as accuracy and the right to reply, the naming of children in court cases, intrusion into grief and invasions of privacy. Newspaper circulations have been in overall decline for several years as more people obtain their news through the *internet*.

**Newspaper Society:** trade body that represents UK local and regional press.

**newsreel:** filmed news reports screened in cinemas up until the 1960s, when they were finally supplanted by television news. Newreels only became redundant when video editing and satellite transmission of stories were introduced, thus bringing reports to TV audiences more rapidly.

**news values:** the values that govern how newsworthy a story is considered to be by the media. Twelve news values were identified by Galtung and Ruge in 1965, and have been accepted with minor modifications ever since. The twelve are grouped under three headings (impact, audience identification, and pragmatics), as follows:

* impact – threshold, *frequency*, *negativity*, unexpectedness and unambiguity

* audience identification – *personalisation*, *meaningfulness*, references to *elite nations*, references to *elite persons*

* pragmatics – *consonance*, *continuity*, and composition.

**next matter:** in print *advertising*, literally anything that is placed next to an advert, which may or may not be linked to it.

**NIB:** (acronym of 'news in brief') a section in a newspaper (commonly a column on the front or inside page) in which news stories are presented in summary form, often with page references to the location of the full story. (See also *NAG*.)

**niche audience:** one with a particular *demographic profile* or special interest, as opposed to a general interest or *mass audience.* With the steady increase in media outlets during the latter part of the twentieth century, the mass audience gradually fragmented, to be replaced by numerous niche audiences. In the digital era, with its cheaper production and distribution methods, the niches have become far more numerous.

**niche marketing:** that which targets a *niche audience* rather than trying to appeal to everybody.

**nickelodeon:** in early twentieth century USA, a small storefront business showing silent films. The nickelodeon was the forerunner of the cinema, charging a nickel (five cents) for entry to see a mixed selection of short films (comedies, *melodramas*, travel films, sporting events) accompanied by a pianist or organist. Nickelodeons died out as they were replaced by purpose-built movie theatres.

**nitrate film:** type of film used for making prints until 1951, when it was replaced by 'safety film'. The use of nitrate film in the first half of the century is a major reason for the disappearance of so many early films, since it tended to deteriorate rapidly and was highly flammable – able to burn even under water.

**noddy shot:** a television camera shot in which an interview subject and/or interviewer 'nods' or reacts in some other small way, apparently in response to what the other person is saying. This gives the editor something to cut to, providing some minimal visual variation to the interview. Noddy shots are often taken before or after an interview has been completed.

**noirish:** having some quality of a *film noir*, for example *low-key lighting* or a dark, crime-oriented theme.

**noise:** generic term for the many possible reasons why even the simplest messages can be misunderstood or not received at all. Noise is a concept forming part of the *Shannon and Weaver model* of communication. It suggests that the message sent is not always the one which is received, since noise – some form of distraction and interference – often gets in the way.

**non-diegetic:** a sound or visual element of a fiction film that does not exist in its *diegesis*, the imaginary world created by the film. For example, soundtrack music and various forms of screen text (captions, titles, credits) are non-diegetic, because they cannot be seen or heard by the characters.

**non-fiction:** any media product whose content is not imagined narrative. This is most easily understood in relation to genres: the non-fiction moving image genres include *news*, *current affairs* and *documentary*. In film, non-fiction films are often documentaries, but can also be abstract or associational – terms used by David Bordwell and Kristin Thompson to refer to *art-house* and *avant garde* films.

**non-linear editing:** *digital video* editing, as opposed to *analogue* editing. Analogue editing requires shots to be assembled sequentially, while non-linear editing, carried out using computer software, allows pictures and sounds to be added or removed at any point on the timeline.

**non-linear time:** that represented in a dramatic *narrative* where events are not shown chronologically. An extreme example is the film *Memento* (Christopher Nolan, USA, 2000), in which the scenes appear in reverse order. Another is *Pulp Fiction* (Quentin Tarantino, USA, 1994), whose narrative structure does not become clear until the end of the film. The American TV drama *Lost* also features numerous instances of past and present events becoming mingled.

**non-verbal communication (NVC):** ways in which people convey meaning in person without the use of words. Also known as body language, non-verbal communication includes physical *gestures*, facial expressions, touch, tone of voice, eye contact, proximity, and even clothing (e.g. the wearing of the Muslim veil). NVC is an important area of study since research has shown that it has a greater impact than words.

**normalisation:** the process of making ideas and practices appear 'normal', for *ideological* or political reasons. Normalisation is a key function of the media, since the media are the fastest and most comprehensive channels of communication. For example, if the government needed to justify using torture on a regular basis – something that is not considered a social *norm* in the UK – it could mount a sustained *propaganda* campaign to make it acceptable to he public. Torture could be justified on the grounds that those to be tortured pose an imminent threat to national security.

**norms:** a society's ideas of correct behaviour, enforced with varying degrees of severity. Failure to observe customs, such as saying 'please', 'thank you' or 'excuse me' usually result in nothing more serious than frowns and mild complaints. More serious breaches of social norms, such as public nudity or acts of violence, are punishable by law. Norms change over time: for example, the wearing of long hair by men was once seen as an act of rebellion or *deviancy*, but is now largely regarded as acceptable. In more recent times, facial piercings and tattoos initially went against the norm, whereas today they are common. The media therefore becomes a site for debate and comment about norms, where traditional-minded and right-wing commentators usually seek to define breaches or changes to norms as signs of deviancy and national decline.

**nouvelle vague:** see *French new wave*

**novelisation:** the process of adapting a film into a novel. This reverses the more common practice of adapting novels into films.

**NPA:** abbreviation of the Newspaper Publishers Association, a trade body that represents the interests of national newspapers in Britain.

**NRS:** abbreviation of the National Readership Survey, an organisation that estimates the readerships of newspapers and magazines in the UK. These figures are arrived at through interviews with a representative sample of the population, and provide publications and advertisers with an objective estimate of the numbers of readers of a publication, as opposed to actual sales.

**NTSC:** technical standard for analogue television transmission in North America, Japan and certain other countries. NTSC (the National Television System Committee) is made up of 525 continuously scanned lines on a television screen, making it less detailed than the European PAL system, which uses 625 lines.

**NUJ:** see *National Union of Journalists*

**nut:** (or house nut): the amount of money that needs to be taken at the *box-office* in order to cover the costs of a cinema's overheads (wages, heating, lighting, air conditioning, general maintenance) during opening hours. Any income beyond the 'nut' is therefore profit.

**NVC:** see *non-verbal communication*

**NVLA:** see *National Viewers and Listeners Association*

**Do you need revision help and advice?**

Go to pages 251–292 for a range of revision appendices that include exam advice and tips.

**OBC:** abbreviation of *outside back cover*, a term used in magazines.

**obit/obituary:** a published or broadcast account of a recently deceased person's life. *Broadsheet* national newspapers run daily obituaries of prominent people.

**objectification:** the practice of treating human beings as if they are objects, without feelings or any sense of dignity. *Feminist* critics have long argued that women are objectified by the media because they are so often represented only in terms of their sexual attractiveness, not as a whole person.

**objective:** the type of dramatic screen *narrative* that positions the *spectator* as a dispassionate observer of the scene, as opposed to a *subjective* sharer of a character's viewpoint. Objective narration is the *norm* in screen *drama*.

**objectivity:** the quality of observing and assessing an issue with personal detachment and a concern to establish the facts, rather than impose one's own opinions or preferences. Objectivity is particularly valued in *news* reporting, where a cool appraisal often sheds more light than a one-sided emotional reaction. However, many reporters argue that true objectivity is impossible, particularly in war zones or other areas where innocent people's lives are in danger from armies or militias, or where people are the victims of government incompetence or extermination campaigns.

**object of the gaze:** a screen character who is looked at by the *audience*. The term is used in studying *spectatorship*. According to critics who draw on *psychoanalytical* theory, the film spectator's gaze involves either *narcissistic identification* with a character or *voyeuristic objectification* of them. (See also *female gaze; male gaze; spectator.*)

**Obscene Publications Act:** law last updated in 1964 to prevent the publication of sexual material that 'tends to deprave and corrupt' (i.e. *pornography*). Although still in force, the Act is rarely invoked today due to the near impossibility of proving in court that a person has been depraved or corrupted by something they have seen or read.

**observational documentary:** one which, according to critic Bill Nichols, allows the film maker to 'record unobtrusively what people did when they were not explicitly addressing the camera'. The style adopted for observational documentary is usually *fly-on-the-wall* or direct cinema, in which participants appear not to be conscious of the camera. This supposedly creates the conditions for an accurate and reliable portrait, but the need to make choices in the editing process make it less *objective* than it might appear.

**obsolescence:** see *built-in obsolescence*

**occult horror:** *subgenre* in which the story involves such themes as Satanism and devil-worship, supernatural evil and demonic possession, e.g. *The Exorcism of Emily Rose* (Scott Derrickson, USA, 2005) or *Rosemary's Baby* (Roman Polanski, USA, 1968).

**Oedipal narrative:** one in which the (usually) male *protagonist* is subject to the psychological pressures outlined by *Freud* of seeking to overthrow the patriarchal power of the father by killing him, literally or figuratively, and taking possession of the mother. Among many examples of the Oedipal narrative in film are those of Alfred Hitchcock; and *Blue Velvet* (David Lynch, USA, 1986). *Feminism* has criticised this kind of narrative for its focus on the male, assertion of male power and the positioning of the female as *'other'*.

**Ofcom:** official body with responsibility for regulating commercial (i.e. non-BBC) broadcasting and the mobile phone industry. Among its many duties, Ofcom handles complaints from viewers and listeners and issues licenses for broadcasting. It replaced five other regulatory bodies, including the *Independent Television Commission* and the *Radio Authority*, when it began operating at the end of 2003.

**off-air:** (i) anything that takes place in a broadcast environment but is not transmitted to the public. Hence, for example, a comment made after the microphones have been switched off in a radio studio is referred to as 'off-air'. (ii) an off-air recording is one made of a broadcast for later viewing or listening (e.g. a television programme).

**Official Secrets Act (1989):** this Act of parliament governs what information may or may not be published in the media or in books, regarding issues of national security or intelligence (among others).

**offline:** (i) when a computer is not currently connected to the *internet* it is referred to as being 'offline'. (ii) offline *editing* of film is done digitally after the original *footage* has been copied, in order to protect it from damage; in video, offline editing takes place as a means of protecting the original analogue tape. In both cases, editing decisions made at the offline stage are acted on during the final *online* edit.

**off-screen action:** any part of a screen narrative that is important to the story but is not seen by the *audience*; for example, the robbery that is the central event in *Reservoir Dogs* (Quentin Tarantino, USA, 1992), but is not shown.

**off-screen sound:** any sound in a screen *narrative* whose source is not visible. A common technique in *continuity editing*, off-screen sound can be used to cue an *audience* to some impending event, such as the sound of a rattling door handle preceding a character visibly entering a room. It can also create slapstick comedy.

**oligopoly:** dominance over a market exercised by a few large organisations. During the *Hollywood studio system* era, the film industry was dominated by the oligopoly of the *Big Five* and the *Little Three*. (See also *duopoly, monopoly*.)

**omni-directional:** see *microphone*

**omniscient:** a film *audience* that knows more about the story than any single character within it is said to be omniscient, or 'all-knowing'. This *narrative* term is at one end of a sliding scale, with *restricted* at the opposite end. Audience knowledge is always somewhere between the two, although towards the end of a typical film, omniscience is the norm.

**on air:** when a *live* television or radio broadcast is in progress, the programme, its presenters and production team are said to be 'on air'.

**on-demand:** see *video on demand*

**online:** (i) when a computer is connected to the *internet* it is referred to as online; computer users also refer to themselves as being online when using the internet. (ii) online *editing* of film or video is carried out once the edit decisions have been made in the *offline* edit.

**op-ed piece:** a newspaper article in which the author expresses a clear opinion about a topic.

**opening weekend:** the make-or-break period at the very beginning of a film's *theatrical release*, which determines whether it will be commercially successful. *Distributors* therefore discover very quickly the likelihood of making a profit on their new release.

**open sign/text:** one which is ambiguous, i.e. not *anchored* by written text or other indications of its *preferred reading*, and hence is open to a variety of possible interpretations. (See also *polysemic*.)

**opinion poll:** a representative survey of public views on any issue or set of issues, including voting intentions. Opinion polls are the lifeblood of modern politics, since they indicate the likely outcome of elections.

**opportunities to see (OTS):** the number of times the *target audience* for an advertisement is exposed to it. Calculating the number of opportunities to see is a key factor in determining the effectiveness of an *advertising* campaign.

**oppositional cinema:** that which argues against established social *norms* and power structures, highlighting the plight of marginalised and oppressed people. Oppositional cinema often makes use of unconventional or *avant garde* techniques, thus distancing itself from conventional *Hollywood* practices. (See also *counter cinema*.)

**oppositional meaning/reading:** meaning or reading that recognises but refuses to accept the *dominant* meaning or reading of a *text*. This does not simply refer to disagreement with the sentiments expressed but also with all the cultural assumptions that go along with it. For example, a newspaper columnist might call for more prisons to be built to ease overcrowding. An oppositional reading might reject the whole idea that prisons are the answer to tackling crime.

**optical effect:** any *special effects* technique in film that is carried out in *post-production* on the film itself. Optical effects include adding *transitions* such as *fades* or *dissolves*, secondary images, *freeze frames*, or the use of *matte* techniques. Today, such effects are usually achieved digitally using computer software.

**optical sound:** sound that is encoded as light patterns alongside the visual images on a film strip. As the film runs through the projector, the light patterns are converted into electrical signals and then back into sound.

**option:** a film or television production company that buys the *rights* to a *property* (usually an original *screenplay* or a book) is said to have 'optioned' it. This means that the company may exercise the right to produce the script or *adapt* the book into a film or TV drama at any point during the period of the option. If no production takes place, the rights revert to the original author and may be sold again.

**original screenplay:** a film script written from scratch i.e. one that did not originate in any other medium (such as a novel, cartoon or television series).

**o/s:** 'off-screen', a scripting term for action that takes place outside the camera frame or sound whose source is not visible.

**Oscar:** the more commonly used term for an *Academy Award*. Presented at an annual ceremony held each February in *Hollywood* since 1928. The Oscars come in 24 categories, the most prized of which are Best Picture, Best Director, Best Actor and Best Actress. Due to the enormous publicity generated by the Oscars, any film that gains one of the top awards following its original release is virtually guaranteed to enjoy a profitable second run, and to sell well on *DVD*.

**OSD:** abbreviation of on-screen display.

**OSS:** an *over-the-shoulder* (camera) *shot*, one in which the subject of the shot is filmed from behind a person's head and shoulders, which are framed to one side in the foreground. An OSS is commonly used in drama when two characters are holding a conversation, or in interviews in factual production, where it can be used in a *shot/reverse shot* sequence.

**'other':** a representation that positions a social group as somehow different and alien from, and inferior to, the *norm* (i.e. those who wield power in any given society). The concept of the 'other' has been influential in feminist criticism, which has suggested that women become 'other' in a male-dominated society. *Homosexuals* and *ethnic minorities* are equally liable to be considered 'other'.

**OTS:** see *opportunities to see*

**out-cue:** in radio scripts, the sound that indicates to the presenter the end of a programme or segment (e.g. the final words of an interview or a piece of music).

**outside back cover:** see *OBC*

**outside broadcast/OB:** a radio or television programme transmitted from a location, as opposed to a studio. In television, the technical centre of any outside broadcast is a mobile studio known as an OB van, in which the crew carry out all the usual functions of vision and sound mixing, recording and editing, and transmit the results back to base.

**out-take:** any scene filmed but not used in the final edit of the programme or film, due to mistakes made within it by cast or crew. Comical out-takes are popular with television *audiences*, and for many years have formed the basis of an entire *genre*, originated by ITV's *It'll be All Right on the Night*. Out-takes have also featured in the end credits of *comedy* films such as *Bend it Like Beckham* (Gurinder Chadha, UK/Ger/USA, 2002), and were included in *Antz* (Eric Darnell/Tim Johnson, USA, 1998), despite the fact that in an *animated* film the 'mishaps' were obviously scripted and *staged*.

**overcrank:** see *film speed*

**overhead shot:** also known as a *bird's-eye view* shot, this camera shot is directed vertically downwards towards the subject. Not to be confused with a *high-angle* shot, which is not vertical.

**overlapping sound:** where sound from one scene continues into the next, or where the sound from the next scene arrives before the accompanying picture. This technique, also known as a *sound bridge*, can be used to improve continuity between scenes. When the dialogue spoken by characters in a drama overlaps, it can create a sense of increased *realism*, since it is closer to the speech patterns of real life.

**overlay:** term used in television production for screen *images* or *captions* that are used to accompany a voiced commentary, as in *news* reports.

**over-the-shoulder shot:** see *OSS*

**ownership and control:** a key issue in *media studies*, since the identity and political agenda of an individual who owns and controls a media organisation is often reflected in the products it makes. When ownership and control of *news* media is concentrated into the hands of a small but extremely powerful *elite*, it can influence the political process.

Notoriously, the *right-wing Sun* newspaper – owned and controlled, along with three other national newspapers, by Rupert Murdoch's *News Corporation* – claimed to have secured the narrow victory of John Major in the 1992 general election. Its relentless personalised campaign against Labour leader Neil Kinnock may have been decisive: the headline it used after the election was 'It Was *The Sun* Wot Won It'.

**What other subjects are you studying?**

A–Zs cover a range of different subjects. See the inside back cover for a list of all the titles in the series and how to order.

A
B
C
D
E
F
G
H
I
J
K
L
M
N
O
P
Q
R
S
T
U
V
W
X
Y
Z

**pace:** the *audience*'s sense of the speed at which events are proceeding. In moving image media, pace is generated by a combination of factors: *editing, cinematography, narrative, soundtrack* and *performance* can all contribute. At extreme ends of the scale, a *high-concept action film* would tend to be relentlessly fast paced, while an *observational documentary* would be consistently slow paced. Most media products, however, make use of a variety of pacing techniques.

**package:** in TV and radio *news*, this is a pre-recorded and edited segment on a news item, which is inserted into a live programme. (See also *packaging*.)

**package-unit system:** the way in which most *Hollywood* films are now made. For each film, the *producers* have to assemble a *package* of necessary elements, such as personnel, equipment, locations, sound stages and catering. These are leased or contracted on a short-term basis from a variety of sources, as needed for the duration of the production. An agency package is where a large creative *agent* can offer a *producer* many of the film's elements in a single deal. For example, this might include a literary *property*, a *screenwriter* and several *actors*. This approach replaced contract-based *unit* production used during the era of the *Hollywood studio system*, which was ended by the *De Havilland decision* and the *Paramount Case.*

**packaging:** (i) a generic term for the overall style and structure of a TV show. It is most often used to describe the enhancement of *news* with dramatic music, *CGI* animations, slick *editing* and charismatic *presenters*. The term tends to be used pejoratively, suggesting an emphasis on style, rather than substance. The packaging of TV news and *documentaries* has been *satirised* by Chris Morris in *The Day Today* and *Brass Eye.* (ii) an important element in the *marketing* of a *media product* can be the type of casing in which it is supplied. Typically, this packaging is designed to make the product seem more interesting or substantial for the purchaser. In the music industry, records and CDs are often elaborately packaged with artwork, lyrics sheets and other material. From the point of view of the *record labels*, a problem with the *digital* revolution is that *downloaded* music comes without any packaging at all, and therefore the power of this element of marketing has been diminished. In some other digital media, packaging is used extensively to compensate for the apparent lack of a product. For example, *video games* are expensive but the discs themselves are very small. Games manufacturers tend to package their products in large boxes, far out of proportion to the size of the discs, with the intention of convincing the consumer that the product is worth its £50 price.

**PACT:** see *Producers' Alliance for Cinema and Television*

**PAL:** one of three systems for colour TV broadcasting, the other two being *NTSC* and *SECAM.* PAL is the commonest, and the form used in the UK, as well as most of Europe.

**pan:** a horizontal *camera* movement left-to-right or right-to-left on a fixed axis. The word is short for 'panoramic movement'. A pan following a moving object suggests that we are viewing it from the point of view of an observer. Pans are also used to reveal elements of the *mise en scène*, for example, during an *establishing shot.*

**panaglide:** a competitor to the *steadicam*, developed by *Panavision* in the 1970s.

**pan and scan:** a technique for presenting *widescreen* films in a 3:4 ratio for presentation on TV. The film would be scanned, with the *camera operator* following the main action on screen (by panning). Since these films had originally been composed for widescreen, most film enthusiasts consider panned and scanned versions to be inferior to the alternative *letterboxing* technique. Since the advent of *DVD* and widescreen TV, panned and scanned versions of films have become less common.

**Panavision:** a major manufacturer and supplier of film equipment, including cameras, to the industry. Panavision operates exclusively as a rental business, and does not sell any of its equipment.

**panel game:** a type of *game show* in which teams are generally composed of celebrities, and the competition is of secondary importance to the entertainment provided by witty and/or knowledgeable talk between the teams. The *genre* has a long history in radio and TV. Examples include *Through the Keyhole*, *Eight Out of Ten Cats* and *Never Mind the Buzzcocks.*

**paparazzi:** photographers whose sole job is to take pictures of celebrities, ideally in private or revealing circumstances. The paparazzi have a reputation for unscrupulous and aggressive intrusion into the lives of the people they photograph. The word derives from the character 'Paparazzo' in Fellini's *La Dolce Vita* (Italy, 1960).

**paper edit:** in film-making and video production, a plan of basic editing decisions, written down in advance of actually editing the work.

**paradigm:** a set of units of meaning, each of which is distinct from the rest, but which can be selected and combined to form different *syntagms.* At a simple level, a musical scale is a paradigm; a tune made by arranging notes from the scale is a syntagm. A *genre* (for example the *western*) can be seen as a paradigm, and each example of a genre product (for example, *How the West Was Won*) is a syntagm.

**paralanguage:** the ways in which an individual can communicate in addition to, or instead of, using words. Physical *gestures*, tone of voice, facial expression, posture, grunts and hesitations are all elements of paralinguistic communication. Paralanguage is a key element of *performance.*

**parallax:** the difference in the way an object will appear against its background when viewed from two different positions. When using a *camera* with a separate *viewfinder*, rather than looking through the *lens*, the photographer needs to compensate for the small parallax between the viewfinder and the actual lens. Motion parallax is the sense of movement created by shifting the observer's point of view; in a *tracking shot* past a stationary object, for example. In early *video games*, motion parallax was often used to create a sense of horizontal movement.

**parallel action/parallel editing:** usually, synonyms for *cross-cutting.* However, parallel action can also take place when the screen is split (i.e. divided into several frames) as in the TV series *24.*

**parallel narrative:** where two stories are presented so that the *audience* can compare and contrast them. For example, the main plot of the *romcom When Harry Met Sally* (Rob Reiner, USA, 1989) depicts two characters each suffering a series of unsatisfactory relationships before eventually realising that they should be married to each other; meanwhile, in a parallel *subplot*, their two best friends fall in love at first sight and immediately embark on a highly successful marriage.

**parallel sound:** see *synchronous sound*

**Paramount:** one of the major studios of the *Hollywood Studio System*. Now owned by *Viacom*.

**Paramount Case:** legal proceedings brought successfully against Paramount Studios in 1948 by the US government. The decision of the court was that the business practices of Paramount, and therefore all of the big studios, were illegal. The main outcome was that the studios were no longer allowed to be *vertically integrated* and were forced to sell off their chains of cinemas. This, along with the earlier *de Havilland decision* effectively ended the power of the studios. The end result was the development of the *package unit* production system of film-making in Hollywood.

**parody:** a comical imitation of a *narrative* or *genre*. *Scary Movie* (Keenen Ivory Wayans, USA, 2000) parodies the *horror* genre; *Hot Shots!* (Jim Abrahams, USA, 1991) parodies *Top Gun* (Tony Scott, USA, 1986). In TV, *Shooting Stars* was a parody *game show*. Sometimes the aim of the parody is merely comic; sometimes it is *satirical*.

**parole:** language as it is actually used. The *structuralist* thinker Ferdinand de Saussure distinguished between parole and *langue*, which is language as a set of rules. A dictionary or grammar book contains langue, while everyday speech is parole.

**passive audience:** the idea that viewers, listeners and readers accept without question the *messages* and *values* presented by the mass media. This view is now regarded as over-simplified and most modern researchers are interested in the ways in which *audience* members are *active*. (See also *hypodermic model*.)

**pastiche:** an imitation (sometimes comical) of a *narrative* or film *genre*. Similar to a *parody*, but more gentle and respectful to the original. For example, Tarantino's *Kill Bill* films, (Vol. 1 2003 and Vol. 2 2004) are mixtures of *French new wave* films, Sergio Leone's *spaghetti Westerns*, Japanese *samurai* epics and Hong Kong *kung-fu* films.

**Pathé:** a major French film company and record label. Internationally, the company was important as a *producer* and distributor of *newsreels* during the first half of the twentieth century.

**pathetic fallacy:** a narrative technique where the weather or other elements of the world mirror the emotional state of a character. The fallacy (or false belief) is that any individual's state of mind could possibly have an effect on meteorological conditions. Pathetic fallacy is a common technique in *expressionist* film styles. For example, towards the end of *Brief Encounter* (David Lean, UK, 1946), Laura finds herself caught in pouring rain just as she reaches a point of complete despair.

**pathos:** direct appeal to the emotions of the *audience*. The term is usually applied to *narratives* and other images that aim to create sadness. Charity advertisements often make heavy use of pathos.

**patriarchy:** male dominance in society. The term means 'ruled by fathers'. *Feminism* is critical of media texts that reinforce patriarchal *values.*

**patriotism:** support for one's own country. An important element of many newspapers' *ideological* positions. Extreme and uncritical patriotism is called 'jingoism'.

**payment by results (PBR):** a way of charging for *advertising* that is increasingly common on the *internet.* Forms of PBR include pay-per-click (PPC), where the advertiser is charged every time someone clicks on an advertisement; pay-per-lead (PPL) where the advertiser is charged only when a potential customer provides a form of contact, such as an email address, and pay-per-sale, which is when a charge is only made if the advertisement leads directly to a purchase.

**pay or play contract:** a legal agreement that fees will be paid whether or not the project goes ahead. In modern *Hollywood*, this type of contract is routinely offered to the highest-paid *stars.* Pay or play guarantees that the star will still be paid if the project is abandoned, or even if he or she is fired. This means that recasting tends only to take place under very extreme circumstances.

**pay per view (PPV):** where a charge is made direct to the viewer for each individual TV set showing a single programme. PPV events tend to be films, pornography, important sporting fixtures or music concerts by major artists. They can be either *scheduled* or *video on demand.* Supplied by *cable* and DST operators, any PPV purchases are added to the customer's monthly bill.

**pay TV:** all TV services for which a charge is made to the user. In this context, the *licence fee* is not considered to be a charge. (See also *free-to-air.*)

**PCC:** see *Press Complaints Commission*

**peak time:** the period when most TV viewing or radio listening takes place. For UK television *audiences*, this is defined by *BARB* as between 6 pm and 11 pm. In radio, peak times differ according to the station's *target audience.* The American equivalent term is primetime.

**pedestal shot:** a *camera* move in which the camera is lowered or lifted; for example, to follow an actor as she stands up. Should not be confused with a *tilt.*

**penetration:** a term used in various media and *advertising* contexts to describe the proportion of a total *audience* or *market* that is reached. For instance, a radio station's marketing pack might tell potential advertisers that it has 'excellent penetration in the lucrative 18–25 student market'. Brand penetration means the percentage of potential buyers who are aware of a specific product – it is the job of advertisers to create brand penetration for their clients. Market penetration is the strategy of pricing a new product so that it becomes widely used.

**peoplemeter:** a device given to each individual household that has agreed to contribute to the *BARB* TV ratings. The peoplemeter registers which members of a household are watching TV at any time. This information is then matched to the programmes viewed throughout the day. The system allows BARB to identify not just what was watched, but who was watching it.

**peplum movie:** a film set in ancient Rome or Greece, usually with a biblical, mythological or historical theme. The peplum is a short tunic that featured in the costume of most of these films. Many *Hollywood epics*, such as *Spartacus* (Stanley Kubrick, USA, 1960) and

*Gladiator* (Ridley Scott, USA, 2000), are peplum movies. They are also known as 'sword and sandal movies' and 'toga films'. The Italian film industry produced a large number of *low-budget* peplums during the 1950s and 1960s.

**perception:** at its simplest, this is the system by which the brain converts information from the senses into *meanings*. For example, the eyes receive light that has bounced off an oak tree; they convert this information into signals which are sent via the nervous system to the brain. These signals are then processed and recognised as an oak tree. However, the more sophisticated the information, the more *subjective* the process of perception becomes. This is important in media texts, which can involve complex *subliminal* or *connotative* messages. An image of an oak tree in an advertisement for a bank, for example, could be **perceived** as connoting stability, tradition, length of time and Englishness. (See also *schema theory*.)

**performance:** the contribution made by an *actor* to a *narrative*. Because of the dominance of *genre theory* and *auteurism* in film theory, performance has been a relatively neglected area of study. However, the work of the actor is a major factor in the creation of meaning. Performance for the camera, or for the radio microphone, requires different skills from stage acting. For example, since an actor's face will be expanded to many times its real size on a cinema screen, even the smallest facial movement can communicate a great deal. There are many approaches to acting, and fashions change over time. For example, James Cagney's performances in *gangster films* of the 1940s appeared gritty and naturalistic when the films were released, but his style seems artificial to a modern audience.

**performative documentary:** see *documentary*

**Performing Right Society (PRS):** the body that collects *royalties* for musicians and composers.

**period drama:** any *narrative* that seeks to recreate an earlier time in history. A characteristic of the period drama is its careful creation of a convincing *mise en scène*. This 'period atmosphere' is a key audience *pleasure* of the *genre*. The setting may be far in the past, as in a *peplum movie*, or relatively recent. The BBC TV production *The Line of Beauty*, which was made in 2006 and set in the 1980s, would certainly qualify as period drama. Sometimes known as *costume drama*.

**periodical:** a magazine that is published at regular intervals. The various categories of periodicals reflect the period between *issues:* weeklies, fortnightlies, monthlies, bimonthlies and quarterlies.

**Periodical Publishers Association (PPA):** the trade organisation for the British magazine industry. The PPA looks after the interests of all British magazine publishers.

**periodicity:** an important *news value*. If a story can reach some point of completion within the news cycle it is more likely to pass through the *gatekeeping* process. For example, a murder is likely to be reported in a daily paper, since it will normally occur between the publication of two *issues*. The economic development of India is less likely to make news, because it occurs slowly over many years.

**persistence of vision** is the scientific principle behind moving images. The human visual system continues to 'see' an image for a fraction of a second after it has disappeared. This means that when we are shown a sequence of images, each slightly different from the last, the illusion of movement can be created.

**personalisation:** an important element in *news values*. The more a news story is built around individual *characters* (rather than abstract issues), the more likely it will be that the *audience* will engage with it. For example, the declining quality of school meals in the UK only became really significant when the *celebrity* chef Jamie Oliver began to campaign for a change in policy. News stories could then be constructed around his personality and public image.

**perspective:** (i) the visual clues that allow viewers to understand *spatial relationships* of depth within an image. A figure in the foreground appears to be much larger than a figure in the background. Perspective is an important element of *composition* and *framing*. (ii) A theoretical, *ideological* or political attitude. We might, for example, say that from a *feminist* perspective, many TV *sitcoms* would be seen as reproducing harmful gender *stereotypes*.

**PFL:** (pre-fade listen) button on a sound mixing desk that enables a channel to be listened to before the fader takes effect.

**PG certificate:** part of the UK age *ratings system* imposed on film and video material by the *BBFC*. Children are allowed in to see PG films unaccompanied, but parents are advised that they should check beforehand to make sure that the film is suitable for their child. In the case of video recordings, many retailers interpret the law as meaning that nobody under 15 is allowed to buy a PG video unless accompanied by a parent. Anyone over 12, however, can buy a video with a 12 certificate, though this is a higher certification than PG. The American *MPAA* system also includes a PG certificate.

**phallic:** concerning the penis or phallus. Many theorists, especially those influenced by *psychoanalysis* and *feminism*, suggest that penis-like images are used to connote masculine power. For example, in the *western genre*, which strongly values the ideas of male authority, strength and freedom, we can identify a large number of common phallic symbols, among which the gun and the horse are the most obvious.

**phallic woman:** literally, a woman with a penis. However, the term generally means a woman who presents certain 'masculine' characteristics, and is therefore seen by men as threatening. Phallic women characters can be found in *queer cinema*, but also in more *mainstream* texts such as the *comic book* and 1970s TV series *Wonder Woman*. In *film noir* and similar genres, the *femme fatale* character can often be described as a phallic woman.

**phatic:** elements of speech or gesture that do not communicate meaning or information, but are considered a necessary part of language. The anthropologist Malinowski gave the name 'phatic communion' to those parts of a conversation whose functions are either to establish that an interchange is beginning, or to keep it going while there is temporarily nothing meaningful to be said. A good example is the phrase 'How are you?' which occurs in many conversations but may not be a genuine request for information about the other person's physical or psychological state. One of the differences between written *dialogue* and real speech is that it tends to contain very little phatic communication, while real conversation uses it a great deal.

**phonograph:** an early form of sound recording invented in the nineteenth century. Phonograph recordings were the first example of a *time-based medium*.

**photographic truth:** the idea that the *camera* never lies. This has always been a myth. From the earliest days of the camera, photographers experimented in creating unreal images. For example, the Cottingley photographs of the 1920s fooled many intelligent people with their 'proof' of the existence of fairies. Today, with digital technology, it is possible to modify photographs much more convincingly. Even without altering the image, the *meaning* of a picture (still or moving) can be changed by *framing* and *composition*, *depth of field*, and *selective focus*. Perhaps most importantly, every photograph is the result of a photographer selecting a small segment of the whole view. In the context of the media, photographs for publication are selected from a range of possibilities, and the *editor* always looks for an image that best fits the message of the story it accompanies. Nevertheless, a photographic (or filmed) image is still likely to be seen by audiences as in some way 'true'.

**photography:** originally a chemical process for creating still, two-dimensional images of the real world. The first black and white photographs were achieved in 1793. The idea was developed commercially by Daguerre in France and later by Fox Talbot in Britain. At the beginning of the twentieth century, the Eastman Company introduced a process using celluloid rolls of film and small inexpensive cameras became available to the general public. Colour film became generally available from the mid-1930s onwards. During the early years of the twenty-first century, chemical film processes were largely replaced by digital photography. Traditional *analogue* photography was a relatively complex, costly process, and unless individuals were willing to invest space, money and time in a darkroom, there was little control over the way the final image would look. Since the introduction of digital photography, which requires neither film nor processing, the photography industry has been revolutionised. It is now possible to take massive numbers of photographs (a memory card can hold hundreds, even thousands, of images) without the prohibitive costs of chemical processing. The ordinary amateur can easily process and modify photographs, using computer software, and the results can either be stored electronically or printed out. Basic cameras are now so cheap and small that they can be attached to a keyring or integrated into a mobile phone. Online communities such as FlickR allow amateurs and professionals to share their images with the rest of the world.

**photo-journalism:** as soon as technology made it practical to print photographs in papers, the photographer became a critical element of the news-gathering process. The *halftone* process introduced in 1915 meant that *black and white* photographic images could be printed with the full tonal range, and this led to an awareness that *news* photographs could be dramatic and interesting in themselves. Thus, the presence of a good photograph became an important element of *news values.* The mid-twentieth century saw the growth of popular magazines based around documentary-style photographic *features*, such as *Life* in the USA and *Picture Post* in Britain. That style of photojournalism has declined, but in today's newspapers only the most minor items and *filler stories* are not supported by a photograph, while many stories are *picture-driven.*

**photomontage:** a trick *photography* technique, originally involving the physical cutting and pasting together of images from different photographs to produce a new image. Photomontage has been used, for example, by artists to create strange and/or meaningful *juxtapositions;* and by hoaxers to 'prove' the existence of UFOs, Bigfoot or the Loch Ness Monster. With the advent of digital image software, it is now possible to create sophisticated montage effects relatively easily.

**photo opportunity:** a chance to take a publishable photograph, usually in a *news* or *celebrity* gossip context. The opportunity may occur without the intention or consent of the photograph's subject (as is frequently the case with the *paparazzi*). Alternatively, the opportunity may be deliberately staged. Two world leaders shaking hands at a *press conference* would be one example of a manufactured photo opportunity.

**photorealistic:** looking like a photograph or filmed image. The term is used to describe computer graphics, such as *CGI*, that have been created with the intention of looking 'real', rather than the stylised images that are used in some productions. For example, the giant ape in Peter Jackson's version of *King Kong* (USA, 2005) is rendered photorealistically, whereas the fish in *Finding Nemo* (Andrew Stanton/Lee Unkrich, USA, 2003) are much more stylised.

**photo-story:** a *genre* of printed narrative, similar to a cartoon strip, but using photographs instead of drawings. Photo-stories were at one time a common feature of teenage girls' magazines. Brief photo-stories can still be found in the *agony columns* of *tabloid newspapers*, where the narrative usually concerns a relationship problem involving an attractive young woman in her underwear.

**picture-driven/picture-led:** a *journalistic* term referring to any story in which the image is the most telling aspect. The *news* coverage of the attacks on the World Trade Centre, for example, was dominated by the image of two planes crashing into the Twin Towers.

**picture editor:** (i) in the publishing industries, a person who has overall responsibility for the selection and placing of pictures within the publication. (ii) a piece of software used for making alterations and improvements to digital images.

**picture palace:** a name for *cinemas* in use during the early days of the industry. The term was probably suggested by the opulent, art-deco influenced design of many cinemas.

**pilot:** a single episode of a TV programme, made as a test so that TV executives can assess the likelihood of success. Sometimes, a pilot leads to the commissioning of the programme, usually it does not. The pilot episode can be broadcast, usually as the first episode of the commissioned series, but often the *production values* are lower than the eventual series, or significant changes, such as recasting, have taken place, making this impossible.

**Pinewood Studios:** a collection of *sound stages* and *back lots* in the grounds of an old manor house on the outskirts of London, used for a variety of film and TV productions, including most of the James Bond films. Although many British films have been shot at Pinewood, it is also often used for *Hollywood* productions such as *The DaVinci Code* (Ron Howard, USA, 2006). Since 2001, Pinewood has been part of the same company as Shepperton Studios, a similar organisation, also on the outskirts of London.

**piracy:** in a media context, refers to the *distribution* and especially sale of unauthorised copies of a product, such as a DVD, CD, MP3 or video game. Digital technology has made the manufacture of high-quality pirate copies easy and cheap. The creative industries are engaged in a constant war against piracy, mostly through the use of *encryption* or digital rights management (DRM) software, which makes it difficult to reproduce the material. However, this approach is controversial. In the first place, most DRM can be beaten by a determined programmer. Second, DRM prevents users from making legitimate copies – for example, the DRM on audio CDs can stop the user from making an MP3 version of the recording. Third, new forms of DRM can prevent discs from working in older machines.

**pirate radio:** unlicensed broadcasting. During the 1950s and 1960s, when the *BBC* held a *monopoly* on UK broadcasting, a number of **pirate stations** operated, often from ships (hence the term 'pirate'), broadcasting mainly *pop music* and financing themselves with *advertising*. When the BBC launched its first pop music station (Radio 1), many of the first *DJs* had previously worked for pirate stations like Radio Caroline.

**pitch:** a basic characteristic of sound, caused by the frequency of the sound's waveform. The effects of pitch on an *audience* depend on *context*. Low-pitched music can be used to reinforce tension or comedy; high-pitched notes can evoke the flight of birds or (as in the famous *Psycho* shower scene) emphasise a stabbing blade. The pitch of an *actor's* voice is an important element of *performance*. For example, the deep, resonant voice of the actor James Earl Jones has led to his being cast repeatedly as authority figures (including Darth Vader in the *Star Wars* series), while Joe Pesci's unusually squeaky, high-pitched voice means that he is generally cast as either a savage psychopath (*Casino*, Martin Scorsese, USA, 1995) or in comic supporting roles (the *Lethal Weapon* series).

**pitching:** selling an idea to someone who will pay to have it developed. In the film industry, a pitch is where a *screenwriter* describes the idea for a film to a *producer* in as exciting a way as possible in the hope that the project will be financed. Similarly, in TV, writers will pitch an idea to station executives, perhaps aiming to have a *pilot* produced. An *advertising* pitch is an attempt to convince a potential client that an agency's idea for a *campaign* will benefit the client's product. Because film producers are notoriously short of time and difficult to impress, while hopeful screenwriters are notoriously desperate, *Hollywood* pitching has developed into an intense process. There are numerous theories regarding the best ways to structure and deliver a pitch, as well as a number of terms for extremely short pitches. An 'elevator pitch' is one that can be delivered while the producer is temporarily trapped in a lift with the writer. Producers will often look for a 30-second pitch, or even a 3-second pitch. Allegedly, the 3-second pitch for *Alien* (Ridley Scott, USA, 1979) was 'Jaws in space'. Some commentators would argue that such short pitches are a symptom of *dumbing down* in Hollywood. It is certainly true that it is an approach best suited to *high-concept* films, which tend to be based around very simple ideas.

**pivot shot:** a *pan* or *tilt*.

**platform:** a specific form of hardware used to deliver media content. The term is most commonly used in relation to *new media*. For example, Microsoft's X-Box 360, Sony's Playstation 3 and Nintendo's Wii are all competing platforms for *video games*.

**platform game:** an early type of two-dimensional *video game* in which the *avatar* must avoid various obstacles, while jumping and/or climbing up a series of platforms in the process. Some 2-D platform games, such as Nintendo's *Donkey Kong* and *Super Mario* were successfully expanded into more sophisticated 3-D adventures, which retained some of the jumping and climbing elements of the originals but added new material, such as puzzles and fighting. Nevertheless, these games will still sometimes be described as platform games or platformers. More straightforward platform games (such as *Super Mario Brothers*) continue to be popular on small hand-held consoles.

**platform release:** a strategy used by the distributors of *low-budget* and *independent* films. A small number of prints are made and released in the hope that good reviews and/or *word-of-mouth* will develop as a consequence, causing the film to grow in popularity. Profits from the initial release can then be used to fund wider distribution. A successful platform release can take several weeks, or even months, to build an *audience*. This approach is the reverse of the *saturation release* and *opening weekend* philosophy used in the marketing of expensive *Hollywood* films.

**player:** *Hollywood* and media slang for a person who is to be taken seriously in the business, such as a *producer*, a studio executive or a big *star* who is also involved in the *production* side of film-making. The term is also used in other industries. Robert Altman's 1992 US film, *The Player* tells the story of the downfall of a studio executive, played by Tim Robbins.

**playlist:** (i) the list of tracks that can be played by *DJs* on a music radio station, as decided by the station managers, and usually updated on a weekly basis. The playlists for different times of the day may vary as part of the station's dayparting strategy. (See also *scheduling*.) (ii) a pre-ordered list of tracks created by an individual user. Playlists can operate on personal computers or MP3 players.

**pleasure:** individual enjoyment. Pleasure is a key element of *spectatorship*-based approaches, especially in film studies. You might, for example, say that an attraction of film *genre* is that the *spectator* can find pleasure in predicting the *narrative* (when it follows *conventions*) and a different kind of pleasure in being surprised (when the narrative breaks conventions). One of the most influential essays in *feminist film theory* is Laura Mulvey's 'Visual Pleasure and Narrative Cinema', in which she argues that the pleasures of conventional cinema are all *masculine* ones.

**plot:** although this term is often used interchangeably to mean *story* and *narrative*, plot is best understood as being somewhere between the two. Story is a basic set of events; plot is an outline of the structure by which these events will be unfolded; narrative is the complete, finished work. Bordwell and Thompson point out that *plot* is what the *audience* see or hear in the presentation of the film (i.e. that which is controlled by the director) and *story* is the sense the audience make of it when they put it all together (which may include events beyond the film's plot). (See also *fabula*.)

**plug:** to promote something (often a related media product) within a broadcast, publication or film. The final pages of most magazines contain a plug for the next issue. *Product placement* is a way of subtly plugging a *brand* within a film.

**plug and play:** a system for adding new hardware to a computer without the need to install extra software. This makes the use of digital media devices, such as video cameras, far easier to manage.

**pluralism:** a concept originating in *sociology* that emphasises the different groups within a society. From a media studies perspective, the idea has a number of applications:

i.    One set of pluralist approaches are *audience*-based ones that explore the ways in which the same *message* or text can have very different *meanings* and consequences according to the *social class*, religion, *ethnicity* or political position of the person who receives the message.

ii.   Another approach questions the extent to which the *producers* of *media texts* reflect the plurality of society, and criticises the media for their predominantly white, heterosexual, middle-class, middle-aged London-centred *perspective*.

iii.  The term also refers to a model of the *ideological* effects of the media. The pluralist model suggests a 'circuit': the audience reacts to media messages and then the media producers react to the audience, producing new messages, which in turn produce new reactions, and so on. This is considered plural because no individual group is responsible for imposing *ideology* on the audience. However, as David Morley has pointed out, this model has to take account of the fact that some groups in society have a more powerful 'voice' than others.

**podcasting:** a form of broadcasting via the *internet*. Most podcasts are similar to speech radio programmes and can be *downloaded* in *MP3* and/or other compressed audio formats. The term combines 'broadcasting' with the name of Apple's popular iPod audio players. Video podcasts include short film or animation clips that can be played on a computer or a video-enabled portable player. The term 'podcast' was probably coined by the journalist Ben Hammersley in a *Guardian* article in 2004.

**point-of-sale advertising:** consists of posters and other promotional materials placed in or around the outlet where a product is sold. The aim is to encourage an immediate purchase.

**point-of-view shot:** a camera angle in which the viewer seems to see with the eyes of a character in the scene. Also called a *POV*.

**policier:** French term for a *genre* of *narratives* (in TV, film and popular literature) about official police investigations. Policiers usually involve detectives rather than uniformed beat officers. The French TV series *Engrenages* (broadcast in the UK as *Spiral*) is an excellent example, as are various US productions, such as *CSI* and *Cold Case*. Also known as police procedural.

**political allegory:** a *narrative* in which characters and events stand for real politicians and political events, usually with a *satirical* aim. The allegory may be direct, as in the animated film of George Orwell's novella, *Animal Farm*, in which individual animals stand for real Russian revolutionaries. Alternatively, the allegorical relationship may be more general. For example, the 1987 *science-fiction* film, *Robocop* (Paul Verhoeven, USA) can be seen as an allegory about the power of technological and media conglomerates in America, but there is no reference to any specific corporation.

**political correctness (PC):** a pejorative term invented in the 1980s, and associated with the left of the *political spectrum*. PC is mostly concerned with equal treatment for women and minority groups such as gay men, lesbian women, ethnic minorities and people with disabilities. The two main characteristics associated with PC attitudes are a belief in *positive discrimination* and the avoidance of offensive or careless language (such as referring to people with disabilities as 'cripples'). The term is mainly used by people on the right, especially when claiming that such attitudes are being carried to ridiculous extremes. During the late 1980s, the *tabloid* press created a *moral panic* about 'loony leftie' London councils, which included claims that the word 'blackboard' had been outlawed in London schools because it might offend black children. Most of these stories were later revealed to have been exaggerated.

**political incorrectness:** the deliberate adoption of non-PC attitudes and language, often for comic purposes and sometimes as a reaction to the idea that political correctness is an attack on freedom of expression. Some political incorrectness is a straightforward expression of attitudes that would now be seen as *racist*, homophobic, misogynistic or unacceptable in some other way. Other examples are more complex, as when the aim is *satirical*.

**political interference:** where the government attempts to influence some element of the media. Usually, the subject of interference would be *news* or news-related. In democratic societies, such as the UK, it is considered unacceptable to *spike* or rewrite stories simply because they might make the government look bad. Some aspects of national security cannot be reported by law. These are covered by the *Official Secrets Act*.

**political spectrum:** the range of views and attitudes held by individuals or institutions regarding the way society should be organised. What follows is a very simplified summary. At the extreme ends of the scale are the far right (fascism) and the far left (communism). Although there are small fascist and communist factions in the UK, British politics tends to be concentrated on the centre ground. The modern British right-wing can be described as having two main characteristics: conservatism and libertarianism. Conservatism is the desire to hold on to established values (e.g. respect for the police, church-going and for some, fox hunting). It is based in deep-seated support for the *social class* structure. Traditionally, members of parliament for the Conservative (or Tory) Party have come from a higher social class background, though over time this has changed, resulting in new attitudes developing. Libertarianism, a strongly individualistic belief that state control and regulation should be minimised, came into force within the new right in the Tory Party during the 1980s. The British *left-wing* is dominated by the Labour Party. Its traditional roots are in the working class and trade unions. Left-wing politics are often connected with higher taxation with the aim of spending more on public services. This idea, that there is a shared social responsibility, contrasts with the individualistic attitude of the libertarian right. A left-liberal approach is one that is not just concerned with social class, but generally wishes to create greater equality, social improvement and change – through reduced racism, more opportunities for women and so on. Those critical of such an approach often describe it as *political correctness.* In recent years, there has been ever greater crossover between the positions of the two main British political parties and the main battle for power has not been between the left and right but for the centre ground. The Labour Party has taken on a number of libertarian ideas and the Conservative Party has adopted traditionally 'leftist' language such as 'social justice'. Also, the Liberal Democrats have been taking positions that are left of Labour.

**politique des auteurs:** the 'auteur policy' suggested during the 1950s by the French *critic* and film *director* François Truffaut. 'La politique' suggests that the director should be seen as the sole creator of each film. It distinguishes between two types of director: the *metteur-en-scène*, who is merely competent in the craft of film-making, and the *auteur*, who is a great artist. The idea was taken up enthusiastically by an American film critic named Andrew Sarris, who created a modified version called the 'auteur theory'. It is often argued that Sarris's influence on film criticism was indirectly responsible for the power and freedom given to such *Hollywood* directors as Francis Ford Coppola and Michael Cimino during the 1970s. Many critics, notably Pauline Kael, have argued strongly against auteurism, pointing out the importance of other factors such as film *genre* and the collaborative nature of film production, and with a few exceptions, in modern Hollywood, *stars* are now much more powerful than directors. However, among *cineastes* the director still tends to be considered the key factor in defining a good film. Most significantly in *independent film* production, where writer-directors like Jim Jarmusch are common, an auteurist approach continues to be central.

**polysemic:** having several possible *meanings*. Polysemy is a characteristic of *symbols* but not of *icons*. For example, a gun can have many symbolic meanings. It might be a *memento mori* (standing for the inevitability of death), it might be a *phallic* symbol (suggesting male power), it might represent hope or hatred or security, it might be an *action code* pointing to some later event in a *narrative*. The actual meaning will depend on the context in which we see the symbol.

A
B
C
D
E
F
G
H
I
J
K
L
M
N
O
**P**
Q
R
S
T
U
V
W
X
Y
Z

**pop music:** although the term is an abbreviation of *popular music*, pop is a particular *genre*, distinct from other forms such as rock or hip hop. The styles of pop music change over time, but we can identify a few common characteristics. The typical pop song is short, around three minutes or less; pop performers are relatively young; the *target audience* is predominantly female and youthful. Songs fall into two categories: bouncy, upbeat danceable tunes or romantic ballads. Pop stars often have very short careers before either disappearing from the public eye (like Andrew Ridgeley of *Wham!*) or changing their style to attract a different audience (like George Michael of *Wham!*).

**popping:** a form of unwanted audio distortion. Popping is a problem particularly associated with digital sound reproduction, where it is caused by the system trying to handle too much data at one time.

**popular culture:** literally, the *culture* of the people. Popular culture includes a vast range of material, including film, pop music, fashion and mainstream TV. The term is used by some cultural theorists (such as the *CCCS*) instead of the more traditional idea of 'low culture'. So-called '*high culture*' would typically include *elite* interests like opera, poetry and classical drama, and would be considered automatically superior to 'low culture'. This view is connected to a cultural decline model of media effects. The term popular culture – or pop culture – avoids this high/low idea and reflects a view that there may well be much that is of value in modern media products.

**popular music:** is any form other than classical orchestral or chamber music. The range of types of popular music is enormous, from traditional folk song to electronic; from the simplicity of two-chord punk to the complexity of free jazz. Some popular music (such as the stadium rock of U2) can attract *mass audiences*, while other *genres* (such as the antifolk performances of Jeffrey Lewis) remain confined to tiny *subcultures*. (See also *pop music*.)

**pornography:** any material in print, audio or *moving image*, whose main purpose is to provide sexual excitement. The distribution and content of porn is more strictly controlled than other genres. (See also *R18 certificate*.)

**portmanteau film:** a film composed of several *shorts*. Also known as an omnibus film, a *vignette film*, or an anthology film. The shorts are usually linked to each other by a frame story, shared theme or linked characters.

**positioning:** the relationship between the *audience* and a *character* in a *narrative*. Sometimes the character is subsequently repositioned. For example, in *Thelma and Louise* (Ridley Scott, USA, 1991), the character of Thelma is positioned as a victim for the first half of the film, but repositioned into a powerful heroine for the last half. The audience first sympathises with her, and then admires her.

**positive:** the final stage in traditional processing of film *stock*. After filming, the exposed *footage* must be developed to produce a stable *negative* in which all values are completely opposite to reality – light appears dark, white appears black, red appears blue and so on. This image is projected onto unexposed film, which is processed to produce the positive. This footage can then be edited.

**positive discrimination:** actively trying to improve opportunities for women and/or minority groups. Many media *institutions* operate a policy of positive discrimination in job interviews, giving preference to (appropriately qualified) people who belong to under-represented groups. There may also be positive discrimination policies in relation to the writing and casting of *fiction genres*, usually with the aim of improving *representation*.

**post-colonial film:** literally any movie made in a country, such as India, that was previously a colony of another. However, the term would usually be applied to a film such as Satyajit Ray's *The Chess Players* (India, 1977) that deals explicitly with issues of colonisation. The study of postcolonial film is part of a more general approach known as post-colonial theory.

**posters:** large sheets of printed paper designed to be stuck to walls in order to communicate a message. Posters need to be understood quickly and therefore tend to depend on visual images and short *slogans*. The famous First World War recruiting poster depicting Lord Kitchener pointing his finger at the viewer and the slogan 'wants YOU' is a classic example. Film posters have developed a particular style of their own, communicating *genre* elements and aspects of *narrative* along with *stars*, *titles*, *taglines* and *proprietary elements* in a concise visual package.

**postfeminism:** a set of approaches to social and cultural studies based on the idea that *feminism* is no longer useful. One line of argument in postfeminism suggests that we are now living in a society whose values have been partly determined by feminism. For example, while traditional *films noirs* presented women quite straightforwardly as dangerous *femmes fatales*, neo-noir films like *House of Games* (David Mamet, USA, 1987) often reflect an understanding of the arguments raised by feminism about the representation of women. Since feminism is now actually an element of these postfeminist *texts*, a traditional feminist reading would be inappropriate.

**post-heritage cinema:** films that seem superficially to belong to the *heritage genre* but which include criticism of the society they represent, often from a *feminist* point of view. The term was first used by Claire Monk in her 2001 essay 'Sexuality and Heritage'

**postmodernism:** a set of ideas that replaced *modernism* as a way of interpreting society and *culture*. Postmodernism covers a wide range of philosophical, sociological, psychological and critical perspectives. Its key characteristic is disbelief in the idea of *objective meaning*. From a postmodernist point of view, there is no such thing as 'truth', only individual ways of interpreting the world. Postmodernist *narratives* tend to be highly *self-reflexive* and make extensive use of *irony*. Postmodernist *criticism* is generally interested in the ways that the appearance of meaning is created.

**post-nationalism:** an aspect of internationalism and globalism. Post-nationalism suggests that the concept of individual nations has ceased to have meaning in a world where media communications over vast distances have become almost instantaneous.

**post-production/'post':** the various processes that take place after filming in order to create the *final cut* of a film. The major element of 'post' is the visual and sound *editing* of the film. The addition of the *score*, *special effects*, *sound effects* and any addition of *captions* all take place in post-production.

**post-synching:** see *dubbing*

**poststructuralism:** a form of *postmodernist critical theory* that challenges the basic idea of *structuralism* and argues that there are no 'underlying structures' to *texts*. From a poststructuralist point of view, structures are created by the *audience* as part of the process of interpretation. The author is unimportant. A key text in poststructuralist thought is Roland Barthes' 1967 essay 'Death of the Author'.

**POV:** see *point-of-view shot*

**power of the media:** the *mass media* have no direct power. Newspaper *editors* cannot, for example, call on armed forces or have individuals thrown into jail. However, the media do have a great deal of influence on the public. Consequently, politicians and other public figures are often keen to maintain good relations, especially with the *press*. It is probably impossible to be elected to government without the support of at least one newspaper. This makes figures such as Rupert Murdoch, with his massive media empire, very powerful indeed.

**power elite:** a group with high status and strong influence on society. The term was originated by the *Marxist sociologist* C Wright Mills in 1967. Control over the *mass media* is an important characteristic of most modern power elites.

**PPL:** abbreviation of Phonographic Performance Limited. PPL collects *royalties* on behalf of music performers and record companies. Anyone, such as a *radio station* or nightclub who plays recorded music in a public setting must first apply for a PPL licence so that royalties can be paid for every track played.

**PR:** see *public relations*

**praxinoscope:** an early form of *animation*, invented in the late nineteenth century. Based on a spinning cylinder, it resembled the earlier *zoetrope* but was a little more advanced in design.

**pre-credit sequence:** see *pre-title sequence*

**pre-echo:** a term used in TV *ratings* and *scheduling* to describe the portion of the *audience* who switch to a channel before their chosen programme begins. Schedulers sometimes try to take advantage of this. They may, for example put carefully selected *trails* into the pre-echo period.

**preferred meaning:** the interpretation that the maker of a *text* expects. Although the *audience* is *active*, and signs can be *polysemic*, there are normally some efforts made by the creators of the text to *anchor* the *meaning*. If you discuss the preferred meaning (also called the 'preferred reading') of a text, you are acknowledging those efforts but accepting the possibility that some or all of the audience might read the text in a different way from the preferred one, finding their own meanings in it rather than the ones that were put there by the makers. According to the sociologist Stuart Hall, the preferred meaning would normally be one that is in line with *dominant ideologies*. Of Parkin's three *meaning systems*, the dominant would be the preferred reading, while *subordinate* and *radical readings* would both constitute *aberrant decoding*.

**prejudice:** a judgement based on neither experience nor evidence. The commonest examples are negative prejudices about particular racial groups, often based on *stereotypes*. Prejudices can be positive or negative, however. For example, TV *presenters* with North-Eastern English or Scottish accents are perceived by the *audience* as more trustworthy. This is no more a fact than the prejudiced belief that a Birmingham accent is a sign of low intelligence. Nevertheless, the existence of these prejudices in the *audience* undoubtedly has an effect on the choice of presenters made by TV stations.

**premiere:** the first time a film is exhibited in a particular country. Premieres are designed to be large-scale media events. Usually one or more of the stars of the film will attend, and the *distributors* will hope to achieve as much *press* attention as possible.

**pre-production:** the period between a film project being given the *green light* and the start of filming. It is a time of detailed planning and preparation. The *shooting schedule* is prepared, any *sets* are built and the crew is assembled. Everything that needs to be done to ensure that the project runs as smoothly as possible takes place during this period.

**prequel:** a *sequel* that tells the story leading up to the previous film. For example, *The Scorpion King* (Chuck Russell, USA, 2002) is a prequel to *The Mummy Returns*, set 5,000 years before the previous film, and based on the *backstory* of one of its minor characters.

**pre-sales:** a key element of modern film financing. In order to raise money to make the film, the *producers* will sell *distribution rights* while the production is still at the *screenplay* stage. A consequence of this is that the distributors, who have invested in the production, will often wish to interfere in such matters as *casting*.

**presence and absence:** being there and/or not being there. An *audience* is often affected as strongly by what is not in a text as it is by what is there. A strong example is the cover photograph of Yoko Ono's 1981 album *Season of Glass* which includes the bloodstained glasses that her husband John Lennon was wearing when he was shot and killed. In this case, the absence of Lennon is suggested by the presence of the glasses.

**presenter:** a term covering a range of roles in TV and radio. For example, radio *DJs* can be described as presenters, as can continuity announcers and the hosts of *game shows*. The role of the presenter is normally to fill the space between other elements with talk or other activities that the *audience* will find interesting. Unlike other forms of TV and radio *celebrity*, being a presenter does not require any specific skill, such as acting, singing or comedy. However, it does require confidence in front of the camera or microphone and a personality that the audience will find engaging.

**press:** a generic term for all newspapers. 'The press' can also be used to mean all news providers: not just the papers but also *news agencies* and *freelance journalists* as well as TV, radio and internet journalists.

**press agent:** a *public relations* worker who deals mainly with the way newspapers represent his or her client.

**press baron:** the owner of a number of newspapers or one very influential newspaper. Press barons have a reputation for using the papers they own to promote their own interests and political views. During the twentieth century, influential British press barons included Lord Rothermere and Lord Beaverbrook. Today, the term is a little old-fashioned, since newspaper owners like Rupert Murdoch tend to control a wide range of media interests.

**pressbook:** a collection of materials sent to cinema managers so that a film could be *marketed* in local newspapers. The pressbook would include stills, plot summaries, quotations, star profiles. The film industry stopped using pressbooks in about 1980 because of a shift towards an *opening weekend* release pattern, which meant that national advertising campaigns became more appropriate.

**Press Complaints Commission (PCC):** the official body, set up by the newspaper industry in 1991, to help maintain its own ethical standards. The PCC Code of Practice has 16 elements: Accuracy; Opportunity to reply; Privacy; Harassment; Intrusion into grief or shock; Children; Children in sex cases; Hospitals; Reporting of crime; Clandestine devices and subterfuge; Victims of sexual assault; Discrimination; Financial journalism; Confidential sources; Witness payments in criminal trials and Payment to criminals. Official complaints to the PCC are investigated and adjudicated. However, since the only punishments resulting from a successful complaint are reprimands or forced apologies, the PCC is sometimes considered a 'toothless watchdog'.

**press conference:** a formal event at which *journalists* (from the newspapers and other media) can ask questions. Press conferences are typically called by politicians, by the police or by *public relations* agencies on behalf of their clients. The aim is to gain some control over the stories that appear in the news.

**press cuttings:** stories or other material cut from a newspaper and kept, usually as evidence. Journalists traditionally kept cuttings of their own work as part of a portfolio to be used when applying for jobs. Actors keep cuttings of reviews for similar purposes.

**press date:** the date a publication is scheduled to be printed. The deadline for *copy* will be some time in advance of this.

**press junket:** a promotional event to which *journalists* are invited. Junkets are much more informal than *press conferences* and are used as part of the *marketing* campaign for many new products. In the *Hollywood* film industry, a typical junket is a catered event lasting two or three days. There are opportunities to interview the stars or other key personnel and special preview screenings of the film. Frequently, the junkets take place in or around an attractive resort. The aim is to create a positive atmosphere around the film so that good reporting and favourable *word-of-mouth* begins to develop.

**press kit:** a collection of materials that can be sent out to newspapers or distributed at a *junket*. Also known as a 'press pack'. It may be targeted at TV, radio and internet institutions as well as the press, hence the alternative terms 'media kit' or 'media pack'. Usually, the press kit contains background information, photographs and artwork. Media kits may also include audio-visual material. The hope is that the pack's contents will be used in a news story or *review*. Businesses with new products to launch, bands on tour or releasing a new album, TV production companies with a series to promote are all likely to have press packs created as part of their *marketing* strategy.

**press office:** the department of a company or official body who are responsible for communication with the media. A press officer is someone who works in this department.

**press release:** a prepared statement that is given to the news media, usually via a *press office*.

**pre-title sequence:** a piece of *footage* shown before the opening *titles* in a film or TV production. Other terms for the same technique are head sequence, cold opening and pre-credit sequence.

**preview:** an opportunity to see a film before its official release. Usually part of a strategy to build *word-of-mouth* in advance of the *opening weekend*, for example by offering free preview tickets to readers of certain newspapers.

**previsualisation:** an attempt to show how a finished *moving image* product will look. The simplest form of previsualisation is the *storyboard*. Other techniques such as *animatics* and software modelling can give a more detailed sense of the potential finished work.

**primary audience:** the target demographic for a media product. For example, the primary audience for *GQ* magazine is middle-aged, middle-class males.

**primary definers:** the main official sources of information, such as the police and government. According to the sociologist Stuart Hall and others, the primary definers are responsible not just for the factual information we receive, but also for the *ideological* and *cultural* interpretation of this material. Secondary definers, especially the *mass media*, pass these messages along to the audience.

**primary level of attention:** full concentration. Media that require a primary level of attention are often those that present complex messages. For example, a *policier* with an intricate *plot* might become incomprehensible if the viewer does not give it a primary level of attention.

**primary medium:** (i) *media* forms of major importance (for example, 'Among younger audiences, the web has become the primary medium.') (ii) media or *media texts* that are likely to be given a *primary level of attention.* (iii) a user's main storage medium (for example a computer hard drive).

**primetime:** see *peak time*

**principal photography:** the period of time when a film is being shot. Also known as *production*, since it falls between *pre-* and *post-production.*

**print:** an individual copy of a film, ready for *distribution* to *cinemas.*

**printing press:** a machine for producing large numbers of identical sheets of text and/or visual images. There are various methods by which this can be achieved, but all require an inked image to be pressed onto paper. The printing press, invented by John of Gutenberg in the fifteenth century, was the first *mass media* technology, enabling messages to reach vast numbers of readers. Print remained the only mass medium until the late nineteenth century, when the *phonograph* and *radio* were invented.

**print run:** the number of copies of a publication that are made, usually based on the number that the publisher expects to sell.

**print space:** the parts of a page on which text or other material can be printed (i.e. excluding the *gutters* and *margins*).

**privacy** is often considered a basic human right. This individual right to privacy is sometimes at odds with the aims of journalists. For example, the *paparazzi* routinely invade the privacy of *celebrities.* The *Press Complaints Commission* Code of Practice states that journalists should respect the privacy of individuals, but adds that this part of the code may sometimes have to be breached in the *public interest.* (See also *invasion of privacy.*)

**private eye film:** a film about an investigation by a private detective. A very common subject of *film noir.*

**privatisation:** the sale of shares in publicly-owned businesses, turning them into private companies. It is sometimes argued that the *BBC* should be **privatised**. The *producer choice* initiative of the 1990s can be considered a step in the direction of privatisation.

**privileged access** can be used in media contexts in a number of ways:

i.   In *documentaries* and other *reality* formats, the term suggests that the *production* team have been allowed freedom to shoot in places that would normally be restricted. For example, 'cameras were given privileged access to the discussions between solicitors and their clients'.

ii.  In *broadcasting*, the term can suggest that some individuals or groups have a better chance of promoting their views than others. The *press baron* Rupert Murdoch, for example, has privileged access to the *news* media.

iii. In *fiction* formats, it can mean that *audiences* are allowed to see characters in private and intimate settings. In *soap opera*, for example, we are given privileged access to the characters' home lives.

**proactive observationalism:** see *reactive observationalism*

**proairetic code:** also known as 'action code'. The proairetic code is a signal of something yet to happen. For example, in *High Noon* (Fred Zinnemann, USA, 1952) we see Amy (Grace Kelly), hiding in the Marshall's office while a gang of gunfighters hunt down her husband. Behind her head, hanging on the wall, is a pistol. This shot prepares the *audience* for the moment a few minutes later when Amy shoots one of the gang in the back. The term was proposed by the French *poststructuralist* Roland Barthes as one of two essential narrative codes.

**problem page:** a *feature* in magazines and newspapers where readers send in problems in the hope of advice. The problems are printed with the advice. Some problem pages deal with medical issues, others with *niche* interests, such as fishing. However, the most popular form of problem page is the 'agony column' dealing with emotional, sexual and relationship problems.

**process shot:** the final image, produced either by filming a subject against a *rear projected/front projected* image, by combining filmed *footage* with a *matte* or by use of *chromakey*.

**producer:**

i.  The *institution* that makes a particular media product.

ii.  In the film industry, the role of the producer is to arrange the business aspects of film-making, such as raising finance, hiring directors and stars and negotiating with distributors. There are various types of producer. The *executive producer*, often the head of a production company, would typically have overall responsibility for the whole *slate* or a large proportion of it, but would not be directly involved in the production process. Each production company, however, has its own structure, so that roles such as associate producer, assistant producer or co-producer can involve a range of responsibilities.

iii. In TV, the role of the producer is similarly to oversee a production. However, particularly in British television, there is also a tradition of strong creative input from the producer.

iv.  A radio producer has a very straightforward organisational and technical role, assisting the *presenters* in practical aspects of the broadcast, such as lining up telephone calls, reminding the presenter of scheduled news breaks and cuing up music.

v.  A music producer is responsible for the overall sound of an album or a single track. This involves creative discussion with the performers, musical arrangements and general supervision of the whole recording process.

**Producers' Alliance for Cinema and Television (PACT):** a trade organisation for *independent* British film and TV production companies. PACT provides support and information for its members, speaks on behalf of independent producers in negotiations with government and is responsible for distributing *Skillset* funding.

**producers and audiences studies:** these are mainly concerned with the relationship between the organisations that make and distribute media products (producers) and the people who consume them (audiences). This is a key concept in the study of film and media. All the *texts* we study are the products of structured organisations which operate in distinctive ways. For example, *Hollywood* functions as a business operation, while the *BBC* operates as a *public service broadcaster.* If we were to compare the Hollywood film *Romeo+Juliet* (Baz Luhrmann, USA, 1996) with the BBC TV production of *Romeo and Juliet* (1978), we would need to take into account the fundamental differences between the organisations that produced the two texts. One of these would be the *demographics* of the audiences targeted, and hence the methods of *marketing* used to reach those audiences. Areas of importance within producers and audiences study include *marketing*, *distribution*, *exhibition*, *genre*, and *media technologies.* It is also important to consider the effect of *regulatory bodies*, government policies and pressure groups such as *Mediawatch-UK.* This broader focus can be described as institutions and audiences study, since it is not solely concerned with media producers.

**producer-broadcaster:** an organisation that both makes programmes and broadcasts them. In the UK, the largest TV producer-broadcaster is the *BBC*. Several ITV stations (such as Granada TV) are also major producer-broadcasters.

**producer choice:** a cost-cutting system introduced in the *BBC* during the early 1990s, where producers were allowed to buy in facilities (for example *costume* or catering) from external organisations. The BBC's own departments therefore had to compete on price in order to survive.

**product:** (i) anything made (and usually sold). Advertising is concerned with encouraging the *audience* to recognise and purchase particular products. (ii) in *media studies*, this is also another name for a *media text.* Generally, we would use 'text' when writing about the *semiotic* and/or artistic aspects of, for example, a TV programme. 'Product' is more often used when we want to focus on the business aspects of the medium.

**product placement:** a form of *advertising*, where a *brand* is integrated into a film narrative: for example, the use of Nokia mobile phones in *The Matrix* (Andy and Larry Wachowski, USA, 1999). The film makers will normally be paid a fee for this service.

**production:** (i) the work done by a *producer* in any medium. (ii) the whole process of making a film. (iii) the period of *principal photography.* (iv) a completed film.

**production code:** see *Hays code*

**production designer:** the artist who creates the overall look for a film, including such elements as colour schemes. Senior to the *set* designer and *art director.*

**production manager:** the person responsible for day-to-day management of the filming process. He or she works on one film at a time, and reports to the *producer*, who is likely to be overseeing several films.

**production quota:** see *quota quickie*

**production schedule:** a plan for the production, designed to make best use of all resources and overseen by the *production manager.* (See also *shooting schedule.*)

**production still:** a still photograph taken during *principal photography* to be used in promoting the film. This is not a still frame from the film itself, but a specially taken photograph, and may include *behind-the-scenes* elements such as crew members and equipment.

**production values:** the amount of money invested in a media product, as reflected in the quality of the item. An example of low production values can be seen in weekly *celebrity* gossip magazines. In general, these publications are circulated on cheap paper, with poor colour printing and sloppy page design. By contrast, the high production values of a monthly fashion magazine include high-quality glossy paper; sharp, rich colour printing and thoughtful *layout*.

**profile:** see *demographic profile*

**profilmic:** according to the French film scholar Etienne Souraiu, the profilmic is the world arranged for the film: in other words, the fictional *mise en scène*. The mise en scène of *documentaries* is therefore considered 'afilmic'.

**profit:** the main aim of most media businesses: to make more money than was originally invested. A particular problem in the film industry, where significantly more films make a *loss* than make a profit.

**programme:** (US 'program') (i) a TV or radio broadcast of any kind (in American English, usually called a 'show'). (ii) a complex set of instructions for a computer used to drive software such as a word processor or video editor. (iii) the list of films to be shown at a cinema during a specified future period. (iv) to plan a cinema programme or a TV *schedule*.

**projection:** the creation of a large picture by passing an intense light source through a small, transparent image onto a *screen*. This technology was first used in the Victorian *magic lantern* and subsequently became the basis for *moving image* film projectors.

**promotion:** any activity designed to spread knowledge about a product. From a media studies perspective, the most important aspects of promotion are *advertising* and *public relations*.

**promo:** shorthand for 'promotional activity'. Pop *videos* are sometimes referred to as 'music promos'.

**proof:** short for 'galley proof'. A printout or electronic copy of a complete, designed publication made ready for checking by the *editor* or the proofreader.

**prop:** short for property. A small item used in a film or TV production to add *realism*, assist with the *narrative* or act as a *motif*. Normally, the term describes an object that is carried or picked up by an actor during a scene. A cane, a bag or a replica gun can all be used as props, but the list of potential examples is endless. The category of props is distinct from *costume* and *set*. They are the responsibility of the **properties manager**.

**propaganda:** any communication designed to persuade, whether to adopt a particular ideology or simply buy a product. The term is normally used pejoratively. For example, a member of the Labour Party might use the term 'Nazi propaganda' to describe a party political broadcast by a far right group, but would not describe a Labour broadcast using the same kind of terms. In wartime, however, the use of propaganda by one's own side is considered acceptable. During the Second World War *propaganda films* such as *In Which We Serve* (David Lean, UK, 1942) and *Casablanca* (Michael Curtiz, USA, 1942) were extremely popular as they were morale boosters to the Allies. The term has also been used in conjunction with critiques of advertising, as all manner of advertising involves attempts at persuasion.

**propaganda film** was particularly important during the first half of the twentieth century, when TV was in its infancy. Some films made with a *propaganda* aim have become regarded as classics of cinema: *Battleship Potemkin* (Sergei Eisenstein, USSR, 1925) is perhaps the most notable of these.

**property:** (i) a *prop*. (ii) short for **literary property**. Any *copyright* material, such as a screen-play or a novel. To use a property (for example, adapting a novel for film) the *producer* must first buy its *rights*.

**Propp, Vladimir (1895–1970):** author of *The Morphology of the Folk Tale* (1928). (See also *characterisation*; *narrative*; *quest*; *seeker-hero*.)

**proprietary elements:** things that are owned by the makers. In the *marketing* of film, pro-prietary elements can be more powerful than generic elements. If we consider, for example, the *genre* of magical fantasy, there are many genre elements that could appear on a poster for such a film, but the *Harry Potter* logo (now owned by *Time Warner*) is undoubtedly a stronger marketing tool than any of them.

**proprietary format:** a means of reproduction that is owned by a particular company. For example, the MP3 audio compression format is owned by Thomson Consumer Electronics, meaning that any businesses wishing to make use of the MP3 *codec* must pay fees to Thomson.

**prosthetics:** fake body parts, attached to an actor and used to simulate injuries or to create *SFX* in the filming process. Sometimes combined with *animatronics*.

**protagonist:** the central character of a narrative. (See also *hero/heroine*.)

**Protection of Children Act 1978:** a British Act of Parliament dealing specifically with the definition of child pornography and specifying punishments for its distribution or ownership.

**PRS:** see *Performing Right Society*

**psychographics:** the grouping of potential consumers according to psychological features. The proprietorial 'Values, Attitudes and Lifestyle System (VALS)' divides people into groups such as 'innovators', 'achievers' and 'survivors'. This approach is an alternative to the *demographic profiling* traditionally used in the *advertising* industry.

**psychological thriller:** a *narrative genre* in which the psychological stability of the *protago-nist* is put under strain. Classics of the genre include many of the films of Alfred *Hitchcock*, such as *Rebecca* (USA, 1940) and *Spellbound* (USA, 1944).

**public access:** the opportunity for ordinary individuals to create and broadcast their own *programmes* on radio or TV. This may be achieved during a dedicated *slot* on a normal channel, or – more often – by the provision of a special, dedicated public access channel. Usually, such channels are provided by cable providers as part of their licence agreement. In the USA there is a long and established public access channel. In the UK, provision has been patchier, but some form of *community TV* is available in many areas of the country.

**publication:** (i) any document that is published: i.e. printed and distributed. Books, magazines and newspapers are all publications. The term is sometimes used to describe some documents placed on the internet. Such documents can be called electronic publica-tions. (ii) the act of publishing: distributing printed or internet material.

**public domain:** any work that is in the public domain is no longer subject to *copyright*, therefore anyone may publish, adapt or otherwise use it free of charge.

**public interest:** for the general good of society. This is the most common justification given for breaches of *privacy* by the *press*, since it is considered useful and important that the public should know certain things. The term does not mean 'things that interest the public'. For example, a news story about a member of parliament having an extramarital affair would be considered a matter of public interest because elected politicians are expected to set a high standard of honesty. A news story about a grocer having an extramarital affair would be considered *invasion of privacy*, unless the affair had led the grocer to commit a crime of some sort.

**publicist:** a type of *public relations* worker who is mainly concerned with creating media *exposure* for his or her clients. Publicists often work closely with the *tabloid newspapers*, setting up 'kiss-and-tell' stories. Max Clifford is the best known British publicist.

**publicity:** making information public. Much media activity, such as *advertising* and *trailers*, constitutes publicity.

**publicity still:** see *production still*

**public relations (PR):** the management of the way a person or an organisation is seen by the public. PR workers can be employed by individuals, by businesses, by political parties or by state institutions (such as the National Health Service). The aim of public relations is to create a positive public image for the client, using such techniques as *press releases* and the planting of *news* stories.

**public service broadcaster:** any radio or television station that is set up by the state rather than as a straightforward business. Usually, a public service broadcaster will be expected to do more than simply provide entertainment. The responsibilities of such an institution often include educational broadcasting, provision of news, exposing the *audience* to the arts and classical music. In Britain, the main public service broadcaster is the *BBC*, which was originally founded on the *Reithian* principles that it would 'inform, educate and entertain' the British public. Channel 4 is also a public service broadcaster, but unusually, it is funded entirely by advertising, while the BBC receives most of its funding from the TV *licence fee*.

**publisher:** an organisation whose business is to make and distribute printed material, such as books, magazines or newspapers. Different types of publishers operate in different ways. For example, magazine and newspaper publishers usually print their own *publications* but book publishers will normally commission a printer to do this work. Magazine and newspaper publishers employ a staff of *journalists*, *editors* and *sub-editors* to produce the *copy*, along with the photographers, and design staff who provide images. Additionally, they will take work from *freelances* such as writers and cartoonists. Sometimes the owner or director of a publishing house is referred to as a publisher.

**publisher broadcaster:** a TV station that makes very few, if any, programmes and instead *commissions* work from production companies. Channel 4 is a publisher broadcaster. Also known as a commissioner broadcaster. The opposite is a *producer broadcaster*.

**puff:** journalists' slang for material that is very complimentary. A 'puff piece' is an article designed to give an uncritical and positive impression of its subject.

**pulling focus:** see *racking focus*

**pull-back:** a camera movement, either *zooming out* or *pulling out*.

**pull out:** the reverse of *pushing in*. The camera *tracks* backwards away from the subject, producing an increasingly *wide* shot.

**punk:** a movement in *popular culture* that began in about 1976. It began as punk rock, a ferocious and uncomplicated style of music, but grew into a spectacular *subculture* whose members sported distinctive and unconventional clothing. The *aesthetic* of punk was aggressive and bold. Punk *fanzines* such as *Sniffin Glue* were made using typewriters, scissors and glue, and then reproduced on photocopiers. They were clearly the homemade work of DIY designers with no artistic training. The attitudes and aesthetics of punk continue to influence *popular music, comic books* and other aspects of *youth culture*, as well as radical perspectives like *queercore.*

**pure cinema:** an *avant-garde* approach to film-making that rejects everything that is not unique to cinema. *Narrative, character* and *representation* can all be found in other media – the novel, the drama, painting – and so none of these are acceptable in pure cinema. Instead, abstract qualities such as rhythm and form are explored. French pure cinema of the 1920s was associated with the *Surrealist* and Dadaist movements, and its artists included Marcel Duchamp and Man Ray.

**push in:** a *camera* movement towards the subject. Often mistakenly called a *zoom in* but actually very different in effect. (See also *dolly.*)

**PVR:** an acronym of personal video recorder. The PVR is a sophisticated form of hard drive recorder that can synchronise itself with broadcast schedules so that it can, for example, be set to record every episode of a particular series or to record every programme of a partic-ular *genre.* The earliest PVR was the TIVO, which required viewers to make a monthly *subscription* to an updating service in addition to paying the cost of the machine. A more popular device in Britain is the Sky+ *set top box* which is a combined digital *satellite* receiver and PVR.

**pyrotechnics:** any *SFX* involving fire that is actually created on *set* (rather than with *CGI*). Pyrotechnics can be among the most dangerous effects in film production, and usually require specially trained *stunt* artists as well as skilled technicians.

A B C D E F G H I J K L M N O P Q R S T U V W X Y Z

**quadrilogy:** a sequence of four. The word was probably invented at *20th Century Fox* for the *marketing* of the *DVD* release of the four *Alien* films. Perhaps the more correct term 'tetralogy' was not used because its meaning would not have been so obvious.

**qualitative methods** examine the detail of individuals' experiences, whether for *market research* or academic purposes. The sample group is small. Two common examples of qualitative research methods are the *interview* and the *tracking study*. The results of qualitative research are considered to have greater validity – that is, they contain more truth. On the other hand, the results cannot be generalised (i.e. applied to the whole population); it is also difficult to compare individual responses within the study or to repeat the research.

**quantitative methods** may, like *qualitative methods*, be used for *market research* or academic purposes. Quantitative research counts the responses of a large sample, usually to a survey questionnaire. The main advantages of this type of research over qualitative methods lie in the fact that the results can be analysed mathematically. Because of this, they are considered more reliable. Quantitative studies can also be repeated easily. However, the data tend to be simplified and lacking in depth compared with those obtained by qualitative work.

**queer:** until the mid-late twentieth century, a colloquial, and usually pejorative, term for 'homosexual'. In recent years, the word has been revived with the new meaning of 'political sexuality'. While many uses of 'queer' are connected to male *homosexuality*, the term now also embraces a wide variety of sexual interests and orientations outside the heterosexual mainstream. **Queercore** (also **homocore**) is a movement predominantly in indie/rock music and associated *fanzines*, but also *comic books*, *film* and the *internet*, combining a highly political approach to sexuality with an aggressive DIY *aesthetic* that owes a great deal to *punk*.

**queer theory:** an approach to culture that rejects traditional *taxonomies* of sexuality which seek to identify individuals as 'gay, 'straight' or 'bisexual'.

i.   A **queer reading** of a media or film text is one that considers it primarily from the point of view of its representation of sexual identity. Queer readings are primarily concerned with uncovering non-mainstream sexualities in apparently heterosexual narratives.

ii.  New **queer cinema** is a film *genre* identified by the American critic Ruby B Rich, in which gay identities are explored, often from a political perspective. Examples include *Boys Don't Cry* (Kimberly Peirce, USA, 1999) and *Ma Vie en Rose* (Alain Berliner, Fr/Belg, 1997).

**quest:** a search for something of great importance to the *protagonist*, often involving a journey. According to various theorists of *story* and *narrative*, the quest is the central element of every story. It is a core component in Vladimir Propp's 1928 book *Morphology of the Folk Tale* and in Joseph Campbell's monomyth or *hero's journey*. A quest may be for an external object: for example, Indiana Jones's search for the Ark of the Covenant in *Raiders of the Lost Ark* (Steven Spielberg, USA, 1981); or it may be internal – for instance when an *existential hero* searches for a sense of meaning. Similarly, the journey may take many forms: physical, spiritual, educational or emotional, for example.

**questionnaire:** a paper or online form designed by market researchers to obtain facts and/or opinions about products and services, such as reading or viewing preferences.

**quick cut:** an *edit* that follows very shortly after the previous one. Depending on how they are used, quick cuts can generate a sense of pace and energy or they can communicate a feeling of disorientation.

**quiz show:** a TV and radio *genre*. Competitors, usually members of the public, are asked questions, most commonly based on general knowledge, but sometimes on a specialist subject. Quiz shows can be considered a *subgenre* of *game shows*, and some game shows contain a quiz element. For example, *Bullseye* combined dart-throwing with quiz questions. Although many quizzes, from *The $64,000 Question* through to *Who Wants to be a Millionaire?* have given out extremely large prizes, others offer mainly prestige for the winner. The latter category includes *Brain of Britain* (radio), *Mastermind* (TV and radio) and *Fifteen to One* (TV). The big prize quiz shows usually involve much more elaborate presentation (dramatic camerawork, huge sets, celebrity presenters) than their prestige-driven counterparts.

**quota quickie:** a cheaply made film produced in Britain by American distributors. The Cinematograph Films Act, 1927 required British cinemas to exhibit a percentage of British films (initially 7.5 per cent and later 20 per cent). In order to meet this requirement, the *Hollywood* industry produced a large number of inexpensive 'British' films for exhibition as **B features** in the UK. Occasionally, these would involve American *stars* on contract, who had been sent to the UK by the *studio* as a punishment for misbehaviour of some kind.

**Do you need revision help and advice?**

Go to pages 251–292 for a range of revision appendices that include exam advice and tips.

A B C D E F G H I J K L M N O P Q R S T U V W X Y Z

**R18 certificate:** an age rating that can be given to a film or video recording designated as *pornography* by the *BBFC*. Unlike the other age classifications, R18 is legally binding on film as well as video. R18 material can only be provided to persons over the age of eighteen, and may only be sold in licensed sex shops or exhibited in private clubs.

**RA:** see *Radio Authority*

**RAB (Radio Advertising Bureau):** see *RadioCentre*

**RACC (Radio Advertising Clearance Centre):** see *RadioCentre*

**race:** a *taxonomy* of human beings based on physical factors such as skin colour. The concept of race is not a very useful one, since it is difficult to separate out different so-called 'races' except in a very simplistic way. When exploring complex social phenomena such as media or film, *ethnicity* (which involves not just a person's genetic background but also his or her *cultural* influences) is considered far more useful.

**racism:** discrimination based on *race*. Within the media, racism can potentially take several forms: offensive *stereotyping*, inappropriate language and under-representation. It is relatively rare for media or film texts to promote straightforwardly racist messages (i.e. explicitly encouraging racial hatred) and discussions or accusations of racism are often quite complex. An oft-cited example is the 1970s British TV *sitcom Love Thy Neighbour* which explored the comic possibilities of a black family moving next door to a white bigot. This series is frequently held up as an example of casual 1970s racism because of the regular use of the word 'nignog' in the script. In fact, almost all the humour is actually directed against the white neighbour, Eddie, played by Jack Smethurst, who is presented as a buffoon, while his black neighbour, Bill, played by Rudolph Walker, is shown to be intelligent, self-controlled and in every way superior to Eddie. Nevertheless, the general tone of the series would now make most viewers uncomfortable, and it is never given repeat broadcasts in Britain. Racism has become a kind of *taboo*, and is now seen as more offensive than depictions of sex, violence, strong language or drug-taking. It has, therefore, naturally become the subject of comedy again. (For example, the character comedian Sacha Baron Cohen has confronted British and American attitudes to race and racism repeatedly in his two *personae*: 'Ali G' – a white youth from Staines who fantasises about being black and 'Borat' – an anti-semitic and woman-hating TV personality from Kazakhstan.) Much cinema and TV shows a tendency to associate *ethnic minorities* with crime, and some commentators have complained that this reinforces a stereotypical view. It would be easy for a TV or film viewer to believe that all Italian-Americans are Mafiosi or that all young urban black men are members of street gangs. The makers of these *narratives* would argue that what they are representing is a social reality; critics would suggest that the media focus on a narrow range within these communities and so create a distorted impression.

**racking focus:** changing the focus while filming so that a new aspect of the *mise en scène* is emphasised. Also known as 'pulling focus'. Can be used in an *eyeline match*, for example, to show that the character has suddenly noticed a particular object.

**radical meaning system:** see *meaning systems*

**radio:** a system for converting sound into electromagnetic waves and communicating without the need for wires. Radio was the first fully developed *mass broadcasting medium*, with experimental stations operating regularly from 1919 onwards. Because it was far cheaper, both in terms of production and the purchase of equipment, radio was a much more important media form than *TV* during the middle of the twentieth century. In the UK, from 1927 onwards the *BBC* operated a national service as a *public service broadcaster*. During this time the BBC were the only legal radio broadcasters in the country, though a number of *pirate radio* stations challenged this *monopoly*, and commercial broadcasting on a local basis, funded by advertising, was finally legalised in 1972. In 1954 the transistor radio was invented. These small, cheap, portable *receivers*, used mainly for listening to pop music stations, became one of the first examples of a new technology being closely linked to developments in youth culture. A subsequent important development was the introduction of *FM* broadcasting, which allowed users a higher quality experience, including the possibility of *stereo* sound. Radio continues to be popular for various reasons. Because it provides sound-only entertainment, it can operate as a *secondary medium* and be enjoyed while the listener is engaged in other activities, such as driving. In less-developed countries, it is often the only reliable medium, and an important source of information. Most radio is cheap to produce, and content can reach an international *audience*, particularly when using *short wave* transmission. The digital revolution has produced many new ways to experience *radio genres*. So-called '*internet* radio' can provide streaming audio, and most *podcasts* are effectively radio programmes. *Cable*, *satellite* and *Freeview* TV services offer large numbers of radio stations along with TV and other types of content. *DAB radio* provides a higher quality, more reliable service than FM, and can support its content with extra material, such as scrolling text.

**Radio Academy:** a professional association for the radio industry. The Academy is a registered charity. Its work includes the encouragement of new radio talent, the organisation of conferences for radio professionals and the publication (both online and in print) of the Radio Directory, which is a comprehensive list of information about radio in the UK. The Academy is also jointly responsible (with the *Sony Corporation*) for the prestigious annual *Sony Awards*.

**Radio Authority (RA):** the *regulatory body* for Radio in the UK until 2003, when its duties were taken over by *Ofcom*.

**RadioCentre:** a trade organisation for commercial radio stations in the UK. The role of the RadioCentre is to work on behalf of all British radio stations in discussion with *Ofcom* and other government bodies. It also provides a forum for radio stations to work with each other. The RadioCentre includes a number of sub-organisations, most of which previously existed as independent bodies. These include:

- **The Radio Advertising Bureau (RAB),** which works to promote radio advertising in general, encouraging potential advertisers to see radio as a valuable medium for advertising. They also provide research-based advice on the best, and most effective, forms for radio advertising content.

- **The Radio Advertising Clearance Centre (RACC),** which is responsible for ensuring that all radio advertising conforms to the *BCAP* (Broadcast Committee of Advertising Practice) code.

The RadioCentre is joint owner (with the *BBC*) of *RAJAR*.

**radio genres:** styles of programming that are used in radio. The most familiar to modern audiences are probably the radio *news;* the *disc jockey* format, in which a presenter plays a series of records, providing spoken links between them; and variations on this formula such as the *zoo format.* There are also large audiences for spoken word genres. In the UK, the most important speech-based radio stations are all provided by the *BBC.* They are as follows:

- **BBC Radio 4** (LW, FM, DAB, internet) offers a very broad range of radio genres, including current affairs and news, radio plays, comedy shows, discussion, drama series, readings of prose works.

- **BBC 7** (DAB, internet) features radio plays, drama series, comedy.

- **BBC 5 Live** (AM, DAB, internet) features sport and current affairs.

The *conventions* of radio genres differ significantly from similar TV genres, because they cannot depend on pictures. For example, when broadcasting football on radio, it is necessary to describe far more of what is happening than would be necessary were the match being shown on TV. Conversely, when nothing is happening (as can often be the case during a cricket match) the commentators must keep talking so as to avoid *dead air.* In radio dramas and *sitcoms* the writers cannot use visuals; consequently, they often need to provide more *exposition.*

**ragged right** (or less commonly **ragged left**) are terms referring to the arrangement of text that is not *justified*, or flush on both sides of the page. Text that is left-justified (or flush left) produces a ragged right; text that is right-justified (or flush right) produces a ragged left.

**Raindance Film Festival:** a major festival of independent film held annually in London. The name is an adaptation of the American *Sundance* festival.

**RAJAR:** an acronym of Radio Joint Audience Research. It is the organisation that has supplied audience *ratings* for British radio stations since 1992. Its figures are based on diaries kept by a representative group of listeners within each station's *total survey area.* RAJAR is owned jointly by the *BBC* and the *RadioCentre.*

**rate card:** a document provided by a magazine or newspaper to potential advertisers, listing the costs of various sizes and positions of *advertisement* in the publication.

**ratings:** the number of viewers to have watched a TV show or heard a radio programme. Broadcasters use various methods to collect and interpret ratings, since raw data may not be especially useful. For example, a smaller number of viewers from the *ABC1* demographic may be as valuable to advertisers as a large audience in the *C2DE* range. In the UK, official TV ratings have been supplied by *BARB* since 1981 and radio ratings have been collected by *RAJAR* since 1992. For *commercial broadcasters*, ratings are important as a tool for selling advertising, while *public service broadcasters* use them to demonstrate that money (raised, for example, by the *licence fee*) has been wisely spent.

**ratings system:** an alternative to *censorship* whereby material is given an age rating. Ratings systems are currently applied to films, videos and video games.

**ratio:** can mean either *aspect ratio* or *shooting ratio.*

**reach:** the *audience* exposed to a media product, expressed as a number of individuals or a portion of the population within a specific period of time. For example, a radio station might have a 'seven-day reach of two million listeners'. Reach figures only count each individual person once; it does not matter how many times he or she is exposed to the product. That figure is counted as *frequency.* The figures for reach and frequency are extremely important in calculating the effectiveness of *advertising.*

**reaction shot:** one in which we see a person's response to whatever happened in the previous shot. For example, if shot 1 is of a man staggering along the street drunk and shot 2 is of a woman laughing as she looks out of a window, we understand that the woman is laughing at the man. Reaction shots are important not only because they show us how characters are responding to each other and to events in the story but also because they create important messages about how we in the audience should respond to them ourselves. For example, in the scene with the drunken man we can understand from the woman's reaction that we are to see the man as comical or perhaps pathetic. If, on the other hand, the woman were to look terrified, his drunkenness would then seem threatening. (See also *Kuleshov effect.*)

**reactive observationalism:** part of an extension to Bill Nichols' *documentary* modes suggested by John Corner. Reactive observationalism is in fact precisely what Nichols described simply as 'observationalism' – that is, a '*fly on the wall*' approach where there is little or no interference by the documentary maker in the natural flow of events. However, Corner contrasts this with proactive observationalism, in which observation is combined with increased control of the *mise en scène* by the film maker.

**readership:** quantitatively, the number of people who read a publication, such as a newspaper or magazine. This is usually a much larger figure than the *ABC* sales figures would suggest, since many purchased copies will be read by more than one person. A readership can also be defined qualitatively – in terms of *gender*, *social class*, *ethnicity* and so on. For example, it might be said that the *Daily Mail*'s readership is predominantly female and traditionalist.

**real-time narration** is the unfolding of a story in the time that the events would actually take. In a real-time film, what we see in 30 minutes will be 30 minutes of the characters' lives. There is no *ellipsis.* Famous examples of films using real time narration include *High Noon* (Fred Zinnemann, USA, 1952) and *Phone Booth* (Joel Schumacher, USA, 2002). The technique is also a feature of the American TV *serial 24*, in which each *season* is composed of twenty-four episodes, each an hour long, forming a whole day in the life of Jack Bauer, the *hero* of the programme. Most real-time narratives involve some 'cheating' to keep the story going. For example, dramatic events can last longer than the time on the clock, while less interesting ones are speeded up. In *24*, characters sometimes travel great distances in unrealistically short periods of time (usually while off-camera) so that the *action* can continue.

**realism:** one of the most complex terms in the study of art and literature as well as media and film texts. The word has been put to many uses over time, and caused much disagreement. There is a fairly clear distinction between the realist and the merely realistic. A 'realistic' *text* is any that seems to the *spectator* to create a believable reality; whereas a 'realist' text is one that is committed to reproducing reality. For example, the *stunts* in an *action film* often seem realistic because of careful choreography, camerawork, editing and use of *special effects*, but they are not realist because they could not happen in real life. Put briefly: most film makers seek to make their work realistic; but realist film makers seek to make their work 'real'. Our understanding of realism changes constantly. For example, the *Italian neorealist* film makers adopted various techniques in order to make their work more 'real' than the glossy products of *Hollywood*. The movement produced some highly regarded films, such as Rossellini's *Paisà* (Italy, 1946) and De Sica's *Bicycle Thieves* (Italy, 1948), but to a modern audience, none of them now look especially like life. The acting can seem awkward and self-conscious, their use of music is extremely manipulative, and the camera-work draws attention to itself. We can see the realist intentions of the film makers, but the films no longer appear realistic. Realism is also subject to *ideological* influences. What is seen as realist depends on the attitudes, beliefs and values of the person looking at the work. A good example of this is the 1980s TV *drama Boys from the Blackstuff*. From a *left-wing* perspective, this tale of life on unemployment benefit seems deeply realist; to a right-wing viewer, it would look like *propaganda*. (See also *documentary realism; social realism; surface realism; realist aesthetic.*)

**realist aesthetic:** the intention of creating art (such as film or TV drama) that reproduces some kind of *objective reality* in its look and sound. A realist aesthetic can be contrasted with an *expressionist* aesthetic, which seeks to reproduce a more *subjective* (i.e. an emotional or psychological) reality. Very few texts are, however, entirely realist or entirely expressionistic in aesthetic terms. For example, the TV drama series *The Sopranos* would regularly break off from its realist approach to Mafia life in order to present such expressionist devices as dream sequences.

**reality effect:** the way in which the *audience* tend to experience films and other audio-visual media texts as if they were reality. The concept is similar to that of *suture*.

**reality TV:** a *genre* in which the 'real lives' of individuals or groups are the focus of attention. The genre is quite diverse, including *formats* such as:

- collections of CCTV or police camera *footage* with an added *expository voiceover* (e.g. *Road Wars*)

- *docu-soaps*

- **reality game shows** in which a group of people are placed in an unusual social environment, watched by the cameras twenty-four hours per day and progressively voted off by the general public (e.g. *Big Brother; I'm a Celebrity, Get Me Out Of Here!*)

- **reality talent shows** involve the hopefuls being coached and developed by professionals over several weeks (e.g. *X-Factor, American Idol*). Usually there is a voting-off structure similar to the game show. The popular series *The Apprentice* is a reality talent show for business people rather than entertainers

- **social experiment formats**: e.g. can a woman live with a family other than her own for a fortnight? (*Wife Swap*); is it possible to gain a completely new skill with a month's intensive training? (*Faking It*) and so on

- **makeover shows**: either for people's homes (e.g. *Changing Rooms*) or their lifestyle and clothing (e.g. *Queer Eye for the Straight Guy*).

The 'reality' element of all these genres is open to debate. In most cases, the programme-makers set up extremely unreal situations so as to encourage *drama* and *conflict*. For example, *Big Brother* has in successive years selected increasingly flamboyant, emotionally intense and/or aggressive competitors in the hope of building up greater levels of drama. The programme's makers have also introduced a series of deliberately divisive *stunts* to encourage conflict among the competitors. Moreover, the material is usually *cropped* (selected and edited) so as to produce the most interesting broadcast possible. Reality shows do not aim to represent any kind of reality in the way a *documentary* would. It seems that the popularity of the genre has little to do with the audience's desire to see the real world, and more with *voyeurism*. Because of their *sensationalist* approach, reality pro-grammes are seen by many commentators as evidence of *dumbing down* and *tabloidisation* in TV as a whole.

**rear projection:** see *back projection.*

**recall:** a measurement of the effectiveness of *advertising;* this is the length of time an advertisement is remembered by people who have been exposed to it, and the amount of detail that they retain. It is particularly important that the subject remembers the *brand* as well as the advertisement.

**reception:** (i) the use of a piece of equipment, such as a radio or TV aerial, to pick up a broadcast signal. (ii) the general response of *critics* to some recent release or event. For example, you might read that 'the critical reception to the new *Spielberg* film was not as positive as the studio had hoped'.

**reception theory:** the idea that a *text's meaning* depends on the person experiencing it, rather than the original intentions of the person(s) who created the text. Reception theory suggests that the cultural background of the *spectator* or reader will mean that the same text has different meanings to different people, and that meanings cannot be *anchored*. This approach has been particularly important in the work of the sociologist Stuart Hall and the *CCCS*. It is a defining factor in David Morley's important study of the 'Nationwide' audience and in Parkin's idea of the three *meaning systems.*

**recce:** abbreviation of 'reconnaissance', it is a term borrowed from military use, used in film-making to describe a visit made to a *location* in order to establish its potential – and any possible obstacles – before *shooting* commences.

**reconstruction:** an attempt to recreate a real event as accurately as possible for film or TV. Most reconstructions use actors in place of the people involved in the real events. For example, on television, *Crimewatch UK* often presents reconstructions of crimes as a more dramatic alternative to simply giving witness accounts.

**redhead:** an 800 watt tungsten light. Redheads are regarded as general purpose lights for filming. Most *three-point lighting* set-ups would use redheads. (See also *blonde.*)

**red top:** see *tabloid*

**redundancy:** see *syntagmatic redundancy*

**reel:** (i) a spool designed to hold a length of film on a camera or projector. Reels are also used for storing film, when they are usually kept inside a canister. The length of film on a reel will run at around 15–25 minutes, depending on frame rate. (ii) a *showreel.*

**re-establishing shot:** a *wide shot* appearing some way into a sequence in which we have already seen a traditional *establishing shot*. Usually there will have been some movement or change in the *spatial* relationships since the beginning, and the new shot will establish this clearly for the audience. Sometimes, especially during a longer sequence, the re-establish-ing shot simply reminds the audience of what they have already seen.

**185**

**reference to elite nations; reference to elite persons:** see *elite*

**referent:** in *semiology*, the thing in the world that is indicated by a specific *sign*. For example, the referent of the word 'bicycle' is a bicycle. Other examples are less straightforward, and depend on *context*. A skull and crossbones on a bottle of unknown liquid refers to 'poison'; the referent of the same sign on a black flag flying from a ship's mast is 'pirates'.

**referential meaning:** one of four types of film meaning proposed by David Bordwell. The referential meanings of a film are *constructed* by reference to the viewer's pre-existing knowledge or attitudes. For example, *In the Heat of the Night* (Norman Jewison, USA, 1967) is set in a small town in Mississippi. The film assumes that the *audience* will have a reasonable grasp of the historical reasons for the racism we see in its characters. It does not, therefore, need to begin with a history lesson about slavery and the American Civil War.

**reflexive documentary:** see *documentary*

**reflexivity:** see *self-reflexive*

**reframe:** in film, to create a new composition by moving the *camera*. Reframing is usually needed because figures move within the *mise en scène*. For example, the camera may follow an actor as he walks across a room.

**region code:** a system designed for restricting the use of *DVD video* material to a specific geographical location. Region coding is intended to give the *distributors* power over the release dates and costs of DVDs in different countries. At the time of writing, seven region codes are in use. The following is a generalised list of their applications: Region 1: USA, Canada and Bermuda; Region 2: Most of Europe, Japan, The Middle East, parts of Africa; Region 3: Southeast Asia; Region 4: South and Central America; Region 5: Russia, India, parts of Africa; Region 6: China; Region 8: International use on ships and aircraft. Region 7 is not in use. Additionally, 'Region 0' is sometimes used to indicate a disc that can be played anywhere or a player that can handle discs from any region. The system is not entirely successful or consistent. Many DVD players are sold as multi-region, meaning that they can play any disc, regardless of region coding. Others can easily have their settings changed to add multi-region capability. There is some debate as to the legality of region coding, since it restricts free trade between countries.

**regional film theatre (RFT):** an *art-house* cinema that receives direct financial support from the *BFI* with the aim of promoting non-mainstream films which would otherwise receive little *distribution* outside of London.

**regional press:** the publishers of local newspapers, or the newspapers themselves. The term tends not be used to describe London's local newspapers, such as the *Evening Standard*. Regional newspapers in the UK vary considerably in style and content, since each is produced with a strong sense of its local *readership*. Many carry a small number of national news stories, but all devote the bulk of their space to local issues. This means that the balance of types of story and the sense of *news values* in the regional press differs somewhat from its national counterparts. Events that would not reach the *threshold* for a national newspaper, such as a burglary, or the retirement of a local headteacher, would be reported by the regional press.

**register:** the effect created by choice of vocabulary and sentence structure. For example, the *gangster* characters in a Quentin Tarantino film adopt an informal register filled with obscenities and slang words, though the structures of this *dialogue* are often very elaborate. The very different register adopted by children's TV *presenters* is also informal, but based on simple vocabulary and structures. Radio 4 newsreaders choose a register that is both complex and formal. A notable characteristic of the *tabloid press* is its use of an extremely simple language register.

**regulation:** see *statutory regulation*

**regulator:** a person or body who applies codes of conduct to an industry. The media industries are subject to regulators of various types. Some are government-appointed (state regulation or *statutory regulation*); some are set up by the media industries themselves (*self-regulation*).

**reissue:** (i) a new printing of a particular edition or series of editions of a publication. (ii) a new version of a music recording, normally with some alterations or enhancements, such as new artwork or extra tracks. Similarly a new version of a video recording with, perhaps, improved visual quality, new director's commentary or other enrichments. (See also *re-release*.)

**Reithian** means 'following the principles of Lord Reith'. John Charles Walsham Reith, 1st Baron Reith of Stonehaven, was the first Director General of the *BBC* (1927–1938) and established its basic principles as a *public service broadcaster:* to inform, educate and entertain. He saw the role of the BBC as being mainly to improve the general culture and education of the country. Subsequently, he has been seen critically, as wishing to reinforce a very traditional idea of *culture* and imposing on the general population his own ideas about what was right and good. However, the post-Reith BBC has also been criticised on occasion for departing from Reithian principles and focusing on the production of mass entertainment in order to chase easy *ratings*.

**release:** to make copies of a film, DVD, album or single available to the public.

**release form:** a legal document, giving the right to use an image of the signatory (a model release), or the signatory's *property* (a property release), for commercial purposes. Release forms are not normally required for *news* images, but are always needed for images used in *advertising*.

**release pattern:** there are a number of variables in a *release* that can affect the success of the product. For example, the *distributor* may wish to release the same product in different countries at different times: this is the thinking behind *region coding* of *DVD* video. In the film industry, different types of film are given different release patterns. The most important distinction is between the *saturation releases* given to *blockbusters* and the *platform releases* that are more common for *independent*, foreign-language and *low-budget* movies.

**remake:** a new version of an older film. Sometimes, the aim of a remake is to take advantage of improved technology, especially in terms of *special effects*. The two remakes of *King Kong* are examples of this. Other remakes seek to bring a story to a new *audience* who might find the style of the original a little dated. Brian De Palma's *Scarface* (USA, 1983), retains the basic plot and characters of Howard Hawks' original (USA, 1932), but is stylistically very different. *Hollywood* quite frequently produces English language versions of films originally made in other countries. Cameron Crowe's *Vanilla Sky* (USA, 2001), for example, is a remake of Alejandro Amenábar's *Abre los Ojos* (Sp, 1997). On occasion, a remake will move the action of the original to a new location, or even change *genres*. Several of Akira Kurosawa's *samurai* films were remade as *Westerns*, while the Western, *High Noon* (Fred Zinnemann, USA, 1952) has been remade as a police *thriller* (*Cop Land*,

James Mangold, USA, 1997) and as a *tech-noir* (*Outland*, Peter Hyams, UK, 1981). In many cases, the remake reflects the film maker's respect for the original. Perhaps the ultimate example of this *homage* approach to remakes is Gus Van Sant's (USA, 1998) remake of Hitchcock's *Psycho* (USA, 1960), which reproduces the original black and white film in colour, almost shot for shot.

**remote control:** an *interface* that can be used at a distance from the device. Though commonplace today, TV remotes were rare until the 1980s. They have been a key factor in reducing the importance of *scheduling* as a way of controlling the *audience*. Since it is possible to switch channels without leaving one's chair, strategies such as *hammocking* are no longer so powerful. Similarly, the volume button on a remote means that the long-standing practice of compressing audio on advertisements to increase audience attention is less effective.

**rendering:** in *non-linear editing* and other *digital post-production* techniques, rendering is the process of creating a final video file out of the edited material. For example, if *special effects CGI* has to be added to filmed *footage*, the final stage in this process will be to create a new rendered file combining the original images with the added special effects.

**repeat:** any broadcast of a television or radio programme after the first time it is aired. A repeat fee is money paid to an actor when a programme in which he or she has appeared is repeated.

**repertoire of elements:** the whole set of possible 'ingredients' that make up a *genre*. The repertoire is a large pool of elements, from which only a few will be selected. For example, the stock *character* of the bossy wife is typical of TV *sitcoms*, but not every sitcom contains a bossy wife; weddings are a common feature of film *romcoms* but not every romcom includes a wedding.

**repertory cinema:** a cinema that shows older films, in contrast to *multiplex* cinemas, which tend to show only *first runs*. The term comes from repertoire, which in this context means the full range of films that are available. At one time, prior to the wide availability of films on video, repertory cinemas were common in the UK, and prints of films would circulate around the country for many years after their original *release*. Today there are far fewer repertory cinemas. They are mainly *art-house* cinemas or *regional film theatres*, catering for a *cineaste* audience.

**repetition and difference:** the defining characteristics of *genres* in all media. The *audience* is made comfortable by that which it has seen before in other examples of the genre, but also wishes to see some elements that are new. The most successful makers of generic works are therefore those who can best judge how much difference and how much repetition to include. The *news values* of consonance and unexpectedness work on similar principles.

**report:** a piece of *news* collected and written (for a newspaper) or presented (for TV or radio) by a *reporter*.

**reportage:** a piece of *news*, usually from a foreign *correspondent*, that presents an individual viewpoint of events as witnessed at first hand by the journalist. The term suggests a more engaged piece and a higher quality of writing than a mere *report*.

**reporter:** a journalist working in TV, radio or the press, whose job is to go out and collect *stories* then to construct *reports*.

**repositioning:** see *positioning*

**representation:** (i) 'showing'. This is a key concept in the analysis of *media products*. At a basic level, we can say that all media are forms of representation. A *news* broadcast **represents** to the *audience* events that have happened; a *science-fiction* film represents things that have not happened. However, the people involved in making the representation (the writers, the presenters or actors, the editors) are all governed by their own beliefs, values and attitudes. This means that no representation in the media is ever *objective*. Most media products tend to reproduce *dominant ideologies* in the way that they represent the world. This has led many *minorities* to complain that they are *misrepresented* in media texts. (See also, for example, *racism*.) (ii) The work of an *agent*. He or she represents the client (an actor or musician, for example) by finding auditions, negotiating fees and so on.

**repressive state apparatus:** the name given by the structural *Marxist* Louis Althusser to institutions such as the army and police force, which can be used to control the population in the event that the *ISA* should be unsuccessful in doing so. Sometimes abbreviated to RSA.

**re-release:** (i) the re-release of a film is the *distribution* of prints to cinemas some time after its *first run*. Some re-releases are simply the original prints, others (for example the 'Special Editions' of the original *Star Wars* films released in 1997) are new versions. Re-releasing used to be a common distribution strategy when most towns had a small *repertory cinema* and films were not available on video. Since the development of the *multiplex* alongside *VHS* and subsequently *DVD*, re-releases have become relatively rare: though they are still a feature of the *art-house cinemas*. (ii) a re-release is also a synonym for a *reissue* – particularly in the music industry.

**research methods:** systems for collecting information. Established and ethical research methods are an important element of the academic study of the media. Depending on the type of research, *qualitative* or *quantitative* methods may be employed. In media industries, it is also important to carry out regular *audience* research using methods such as *ratings* collection, *questionnaire* surveys and *test screenings*.

**residuals:** another term for repeat fees.

**resolution:** the *denouement* of a narrative.

**restricted code:** according to the language theorist Basil Bernstein, this is a simple, informal way of speaking, using limited vocabulary and sentence structures. It contrasts with the more complex and sophisticated *elaborated code*. According to Bernstein, *middle-class* children have access to both restricted and elaborated codes, while *working-class* children tend only to use the restricted code.

**restricted and unrestricted narration** are two basic forms of *narrative*. Restricted narration presents the story from one person's point of view. This means that the viewer often has to work a little harder to piece together the evidence. A perfect example of more or less completely restricted narration is Christopher Nolan's film *Memento* (USA, 2000) in which we see a sequence of events as experienced by a character suffering from short-term memory loss. Unrestricted narration gives the viewer a god-like overview of all events and does not confine us to one character's perspective. It is, for example, the main form of narration in *soap operas*, in which the viewer is given the opportunity to move from place to place, watching the various lives of the characters unfolding and intersecting. Many narratives adopt both approaches, moving between restricted and unrestricted modes to suit the needs of the story that is being told.

A B C D E F G H I J K L M N O P Q **R** S T U V W X Y Z

**retake:** a second or subsequent attempt at a *take*.

**retrospective:** a series of films shown (usually at an *art-house* cinema) to honour the past work of a person (such as a director or an actor) or an institution (such as a studio).

**return on investment:** see *profit*

**reveal:** a *camera* movement, *edit* or other on-screen event that shows the *audience* something previously hidden.

**revelation:** in the (mainly *tabloid*) press, used in *headlines* and other stories to suggest that the material is amazing, unexpected and until this moment has been a secret.

**reverse:** any *shot* representing the view that was behind the camera in the previous shot. Can be called a 'reverse shot' or a 'reverse angle'.

**reverse motion:** running film backwards so that events appear to happen in reverse.

**reverse track:** a *camera* movement. An object (usually an actor) moves towards the camera, which moves backwards at the same pace. Sometimes achieved using *steadicam*, sometimes using a *dolly*. Used frequently in the TV drama *The West Wing* to show characters engaged in discussion while walking along corridors.

**reverse zoom:** the opposite of *zooming in*. A reverse zoom typically begins with a small section of the *mise en scène* and then shows us more and more. It is sometimes used as a type of *reveal*. Should not be confused with a *pull out*.

**review:** originally a piece of *journalism* in which a critic expresses his or her opinions about a recent *release, publication, broadcast* or live performance. Readers certainly look to trusted **reviewers** for guidance: they may decide, for example, whether or not to see a particular film on the basis of the reviews it receives. Positive reviews are a therefore useful *marketing* tool, and film *distributors* are noted for the *misrepresentation* of reviews by careful selection of only the positive words. The *audience* for a review does not simply consist of people who are using it as a selection tool. Some will be using it to compare with their own impression, having already seen the film, bought the album or whatever; some will use the review itself as a form of entertainment. The latter is particularly true of television criticism. The *internet* has created many opportunities for members of the general public to become reviewers without the need to be employed as journalists.

**RFT:** see *regional film theatre*

**rhetoric:** the language of persuasion. Often used pejoratively to accuse the speaker or writer of producing language that sounds impressive but means little. (See also *sound bite.*)

**rhythm:** creating a pattern over time. Rhythm is an important characteristic of all good film *editing*. It is created by various factors, for example, the balancing of different *shot lengths* during a *sequence* or returning repeatedly to a particular shot. The term 'rhythmic editing' is used to describe editing that pays particular attention to the duration of shots – typically, speeding up or slowing down the pace of the film by increasing or decreasing the number of cuts per minute.

**riff:** a short, distinctive sequence of notes, often played repeatedly. Riffs are a common feature of most *pop music*. For example, much dance music relies on strongly rhythmic bass riffs.

**rifle mic:** a long, highly *directional microphone* used for recording sounds at some distance from the camera (e.g. in wildlife filming) or for picking out a specific sound where there is a lot of surrounding noise. Useful, for example, for recording interviews on the street where traffic noise would otherwise be a problem.

**right of reply:** the power, under the law, to answer a statement made in the press about an individual. Apart from the *libel* laws, UK residents have very little right of reply when a newspaper publishes material that is inaccurate and/or harmful. A number of individuals and organisations, including MediaWise, continue to campaign for a more effective way for individuals to take legal action against newspapers who *misrepresent* them.

**rights:** the legal ownership of some aspect of a copyrighted *property*. For example, film companies often purchase the film rights to a novel. This means that the copyrighted text still belongs to the writer, except for the right to make a film from it. (See also *copyright*.)

**right to know:** an important principle of *journalistic* freedom. The press, radio and TV news frequently come into conflict with organisations who wish to keep secrets. Journalists will then argue that the general public have a right to know about matters that affect them. Governments, particularly, tend to argue that the right to know does not always fit comfortably with national security. One result of this is the *Official Secrets Act.*

**right-wing:** see *political spectrum*

**RKO (Radio-Keith Orpheum):** see *studio system*

**road movie:** a film that follows characters on a journey by road. Usually, the characters are driving, but occasionally they travel on foot. There are many types of road movie, and the classification is probably too loose to be called a *genre.* Examples include *The Wizard of Oz* (Victor Fleming, USA, 1939) (fantasy genre); *Thelma and Louise* (Ridley Scott, USA, 1991) (outlaw genre); *Road to Singapore* (Victor Scherzinger, USA, 1940) (musical comedy genre).

**rockumentary:** a slightly jokey term for a *documentary* about a rock band. A good example is *End of the Century: The Story of the Ramones* (Jim Fields, USA, 2003). The genre was *satirised* in *This is Spinal Tap* (Rob Reiner, USA, 1984).

**role-play:** the taking on of an identity other than your own. This is sometimes considered an element of *video gaming.* Most games are written with the intention of increasing player *immersion* and this is often achieved by giving the player a role in the narrative. For example, Nintendo's *Legend of Zelda* series is based around a character called 'Link', who automatically takes on the name of the person playing the game. First-person adventures such as *Metroid Prime* give the player the opportunity to see from the perspective of the central character, and in what is perhaps the ultimate example of role-play, *Black and White* allows the player to 'be' a 'god'.

**rolling credits:** as cast and crew on film and TV productions grew in number, it became necessary to find a way of fitting everyone's name onto the screen at the end of the finished product. A common solution is to roll the credits (i.e. for the names to be shown rising from the bottom of the screen and eventually disappearing off the top). For workers in the media industries, it is very important to have your work credited, since this serves as proof of previous experience. The rolling credits system has the advantage of keeping each person's name on screen for a reasonably long time.

**romance; romantic:** complex terms with a range of meanings. As a *genre*, romance covers a variety of types of *narrative* in which love is the central concern source of interest. Frequently in romance films there is an element of *tragedy*. *Love Story* (Arthur Hiller, USA,

1972), and *Titanic* (James Cameron, USA, 1997) are very good examples. Many films that are not romances include a romance *subplot* such as that between A J (Ben Affleck) and Grace (Liv Tyler) in *Armageddon* (Michael Bay, USA, 1998).

**romantic comedy (romcom):** a film *genre* targeted predominantly at a female *audience*. There are many variations on this popular formula. Romcoms tend to be mid-budget films. They are usually set in glamorous metropolitan locations, such as Manhattan. The central characters tend to have enviable lives doing interesting jobs, frequently in a creative industry of some kind. They are surrounded by witty friends; they are physically attractive, but they are also searching fruitlessly for the right partner. The *narrative* may focus on the man or the woman. It will present the difficulties that they overcome before finally uniting as a couple. These will certainly include some misunderstandings and mistakes. Usually, one partner must make a 'grand gesture' such as running through the rain, or making a public speech, just before the couple are reconciled forever. This genre can be seen as a descendant of the *screwball comedy*.

**rostrum camera:** a camera mounted on a frame with its lens pointing downwards towards a flat surface on which a piece of artwork is positioned. Rostrum cameras were frequently used in traditional *animation*. Another common use is for filming paintings. The rostrum camera can *track* in and out and from left to right, but cannot *tilt* or *pan*.

**rotoscope:** a technique for creating *animation* by tracing over filmed *footage*. Rotoscoping has a long history in film, and can now be achieved digitally, as it is in *A Scanner Darkly* (Richard Linklater, USA, 2006).

**rough cut:** the first full *edit* of a film. Following the rough cut, further edits may only be fine-tuning the film. On some occasions, however, a rough cut reveals serious problems and the film must be substantially re-edited.

**royals:** a slang term for kings, queens, princes and princesses in general, and the British royal family in particular. Royalty is now a form of *celebrity* and royals are of great interest to the *mass media*, especially the *tabloids* and the *paparazzi*.

**royalties:** in the music and book publishing industries, money paid to writers or performers. Royalties are collected as a percentage of the retail price of each CD, download or book sold. Any business, such as a nightclub or radio station that plays a recording must then pay royalties to the *copyright* holders. They are also payable to songwriters if another artist performs or records his or her composition.

**'R' rating:** An age *rating* used in American cinemas. 'R' stands for 'Restricted'. Nobody under the age of 17 can be admitted to an 'R' film unless accompanied by an adult.

**RSA:** see *repressive state apparatus*

**RSL:** a **radio special licence** that allows the holder to broadcast on radio frequencies for a specified time at a particular event (e.g. an air show), or over a limited area (e.g. a university campus).

**rule of thirds:** a principle of *composition* based on dividing the frame into horizontal and vertical thirds, producing nine segments. Using the rule of thirds produces more interesting compositions than dividing the frame into halves, but still retains a sense of balance. It can be applied to *cinematography*, still photography and to overall page design.

**running gag:** a joke that is developed over a period of time. A running gag might be confined to a single episode of a TV programme or may appear repeatedly during a series. They are also common in *comedy* films. For example, in *Austin Powers, International Man of Mystery* (Mike Myers, 1997), there is a running gag where the death of each minor henchman is followed by a sequence showing its consequences: the news being broken to his family or friends.

**running order:** in a TV and radio *news* broadcast this is the sequence in which *stories* are organised. There is an element of hierarchy in the creation of the running order, particularly with regard to the first two or three stories, which are considered the most important of the day. However, there will also be attempts to balance material – grim stories and more upbeat ones, complex and simple – and also to keep back interesting material to be used as *still-to-comes*.

**running time:** the length of a recording, expressed in hours, minutes and seconds.

**rushes:** a print of the day's shooting on a film, produced for immediate checking. They are called rushes because they have to be rushed through processing in order to be ready on time. Also known as 'dailies' because they are produced on a daily basis.

### What other subjects are you studying?

A–Zs cover a range of different subjects. See the inside back cover for a list of all the titles in the series and how to order.

A B C D E F G H I J K L M N O P Q **R** S T U V W X Y Z

**safety shot:** see *master shot*

**sales revenue:** in *magazine* and *newspaper* publishing, the money earned by the company from the *cover price* of the publication. In most cases, *advertising revenue* is a much more important source of income.

**salience:** (i) the extent to which certain issues are seen as important and relevant (salient) by members of the public may be determined by the amount of attention these issues are given in the *mass media*. In their research into several US presidential elections in the 1960s and 1970s, McCombs and Shaw called this effect of the media *agenda-setting*. (ii) in advertising, much attention is paid to the way that, because of their positioning, colour and size, some elements within an advertisement will seem more salient than others.

**samurai film:** Japanese film *genre*, also known as 'jidai geki' (historical drama), mostly set in the Edo period (1600–1868). This genre, which made use of strong *conventions* to the point of *cliché* was very popular in Japan during the first part of the twentieth century. For a short time after the Second World War, the American forces occupying Japan banned samurai movies because they were seen as encouraging a war-like attitude. During the 1950s they emerged again, now showing the influence of Hollywood *Westerns*. The greatest *director* of samurai films in this period was Akira Kurosawa, whose works such as *Seven Samurai* (1954) and *Yojimbo* (1961) found an audience not only in Japan but also in Europe and the USA. Samurai films continue to be made in Japan, and there have been attempts in other countries to work in or around this genre, including *Le Samouraï* (Jean-Pierre Melville, Fr, 1967) and *Ghost Dog: The Way of the Samurai* (Jim Jarmusch, USA, 1999).

**sans serif:** see *serif*

**satellite:** an object in orbit around a planet. A communications satellite (comsat) is an electronic information *transceiver* in orbit around the earth. The first satellite of this type, called Telstar, was launched in 1962 to carry telephone and television signals. Today there are a large number in orbit, serving a wide range of purposes. Comsats are still used for international telephony as well as carrying *internet* and other signals. In isolated locations, it is sometimes possible to access *broadband* internet by connecting directly to a satellite during the short period when its orbit brings it within range.

**satellite broadcasting:** a *television* system that uses a *direct broadcasting satellite* (DBS) to transmit signals to specialised receiving equipment within a specific geographical area. The first fully commercial DBS system operating in the UK was *Sky TV*. In some countries, such as Germany and India, DBS services operate *free to air*.

**satire:** an attempt to present a powerful figure or institution as ridiculous. Satire involves an element of humour, especially *irony*, though the subject is usually a serious issue. The *documentary* film maker Michael Moore uses satire extensively in his film *Fahrenheit 9/11*

(2004) in which he represents President George W Bush as idiotic and the second Gulf War as an absurd venture. **Satirical** TV shows in the UK include *panel games* such as *Have I Got News For You* and *sketch shows* like *Bremner, Bird and Fortune.* The 1980s satirical Channel 4 TV *sitcom Drop The Dead Donkey* was recorded the day before transmission so that its content would be as *topical* as possible.

**saturation release:** a pattern of film *distribution* commonly associated with *blockbusters.* With the aim of attracting huge *audiences*, the *distributors* release a massive number of *prints* for the *opening weekend*, supported by an enormous *marketing campaign.* Saturation releases were in occasional use from the 1960s, mostly for films expected to be *event movies*, but have now become common practice for distributing *high-concept* movies and other major releases to *multiplexes.* This model is almost the exact opposite to the *platform releases* given to *art-house* and *low-budget* films. For example, *Batman Begins* (Christopher Nolan, USA, 2005) opened simultaneously on 3,858 American screens and 514 in the UK. As a comparison, the British art-house drama *Vera Drake* (Mike Leigh, UK, 2004) opened on two US screens with a later UK release of 65 prints.

**de Saussure, Ferdinand:** see *semiology*

**scanner:** a mobile control unit used like a TV *gallery* for *outside broadcast* work. For many years, this was bulky equipment requiring its own van, but the same tasks can now be accomplished using a laptop-sized unit.

**scenario:** an alternative term for *screenplay.* Sometimes also used to describe the overall *concept* for a film or TV series.

**scene:** (i) a subsection of a *script* or *screenplay* in which all the events have *spatial and temporal contiguity.* If there is a change to a new location, a different point in time, or both, a new scene begins. (See also *space and time.*) (ii) any place in which the story is set. This is to be distinguished from *location*, which is where the story is filmed. For example, in *Get Rich or Die Trying* (USA, 2005) the scene is New York City, but the location was actually Toronto.

**schadenfreude:** literally 'shameful pleasure', the term refers to the enjoyment of other people's misfortunes. *Drama* is usually based around characters suffering distressing events, and though the audience may sympathise or *empathise*, they also enjoy the *drama* that is built around what are often terrible experiences for the characters. Many *sitcoms*, such as *One Foot in the Grave*, and *The Office*, depend on schadenfreude for their comic effect.

**scheduling:** placing TV or radio programmes in *slots.* During the first few decades of TV broadcasting, the planning of schedules was of critical importance, though it has become less useful as a way of controlling *audiences* thanks to such developments in *media technologies* as the *remote control* and *time shifting* alongside the introduction of multiple *cable* and *satellite* channels. Nevertheless, broadcasters still rely on scheduling techniques in an attempt to attract and retain audiences. The most basic of these is 'dayparting', which consists of identifying which *demographic* is most likely to be watching or listening at particular times and adjusting output accordingly. Channel 4's targeting of an elderly audience during the late afternoon is the product of a dayparting strategy, as are the 'drivetime' programmes broadcast on many commercial radio stations. Other common strategies include:

- **stripping** – running a TV *series* every day of the week. Often the term refers to a *repeat* of a show originally broadcast weekly. This technique is very common on *cable* and *satellite* channels

- **stranding** – showing programmes of the same or a similar *genre* at the same time each day

- **stacking** – running similar programmes in succession, for instance three daytime *soaps* in a row or a triple bill of *lifestyle shows* in the hope that the audience will stay with the channel

- **tentpoling** – placing two 'weaker' programmes either side of a strong (i.e. popular) one

- **hammocking** – placing two stronger programmes either side of a weak one – or one for which the station hopes to build up an audience

- **theming** – building a period of programming around a single idea. Usually this would be restricted to a single night, probably during a weekend. Channel 4 have experimented with numerous theme nights as, to a lesser extent, have BBC2. The main *terrestrial* channels are less likely to present themed nights aside from charity telethons.

There are a number of important restrictions on British schedulers. Successful regular programmes such as major soaps will occupy a fixed position. The time and length of the *news* is controlled by *Ofcom*. There is also the 9 pm *watershed*. (See also *echo, pre-echo*.)

**schema theory:** a psychological explanation of the ways in which individuals understand the world. First proposed by F C Bartlett in 1932, it suggests that we develop schemata (sometimes called schemas) which are sets of expectations about the world based on our previous experiences. Schemata define our understanding of social situations and our behaviour. When we come across a new situation, we try to apply an existing schema to it in order to understand it quickly. If the schema fits, it is used; if not, it may be modified or a new schema may be created. For example, a student entering a classroom in a college for the first time after leaving school will apply the school classroom schema and try to behave accordingly. However, it will quickly become apparent that not all elements of the school classroom schema apply in the college classroom, so the schema will be modified. This is an example of a 'social schema'. According to schema theory, we also use 'textual schemata' to create our expectations about broader structures (such as *story, narrative* and *genre*) and formal *conventions* (for instance camera and editing). Usually, our understanding of a *text* combines social and textual schemata. When watching a hospital *drama* like *Casualty*, the viewer will apply textual schemata to the story and the way it is told, while social schemata will create understanding of the hospital environment, the family and friendship relationships shown, the status of doctors and so on.

**science fiction:** an important *genre* in *film, TV* and *radio drama*. Typical genre indicators include: imagined technology, future events or alternative realities, aliens, time travel, mutation and telepathy. Examples of science fiction film date from the earliest days of the *moving image*, the most famous of which is Georges Méliès' *A Trip to the Moon* (Fr, 1902). There are many subgenres of science fiction, often the product of hybridisation with other genres, such as *horror* in *Alien* (Ridley Scott, USA, 1979), *film noir* in *Total Recall* (Paul Verhoeven, USA, 1990), or the *western* as in *Star Wars* (George Lucas, USA, 1977). This capacity to change and develop partly accounts for the continuing success of the genre. It is also particularly good at showcasing the latest *special effects* and providing *spectacle* for the *audience*. TV science fiction series often inspire *cult* audiences. Among the most significant of these have been *Doctor Who* in the UK, and the *Star Trek franchise* in the USA. The definition of science fiction is the subject of some debate – some argue that there need to be imaginary products of science (spacecraft, ray guns and so on). Others would include films about a future society, like that represented in *The Handmaid's Tale* (Volker Schlöndorff, USA/Ger, 1990). This, along with the sometimes uncertain boundary between science fiction and *fantasy*, has led some to use the alternative term *speculative fiction*.

**scoop:** a major *news story*, especially an *exclusive*.

**scopophilia:** literally the love of watching. The term is used in psychology to describe a particular form of *voyeurism*. Scopophilia is a fairly common *theme* in film, most famously Hitchcock's *Rear Window* (USA, 1954). The term also describes the relationship between *pornography* and its audience. According to the *feminist film critic*, Laura Mulvey, the way most films represent women puts the viewer in the position of a scopophile. This is what she means when she suggests that the camera constructs a *male gaze*.

**screen:** (i) any surface on which an image is produced by projection or other means. (ii) an influential British academic journal of *film studies*.

**screen direction:** the direction in which a figure moves across the screen. Usually this is expressed in terms of the viewer's left and right, using the terms 'screen left' and 'screen right' or the abbreviations 'screen L' and 'screen R.' Since a figure can be filmed from either side, it is possible to show the same movement as 'screen L-R' or 'screen R-L', depending on where the camera is positioned. Consistent screen direction is very important in *continuity editing*. Within a single scene, the audience can understand spatial locations because edits do not *cross the line*. If *characters* are shown to be approaching each other in a *cross-cutting* sequence, they would usually maintain opposite screen directions. If a character is following another, both will move in the same screen direction. More widely, if a film shows a journey out and a journey home, the two stages will predominantly use opposite screen directions. Most commonly, the journey out is L-R and the journey home is R-L.

**screenplay:** a *script* for a film. This is the basic script produced by the *screenwriter*. It has to follow very strict layout rules so that the amount of screen time can be estimated. Screenplays contain dialogue and directions for the *actors*. They should include as little camera direction as possible. (See also *scenario*; *shooting script*.)

**screen test:** a short piece of filmed performance used in the process of auditioning *actors* for films.

**screen time:** time on-screen. Leading characters typically have more screen time than minor characters.

**screen violence:** see *media effects*; *censorship*; *violence*

**screenwriter:** a writer of *screenplays* for films. Syd Field is a US screenwriting theorist whose various books, based on his experience as a professional *script* reader, have been highly influential in defining basic principles for constructing *Hollywood* scripts. Most importantly, he described the standard 'three-act structure', which states that the following elements are essential to a successful film story:

i.   a thirty minute 'set-up' (act 1), followed by...

ii.  a 'plot point' or *turning point*, which begins a period of confrontation (act 2) during which the *protagonist* has to overcome various problems on the way to his or her goal until...

iii. a second 'plot point' occurs, which makes achieving the goal even more difficult for the protagonist. During the final 30 minutes the film reaches its most dramatic moments.

**screwball comedy:** a film *genre* that was particularly important during the *Hollywood studio system* of the 1930s and 1940s, but which has influenced many subsequent films.

Screwball comedies usually concern a wealthy and sophisticated young woman who becomes involved with a man from outside her social circle. The dialogue is generally witty and somewhat cynical. Divorce and remarriage are often important plot devices. Good examples include *It Happened One Night* (Frank Capra, USA, 1934), *Bringing Up Baby* (Howard Hawks, USA, 1938) and *The Philadelphia Story* (George Kukor, USA, 1940).

**script:** any written text intended for performance. Most film and television productions are scripted, as are many radio programmes. See also *ad lib* and *improvisation.*

**script development:** the process in *Hollywood* between *optioning* an original screenplay or other filmable idea (such as an *adaptation*) and *greenlighting*. It includes lining up *directors*, *stars* and other key personnel as well as rewrites. Sometimes a project is stuck for a very long time in development and may never reach greenlighting stage. Industry slang for this phenomenon is '*development hell'*.

**script writer:** a writer of scripts for TV or radio.

**scuttlebutt:** see *word-of-mouth*

**season:** American term for a sequence of *episodes* of a TV *series* or *serial* recorded and broadcast as a group. Most US TV shows broadcast one season per year. Seasons can be up to 26 episodes long.

**SECAM:** one of three colour broadcasting systems in use throughout the world. The other two are *PAL* and *NTSC*. SECAM is the least widespread system, confined mainly to France (where it was invented) and Eastern Europe.

**secondary definers:** see *primary definers*

**secondary level of attention** describes the way in which some *media products*, particularly radio and TV, are consumed alongside other activities. A person who is ironing at the same time as watching television, or doing homework while listening to the radio, is giving the media text secondary attention. Some texts, such as daytime *soap operas*, are produced with the expectation of secondary levels of attention in the *audience*, and provide extensive and repeated *exposition*. The result can often be seen as *syntagmatic redundancy.*

**secondary medium:** (i) *media* of lesser importance, as in, for example, '*Newspaper* editors tend to see the *web* as a secondary medium.' (ii) media or *media texts* that are likely to be given a *secondary level of attention*, as in 'Drivetime radio is, by definition, a secondary medium.' (iii) a medium used for backup storage, such as a writable CD, portable hard drive or data stick. (See also *primary medium.*)

**second unit:** a small film crew that is responsible for less important material such as *footage* of scenery, *cutaways* and *insert shots*. They may also shoot *stunts* and other material involving *doubles*. Directing the second unit is an important creative role in film production, and often acts as the final career step towards first-unit direction. The second unit director should not be confused with the *assistant director*, who is essentially an administrator.

**seeker-hero:** according to Propp's 1928 book *The Morphology of the Folk Tale*, this is another name for the *protagonist*. The term emphasises the idea of the *quest*.

**segue:** a smooth transition from one part of a broadcast or other media product to another. For example, between the news and sport sections of a *bulletin*. Also used to describe the change from one level to the next in a *video game*, often using a *cut scene* to advance the *story*.

**selective focus:** using the camera lens to emphasise a particular object or set of objects, by keeping them sharp, while other elements, more distant and/or closer to the camera, are blurred. The technique is used both in still and *moving image* photography. (See also *pulling focus*.)

**self-actualisation:** see *Maslow's hierarchy of needs*

**self-reflexive** or **self-referential texts:** texts that deliberately draw attention to their own fictional nature. Self-reflexivity is a characteristic of *postmodernism* but also occurs in other types of *text*. Some **self-reflection** serves comic purposes, as when the comedy *Western*, *Blazing Saddles* (Mel Brooks, USA, 1974) ends with a chase sequence bursting into the sets of other films of different *genres* apparently being made at the same *studio*. The *screenwriter* Charlie Kaufman is well known for his self-referential approach: in his film *Adaptation* (Spike Jonze, USA, 2002) the central character is a screenwriter called Charlie Kaufman.

**self-regulation:** voluntary controls over a sector of the media industries, usually adopted out of fear that *statutory control* would be more severe. The PEGI age ratings on most *video games* are a good example, as was the *Hays code* that operated in *Hollywood* during the 1930s.

**sell lines:** the lines of text on a *magazine* cover that describe some of that particular issue's contents. Also called 'cover lines'.

**semantics:** the study of *meaning* and how it is formed by *language*.

**seminal:** a critical term describing any work from which others have developed or grown. For instance, 'The original *King Kong* is the seminal monster movie.' Sometimes now used to mean the greatest example of a *genre*, whether or not it has been very influential.

**semiology:** the study of meaning and how it is formed by '*signs*' such as words, images or music. The most important figure in semiology was the Swiss thinker Ferdinand de Saussure (1857–1913), who proposed the idea that signs could be arbitrary – that is that there need not be a connection between the '*signifier*' (for example the word 'fish') and the 'signified' (a fish). Another important figure was the American Charles S Peirce (1839–1914), who distinguished between iconic signs (*icons*) which represented the signified (for example a picture of a fish to represent a fish) and symbolic signs (*symbols*) which did not (for example a picture of a fish placed on a car to indicate that the driver is a Christian). Much analysis of *media texts* makes use of semiology, looking for the culturally defined meanings of words, typefaces, colours, images and so on. (US sources refer to 'semiotics/semiotician', whereas 'semiology/semiologist' are European.)

**sensationalism:** the reporting *style* of the *tabloid press*, especially the red tops. The first stage in sensationalising the news is the selection of *stories* dealing mainly with sex, violent crime and other vivid material. The presentation of these stories through lurid images, *splash headlines* and exaggerated, though simple, language aims for maximum dramatic effect on the reader.

**Sensurround:** a short-lived process for augmenting action sequences in *Hollywood* films during the 1970s. Very loud low-frequency sound was generated by massive subwoofers. The sound was inaudible to the human ear, but could physically shake the audience in their seats. It was designed for *Earthquake* (Mark Robson, USA, 1974) as part of a strategy to draw declining *audiences* back to the cinema by creating more of a sense of 'event' around cinema films. Like other gimmicks, such as *3-D*, it was not of lasting interest to audiences and has only been used in a small number of films.

**sequel:** a *narrative* that follows on from another, previously complete narrative, usually a film. Sequels have become a much more significant element of *Hollywood* film-making in recent years, since it is recognised that seriality (the production of one or more sequels) is an even better guarantee of success than *genre*. Consequently, many film narratives are now constructed with the idea of a sequel already built in.

**sequence:** a series of *shots* that have been *edited* together to produce *meaning*. Sometimes the term refers to a segment of a *film* or *TV programme* that has been extracted from the whole. Sequences are used in *marketing*; for example, they are provided to broadcasters to support promotional interviews. In academic work, sequences are commonly used for close analysis or demonstration. During *storyboarding*, filming and *editing* film makers will use terms such as '*action* sequence' and '*dialogue* sequence' to identify distinct segments of the *narrative*.

**sequencer:** a piece of *digital* music hardware or computer software designed to remember sequences of musical notes and play them back on a synthesiser. Many audio editing programmes can combine sequencing with digital audio recording and editing, giving such high-quality results that it has been possible for artists such as The Streets and Daniel Bedingfield to produce marketable *singles* or even *albums* using home computers without the need for a large studio or *record label*.

**sequence shot:** a long, complex *take* involving substantial camera movement, such as the *dolly shot* near the start of Spike Lee's *Summer of Sam* (USA, 1999) which follows John Leguizamo and Mira Sorvino as they arrive in a car outside a disco, walk to the front of the queue, head down a flight of stairs and onto the dance floor where they begin to dance. Robert Altman's *The Player* (USA, 1992) begins with a sequence shot lasting longer than eight minutes. Also known as 'plan sequence'.

**serial:** a *narrative fiction* that develops its story towards a *dénouement* over a number of *episodes*.

**series:** a sequence of self-contained *episodes* on radio, TV or film. A series may be *fiction* or *non-fiction*. The episodes of fictional series are usually connected by *characters and/or location* (*Friends*, for example) or a *theme* (*Tales of the Unexpected*) or *genre* (the *Twilight Zone*). Non-fiction series are usually connected by *presenter* (*Richard and Judy*) and/or genre (for example, talk show, consumer affairs, gardening). (See also *story arc*.) Slightly confusingly, in the UK the term is also used (as *season* is used in America) to mean each individual run of a recurring episodic programme. In that context, a *serial* can also be referred to as a *series*. For example, in Britain it would be perfectly correct to say, 'there's a new series of that drama serial you liked last year'.

**serif:** a slight projection finishing off a stroke of a character in a *typeface*. Typefaces are often divided into two basic varieties: 'serif typefaces' have letters that are more ornamented, not just with serifs but also extra curves, loops and other details; 'sans serif typefaces', like the one used in this book, are much plainer and simpler in appearance. These two basic styles have developed *semiotic* meanings. Generally, for example, sans serif is associated with modernity and progress, while serif is associated with tradition and conservatism. For this reason, *The Independent* uses predominantly sans serif and *The Daily Express* uses predominantly serif. These choices reflect the *values* and *target readership* of each paper.

**set:** (i) to identify the time and place in which a *narrative* will unfold: for example, Paris, 1689. The setting will usually require appropriate production design. (ii) an interior that has been constructed to look like a real place when filmed. Sets are used in TV and film to overcome some of the difficulties involved in filming on *location*. For example, because they only have two or three walls, sets can accommodate bulky camera equipment. *Sound stages* and TV *studios* in which sets are constructed are purpose-built to give control over sound and lighting. Using a set also means that the look of the scene is under the control of the film makers. Set designers are highly skilled at translating the *production designer*'s ideas into convincing sets. They are assisted by set decorators and set dressers. Today, sets are almost exclusively used for *interiors*, but during the 1930s and 1940s many filmed 'exteriors' were actually filmed on sets.

**set-top box:** a device for decoding digital TV signals from *DST*, *cable* or *Freeview*. Despite the name, they are rarely placed on top of the television set.

**set-up:** an arrangement of film or TV cameras and lighting equipment prepared in advance of shooting. Some scenes will require several different set-ups to achieve all the *angles* required for *editing*.

**sex:** (i) the biological difference between male and female. (See also *gender*.) (ii) intimate physical contact. The presentation of sex in this sense is a key issue in *censorship* and control of film and *media texts*.

**sexism:** any unequal treatment of individuals or groups based on their biological sex. In film and media, sexism usually refers to issues of *representation*, where women are shown conforming to *stereotypes* as weaker, inferior, sexually available, only interested in housework and so on, while men are presented as *heroic*, determined, powerful, creative figures. Partly because women have become more powerful in the media industries, and partly because of general changes in society, sexism is arguably less prevalent in the media than it once was.

**sexploitation:** anything that exploits its audience's interest in sex, but which is not straight-forwardly presented as *pornography*. The term 'sexploitation film' is used to cover a wide variety of products, including 'documentary' films about nudism, 'sex comedies' such as *Come Play With Me* (George Harrison Marks, UK, 1977) and women's prison films. Usually sex-ploitation films were marketed with the promise of far more sexual material than they actually contained. Famously, the pornographer Bob Guccione transformed the historical *epic*, *Caligula* (Tinto Brass, 1979) into a sexploitation film by editing in several scenes of pornography during *post production*. Since *censorship* laws have been relaxed, making genuine pornography readily available, sexploitation as a film *genre* has died out. Other media products, particularly *advertising* and pop video are still occasionally accused of sexploitation.

**sexuality:** (i) the general realm of sexual behaviour – things to do with sex as an act rather than simply the state of being male or female (as in, for example, 'A significant element of Marilyn Monroe's *star identity* was her sexuality.') Similarly, asexuality is an absence of sexuality (as in, for example, 'Tom Hanks presents a rather asexual persona, which works to his advantage in his typical father-figure or adult child roles.') (ii) sexual orientation: whether a person is heterosexual, homosexual or somewhere between. Many media texts make use of *stereotypes* associated with sexuality.

**sexy:** aside from its obvious meaning, 'sexy' is sometimes used *metaphorically* in media contexts as slang for 'exciting'. Journalists might refer to a 'sexy story' even if it contains no sexual content, for example, a 'sexy political story'. TV executives might refer to 'sexy ratings' for a programme.

**SFX:** see *special effects*

**Shannon and Weaver's model:** a simple outline of *communication*, created by Claude Shannon and Warren Weaver in 1947, which can be applied to all media: the '*message*' begins at a 'source', and passes on to an 'encoder'. It is sent along a '*channel*' to a 'decoder' before it is understood by the 'receiver'. Between the encoder and decoder, it may be subject to '*noise*' which distorts it to some extent. (See also *decode; encode.*)

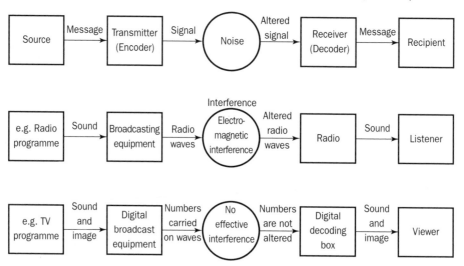

*Shannon and Weaver's model of communication (top) applied to analogue signals (middle) and digital signals (bottom)*

**shallow focus:** the opposite of *deep focus*. In film, TV and photography, a lens with little *depth of field* is used so that most of the image is blurred and only objects within a narrow range appear sharp. (See also *selective focus.*)

**Shepperton Studios:** see *Pinewood Studios*

**shocking cinema:** film that either intentionally or unintentionally shocks at least a section of the *audience*. We can divide shock into two basic categories: pleasurable shock, which is sought by the audience, for example of a *horror film*, and controversial shock, which creates public hostility, sometimes causes a *moral panic* and often leads to the film's *censorship*. The most obvious sources of controversial shock are extreme presentations of *violence* and/or *sex*, as in *Salò* (Pier Paolo Pasolini, Italy/Fr, 1975), but controversy can also be sparked by the film's subject matter, as with the representation of religious figures in Martin Scorsese's *The Last Temptation of Christ* (USA, 1988) or drug use in *Trainspotting* (Danny Boyle, UK, 1996).

**shoot:** (i) to photograph material using a *moving image* or still *camera*. (For example, 'We shot the film in four days.') (ii) a film or TV shoot is the whole process of filming, or a defined segment of it (as in, 'The jungle sequence was completed in a four-day shoot.')

**shooting ratio:** the mathematical relationship between the amount of film shot and the amount that was used in the final *edit*. If the director shot eight times more *footage* than was used, say 720 minutes for a 90 minute film, this would result in a shooting ratio of 8:1, which is fairly typical for a production shot on film *stock*. Much higher ratios are possible when using *video tape* because it is cheaper and reusable.

**shooting script:** the version of a *screenplay* or TV *script* that is used on *set*. Shooting scripts are prepared under the supervision of the *director* and can include instructions about such matters as *angles*, *blocking*, and *lighting*. They will often be ordered to reflect the *production board* and *shooting schedules* rather than the order of the *narrative*.

**shooting schedule:** a daily plan produced by the assistant director of the work to be done on a film *shoot*.

**short film:** any film shorter than a *feature film*. There is some crossover between a long 'short' and a short feature. For example, Richard Linklater's *Before Sunset* (USA, 2004) runs for 77 minutes and Christopher Nolan's *Following* (UK, 1998) is 69 minutes long: each could be considered either a short or a feature film. Most shorts, however, are less than 40 minutes long. The best short films are written and directed to take advantage of their smaller size. Often they are made as student projects or as 'calling cards' to gain interest for a film maker, and *exhibited* at *film festivals*.

**short wave:** a *radio* wavelength that produces relatively low-quality *analogue broadcasts* but which is particularly useful for international broadcasting. A short-wave radio can pick up signals from all over the world.

**shot:** (i) a single unedited piece of filmed material. (ii) a photograph.

**shot duration:** the length of time between two *edits* in a film or TV piece.

**shot length:** see *cinematography*

**shot-reverse-shot:** a *convention* for showing a *dialogue* sequence. We *cut* between the two speakers, showing each person's point of view. The shot lengths may be varied for effect.

**showing:** a single *exhibition* of a film in a cinema.

**showreel:** a collection of examples of filmed material used for *marketing* purposes. Usually now provided on *DVD* rather than a reel of film. *Advertising agencies* often provide a showreel of their previous work to prospective clients; actors sometimes send showreels of their performances to *agents*.

**sidebar:** supplementary material on the same page as a main article, and related to it, but boxed off or given another *layout* feature such as a coloured background to separate it from the *body copy*. For example, a *spread* in which the body copy is an interview with a footballer could include a sidebar giving statistics about his career – teams played for, goals scored and so on.

**sight gag:** a visual joke. There are three basic types of sight gag: *slapstick*, or exaggerated violence; visual puns, which exploit the similarity between two objects and absurd or *surreal* images.

**Sight & Sound:** a film magazine published by the *British Film Institute*. Its approach is predominantly academic and serious.

**sign:** any image, sound or word that communicates *meaning*. (See also *semiology*.)

**signal:** (i) in *broadcast media*, the signal is the stream of electromagnetic waves between the transmitter and receiver. (ii) In *semiotic analysis*, to signal is to use *coding* in order to communicate messages to the *audience*.

**signature:** a feature of form or content that is strongly associated with a particular performer or other creative artist. For example, the *catchphrase* 'I'll be back' has become a signature of the actor Arnold Schwarzenegger. The idea that a film *director* can leave a distinctive signature on a movie is an important element of *auteurist* approaches to cinema.

**signature tune:** a piece of *theme* music, normally the music over the titles and/or credits of a TV programme, but can also be used to mean a *leitmotif.*

**signifier:** an alternative term for *sign* in *semiology.* The signifier can be a word, an image or a sound. The term is used to emphasise the fact that the signifier only exists to represent the 'signified' (i.e. the thing itself).

**sign-off:** (i) the closing words in a broadcast. See also standard out cue (*SOC*). (ii) the once-common practice of closing down a TV station for the night.

**silent film:** a film with no recorded sound. Although not technically impossible, it was so difficult to achieve *synchronised sound* before the late 1920s that almost all films of this period were silent. Music would be provided by a cinema pianist, and occasional *captions* would overcome problems with advancing the narrative. The lack of *dialogue* had a strong effect on early *genres*, which tended to be action driven (*westerns* and *slapstick comedy*) or *melodramatic* (*tragic romances*). The first full 'talkie' was *Lights of New York* (Bryan Foy, USA, 1928), and silent cinema continued into the 1930s, but had mostly died out by 1940. Silent films are still made occasionally, as artistic experiments.

**silly season:** the period in late summer when there tends to be little real *news* and so the newspapers have to fill their pages with *stories* which would not be selected at other times of the year.

**sim:** a *video game genre* in which some aspect of reality is simulated. Examples include *Football Manager* where the player is the manager of a football team in an imaginary league; *Sim City* in which the player 'builds' and maintains a whole city and *The Sims* where the player controls a set of families in a *virtual* suburb. Sim games often have no set outcome or *narrative* – the player does not try to win, but merely explores the effects of various decisions on the virtual world and tries to avoid doing anything too catastrophic to it.

**simulacrum:** the straightforward meaning of this word is 'a realistic copy'. Sometimes it is used pejoratively by *critics* to suggest an empty or sham version of something more substantial, something which is more style than substance. For example, a critic might write, 'The boyband 'Busted' are simulacrum punk rockers'. The philosopher Jean Baudrillard used the term to mean a copy of a copy that no longer has any relationship with the thing it was originally copied from. It can be argued that the media are full of simulacra in this sense, since they are constantly engaged in reinventing past products. For example, Don Powell's 1978 film remake of *The Thirty-Nine Steps* followed Ralph Thomas's version of 1959, which was itself a remake of Hitchcock's 1935 *adaptation* of John Buchan's 1915 novel.

**simulcasting:** a contraction of 'simultaneous broadcasting', meaning being broadcast on two media at the same time. Simulcasts were often used to enhance the *audience* experience when broadcasting music at a time when an *FM* radio tuner could deliver much better sound than a TV set. The viewer could listen to the *performance* on the radio while viewing it on television. Advances in broadcast audio and the time lapses involved in different broadcasting technologies have made the practice rare, though the annual BBC Prom concerts are still simulcast in this way. In the early days of television, many sports commentaries were broadcast on radio and TV simultaneously as a way of keeping down costs. Many radio stations simulcast as a way of extending their audience. For example, BBC Radio 4 is now broadcast on FM, long wave, *DAB* and over the *internet.*

**single:** a song sold as an individual recording on record or CD. In fact, all so-called singles carried more than one track. The 7" singles that were extremely important in the pop industry from the 1950s to the 1990s were all pressed with at least two songs – the A side and the B side. Other variants included the double A side, on which both tracks had equal status, and the 12" single, which delivered higher quality and often more material. CD singles similarly would tend to contain three or more tracks, but never achieved anything like the enormous popularity of the vinyl singles that they replaced. The development of music *downloads* has now effectively destroyed the market for singles.

**single-shot film:** a short piece of *footage* from the point of view of one *camera*. Many very early films were single-shot pieces depicting scenes of interest, such as Louis *Lumière's* one-minute film made in 1895 of workers leaving his factory.

**single-shot narrative:** a story told without a single cut. The most impressive example is *Russian Ark* (Alexandr Sokurov, Russia/Ger, 2002).

**sitcom (situation comedy):** a TV *genre* in which humour is built around a set of characters connected by their social circumstances (e.g. a family or a group of co-workers). Styles of sitcom range widely. Although the standard British sitcom offers a conventional representation of *middle-class* family life (for example, *My Family*), Britain has also produced *surreal fantasy* (*My Hero*); social realist sitcom (Early Doors); documentary realist sitcom (The Office); an anarchist sitcom (*The Young Ones*) and a *period* sitcom (*Blackadder*). By contrast with British sitcoms, which mostly last only for two or three *series* with fewer than ten *episodes* each, successful American sitcoms can run for several *seasons* of twenty-four episodes. This is because they tend to be written by large teams whereas British sitcoms are usually scripted by a single writer. Some of America's most successful TV products have been sitcoms with *ensemble casts*, notably *Cheers*, *Frasier*, *Seinfeld* and *Friends*.

**sketch:** (i) in a newspaper, a parliamentary sketch is a brief, often witty, account of an interesting event in the House of Commons or House of Lords the previous day. (ii) short comic performance on TV or radio involving two or more actors playing roles. A sketch show is a *comedy* programme composed of (probably) unrelated sketches, though often (as in *Little Britain*), there will be repeated use of *characters*, jokes and *catchphrases*.

**Skillset:** a body funded by the National Lottery. It aims to develop the British film industry by giving financial support to people who want to train as film professionals.

**slander:** spoken statements about a person that are untrue and which 'defame' his or her character. Distinct from *libel*, which describes written statements with the same effect. Because libel and slander are illegal, media institutions employ lawyers to carry out libel checks and/or slander checks on any potentially sensitive material.

**slapstick comedy:** a type of *sight gag* involving elaborate *violence*, usually accidental. Although the violence is often extreme, more than severe enough to kill its victim in real life, the exaggerated style of slapstick removes any suggestion of *horror*. Slapstick is a popular element in *silent film*, cartoons and in media products aimed at children, such as the *Home Alone* film *franchise*.

**slasher film:** a *subgenre* of *horror*, related to the *splatter movie*. The villain, a blade-wielding serial killer, often has apparently supernatural powers of survival. The victims are usually young, attractive and sexually active. Early examples include *Peeping Tom* (Michael Powell, UK, 1960) and *Psycho* (Alfred Hitchcock, USA, 1960). The genre really developed its identity in the 1970s and 1980s with *Halloween* (John Carpenter, USA, 1978) *Friday the 13th* (Sean S Cunningham, USA, 1980) and *A Nightmare on Elm Street* (Wes Craven, USA, 1984). By the 1990s the slasher movie was seen as a format that had run out of ideas, but the *postmodernist* series of *Scream* films briefly revitalised the genre.

**slate:** (i) in film production, the filmed marker at the beginning of a *take*, normally using a *clapperboard*, to identify *scene* and take number. (ii) the list of films a production company intends to make and release during a specified future period. For example, 'Pixar's slate for next summer includes *Toy Story 3* and *Finding Nemo... Again.*' (iii) to give a particularly bad review (as in, 'Critics have slated the new Eminem album.')

**sleeper/sleeper hit:** a *slow burner*, particularly in the film industry. A film that does little business on first release but builds a large audience through *word-of-mouth*. Sometimes sleeper films become successful during their *theatrical run*. Increasingly, they achieve this status on their *home video* release. The most celebrated example is *The Shawshank Redemption* (Frank Darabont, USA, 1994).

**slice-of-life:** any TV *drama* or *documentary* concerned with showing, or seeming to show, everyday life. *Docusoaps* are a recent development in slice-of-life TV. Slice-of-life *advertisements* use this approach to sell products.

**slogan:** a short, memorable phrase, usually one associated with a particular product in advertising or a political campaign. Effective slogans often make use of techniques such as:

- rhyme – 'Beanz Meanz Heinz'
- half-rhyme – 'New Labour: New Danger'
- puns – 'Brilliant cleaning starts with *Finish*'
- neologisms – (invented words) 'Drinka pinta milka day'
- absurdity – 'You *know* when you've been Tangoed!'
- assonance or consonance – 'Intel inside'
- balanced ideas 'A dog is for life, not just for Christmas'
- rhythm – 'A hazelnut in every bite'
- Many slogans, however, are memorable for reasons that are less easy to quantify, for example, Nike's 'Just do it', Sony's 'Do not underestimate the power of Playstation' or Audi's 'Vorsprung durch technik'.

**slot:** segment of time where a programme might be positioned in *scheduling* for TV or radio, such as 'an early evening slot' or 'a primetime slot'.

**slow burner:** (i) a media product that takes some time to become successful. For example, the UK *sitcom The Office* drew relatively small audiences during its first series on BBC2. It later developed massive popularity as a consequence of good *word-of-mouth*. (See also *sleeper.*) (ii) used by critics to describe a song, album, film, TV show etc. that makes a less impressive first impression but gradually grows on the listener/viewer. (iii) a narrative in which there is not a great deal of dramatic action.

**slow motion/slo-mo:** film/video effect where action on screen is reduced in speed. This can be achieved in *editing* by slowing down film shot at the normal *frame rate*. Better quality results are achieved by shooting the original *rushes* at a faster frame rate, say 48 frames per second (fps), and then playing back at the normal 24 fps speed.

**slug line:** the *scene* heading in a *script* identifying the important information necessary to shoot the scene. For example:

### EXT. AHMED'S GARDEN. NIGHT

**sneak preview:** a *marketing* technique suggesting *privileged access* to an eagerly awaited product. For example, a film *distributor* might circulate a 'sneak preview' *trailer* of a movie. The preview is not 'sneaky' at all – the purpose is to fire up interest in the coming product.

**soap opera:** popular TV *genre* usually built around a community and focusing on the inter-personal relationships among a large cast of *characters*. There are several overlapping *narratives* in any *episode*, offering a variety of *audience* experiences, such as tragedy, comedy and romance. Originally, a *radio genre* in the USA during the 1930s, the nickname 'soap opera' was coined because the shows were *sponsored* by manufacturers of cleaning products and presented *melodramatic* storylines for an audience of housewives. Today, with the exception of Radio 4's *The Archers*, this is largely a TV genre and its audience has broadened to include male viewers and young people. Soap operas from the USA have tended to be more glamorous and unrealistic than their UK counterparts, some of which, especially *Coronation Street*, were strongly influenced by *social realism*. In recent years, com-petition for ratings has led British soaps to introduce much more dramatic plot elements, such as organised crime, gender reassignment and serial killers. Because of their regular broadcast times and loyal audiences, soaps are an important element in TV *scheduling*.

**SOC (standard out cue):** any phrase used in radio broadcasting to indicate clearly that a piece of recorded *copy* has ended. The conventional SOC for a *news* report is something like, 'Stephen Tompkins, for Radio Ten News, Birmingham.' This allows radio *producer*s, *editors* and *presenters* to *segue* into the next item without *dead air*.

**social class:** layers in society based on economic divisions. For media and film students, social class is important because:

- *audiences* have traditionally been divided into social classes, both by media *institutions* for *marketing*, and by academics for analysis

- *media texts* can often be analysed in terms of their *representation* of social class groups, particularly through *stereotyping*

- British society has traditionally been broken into '*working class*', '*middle class*' and 'upper class', but these are not clear divisions. Class is a complex issue involving the *cultures* of particular social groups as well as their economic status. (See also *ABC12DE*.)

**social construct:** a thing that only exists because society exists. According to the sociolo-gists Berger and Luckman in their book *The Social Construction of Reality* (1966), we can divide reality into brute facts, such as 'the Earth revolves around the sun', and institutional facts, which are facts only because people in society agree about them. The *mass media* are important in this process because they provide the opportunity to share concepts with enormous numbers of people.

**socialisation:** the process through which, mostly during childhood, individuals learn how to fit in to society by following *norms* in attitude and behaviour. Many right-wing thinkers (e.g. F R Leavis) see the *mass media* as a harmful force in socialisation. They claim that the media encourage violence, vulgarity and selfishness, thus producing an overall decline in *culture*. Some on the *left* (e.g. the *Marxist* Herbert Marcuse) argue that the media socialise the *audience* into unthinking acceptance of *capitalism*. Alternatively, some thinkers, including members of the *CCCS*, have argued that the mass media can have positive effects in social-isation. (See also *effects model*.)

**social problem film:** a film *genre* dramatising a contemporary issue such as drug abuse or prison conditions and particularly associated with the *Warner Bros* studio during the era of the *Hollywood studio system*. One of the earliest examples was *I Am a Fugitive from a Chain Gang* (Mervyn LeRoy, USA, 1932). Many early *gangster films*, such as *Scarface: The Shame of the Nation* (Howard Hawks, USA, 1932) can be described as social problem *thrillers* because they combined social comment with action and suspense. The genre continues in more recent productions such as *Traffic* (Steven Soderbergh, USA, 2000).

**social realism:** a *narrative fiction genre* in novels, plays, film and TV displaying most or all of the following characteristics:

- *left-wing* political *bias*
- contemporary urban and/or industrial setting among ordinary, *working-class* people
- story of ordinary life
- hostility towards the traditional *establishment*, such as the church, education, the army, the police and prison system
- presentation of business and industry as exploitative of its workers
- downbeat, somewhat pessimistic tone
- simple camerawork and *editing* – often close to *documentary* in style
- untrained *actors*.

**social realist film:** a film made in a *social realist* style, particularly important in British cinema. Examples include: *Saturday Night and Sunday Morning* (Karel Reisz, UK, 1960); *Kes* (Ken Loach, UK, 1969); *Rita, Sue and Bob Too* (Alan Clarke, UK, 1986).

**sociology:** the academic study of human society. Since the term was first used by the French thinker Auguste Comte in the early nineteenth century, sociology has developed into a complex and wide-ranging set of theories and debates. There is no single 'sociological' interpretation of the world. Sociological approaches are important in media and film studies, and the sociology of the *mass media* is regarded as a major sub-discipline within sociology. Particular areas of sociological interest in the media include: representation of *gender*, *ethnicity* and *social class*; *ideology*; media *consumption*. The approaches to these topics taken within media studies have been heavily influenced by sociology. Typically, a theoretical position will be proposed, which can then be tested using accepted sociological *research methods*.

**soft focus:** slightly blurred effect that can be created with a specially designed *lens*, a *filter* or in *post-production*. The use of soft focus to create a dreamy or romantic effect has become a cinematic *cliché*.

**soft light:** artificial light that has either been filtered (*diffused*) through a sheet of white cloth or bounced off a surface to reduce its harshness and produce a gentler, more rounded appearance when filming.

**soft news:** unchallenging, inconsequential, often positive news. Typical soft news subjects include charity events, strange coincidences, animals, *celebrities* and *human interest*. In broadcasting and print journalism, these stories are included for *balance* with the *hard* *news.* The final *story* in a news broadcast will almost always be soft news, included to give the programme a light-hearted conclusion.

**soft sell:** An *advertising* technique which avoids giving the impression of selling the product. A gentler tone is taken and the qualities of the product may be understated or even ridiculed. Opposite of the *hard sell.* Often the idea is to suggest that the advertiser is being honest with the viewer.

**solus position:** where an advertisement appears on a page with no other *advertising.* Usually sold to advertisers at a premium rate. Also a *billboard* or other location where the advertisement will appear on its own.

**Sony Awards:** annual prizes funded by the *Sony Corporation* and given in various categories for radio programmes. The equivalent of the Oscars or Baftas for British radio.

**Sony Corporation:** Japanese-based *multinational* company, one of the so-called *Big Six.* Sony has introduced a number of significant media *consumption* products to the mass market. The portable Walkman cassette player of the 1980s revolutionised the consumption of music, and the Playstation dominated the *video gaming* market since the 1990s. Sony has *diversified* into media production and distribution, mostly through the acquisition of existing companies. The company has often been at the forefront of developments in *new media technologies.* For example, they introduced the 3.5" floppy disc that was the standard for portable data storage during the 1990s and, together with Philips, the company developed the current domestic DVD format. It has also been responsible for less successful innovations such as the minidisc and *Betamax.* The massive *marketing* power of Sony plays its part in the company's success. As a diversified company it is able to cross-promote its own products, and has a clear aim of *convergence* based on *proprietary formats.* The *PS2,* which was designed to be a *DVD* player, music player, *internet* connection and games machine, was the company's first attempt to create a fully converged *platform.*

**sound bite:** In radio *editing,* this term originally referred to any editable segment of *interview* material. It has come to mean any short, quotable statement, usually in a *news* or *current affairs* context. Increasing dependence on sound bites is a result of changes in *broadcast news* styles, with ever-shorter *bulletins.* The term is used pejoratively, as in 'sound-bite politics' to suggest a dependence on impressive sounding *slogans* rather than meaningful policies or ideas. The creation of sound bites for politicians by speechwriters is a key technique of *spin.* Famous examples of effective sound bites include Margaret Thatcher's 1980 assertion: 'You turn if you want to; the lady's not for turning!' and Tony Blair's 1996 statement that his top three priorities were 'Education, education, education.'

**sound bridge:** film and TV *editing* technique in which visual *cuts* are deliberately not matched with audio cuts. For example, the *editor* may cut to a completely new *scene,* but allow sound from the preceding scene to run on for a short time. Alternatively, we may hear the sound of the next scene before we see it. The device is used for various purposes: for example to smooth over breaks in *spatial and temporal contiguity,* to avoid a *jump-cut* or to create variation and interest during a *dialogue* sequence.

**sound crew:** the team of technicians responsible for all aspects of a film's sound during *production* and *post-production.* The **sound designer** has overall responsibility for audio from *pre-production* through to *final cut.* At *production* stage, members of the sound crew include the *boom* operator who controls the boom *microphone;* the sound recordist, who operates the recording machinery; and the sound mixer, who is responsible for the balance of sound achieved on set. *Post-production* sound crew roles include sound editor, *sound effects* and *foley artists*.

**sound effects** are usually added to film in *post-production*. Usually, they are given a separate credit from the work of *foley artists*, though they have similar results. Sound effects in radio, film, television and video games can be added either by using stored *library* material or digitally created sounds. They may be used to build up *ambience* or to reinforce *action*. Radio sound effects are often essential in creating the *sound image*.

**sound image:** the 'picture' that is created in the mind of a radio listener by various *codes* in a radio broadcast. Types of sound image vary according to the *radio genre.* For example, a radio *drama* uses ambient and other *sound effects* to create an imaginary environment. The *audience* can be made to picture a Victorian street scene or a space station far from Earth simply by careful use of the appropriate sound effects from the *library*. In other genres, different types of codes are used. A debate programme such as *Any Questions?* uses *microphone* positioning and *exposition* from the host to create a vision of the location and the audience; *disc jockey*-led music shows often include discussion about the studio environment. The sound image is much more subjective than the pictures constructed by visual media, but it is an important part of the audience experience and a key factor in the *pleasure* of radio listening.

**sound stage:** a building constructed for filming while recording simultaneous sound. These huge soundproof structures can contain several movie *sets* and offer highly controlled conditions for filming. Under the *Hollywood studio system* most filming, including many 'exteriors' took place inside sound stages. Today, sets on sound stages are still used for many interior shots and for *chromakey* work.

**soundtrack:** (i) the complete audio component of a film, TV production or other screen *media produc*t, such as a video game or advertisement. The soundtrack includes all *diegetic* and *non-diegetic* sound, as *dialogue, music, sound effects* and background *ambience.* (ii) specifically the music track, especially when sold separately as an audio recording.

**Soviet montage:** at its peak of importance in 1920s communist Russia, this was a key development in the history of film-making. Lev Kuleshov (1899–1970) and Sergei Eisenstein (1898–1948) were its most important theorists, promoting the idea that film's unique quality as a medium was in the way it gave artists the ability to order images in time, creating new meanings out of the relationships between them. Eisenstein's experimental films, such as *October* (USSR, 1928) broke many of the rules of the *continuity* system in order to create *metaphorical* meanings.

**space and time** are key elements of *continuity. Cinematography* and *editing* constantly work to tell *audiences* where and when events are taking place. For example, the wide *establishing shot* allows us to see where everything is located; *cross-cutting* tells us when events are taking place simultaneously in two locations.

**spaghetti Western:** a film *subgenre* of the *Western*, popular during the 1960s. Shot in Europe, characterised by strong *violence* and amorality, spaghetti Westerns were highly stylised in *cinematography, editing* and use of *music*. Sergio Leone was the most notable director of this genre.

**spam:** an unsolicited e-mail containing a real, or more commonly bogus, advert (commonly for pornography, pirate software and counterfeit medicines). It may also be used to try to gain personal information which can result in identity fraud or theft by bogus e-mails purporting to be from banks etc., known as 'phishing'.

**spatial and temporal contiguity:** if two *shots*, when *edited* together, seem to follow on directly in time, they are said to have temporal contiguity; if they have a clear relationship in *space*, they have spatial contiguity. *Continuity* requires that one or both of these elements are present.

**spatial relationships:** the arrangement of figures and objects within the *mise en scène*. To make sense of moving images, the *audience* must be given a clear understanding of the physical distance between *characters* and other characters or objects. An *establishing* shot is often used to communicate this information.

**special effects (SFX):** technology that has been used to create illusions throughout the history of the *moving image*. Sometimes the illusion is ordinary – for example, *back projection* during a car journey. Sometimes it is spectacular, like the *stop-motion* animated monsters created by Ray Harryhausen for *Jason and the Argonauts* (Don Chaffey, UK/USA, 1963), or the puppets and *animatronics* of George Lucas's original *Star Wars* trilogy (USA, 1977–83). Today, *CGI* has made amazingly realistic spectacular scenes into a commonplace cinematic experience, and it is much more difficult in many cases to separate special effects from *live action*. SFX are central to the success of many modern *genres* including *action* films, comic-book *adaptations* and large-scale *fantasies* such as the *Lord of the Rings* trilogy, (Peter Jackson, NZ/USA, 2001–03).

**special feature:** (i) in *DVD* video, special or bonus features are extra material included to enhance the *audience* experience. These may include *documentaries*, alternative audio tracks (director's or cast commentaries on the film) and *Easter eggs*. (ii) in the newspaper and magazine industries, a special feature is some element of the magazine that is promoted in the *sell lines* as being of particular interest. A typical special feature sell line might read 'Special feature: summer fashions pullout – 20 pages of the latest high-street styles.'

**special issue** or **special edition:** usually an issue concentrating on a specific area of interest. For example, a football magazine might devote a single edition entirely to the World Cup. Sometimes referred to simply as a 'special'.

### spectacle/spectacular:

i.   in its common use, a spectacle is a visually impressive and/or complicated media event. Films that mount enormous battles or depict natural disasters are described as spectacles. 'Spectacular' can be used either as an adjective or a noun:

    a.   'That scene with the parting of the Red Sea was certainly spectacular.'

    b.   'The latest C B DeMille spectacular is called *The Ten Commandments.*'

ii.  the situationist philosopher, Guy Debord, referred to everything in modern *capitalist culture* – including the *mass media* – as 'spectacle'. He argued that instead of living in the real world, we have all been turned into *spectators* by capitalist society.

**spectator:** an individual member of an *audience*. Spectatorship is an important concept in film theory. Traditional models of audience response (such as the *hypodermic model*) tend to treat viewers, readers or listeners as groups, spectatorship study suggests that the film builds a specific relationship with every individual who experiences it. Rather than being concerned with *media effects*, spectatorship study focuses on understanding the ways films can produce *pleasure* in their viewers.

**spectrum:** the range of electromagnetic frequencies available for communication purposes such as TV, radio and mobile phone networks. *Analogue* media technologies were very inefficient in their use of the spectrum, leading to spectrum scarcity, or the 'overcrowded airwaves (i.e. the problem that there was more demand than could be supplied). Governments have therefore imposed tight controls on the spectrum, usually through licensing. Because *digital media technologies* are much more efficient, some commentators argue that there is now little need for spectrum regulation.

**speculative fiction:** a term coined by the science fiction writer Robert A Heinlein to include all *narratives* that deal with events outside *realism*. It includes *science fiction* texts, but also other non-realist *genres* (e.g. *fantasies* like the *Harry Potter* series and *dystopias* like Terry Gilliam's 1985 film *Brazil*).

**spike:** *journalists'* slang. To spike a story is to drop it from publication. The term derives from the wooden-based metal spike onto which journalists would stick rejected stories.

**spin:** a negative term for *public relations*, based on the idea that it is the job of some PR consultants, especially those employed by politicians, to make bad news seem good. Spinning the *news* is seen as a dishonest activity because, although it avoids actual lying, it deliberately misdirects the public away from the truth. A 'spin doctor' is a pejorative term for a political PR consultant. (Alastair Campbell, who worked for UK Prime Minister Tony Blair between 1994 and 2003 was often described as a 'spin doctor' by the British press.)

**spine:** the point where all the pages of a publication are joined together. More expensive and bulky magazines, usually monthlies and quarterlies, have a glued flat spine printed with the name and date of the issue. This increases their status because it suggests that they will be kept for longer, possibly on a bookshelf. Cheaper weeklies tend to be stitch bound (i.e. folded and stapled).

**spin-off:** a media product in which an element from a previous media product is the main attraction. For example, the central *character* of the *sitcom Frasier* had previously been a secondary character in *Cheers*.

**splash:** a big, dramatic story in the *tabloid press*, usually the lead. Hence a splash headline is the typical headline style found on the front page of a tabloid, combining very large, bold *typefaces* with attention-grabbing language. The *Sun* has a history of memorable splash headlines, including the unforgettable '**FREDDIE STARR ATE MY HAMSTER**' from 1986.

**splatstick:** combination of *splatter movie* and *slapstick comedy*, as seen for example in *Shaun of the Dead* (Edgar Wright, UK, 2004).

**splatter movie:** film *subgenre* of *horror*, involving copious violence and bloodletting. Also known as '*grand guignol* horror' or 'gore film'. The splatter movie differs from other types of horror in the sheer volume of blood, gore and severed body parts shown on screen. George A Romero's *Dawn of the Dead* (USA, 1978) is often seen as the archetype.

**splice:** to join two pieces of tape or film together in traditional *linear editing* of film, VT and audio. Also used to mean the join that is made in this way.

**split screen:** the presentation of two or more distinct moving images on the same screen at the same time. After a brief period of heavy use in 1960s films such as *The Thomas Crown Affair*, split screen became unfashionable, partly because it was expensive and difficult. Since the advent of *digital editing*, the technique has become cheap and easy. The popular TV *thriller* series *24* uses split screen extensively.

**sponsorship:** in media contexts, sponsorship usually means providing money in return for an association with a particular *media product*. Sporting events prominently display the *logos* of their sponsors. Broadcasters play a short *ident* for the sponsor before, after and during the commercial break of a sponsored programme. A more subtle form of sponsorship is the *product placement* practised in many *Hollywood* films. Often, a firm will sponsor media products that it feels enhance its profile. Stella Artois' decision to sponsor films on *Channel 4* and *Film Four* was part of an attempt to create an elite, sophisticated image for its lager. *Ofcom* maintain strict controls over sponsorship of television programmes. Sponsors are not allowed influence over the content of programmes. Sponsorship of the *news* is not allowed, though some elements of the news broadcast, such as the weather forecast, may be sponsored.

**spot:** industry slang for a 15- or 30-second *advertisement* on radio or television.

**spot advertising:** a different approach from a national *campaign*: advertising material is placed in carefully targeted geographical areas.

**spot colour:** any of the four basic coloured inks used in *printing* – cyan, magenta, yellow or black. Printing at lower costs will make use of only one or two spot colours.

**spotlight:** a light that produces a strong, circular beam, which is used to emphasise a particular point in the *mise en scène.*

**spot rating:** the estimated TV *audience rating* of an advertising *spot* at a particular time. Important in calculating the spot's price for a client.

**spread:** two facing pages in a magazine or newspaper on which a single article, image, or set of material has been printed. Sometimes referred to as a '*double-page spread*' or, if it appears in the middle pages, a 'centre spread'.

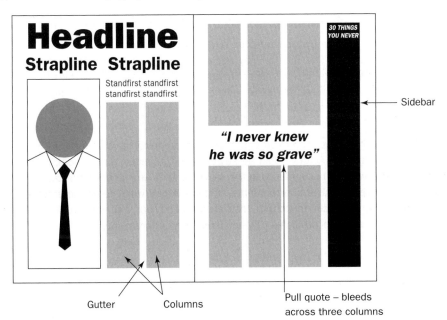

*Typical elements of a spread layout*

**spy film:** a film *genre* dealing with espionage. Spy films were popular during the cold war period. They range from flashy fantasies such as the James Bond *franchise* to more 'realistic' portrayals of the secret service like *The Ipcress File* (Sidney J. Furie, UK, 1965). The genre was *parodied* in the *Austin Powers* series.

**stab:** a short dramatic burst of *music* on a film or TV *soundtrack.*

**staffer:** *journalist* who is employed on contract – as opposed to a *freelance* or *stringer.*

**staged:** of photographed or filmed events, set up or *constructed* rather than occurring naturally. Obviously, all *fiction genres* are staged; but many *non-fiction* genres also include staged elements. For example, during a *news* report about A levels, the *producer* may require some *footage* of candidates sitting their exams. Taking a film crew into a real exam would be unacceptably disruptive, so a group of students might well be asked to pretend that they are sitting their exams for the cameras. Since they do not have any impact on the presentation of the facts, such staged elements are not considered dishonest by many news producers.

**standfirst:** a brief introduction to a *news* story or magazine article, usually printed in bold type and positioned between the *headline* and the *copy*. Also called a 'kicker'.

**stand-in:** a person who takes the place of an *actor* during technical set-ups for camera and lighting. The stand-in has a basic physical resemblance to the actor, similar height and colouring being the most important. (See also *double.*)

**star:** a media performer who has gained very high status with the *audience*. Stardom could be described as an exaggerated form of *celebrity*. Although there are stars in *pop music*, *sport*, and *TV*, the term is most closely associated with film.

**star bankability:** the idea in modern *Hollywood* that *casting* certain *stars* can guarantee that a film will go into profit. At present, bankable stars include Tom Cruise, Julia Roberts and Tom Hanks. Any of these names are enough to ensure that a film will be *greenlighted.*

**star image/star persona/star identity:** terms used to describe the way a star is perceived by the public. This may or may not reflect the actual personality of the actor. Factors that *construct* a star include his or her physical characteristics, the roles in which he or she is cast, as well as news stories about the star, interviews and other media material. (For example, the star persona of the Hollywood actor Russell Crowe has been built around a 'bad boy' image, reinforced by news stories about his violent behaviour.)

**star system:** the methods used to create, promote and control *stars* during the time of the *Hollywood studio system*. Actors would be selected and groomed for stardom, often given new names and invented backgrounds in the process. They were schooled in correct public behaviour and given physical improvements such as dental work. Stars were strictly con- trolled, with tight contracts to control their public behaviour and the studio's *PR* staff working hard to cover up problems. To encourage *fan* interest, the studio would either publicise the star's personal relationships, or more often invent one – setting up fake romances between stars for the benefit of the press.

**star vehicle:** a *media product* – most commonly a film – in which the main aim is to showcase the talents of a particular star.

**status quo:** the existing social order, things as they are. *Dominant ideological* positions are often concerned with reinforcing or protecting the status quo.

**statutory regulation:** control by laws set out in parliament. Since the 1990 *Broadcasting Act*, British governments have sought to *deregulate* many aspects of TV and radio broadcasting, but there are still many regulations, which are now enforced by *Ofcom*.

**Steadicam:** a brand of camera whose harness had a system of weights and balances to minimise unwanted movement when filming *handheld*. Invented in the early 1970s, the Steadicam revolutionised film-making.

**stereo:** the distribution of an audio signal between two speakers. Stereo can create the illusion that sound is coming from more than two sources. It is still the commonest format for recording music, for high-quality radio and for the sound element of broadcast television. In cinemas, and in home cinema, it has been superseded by *surround sound.*

**stereotype:** simplified portrayal of a social group, often used as a quick way to establish characters in *media texts*. For example, IT technicians are often portrayed in TV comedy as obsessive social incompetents with a strong interest in *Star Wars*. Some media texts have been criticised for constructing offensive and/or damaging stereotypes, such as *Hollywood*'s representation of the Italian-American community as being dominated by Mafiosi. Similarly, *feminism* has criticised the use of *gender* stereotypes in *lifestyle magazines* – from the physically attractive, constantly available women who adorn the pages of *lad mags* to the perfect wife and mother figures strongly present in many *women's magazines*.

**sticky content:** *internet* jargon describing any material that encourages the user to stay on a website for a longer time.

**stills:** individual frames from a film or TV product. Often these are used in promotion. For example, they are sent to newspapers as part of a *press pack* in the hope that they will be used to illustrate reviews.

**still-to-come:** material that is flagged up during a TV or radio programme as appearing later during the same broadcast. The announcer may or may not actually use the phrase 'still to come'. The still-to-come technique is used frequently in *news*, *talk* and *magazine format* programmes, usually aiming to tantalise the viewers with an item that sounds interesting and prevent them from switching channels. A typical still-to-come would run: 'Later on *Britain Today:* the farmer who says he's building his own moon rocket; the worst school in the country; and is this Leicestershire pub haunted by the ghost of Anne Boleyn?' In *commercial broadcasting*, still-to-comes were traditionally announced before the *advertisements*. Now that viewers have more choice and power to change channel easily, the technique is often used heavily throughout programmes.

**sting:** an technique of *investigative journalism* in which the reporter sets up an elaborate trick to deceive his subjects into incriminating themselves. Mazher Mahmood of the *News of the World* is a celebrated sting journalist. It can be argued that sting techniques break the rules of journalistic *ethics*.

**stock:** the physical *film* used in a movie camera. There are many types of film stock, varying in size from the amateur's 8 mm to the 70 mm film used for *IMAX* presentations. Moreover, film from different manufacturers and using different developing processes looks different, as do different grades of film from the same manufacturer. The choice of film stock was an important *aesthetic* decision. Because many changes can now be made to the look of film in digital *post production*, and also because much 'film' is now digital video, choice of film stock is less important than it once was.

**stock footage/shot:** pieces of film, kept in a *library* and used where necessary. Useful because it is much cheaper than filming. Stock footage may be of general use – for example, a scene of trains in motion might be used in a drama or to fill out a news report. Alternatively, it may have a specific purpose: for instance, the 1980s TV series *Manimal* repeatedly used the same two pieces of stock *special effects* footage in which the *hero* was transformed into a hawk or a panther.

**stop-motion photography:** technique for *animating* 3-D models, paper cut-outs or other objects. The illusion of movement is created by photographing each individual frame separately, and moving the subject slightly between each shot. The Czech *surrealist*, Jan Svankmajer, and the British Aardman studios have both used the technique to make *feature films*. It was employed extensively in British children's television programmes between the 1960s and 1980s for such series as *Bagpuss* (animated by Peter Firman) and *Trumpton* (animated by Bura and Hardwick).

**story:**

i.    In print, radio and TV *journalism*, a story is any individual item of *news* that appears in a *publication* or a *bulletin.*

ii.   In analysis of *fictions* such as TV *drama* or film, the story is a sequence of connected events that are related in a *narrative.* Story is the thing that is told; narrative is the act of telling a story. Compare the following two examples:

● (story with little narrative) A girl was sent through the woods to take food for her sick grandmother.

● (story with much narrative) There was once a pretty girl who lived with her mother in a little old house at the edge of a dark, oppressive wood. On the opposite side of the wood lived the girl's grandmother, whom she dearly loved, but who was not always in the best of health. It was an autumn day when a tinker, who often passed through the wood, brought a message: poor grandmother was sick and in need of some sustaining soup and cakes. The mother was busy, as mothers often are, and so she called the girl, who was playing in the meadow with her friends...

The film academics Bordwell and Thompson make the distinction that if *plot* is the presentation of events in the film itself, story is the sense the *audience* make of them. The story would therefore include events seen/heard by the audience as well as those inferred by the audience.

**story arc:** a sequence of *narrative* development. This is a very important concept in narrative TV *genres.* In *soap opera*, it has always been normal practice to include several different stories within each episode. Each of these stories will be at a different point in its arc – some will just be starting, some will be developing, some will be concluding. In TV from the 1990s on, story arcs have been used to draw together the advantages of both the *serial* and *series.* Each *season* of an arc-based *drama* will be composed of discrete *episodes* (like a *series*) or two-parters, but the *audience* will be aware of longer story arcs, including an overall arc which will reach its peak in the *season finale.* Examples of arc-based dramas include *Buffy the Vampire Slayer*, *Six Feet Under* and the newest version of *Doctor Who.* Some more recent *sitcoms* such as *Curb Your Enthusiasm* and *The Office* also make use of this structure.

**storyboard:** a tool for planning a filmed sequence. Storyboards represent the sequence as it is likely to appear on screen, but in a form similar to a strip cartoon. They are often used in *pitching* an *advertising* idea to a client or (less often) a film to a potential *producer*. During the film-making process, *directors* will often make use of fairly rough storyboards to explain an idea to others in the *crew*. When more detailed storyboards are required – for instance to plan a complex action sequence – professional storyboard artists are employed.

**straight-to-video** describes what happens when a film is not given a *theatrical release* by its *distributors*. This is usually an indicator that the distributor does not have much confidence in the film. However, release patterns are changing, and most films now make more in *home video* rentals and sales than at the *box-office*. *Disney* has for many years released *sequels* such as *Lilo & Stitch 2* (Michael LaBash/Anthony Leondis, USA, 2005) exclusively on home video.

**strand:** a regular broadcast of a factual type (e.g. ITV's arts strand, *The South Bank Show,* and BBC2's debate strand, *Question Time.*)

**stranding:** see *scheduling*

**strapline:** (i) in the *advertising* industry, the *slogan* attached to a particular brand name (e.g. Nike's strapline is 'Just do it'). (ii) in *print journalism*, a subheading above or below the main headline.

**strap titles:** *captions* at the bottom of a TV screen with a contrasting background. Used extensively in *news* broadcasts to provide information such as the reporter's name and location. Moving strap titles provide constant on-screen updates during 24-hour news broadcasts and on special events such as telethons.

**streaming content:** a method of delivering audio and/or video over the *internet*. Instead of being *downloaded* to a file on the user's computer, the material is played from a file on the source site. Streaming content can overcome copyright problems, since no copy of the material is kept by the person who receives it. This means, for example, that radio stations can include music recordings in the streamed versions of their programmes, but must edit them out of the *podcast* versions. The technical quality of most streamed content is relatively low. However, streaming content is also used for higher-quality services such as *video on demand*.

**streaming video:** see *streaming content*

**stripping:** see *scheduling*

**stringer:** *freelance journalist* who regularly submits *copy* to the same *news* institution.

**structuralism:** general term for an academic approach to analysing culture and society, including *media texts*, by looking for their shared underlying *structures*. Structuralism began as an approach to linguistics during the early twentieth century and developed many variations, most of which tended to suggest that human beings were at the mercy of structures. *Propp* and *Todorov* presented structuralist theories of *narrative* that continue to have some influence today. For the most part, however, structuralism has been replaced by *poststructuralism*, *postmodernism* and *deconstruction*.

**structure:** (i) in *structuralism*, a 'structure' is a pattern of meaning that has strong cultural or psychological importance. (ii) in more general terms, a structure is the way in which the material in a media product has been organised. All *texts* need to be structured so that the *audience* can make sense of them, but every *genre* has its own structural *conventions*. Consider, for instance, the difference between the structures needed for a *sitcom* and those required for a *news bulletin*.

**studio:** derived from the name for an artist's workplace, this term has come to have two main meanings in media and film contexts: (i) a specialised interior in which media products are made. For example, a TV studio is a large hall designed for recording and broadcasting TV programmes; a recording studio is an interior space designed for recording music. (ii) the large *Hollywood* film-making companies established in the 1920s and 1930s.

**studio system:** a *Fordist* method of film *production* developed before 1930 by the *Big Five*, or major, studios – *Paramount, MGM, 20*th *Century Fox, RKO* and *Warner Bros*. Because they *distributed* the films they made, and showed them in their own theatres, the 'majors' were an *oligopoly* – a *cartel* of great power and prestige. They developed the systems of *continuity, narrative* and *genre* still in use today, and employed teams of specialists – *producers, script writers, directors, actors, editors* and *publicists* – who worked nine-to-five on a production line, under a contract system of employment.

**stunt:** (i) a difficult and/or dangerous event in a film or TV production, often performed by a trained stunt *double* rather than the actor. Common stunts include falls from high places, scenes involving *pyrotechnics* and car crashes. Some performers, Jackie Chan for example, are noted for doing their own stunts. (ii) a media stunt is an activity designed to draw the attention of the *mass media* in order to publicise a cause. The technique is a cheap alternative to *marketing* and has been used by many pressure groups. For example, 'Fathers 4 Justice' in the UK have organised a number of stunts, most significantly an attempt by a man in a Batman costume to climb the walls of Buckingham Palace.

**stunt double:** see *double*

**style:**

i.  all elements of *form*, rather than content, in a *media text*. This covers a massive range of contributory factors – the techniques used by directors and performers, music, graphics, the language of the script and so on. Some products (for example the films of Quentin Tarantino or Baz Luhrmann) emphasise style very strongly. Others (such as British TV *soap operas*) avoid drawing attention to style because they wish to create a strong illusion of *naturalism.*

ii. the recognisable and distinctive characteristics of a particular artist's work. This is a particularly important concept in *auteurist* approaches to film analysis.

iii. the ways in which an individual presents him- or herself to the world through various elements, including media use. For example, an individual's style might include their choices of newspaper and music. *New media technologies* such as mobile phones and MP3 players have become extremely important elements of individual style.

**subculture:** a social group composed of individuals who share interests and values that distinguish them from *mainstream* society. *Youth subcultures* are often based around *popular music* and fashion. Since the 1950s, examples have been numerous, including teddy boys, hippies, punks, casuals and skaters. Often these are spectacular subcultures in which a rebellious attitude is conveyed through the wearing of highly distinctive clothing. The *mass media* are often very interested in youth subcultures; sometimes, as in the cases of mods and rockers or more recently hoodies, this interest leads to *moral panic*.

**sub-editor:** a member of staff on a newspaper or magazine, responsible for basic checks on *journalists'* *copy* before publication. The 'sub' makes sure there are no errors in spelling, grammar and *house style*, and may edit (i.e. shorten) articles as well as identifying any potential legal problems, such as *libel.*

**subgenre:** a variation of an already established *genre* with features recognisable in a number of examples. For example, the *horror* genre includes many subgenres, including *splatter*, *monster*, vampire, *gothic*, *occult*.

**sub-head(line):** an additional, smaller headline beneath the main headline. Shorter than a *standfirst*. (See also *strapline*.)

**subject:** the person who receives a media *message*. Some theories of *audience* emphasise *subjectivity* (i.e. the importance of the way an individual responds to the *media text*).

**subjective:** seen from the perspective of an individual. The opposite of *objective*. Many *narratives* are presented from a subjective point of view, in that we identify with a particular character. This does not necessarily mean that we see with that *character*'s eyes throughout, but that we follow that person's story and identify most with him or her. The focus of subjectivity can change during a narrative. For example, in *The Sixth Sense* (M Night Shyamalan, USA, 1999) we spend most of our time following Malcolm Crowe (Bruce Willis) but there are also periods when the psychic child, Cole (Haley Joel Osment) is the focus, and also a small number of scenes where his mother (Toni Collette) has her subjective position emphasised. Factual material, such as *documentary*, is sometimes criticised for taking a subjective approach. However, it is probably impossible to be anything other than subjective when presenting anything more than the simplest factual material.

**subjective camera/subjective shot:** any filming technique that places the viewers within the *action*, as if we are seeing events from a character's point of view.

**subliminal:** having an effect without being noticed consciously by the *audience*. A subliminal cut/cut-in is an image which appears on screen for only a few frames so that the audience barely notice its presence. The technique was used to disturbing effect in *The Exorcist* (William Friedkin, USA, 1972).

**subliminal advertising** is designed to have a subconscious effect on the audience. For example, if the words 'buy baked beans' appeared in a song played as background music at supermarkets, shoppers might follow the instruction without knowing why they had done so. The technique is not allowed by the *ASA* but is sometimes hard to define. For example, *product placement* in films could be seen as a form of subliminal advertising.

**subordinate culture:**

i.   any culture that differs from the dominant one, but has to adapt to its rules. In the UK, for example, Islam can be described as a subordinate culture, since many of the laws of Islam do not appear in the British legal system, and many of the expectations of Islamic culture are rejected by British society. Similarly, in Saudi Arabia, where Islam is a dominant cultural force, westerners operate a subordinate culture

ii.  in colonial societies, the subordinate culture is usually that of the indigenous people. For example, during the British rule of India, all Indian cultures were treated as being of secondary importance to the British imperial culture that was dominant there

iii. according to Antonio Gramsci, subordinate cultures are those groups whose ideas, beliefs, interests and/or behaviour are counter to *hegemony*. Gramsci believed that it is in the interests of the dominant culture to accept such groups because it demonstrates that their society is free.

**subordinate meaning system:** see *meaning systems*

**subplot:** a *story* in a narrative fiction usually involving secondary *characters* which runs alongside the main *plot*. Subplots are added to create extra interest, and can either contrast with or reinforce the main plot's *themes*.

**subscription:** the making of regular payments by a consumer. Some *magazines*, mostly *niche titles*, can be bought for an annual subscription charge instead of paying the *cover price* for each issue. Many *DST* and *cable* TV channels are *broadcast* to subscribers, who usually pay a monthly fee for the service. This is an alternative to the advertising-funded *commercial broadcasting*. Subscription channels often show little or no advertising.

**subsidiary rights:** the legal 'ownership' of various aspects of a creative product. For example, the right to produce *merchandise* or books based on a film or TV series. George Lucas famously became very rich because his contract for *Star Wars* included ownership of the film's subsidiary rights.

**subsidy:** funding from an official source. For example, the *UK Film Council* uses money raised by the National Lottery to provide subsidies for film makers.

**subtext:** any *connotative* message: i.e. one that the *audience* can discover without being told directly. Usually, textual analysis is an attempt to reveal the subtextual *messages* in a *text*.

**subtitles:** *captions* that appear in the bottom part of a screen, commonly used as an alternative to *dubbing* when foreign language films are exhibited. Subtitles are also used when characters speak a language other than the main one in which the film has been made or, for example in *documentaries*, when the audio quality or accent of the speaker might make the words hard to understand. TV broadcasts and *DVDs* often include subtitle options for hearing-impaired viewers.

**suburban gothic:** see *gothic*.

**subversion:** (i) the undermining of *dominant ideologies*, usually in a covert way. *Media texts* can be used for subversive purposes. In repressive societies such as Nazi Germany or Soviet Russia, the media were controlled by the state in order to prevent them from being used subversively. The *HUAC* in the USA in the 1940s investigated so-called communist 'subversives' in Hollywood. (ii) the undermining of the conventions of a *genre*. For example, *Brokeback Mountain* (Ang Lee, USA, 2005), which centres on a *gay* romance, can be described as subverting the traditional *values* of the *Western*.

**Sundance Film Festival:** a major event for *independent cinema* held annually in Utah, USA. Sundance has been strongly supported by the film actor Robert Redford and is named after his character in the 1969 film *Butch Cassidy and the Sundance Kid*.

**super 8/super 16:** types of film *stock*. Super 8 offers slightly higher quality than standard 8 mm film and was a popular format for amateur use during the 1960s and 1970s. Super 16 gives a wider *aspect ratio* than conventional 16 mm film, which was for many years used extensively in *low-budget* film-making and for TV production. Digital processing now means that super 16 films can look close to 35 mm in quality, and many lower-budget film makers are now choosing to work in this format. *Vera Drake* (Mike Leigh, UK, 2004) is one such film.

**superimpose:** to place one image over the top of another on the screen. A common use of superimposition is adding *titles*, *captions* or *graphics*, such as a visual representation of the current scores in a TV *game show*.

**superstructure:** a concept in *Marxist* thinking. According to Marx, the superstructure consists of all those aspects of society, such as religion and education, that help *socialise* individuals into accepting the inequalities of *capitalist* society. Later Marxists, such as Marcuse, have placed much emphasis on the mass media as a key element of the superstructure.

**surface accuracy:** the level of convincing detail, based on research, in a *narrative*. For example, the following of more-or-less correct police procedures in the TV series *The Bill*.

**surface realism:** all the factors which combine in a *media text* to give the *audience* a sense that the events they are witnessing are 'real', even though they may not be very believable or have much *message realism*. For example, the *Harry Potter* film series uses *SFX* to make events look realistic on the surface, though the audience are never expected to believe that what they are seeing represents reality.

**surfing:** using a web browser to explore the *internet*.

**Surrealism:** an *avant-garde* movement of the 1920s in painting, poetry and other art forms. The Surrealists were interested in the ideas of Sigmund *Freud*, and sought to use the sub-conscious in creating their artworks. Surrealist images are deliberately strange, often violent and/or sexual. Many *art-house* film makers, such as Luis Buñuel, David Lynch and the *stop-motion* animator Jan Svankmejer can be described as Surrealists. The movement was also influential in *mainstream* cinema; for example, Alfred Hitchcock's *Spellbound* (USA, 1945) included a dream sequence designed by the Spanish Surrealist painter, Salvador Dali.

**surround sound:** a technology for distributing audio across four or more speakers (current systems can use up to seven) so that the sounds appear to come from all around the listener. Initially, this was one of the major attractions of *multiplex cinemas* exhibiting *high-concept films*, since surround sound could enhance action *set-pieces* by increasing audience *immersion*. Today, *digital technology* means that surround systems such as Dolby 5.1 can form part of a *home cinema* system for relatively little cost.

**surveillance:** a form of media use whereby the media (particularly news and fact-based genres) are treated by their *audiences* as a 'window' through which one can gather information about and keep watch over the real world. (See also *uses and gratifications*.)

**surveillance society:** the possible consequence of increasing use of technologies to monitor the activities of individuals: a society in which everyone is watched nearly all the time. Tracking *internet* activity and placing CCTV cameras in public places are two important examples of common surveillance techniques. Government agencies argue that these technologies prevent terrorism and other serious crimes, but many citizens believe that their use reduces individual freedom and leads to unnecessary *invasion of privacy*.

**suspense:** an important *narrative* technique in which the *spectator* is kept waiting for the outcome to a sequence of events. Sometimes, suspense depends on an *enigma* which we wait to see *resolved;* sometimes it is created by our expectation that something horrible or unwanted is about to occur on-screen. This feeling is the main *pleasure* that is sought by audiences of the **suspense thriller** genre. The film *director* Alfred *Hitchcock* is credited with having created a wide range of suspense techniques.

**suspension of disbelief:** see *willing suspension of disbelief*

**suture:** a term based on the *psychoanalytical* ideas of Jacques Lacan which is often used in film *theory* when discussing *spectatorship*. Film *spectators* are aware of the unreality of the events they are watching, but at the same time they wish to experience the film as if it were reality. Suture is the process by which the mind of the spectator draws together (or 'negotiates') these two contradictory states. Suture (literally meaning sewing/stitching) can also be used to refer to techniques such as the *continuity system* that are designed to enable the *spectator* to negotiate this problem.

**swashbuckler:** a bold, sword-wielding male *hero* in an *adventure film* with a *period* setting. The actor Errol Flynn was noted for swashbuckling roles in the 1930s and 1940s. The term also refers to the *genre* of films in which such characters appear, and was recently revived by *Disney*'s successful *Pirates of the Caribbean franchise.*

**swish pan:** see *whip pan*

**sword and sandal movie:** see *peplum movie*

**symbol:** in *semiology*, one of two types of *sign:*

i.    one that has no direct *iconic* referent. For instance, the letter 'X' does not operate as an *icon* but can **symbolise** many things, including a kiss, a wrong answer or the place where treasure is buried.

ii.   one that refers to something other than its *iconic* referent. In the *Western* genre for example, an image of a horse on the screen can communicate numerous *meanings* other than the obvious 'here is a horse'. Its **symbolic meanings** include, among many other things, masculinity, power and freedom.

**symptomatic meaning:** one of four types of film meaning defined by David Bordwell in his book, *Making Meaning* (1989). (The others are *referential meaning; explicit meaning* and *implicit meaning.*) Symptomatic meanings are those that the film reveals because of its social and historical context. For example, a symptomatic meaning of *The Godfather* (Francis Ford Coppola, USA, 1972) could be that America had lost much of its self-confidence after the Vietnam War. This meaning arises because of when the film was made (in 1972) rather than any elements of its *period setting* (in 1949).

**synchronising motifs:** repetitive actions, phrases or *icons* whose function is to draw the whole *audience* together. A common example is the *catchphrase* in a traditional *sitcom* which is not intrinsically funny but provides a reassuring moment of recognition for the audience. Synchronising motifs help construct a common *message* of the sitcom *genre*, which is that life is largely unchanging.

**synchronous sound:** audio which is directly matched to a *moving image.* The term is used in two ways in different sources:

i.    sound recorded at the same time as the images – for example, *dialogue* spoken by the *actors* on *set.* This does not include any sound added in *post production.*

ii.   sound which appears to the *audience* to come from the *scene*, whether or not it was actually recorded with the images. This includes *post-synched* dialogue, *sound effects* and *foley.* Also known as parallel sound.

Both definitions exclude sound that does not appear to arise directly from the scene, such as *soundtrack* music or *voice-over.* These types of sound would be described as 'asynchronous'.

**syndication:** selling or giving *rights* over a media product to multiple agencies:

i.    In radio and TV, syndication is the sale of broadcasting rights for a programme to individual stations rather than to a *network.*

ii.   In print it is the *licensing* of material such as *comic strips* or regular *columns* to individual *magazines* or *newspapers.* The popular cartoon strip *Garfield* holds the world record for syndication, and is currently published in over 2500 newspapers and magazines.

iii. On the *internet*, syndication means the direct sharing of material with other websites, particularly through the use of web (or RSS – an acronym of Really Simple Syndication and other synonyms) feeds.

**synecdoche:** a *symbol* that can take one of two forms:

i. a single part of a larger phenomenon that stands for the whole thing. For example, in Leni Riefenstahl's Nazi *propaganda* film *Triumph of the Will* (Ger, 1934), *close-ups* of enthusiastic, healthy individuals are used to represent all young Nazis and by extension the whole of Hitler's Germany.

ii. a whole group, structure or other phenomenon that is used to stand for a smaller group within it. This is a common structure in *news journalism*, where, for instance, 'the police arrived at the scene' would actually mean 'a number of police officers arrived at the scene', though, taken literally, it would mean the whole police force. (See also *metonym*.)

**synergy:** the relationship between *media products* that cross-promote each other. For example, there is a synergy between the James Bond film *franchise* and the *video games* (such as *Goldeneye* and *Nightfire*) based on its *characters* and *tropes*. The games are more saleable because the *audience* is attracted to elements they recognise from the films, while the games act as a kind of *advertisement* for the films. Effectively, the two types of products *market* each other. Where media organisations such as the *Sony Corporation* are *diversified* or *horizontally integrated*, they can create synergies more easily and profitably.

**synopsis:** a brief summary of the main elements in a *text*. Most commonly used to mean an outline of the *plot* points and *characters* in a film.

**syntagm:** a set of individual meanings selected from *paradigms* and assembled to produce a larger *meaning*. For example, a vocabulary is a paradigm; a sentence is a syntagm. The repertoire of *shot-lengths* is a paradigm; a sequence of shots edited together is a syntagm. Within *moving image* media, very complex syntagms are often constructed. For example, a sequence in a *horror* film would combine *continuity editing* with *codes*, *conventions* and *narrative* to produce the overall syntagmatic effect.

**syntagmatic redundancy:** the presence of more *meaning*, usually *exposition*, than the *audience* needs. For example, we may be shown a shot of a tractor ploughing a field, over which we hear the Cliff Richard song 'In the Country'. A *caption* appears. It says: 'The Countryside'. Often, syntagmatic redundancy occurs because the creator of the media product is concerned that the audience may only be giving the text a *secondary level of attention*. In *soap opera* it is also expected that some viewers may be new, and others will have to familiarise themselves with narratives after a break from the programme.

**syntax:** a term from linguistics, meaning the rules by which the words in a sentence are ordered. It is sometimes used to describe the structures used to create meanings in media texts. For example, the ordering of *shots* in *continuity editing* can be seen as obeying syntactical rules. At a larger scale, the arrangement of *codes*, *conventions* and *symbols* in a *genre* is sometimes called its 'syntax', suggesting that the makers of genre products follow an agreed set of rules.

**syuzhet:** see *fabula*

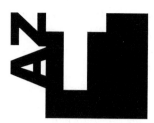

**tabloid:** a newspaper measuring approximately 300 mm x 395 mm per page. For many years, the tabloid format was associated with lower quality, more sensationalised news than would be found in the *broadsheets.* Tabloids were originally cheap newspapers, easy to carry and convenient to read, and aimed at a working-class readership. They are by far the biggest-selling papers in the UK, and some would argue that this is because they adopt a 'lowest common denominator' approach. In the UK there were historically two types of tabloid: 'red tops' such as *The Sun*, which are targeted at a working-class C2DE readership and *mid-market tabloids* like the *Daily Mail* whose *audience* are largely upper *working class* and lower *middle class*. There is a distinct difference in tone between the two types, with the red-tops emphasising *sex, celebrity, human interest* and taking an extremely simplistic approach to the telling of their stories. The mid-market tabloids cover some similar material alongside more serious broadsheet-style content and adopt a more sophisticated language *register.* In recent years, three of the major British broadsheets (*The Independent, The Times* and *The Scotsman*) have adopted the tabloid format, because it is easier for readers to handle, especially when commuting. The publishers of these former broadsheets prefer to describe their publications as *compacts* because the word 'tabloid' has come to mean not only the *format* but also the *style* and *values* associated with the tabloids, and particularly the 'red tops'.

**tabloidisation:** a pejorative term meaning 'taking on the *values* of the red-top *tabloid* newspapers'. To say that 'TV news is suffering from increased tabloidisation' would mean that it is showing many of the characteristics associated with the tabloid press, such as an obsession with celebrity, a tendency to select lurid, sensational stories and a generally simplistic approach.

**tabloid television:** a pejorative term for TV which is seen as having the *values* of the *tabloid* press. In the UK, the ultimate example of tabloid TV was the short-lived *cable channel* L!ve TV, which was headed by Kelvin MacKenzie, a former editor of *The Sun*. Programmes on L!ve TV included 'Topless Darts' and the 'Weather in Norwegian' read by a model in a swimsuit. In the USA, lurid and sensationalist *talk shows* such as *Jerry Springer* are called 'tabloid talk shows'.

**taboo:** a subject that the *audience*, or a portion of the audience, do not wish to see or hear about, or which *gatekeepers* do not allow to appear as a matter of good taste. Today, most taboo material is in one way or another connected to *sex*. There are far fewer taboos operating on the UK media than in the past. For example, it would not have been acceptable to report on the many extra-marital affairs of Queen Victoria's son Prince Edward when he was Prince of Wales in the late nineteenth century, whereas the Prince of Wales' affair with Camilla Parker-Bowles (now his wife) was extensively discussed in the media. This breakdown of taboos is partly attributable to the *internet*, which is a medium that is largely free from institutional controls.

**tagline:** a memorable *slogan* or *strapline* attached to a movie or TV title e.g. 'The toys are back!' for *Toy Story 2* (John Lasseter/Ash Brannon USA, 1999) and 'In space, no-one can hear you scream' for *Alien* (Ridley Scott, USA, 1979).

**take:** (i) an individual attempt to film a single *shot*. Each shot may require several attempts before it is completed satisfactorily. These **retakes** are numbered, using a *clapperboard*. Takes that are not used because of errors are called **out takes**. If they are considered entertaining, they may be used in a 'blooper' reel or shown in a compilation of out takes such as ITV's long-running *It'll be Alright on the Night* series. (ii) in music recording, an attempt to perform and record either a whole piece or a part of it.

**talent:** slang used in film and TV productions to mean the *actors* (as opposed to the *crew* and *extras*). Sometimes the cast are referred to less respectfully as 'the turns'.

**talent show:** a TV *genre* designed to give new performers an opportunity to find national fame. Originally, talent shows such as *Opportunity Knocks* would include a wide variety of performers – comedians, acrobats, singers, musicians, even bodybuilders. The winner would be decided by public vote and/or a studio panel. Talent shows were an important route to fame, particularly for variety performers during the 1960s, 1970s and 1980s, after which they largely died out. The genre was revived as a *reality TV format* in 2001 with the series *Popstars* which, like subsequent variants (*Popstars: The Rivals*, *Pop Idol*, *X Factor*), focused exclusively on pop singers. Various other reality formats such as *Big Brother* can also be seen as talent shows, in which the 'talent' is simply the personality of the competitor.

**talkback:** (i) in music recording studios and in TV and radio studios or *outside broadcasts*, a communications system that allows the *producer* or engineer to give *cues* and other instructions to presenters, performers and to other personnel, such as *camera operators* and *floor managers*. (ii) responses from (usually TV) audiences, especially those *posted* to the *internet* on either official or unofficial *sites*. When used in this way, the term is frequently styled 'TalkBack'. (iii) In Australia and New Zealand, *talk shows* are called 'talkback shows', and studio discussion of items, for example in sports or news *magazine programmes*, is called 'talkback'.

**talkie:** colloquial term for a film with *synchronised sound*. Short for talking picture, this word was mainly used in the late 1920s and early 1930s to distinguish sound films from *silent* films.

**talking head:** (i) a medium, or *medium close-up*, *shot* of the head and shoulders. When discussing film, the term is often used critically to suggest an undramatic or uncinematic scene. (ii) anyone who regularly appears in such shots in the news. This might be part of the broadcasting team, such as a news presenter or pundit, or it might be a government spokesperson or a *PR* worker. Often, calling someone a 'talking head' is pejorative – implying a lack of substance in what is being said.

**talk radio:** the American term for speech radio (see *radio genres*).

**talk show:** any programme on TV or radio in which the main activity is speech. There are various genres of talk show:

- the serious face-to-face style of programme in which an interviewer encourages an interviewee to speak at length and in detail about the things that are important to him or her

- lighthearted *celebrity chat shows* such as *Friday Night with Jonathan Ross*
- *current affairs* discussion programmes like *The Wright Stuff*
- studio audience discussion programmes covering relationship issues (*Trisha, Jerry Springer*).

**target audience/target readership:** the *demographic group* at which a media product is aimed. A target audience can be defined by a shared interest such as fishing or DIY or by other factors, such as *gender*, age, *social class*, *ethnicity* or location. The target audience has a strong effect on the style and content of the product. For example, a magazine aimed at urban *working-class* males aged 18–30 would be very different from one aimed at rural *middle-class* females aged 40–55. Language, images, layout and other design features such as typefaces, as well as the subject matter of articles, would be tailored to the audience. Prior to launch, many *media products* are the subject of exhaustive research, both to identify the target audience and to ensure that the product will meet with their approval.

**target group ratings (TGRs):** a combination of *BARB* ratings and precise survey data to produce information that can be used when analysing TV *audiences* for market research and other purposes.

**taxonomy:** originally the system of giving Latin names to living organisms in biology, now used more generally to refer to any organised set of classifications. *Genre* is a **taxonomic** system.

**tear-jerker:** a film, usually aimed at a female *audience*, with a strongly emotional storyline designed to make the *spectator* cry. A classic example is *Love Story* (Arthur Hiller, USA, 1970).

**teaser campaign:** an *advertising* technique that aims to tantalise the *audience*, often using *enigma codes* that gradually reveal their meaning as the campaign progresses. Typical teaser advertisements include TV ads that do not mention the product, or posters carrying a mysterious message. The UK Food Standards Agency, for example, ran a very successful teaser campaign in 2004 with posters carrying the question 'Who is Sid?': this prepared the audience for a health campaign to lower salt consumption. *Internet* teaser campaigns often take the form of mysterious links, *games* or puzzles. (For example, Microsoft's 'Haunted Apiary' teaser campaign for the X-Box game *Halo II* was an elaborate game involving various websites and automated telephone calls which only revealed its true purpose after several weeks.)

**teaser trailer:** a film *trailer* designed to build early *hype* about a forthcoming film. Unlike conventional trailers, teasers do not make much use of actual *footage*. Sometimes they contain little more than an animated *logo*; sometimes, as with early trailers for *The Incredibles* (Brad Bird, USA, 2004) and *War of the Worlds* (Steven Spielberg, USA, 2005), they are constructed from specially filmed footage that does not appear in the eventual film. This is often necessary because the teasers are shown in cinemas at a very early stage in *production* and there is not yet any real footage ready for use. The increased use of teasers, mostly for big-budget films, is a consequence of the industry's need to *promote* its films ever more heavily and as early as possible in anticipation of the *opening weekend*.

**tech-noir/techno-noir:** hybrid film *genre* combining elements of *film noir* and *science fiction*. *Blade Runner* (Ridley Scott, USA, 1982) and *City of Lost Children* (Marc Caro, Jean-Pierre Jeunet, Fr, 1995) are good examples.

**technological determinism** has two basic principles: first that technological development follows a predetermined path that is not controlled by humanity; and second, that all social change is caused by technological change. This is not a view that is taken seriously by scientific or sociological academics, who tend to prefer the view that technological change and social change are connected, and interdependent, but that technology is merely one of many factors leading to social change. Technological determinism is, however, present in much *science fiction*, particularly *tech-noir*. There are also elements of technological determinism in many *moral panics* related to new developments in *media technologies*, such as the idea that the *internet* is creating increased levels of paedophilia.

**teen movie/pic:** a film about and for teenagers. Because the teenage market is a key one for *Hollywood*, there are many *subgenres* of the teen movie, including: the high-school movie (e.g. *Heathers*, Michael Lehmann, USA, 1989); teen *horror* (e.g. *I Know What You Did Last Summer*, Jim Gillespie, USA, 1997); teen *musical* (e.g. *Grease*, Randal Kleiser, USA, 1978) and teen *science fiction/fantasy* (e.g. *Pleasantville*, Gary Ross, USA, 1998).

**telephoto:** a type of *lens* that makes distant objects appear close-up. Used for *moving image* and still shots in which it would be difficult to get close to the subject, such as *news footage* of very high buildings. The Japanese film *director* Akira Kurosawa sometimes used telephoto lenses so that he could keep the camera at a distance, reducing the *actors'* camera consciousness and obtaining more natural performances.

**teleplay:** a *script* for TV. The term is mainly used in the USA. British TV scripts are usually called scripts.

**teleprompter:** a machine that displays the *script* so that it can be read out rather than learned in advance. A technologically advanced version of the *idiot board*. Teleprompters are usually attached to the camera to which the presenter is speaking. Teleprompters are often used by presenters, newsreaders and for scripted parts of *talk shows*, *chat shows* and *game shows*.

**television (TV):** a word combining Greek (tele – long distance) and Latin (visus – sight) elements to mean 'see over a long distance'. This reflects the fact that originally, and for the first few decades of its popular use, television was simply equipment for *broadcasting*, receiving and displaying *moving images*. While this remains an important element of TV usage, changing technologies have broadened the ways in which this equipment is now employed in the home. Playing *video games* and showing *DVDs* are significant new uses for television. The TV set is also becoming an important portal for *interactive* content.

**television studies:** a branch of *media studies* focusing specifically on television: its *genres*, styles and content; its social effects; its organisation as an industry.

**tempo:** a musical term meaning the pace at which a piece is played. In film and video *editing* it has a similar meaning. An *editor* will seek to produce a tempo which matches the emotional intention of the scene. At a basic level, more cuts tend to produce faster tempo. Rhythmic editing can build up or slow down a scene by progressively increasing or decreasing the number of cuts.

**temporal:** see *spatial and temporal contiguity*

**tentpole movie:** an industry term for a strongly promoted film, usually a summer or Christmas *blockbuster*. The term suggests that the *studio* is relying on this film to provide most of its income, since the rest of the *slate* will not necessarily do so well at the *box-office*.

**terrestrial television:** TV from a non-*satellite* or *cable* source. The five terrestrial UK channels are BBC1, BBC2, ITV1, Channel 4 and Five. These are currently *broadcast* using *analogue* technology. The UK also has a terrestrial *digital* service.

**tertiary text:** talk and writing about *media texts* by members of the *audience*, such as *TalkBack*. The term was invented by the *theorist* John Fiske and is a key idea in audience research that looks for the ways in which audiences resist *preferred readings*.

**test screening:** a technique mostly used in the film industry, but also occasionally for TV *pilots*. A selected *audience*, usually representing a cross-section of the public, is shown the film and asked to complete a *questionnaire*. Frequently, parts of films are re-edited, reshot or otherwise altered in response to comments from test audiences.

**text:** see *media text*

**TGRs:** see *target group ratings*

**theatrical release:** the distribution of a film to cinemas, which are often called 'movie theaters' in the USA. Also referred to as theatrical run, cinematic release, cinematic run, first run, second run.

**theatrical run:** see *theatrical release*

**theme:** (i) a concept that is explored in a *text*. For example In the drama series *Six Feet Under*, the **key themes** are death and the family. (ii) *theme music*, particularly when released as a *single*, as in Ennio Morricone's *Theme from The Good, The Bad and the Ugly*.

**theme music:** (i) an instrumental or song that introduces and/or closes a film, TV programme or radio show. For example, the British TV *sitcom Only Fools and Horses* had two theme songs: 'Only Fools and Horses' at the start of most episodes and 'Hookie Street' at the end. (ii) a musical piece that repeatedly accompanies a particular character, group of characters or event. A famous example is Darth Vader's 'Imperial March' composed by John Williams for *The Empire Strikes Back* (Irvin Kershner, USA, 1980). This type of theme is also called a *leitmotif*.

**theory:** an idea that is proposed by a theorist as a way of explaining a phenomenon, but which has not (or cannot) be proved *empirically*. In media and film studies, theories or theoretical positions based on them are often complex and abstract. The term is sometimes used as shorthand for 'critical theory' which refers to a set of *structuralist* and *poststructuralist* approaches.

**thesis:** an argument or intellectual position. The term is often used to identify a central idea in a *text*: for example, 'Paul Greengrass's central thesis in *Bloody Sunday* is that the British army committed mass murder on the day of the Derry march and that this was subsequently covered up.' 'Thesis journalism' is a pejorative term, suggesting that the journalist has written a piece with a particular thesis in mind and is not showing proper *objectivity*.

**think piece:** any *article* devoted to expressing a point of view on a current affairs issue. (See also *editorial* and *op-ed*.)

**third cinema:** a *Marxist* approach to film-making proposed in 1969 by Fernando Solanas and Octavio Getino. Their proposition was that (the 'first cinema') *Hollywood*'s influence as a promoter of *cultural imperialism* must be resisted; that European *auteur* film (the 'second cinema'), such as the *nouvelle vague*, was merely a by-product of Hollywood, and so a new 'third' cinema was required. Although third cinema was conceived in Latin America, which was part of the 'third world', it can be produced anywhere. For example, many of the films of Ken Loach, a British *social realist*, can be described as 'third cinema'.

**third world cinema:** films from the so-called 'third world'. Not to be confused with *third cinema*. 'Third world' is an outmoded term for the countries of Africa and Asia, based on the idea that Europe was the 'first world' and America the 'second world'. Third world cinema would therefore include *Bollywood* and other highly successful film industries (such as that of Korea) as well as the work of much less economically and technologically powerful film makers in countries such as Iran, Afghanistan or small African nations. It is not, therefore a particularly useful term.

**three-point lighting:** the commonest arrangement of lights for filming. The key light is pointed directly at the main subject of the shot (for example an actor); the fill light is used to soften and round out shadows; the back light makes the subject distinct from the background, by creating a glowing halo around it. The technique is also called high-key lighting and is designed to make filming easier by eliminating shadows and so reducing the differences between *angles*.

**three-shot:** a shot in which three figures appear in the frame.

**threshold:** see *news values*

**thriller:** a set of *genres* in film and television (as well as popular literature) which offer the audience *pleasures* built around tension and violence. Thrillers often have a strong male bias with a masculine hero and plenty of action, as in the James Bond or Harry Palmer *spy films*. Other types of thriller, such as the serial-killer drama *The Silence of the Lambs* (Jonathan Demme, USA, 1991) and the British TV series *Prime Suspect* put women at the centre, as investigators, potential victims, or both.

**through-the-line advertising:** a campaign using both *above-the-line* and *below-the-line* strategies.

**THX:** a system for film sound reproduction developed by George Lucas's company Lucasfilm. It is a set of standards designed to ensure that the film sounds as desired by the makers when it is shown in cinemas or on DVD.

**tie-in:** an ancillary product connected to a film or TV series. For example, a *novelisation*, *soundtrack* album, action figure, pencil case. Some media products, such as the *Star Wars* film franchise, generate enormous numbers of tie-ins.

**tilt:** a *camera* movement up or down on a horizontal axis.

**timbre:** the distinctive qualities of a sound. For example, a violin and a pipe organ can play the same note (pitch) at the same volume for the same length of time, but we can still tell the difference between them because they have distinctive timbres. Timbre strongly influences the choice of instrumentation for *soundtrack* music, since different timbres help to construct different moods. In *performance* the timbre of an *actor*'s voice is an important element he or she brings to the role.

**time-based media:** all media in which time is a subject of the *editing* process. Film, radio, TV and video games are all time-based; *print media* are not. *Multimedia texts* usually contain a mixture of time-based and non-time-based elements.

**timecode:** a marker on a film, video or audio recording to indicate the time elapsed since recording began. Essential for editing, timecodes on film and video follow the SMPTE (Society of Motion Picture and Television Engineers) format Hour:Minute:Second:Frame. For example, 00:10:06:15 would mean 'no hours, ten minutes, six seconds and fifteen frames.

**time code:** a *narrative* device used to enable the *audience* to understand relations of time. For example, we see *characters* having breakfast and deduce it is morning; a *caption* reads 'ten years later'; a *close-up* of a clock shows that an hour has passed; a fade to black indicates that a period of time has passed between two scenes.

**time lapse:** (i) a film technique to speed up time. Individual *frames* are shot very slowly, perhaps once every ten minutes rather than twenty-four times per second. When the film is played back at the normal rate, events pass very quickly. We could, for example, see the sun rise, cross the sky and fall in a few seconds instead of twenty-four hours. The technique, using a device called an *intervalometer* (sometimes incorrectly spelled 'inter-velometer') is used extensively in *Donnie Darko* (Richard Kelly, USA, 2001). (ii) an *ellipsis*.

**timeline:** the correct *diegetic* order of events in a *narrative* (as opposed to the narrative order) which may be disturbed by *flashbacks*, *flash forwards* or other alterations to the order of time. In *Saw II* (Darren Lynn Bousman, USA, 2005), for example, a *twist* is created after the *audience* is tricked into believing that they are viewing events in the correct timeline, when they are actually watching a video recording made much earlier in the narrative.

**time shifting:** using video equipment to record a TV programme and view it later. This technology has given the *audience* control over their own viewing, reducing the importance of traditional *scheduling techniques* and making TV *advertising* less effective.

**time splice:** a piece of video *footage* constructed by using a large number of cameras shooting the same image from different points of view and then assembling the *shots* into what looks like a single camera *tracking shot*. The technique was used to produce the 'bullet-time' sequences in *The Matrix* (Andy and Larry Wachowski, USA, 1999).

**Time Warner:** describes itself on its website (www.timewarner.com) as 'the world's first fully integrated media and communications company', with its history beginning with the Warner Brothers Inc film studio in 1923. It is now one of the *Big Six* international media *conglomerates*.

**Tinsel town:** journalistic term for *Hollywood*, which suggests that, like Christmas tree tinsel, 'all that glisters is not gold'.

**tint:** a colouration process applied to the whole of a piece of film. *Black and white* films, particularly *silents*, were sometimes tinted for effect. For example, D W Griffith's silent epic *Intolerence* (USA, 1916) was tinted using four different colours to help distinguish between four distinct narratives and to contribute to the mood of each. This is an early version of the effect later achieved by using coloured *filters*.

**title:** (i) a magazine or newspaper. For example, 'EMAP currently publish fifteen separate titles aimed at female readers.' (ii) a *caption* on film or video.

**titles:** (i) the opening sequence of a film or a TV programme with *captions*, usually including the title of the production as well as *star* names and possibly the *director* or other personnel. Distinct from the *credits*. (ii) the captions that appear in such a sequence.

**title sequence:** a piece of film over which the *titles* appear. Some title sequences for films, such as those designed by Saul Bass, are considered works of art in themselves. Television title sequences are often constructed out of extracts from the series and/or specially filmed *footage*. Together with the *theme music* these images can operate as important *synchronising motifs*. An excellent example of this is the opening sequence for the American sitcom, *Friends*.

**Todorov, Tzvetan (1939–):** see *narrative*

**toga film:** see *peplum movie*

**tokenism:** a pejorative term for half-hearted attempts to bring in under-represented groups. For example, British TV *soap operas* are sometimes criticised for including 'token' black characters. In *Not Another Teen Movie*, the character Malik is used to *satirise* tokenism by complaining that he is the 'token black guy' and has no proper role in the film. Tokenism is not confined to *ethnicity*, however. There can be token disabled characters, token female characters, token *working-class* characters: anyone, in fact, whose only role is to represent a social group. The same kind of criticism can also be levelled at factual genres – the inclusion of a token woman on a news team, for example.

**tone:** a term used in criticism to define the overall effect of a *text*. For example, the film *American Pie* (Paul Weitz, USA, 1999) could be described as having a 'vulgar tone', while the tone of the TV *news* would normally be 'serious and authoritative'. Factors affecting the tone include the language *register*, choice of subject matter, casting, style of delivery, use of music, colour schemes – in fact, almost everything that contributes to the text's *address*.

**topical:** dealing with issues that are currently in the news. *Have I Got News for You* is a topical *comedy* programme.

**top ten/top twenty:** the official weekly list of the best-selling *singles* in the country. For most of the latter half of the twentieth century, the release of this information was a major weekly event for teenagers (though less so at the beginning of the twenty-first century).

**top lighting:** *lighting* from above, used in a similar way to *back lighting* to distinguish the subjects in the foreground clearly from the background.

**TOT:** journalist's slang for **triumph over tragedy**. A type of *human interest* story about individuals who survive terrible misfortune and rebuild their lives. The *genre* is common in *tabloid newspapers* and *women's magazines*.

**total cinema:** a hypothetical form of film which is indistinguishable from reality. According to the influential French film theorist André Bazin (in his article 'The Myth of Total Cinema' published in 1946) the desire to develop cinematic *realism* to this point was a mistake for two reasons: first, it was not possible; second, if it were possible, what would be produced would not be cinema any more.

**total survey area:** the official geographical area covered by a particular radio station. Used when providing *audience* figures to sell advertising.

**tracking shot:** a *camera* movement that could be achieved by mounting the camera on a *dolly* and moving it along a track. Many tracking shots are achieved in other ways, for example with a *hand-held camera* or one mounted on a vehicle. Typically, tracking shots are used to follow characters or other objects in motion.

**tracking study:** (i) *market research* following a product's success (sales and public awareness) over a period of time. Used to monitor the effects of *advertising*. (ii) research which follows (tracks) the same group of people over a long period, monitoring changes to their attitudes or behaviour. May be used as part of an academic *audience* study.

**trademark:** (i) as identified by the ™ symbol, indicates that a particular word, image or logo has been registered as the legal *property* of a particular company. This is often important in the film industry where secondary *rights* to use trademarked elements of the film can be sold for large amounts of money. For example, many of J K Rowling's invented words for the *Harry Potter* series are now trademarks of *Time Warner*. (ii) a director's *signature* or a distinctive quality associated with an actor: for example, 'Sean Connery's trademark Scottish drawl'.

**trade papers:** newspapers or, more usually, magazines produced for an *audience* of workers in a particular industry. The media industries have a large number of trade papers. Some key examples are:

- *Campaign* – for the *advertising* and *marketing* industries
- *Variety* – for *actors* and other workers in the entertainment industry
- *Screen International* – covers the film business
- *Broadcast* – dedicated to the British television industry.

**tragedy:** a traditional *narrative structure* in which a *heroic*, noble or good person is destroyed by a combination of fate and a personal weakness. The term is used routinely in *journalism* to mean any awful event that befalls an individual – usually an accident or disease rather than crime. The death of TV naturalist Steve Irwin after a stingray attack was presented as *tragic*. To call an event a tragedy suggests that fate, rather than any individual or organisation, was to blame. Thus, in representing the death of Princess Diana as a 'tragedy', the press shifted attention away from the fact that her car was possibly being driven at high speed to escape press photographers. (See also *TOT*.)

**trailers:** short films that give previews of movies not yet released and shown in cinemas. Usually, apart from *teaser trailers*, a trailer is composed of exciting or interesting clips from the film it is promoting; these are often supplemented with *voice over* and/or *captions*. In the past, these previews were shown at the end of a second feature or a *newsreel*, which is why they came to be known as trailers, but now that most films are shown without supporting features the trailers are shown at the start of the programme. They are also frequently added to *DVDs*.

**trailing:** the use of *trails* or announcements on TV or radio to promote upcoming programmes. When one station is used to promote another, this is known as 'cross-trailing'. For example, the *BBC* frequently promotes its *digital* services on its *analogue* stations. This may take the form of a specially constructed trailer, or the *continuity* announcer might simply tell viewers that a particular programme is 'coming up on BBC3'.

**trails:** a term for *trailers*, used in TV and radio.

**transceiver:** any device that can both transmit and receive messages – usually used for wireless devices. A mobile telephone is a transceiver, and so is a communications *satellite*.

**transition:** any means of *editing* from one *scene* or *shot* to another. The simplest and commonest transitional device is the *cut*. Others, such as *dissolve*, *wipe* or *cross fade* are used to create specific effects. Also called a 'transitional device'.

**transnational:** a business that operates in many countries. The *Big Six* media corporations are all transnationals.

**transparency:** a slide photograph. (See also *light box*.)

**travelling shot:** any shot in which the *camera* travels on a vehicle, *dolly* or carried by a *camera operator*. There are many types of travelling shot, including *tracking shots*, *crane shots* and *aerial shots*. They are distinct from fixed-position motions (*pans* and *tilts*) in which the camera moves but does not travel.

**travelogue:** a *documentary* about some type of journey, or a *fictional* film in which the main attraction is a series of exotic locations.

**treatment:** a prose version of a film's *narrative* in a format similar to a short story, but following the *scene* structure of the film. Treatments can be produced at many stages in the development of the *screenplay* and are often used in the process of *pitching* a film.

**trilogy:** in film, a set of three connected *narratives*. A trilogy may be no more than a film repeating a successful *formula* in two sequels before running out of steam (for example the *Die Hard* series). It may be conceived of as a single narrative developed over three films, perhaps based on an existing literary trilogy (as in the *Lord of the Rings* trilogy). Alternatively, the films may be united by an idea, (for example, Baz Luhrmann's 'red curtain trilogy' and Krzysztof Kieslowski's *Three Colours* films).

**tripod:** a three-legged stand on which a camera can be mounted.

**trope:** any *code* or *convention* regularly found in a *genre*. If we take the example of the High School Romance film genre, tropes include:

- visual *images* – e.g. a group of young people in an open-topped car
- *character* types – e.g. the self-absorbed, shallow cheerleader
- *narrative* events – e.g. someone agrees to do something for a bet
- types of *shot* – e.g. a shot from inside a locker as it is opened
- *soundtrack* – e.g. indie rock songs.

All genres are effectively collections of tropes. Not all tropes will appear in all examples of the genre.

**turnaround:** a *film industry* term for what happens when the studio that initially developed a project decides not to continue with it. A film 'in turnaround' may be sold to another studio who will redevelop the script with new personnel.

**turning point:** an important moment in a *narrative* after which the main *character*'s goals, attitudes or expectations are changed. According to the screenwriting teacher Syd Field the major turning point should occur at the end of the first act or set-up, but the character may experience further turning points later in the film. A good example is *Thelma and Louise* (Ridley Scott, USA, 1991). The key turning point occurs at the end of Act 1, when a man who has attempted to rape Thelma is shot dead by her best friend, Louise. However, there are several further turning points as Thelma is transformed by stages from a suburban housewife into a fully-fledged outlaw.

**20th Century Fox:** see *Hollywood*; *News International*

**twist:** a *narrative device* in which something unexpected is revealed to the *audience*. Often, though not exclusively, placed at the ending, as in many films by M Night Shyamalan, beginning with *The Sixth Sense* (USA, 1999). A characteristic of *film noir* is often that there are many twists throughout the whole narrative.

**two-shot:** a shot in which two figures appear in the frame.

**two-step flow theory:** a theory of how communication works, proposed by sociologists Lazarfeld and Katz in the 1950s, whereby opinion leaders (those with the greatest access to information) channel it to others, who form the second step or tier in the process.

**TVR (Television Viewing/Viewership Ratings):** a way of calculating and expressing the *audience* achieved by a TV programme, or by an *advertisement*, in relation to the *target audience*. A TVR is equal to 1 per cent of the target audience, so if a programme has a TVR of 8.5 it was seen by 8.5 per cent of the target population.

**TV spot:** a film *trailer* produced for television. Usually very short (i.e. 15 or 30 seconds). Frequently, TV spots use similar techniques to the *teaser trailer*.

**TV version:** a film that has been specially edited for broadcast on *television*. This may mean that some violent or sexual scenes are either reduced or completely cut. It can also mean that expletives are overdubbed with other words. 'Freaking' and 'Melon Farmer' are two common substitutions for strong swear words in TV versions.

**typeage:** the use of either *stereotypes* or *archetypes*. This term normally suggests a system or group of related types. For instance, 'Within the action movie genre as a whole there is fairly consistent typeage among villain characters: they are all outsiders in some way, and the commonest symbol for this is physical disability and/or foreign nationality.'

**typecasting** is where an *actor* is given a series of very similar roles. The British actor Vinnie Jones, for example, is usually cast as a thug. During the era of the *Hollywood studio system*, typecasting of actors within particular *genres* was standard practice, since it made the making of films a more reliable and speedy process, though not all actors were keen on being typecast. It was Olivia de Havilland's refusal to be typecast that eventually ended the use of seven-year contracts in Hollywood. For many actors today, typecasting is seen as a limitation, and they seek to avoid it. Tom Cruise is a good example. He has taken a diverse variety of roles in addition to the heroic parts for which he is best known. For instance, he plays an emotionally damaged motivational speaker in *Magnolia* (P T Anderson, USA, 1999) and a cold-hearted assassin in *Collateral* (Michael Mann, USA, 2004).

**typeface:** a set of letters, numbers and punctuation marks with a unified design, as used for printing, desktop publishing, *moving image* captions and other such purposes. Also now known as a 'font'. Choice of typeface is an important element of design in any medium that uses lettering, since different styles communicate different *semiotic* meanings.

---

**Do you know we also have A–Zs for:**

- ICT & Computing
- Psychology
- Sociology
- Travel & Leisure?

Ask for them in your local bookshop or see the inside back cover for ordering details.

**U certificate:** the lowest level of age *certification* awarded to films by the *BBFC*. U is an abbreviation of 'universal', meaning 'suitable for all'. The decision to give a U certificate is based on the film containing nothing that is likely to cause a four-year-old child to be disturbed: no sex or drug-related content, only very mild swearing and a 'positive moral framework'. Most films certificated U are designed for children, but the certificate is also awarded to other films which may be too complex in their subject matter for children but do not contain any content that would require a higher certificate. This reflects changes in what is considered acceptable in films for older audiences. For example, *12 Angry Men* (Sydney Lumet, USA, 1957) was passed *uncut* as U on its original release. The 1998 *remake* (William Friedkin, USA) received a 12 certificate when released on video in the UK because it contained one use of 'strong language'. Because the U certificate is associated in the minds of audiences with children's films, movies aimed at an older age group often deliberately include elements that will prevent the film from being given a U (or even *PG*) certificate.

**Uc certificate:** a subdivision of the *U certificate*, used only on *home video* recordings to indicate that the content of a film is especially suitable for children under school age.

**UK Film Council:** a government body under the direction of the *DCMS* that distributes money to support British film. It describes its main aim as 'to stimulate a competitive, successful and vibrant UK film industry and culture, and to promote the widest possible enjoyment and understanding of cinema throughout the nations and regions of the UK'. In addition to funding and co-funding new feature films, the UK Film Council also invests in distribution and exhibition, including an innovative programme to equip cinemas with digital projection equipment. It also funds *short films*, gives a substantial grant to the *BFI* and works in partnership with *Skillset* to provide training for film professionals. The purpose of the UK Film Council is to overcome the problems that have traditionally beset the British Film Industry. Because the UK Film Council is spending mainly public money, in particular a substantial amount raised by the National Lottery, its activities have attracted a good deal of press attention, often focusing on how badly many of the films have done at the *box-office*. Most notorious of these was the comedy *Sex Lives of the Potato Men* (Andy Humphrys, UK, 2006), which cost approximately £1.8 million but *grossed* only £673,328. This is to some extent an unfair criticism, however, since many of the 'failed' films have subsequently done well through sale of TV rights and distribution on DVD.

**undercrank:** running a film camera at a slower speed in order to produce fast motion when the footage is played back. The term comes from the earliest days of film when cameras were cranked by hand. The opposite of overcrank.

**underground film:** a term used in various ways since the 1950s to mean types of non-mainstream film-making. During the 1960s, like the *underground press*, underground films were small productions that challenged conventional social taboos and authority figures, often championing drug use and sexual liberation. Later it came to refer to *micro-budget* film (as opposed to the larger budget *independent* films) with an unconventional attitude. Some underground film makers, such as John Waters, have progressed into the *mainstream.*

**underground press:** any publication produced and distributed independently, usually with an anti-*establishment* agenda. Also known as 'samizdat' publishing. In countries where freedom of speech is limited, the underground press is often an important means of resistance and subversion. The people who publish them risk punishment under the law, and in many cases violent repression. In Britain and the USA during the 1960s, underground magazines were part of a more general challenge to authority and *taboo*. The most famous of these was *Oz*, the publishers of which were sued under the obscenity laws in 1971.

**underlighting:** (i) placing lights below the subject. This technique is sometimes used to create dramatic, eerie effects, but can also suggest that the light is coming from a real source below the line of sight, such as a fireplace or an instrument panel. Shots of people inside cars at night are lit from below because it is often the only place a light can be placed within a vehicle. (ii) another word for underexposure.

**unique selling point (USP):** the feature of a product that makes it distinct from any potential competitors and therefore particularly attractive to the audience. The USP is emphasised strongly in *advertising*. (For example, the Nintendo Wii *games console* is distinguished from its competitors because it uses two motion-sensitive remote controls rather than a traditional *game controller* handset.)

**unit:** a team of film or video workers. In the era of the *Hollywood studio system* a production unit would work together under the same director on a series of films in the same *genre*. This was thought to create greater efficiency. Television companies often adopt a similar structure of unit-based production with specialist teams working on *news*, *drama*, *outside broadcasts* and so on.

**universal service:** a philosophy of media provision based on the *Reithian* idea that communications are an important social right and everyone must receive the same level of service, regardless of profitability. Rural populations, for example, must be given the same level of access to the service as urban ones, though it may be expensive and unprofitable to provide it. Access to the *internet* has become such an important element of modern life that the British government has set targets for the time by which it wants the internet to have become a universal service.

**unrestricted narration:** see *restricted and unrestricted narration*

**unstaged:** of photographed or filmed events, not set up or prepared in advance. In *moving image* genres, unstaged material is composed of events in the world simply filmed with no interference from the film maker. Many (but by no means all) *documentaries* contain predominantly unstaged material.

**uplink:** (i) the connection on a *satellite* that receives information from Earth. (ii) the connection between a mobile telephone and the *network.*

**upper case:** capital letters. The term derives from traditional printing, when the capital letters would be kept in a case above the others. Aside from their conventional use to indicate beginnings of sentences and proper nouns, capitals are frequently used for emphasis, in *headlines* and *titles*.

**urban gothic:** a *narrative* genre combining inner city settings with traditional *gothic* tropes such as sexual obsession and perversion, the supernatural, physical decay, sickness, violence and shadows. There is often some crossover with *film noir.* Examples of the genre often acquire *cult* audiences. It is a style particularly suited to *comic books* and comic book adaptations such as Tim Burton's *Batman* (USA, 1989) and Frank Miller and Robert Rodriguez's *Sin City* (USA, 2005). Examples from TV include Joss Whedon's *Angel* and the British TV series *Urban Gothic.*

**usage and attitude:** a *tracking survey* that analyses the relationship between the general public and a specific product, also known as U&A, A&U, or AAU. Used as a means of monitoring the effectiveness of *advertising.*

**user-friendly:** easy to understand and control without the need for complex instructions. The success or failure of many new media technologies depends on their degree of user-friendliness. For example, the massive success of Apple's iPod is partly due to the extreme simplicity of its *user interface.*

**user interface:** the means by which an electronic media product is controlled. For example, most video recorders now have an interface composed of a *remote control* and an on-screen display. This allows the user to give commands and to receive information about what the machine is doing. The level of complexity of the user interface defines its degree of *user-friendliness.*

**uses and gratifications theory/model:** an *audience*-centred approach to the study of *media effects.* Opposed to *passive audience* models like the *hypodermic model*, it suggests that audience members are *active* in the ways that they choose and experience media texts. The four main categories of use and gratification were listed by McQuail, Blumler and Brown in 1972, as follows:

i.  **diversion** – or the escape from the troubles and stresses of an individual's life.

ii. **personal relationships** – where media products are used as subject matter for conversation or where the individual has a sense of a personal relationship with, for example, characters in a soap opera.

iii. **surveillance** – the use of media texts to find out about the world, most obviously via the news, but also through other types of media text, including fictional ones.

iv. **personal identity** – where an individual uses media products to help construct a sense of self. This can take many forms, such as defining oneself as 'a *Star Trek* fan', seeing media personalities as role models or simply comparing the way a character deals with a problem with the way one would handle it oneself.

This approach can be criticised as being descriptive and individualised. It is good at creating a *qualitative* picture of the way in which one person experiences media texts, but the results cannot be generalised, since the starting point is that everyone's experience of the media is different.

**USP:** see *unique selling point*

**utopia:** an (imaginary) ideal society. Because they would produce little *conflict* there is not much story potential in utopias. There are, therefore, far more narratives dealing with the opposite: a *dystopia.*

**values:** the beliefs and attitudes held by an individual, a social group or a whole society. A person's values are gained through a process of *socialisation*. *Media texts* are constructed to reflect and reinforce the values of their *target audiences*. For example, the British newspaper *The Guardian* is read mainly by educated left-liberals. Consequently, the attitudes expressed by its journalists in *columns* and *think pieces* are generally in tune with the beliefs of that audience. By contrast, Rush Limbaugh's US radio *talk show* has a strongly conservative audience, and the content of his programme tends to reinforce their values.

**variable focus:** the ability to change the subject of *focus* within the lens's depth of field, as used in *racking focus* and follow focus. Should not be confused with variable focal length, which is characteristic of *zoom lenses*.

**VCU (very close up):** see *cinematography*

**verbal discourse:** the transmission of messages through words. Verbal discourse may be spoken, written or printed.

**verisimilitude:** the appearance of reality. The term may be used to refer to *surface realism*.

**vertical integration:** where a single company controls both the production and supply of a product. During the *Hollywood studio system* era, the *Big Five* studios were fully vertically integrated because they made films, which they also *distributed* and then *exhibited* in their own *cinema chains*.

**VHS:** the first commercially successful *home video* tape cassette format. VHS, which originally stood for **vertical helical scan** but soon became known as *home video* system, was introduced by JVC in 1978. Able to provide up to three hours of viewing on a relatively small cassette, it won a *format* war against the competing *Betamax* and V2000 systems and became the dominant home video technology until it was eventually outstripped by *DVD* in the early twenty-first century. Initially very expensive (the earliest players cost the equivalent of over £2000 today) the consumer costs declined quickly until *VCRs* became commonplace items in every home. VHS revolutionised TV viewing. Instead of waiting months or years for films to be broadcast on TV, viewers could simply buy or rent them; instead of being controlled by *scheduling*, viewers could *time shift* programmes to view them as and when it was convenient to do so. VHS can be seen as the most significant development in TV technology and use since the invention of the medium.

**Viacom:** see *Big Six*

**victim-hero:** (i) a technique of *tabloid journalism*, representing people who are victims of disease, disaster or terrorist attacks as 'heroes' though they have done nothing heroic. For example, the press will frequently report someone's 'battle against cancer', since this seems more dramatic than 'terrible misfortune and medical treatment'. Perhaps the ultimate victim-heroine of recent times is Princess Diana, who had become something of a hate figure in the British newspapers before her death in a car accident, after which the press immediately began representing her as the noble, gentle and heroic 'people's princess'. (ii) a character conventionally seen in *film noir*, the victim-hero is commonly the central male character who is initially the victim of the *femme fatale* but who ultimately acts in a heroic way at the end of the film.

**video:** moving images that have been recorded electronically. Video images have a very different appearance from film, which is recorded chemically. Because of its 'cheap' look, video was traditionally associated with low production values in the TV industry. It tended to be used for disposable, high-turnover *genres* such as soap operas and news. However, video also has many advantages over film. It does not need to be processed, is easier to edit, and takes up much less space. These advantages have been multiplied by the development of *digital video*, which does not even require tape, produces extremely high-quality images, is very easy to edit using *non-linear* technology and can be processed to produce a *film look*. Digital video is now used extensively not just in television, but also in the film industry, from *blockbusters* like *Revenge of the Sith* (George Lucas, USA, 2005) to *micro-budget*, *independent* and *underground* films.

**video game:** a *game* played on a TV, using a console or on a computer screen. Video games have developed numerous *genres*.

**Video Home System:** see *VHS*

**video nasties:** a *moral panic* of the early 1980s which was inspired by the rapid growth in *home video* ownership and lack of regulation of video material leading to a small boom in *exploitation films* from Italy and the USA combining *violence* with soft-core *pornography*. The *Daily Mail* and other *tabloid* newspapers began reporting on these 'video nasties', presenting them as a social danger. For the most part, the films were far less *shocking* in reality than their covers and publicity suggested. In June 1983 the Department of Public Prosecutions produced a list of films considered potentially obscene, 39 of which were banned under the *Obscene Publications Act*. The banned list was mostly composed of trashy exploitation films, but also included some critically regarded *horror* films such as *The Last House on the Left* (Wes Craven, USA, 1972) and *Tenebrae* (Dario Argento, Italy, 1982). Many of the banned films have now been given certificates by the *BBFC*.

**video on demand (VOD):** a system offered by digital *cable* services for allowing viewers to receive and immediately view video material at any time they choose, rather than following a *schedule*. VOD is either *downloaded* to a *set-top box* or *streamed*. It is normally a *pay-per-view* service.

**Video Recordings Act 1984:** the act of parliament that gave the *BBFC* authority to *certificate* video recordings. It was a reaction to the *video nasties* scare.

**video tape recorder:** any machine for recording and playing back *moving images* on video tape. In TV production, the phrases 'roll VT' or 'go to VT' are *cues* to show pre-recorded *footage*.

**viewer:** an individual member of the TV audience. A television *spectator*.

**viewfinder:** part of a camera, or a piece of equipment attached to a camera, used to show the image as it will eventually appear on film. A director's viewfinder is an apparatus used (mainly by *cinematographers*) to look at potential *shots* in preparation for the actual positioning of the camera.

**vigilante film:** a film *genre* in which the *hero* is a member of the public who takes on criminals independently when the official forces of law and order have failed. Usually revenge is an important motivating factor in the plot. There is a tradition of violent, politically right-wing vigilante films, such as the *Death Wish* series made during the 1970s and 1990s, starring Charles Bronson. Many superhero films, such as *Spider-Man* (Sam Raimi, USA, 2002) can also be described as vigilante films.

**vignette:**

i.  a short film can be described as a film vignette, or simply as a vignette, especially if it does not contain much, or any, *narrative*.

ii. a vignette film is one made up of a number of smaller *stories* which connect to construct the whole. *Crash* (Paul Haggis, USA, 2004) presents the audience with a set of interconnected *narratives* taking place in a single day in Los Angeles. *Dead of Night* (Cavalcanti *et al.*, UK, 1945) uses a *frame story* in which various characters in a country house each tells a supernatural story. *Night on Earth* (Jim Jarmusch, USA, 1991) presents a series of five taxi journeys, each in a different country on the same night.

iii. in *print*, a vignette is an image which has been processed to fade out at the edges rather than having a clear border.

iv. in *TV advertising*, a vignette ad is a *montage* of very short *scenes*. These may be connected by a *narrative*: for example, several different frustrating events in the same woman's day could be shown before a final scene in which she enjoys a relaxing bubble bath. Alternatively, the scenes may be relatively disconnected, showing different people enjoying, or benefiting from, the product.

**violation of expectation:** an important concept in *cognitive psychology*. Once individuals develop a set of beliefs about *cause-and-effect* they are uncomfortable with images or statements that do not fit (i.e. they violate) these *expectations*. In mainstream *narratives*, the commonest violation of expectation is the *twist*, where the *pleasure* for the *spectator* is in re-forming a consistent understanding of preceding events in the light of new information. *Surrealist* films take a more radical approach, deliberately and repeatedly violating the audience's expectations without offering any way of understanding what has happened. For example in Luis Buñuel's *That Obscure Object of Desire* (Fr/Sp, 1977), the part of Conchita is played by two different actresses alternating in the role, but this is neither acknowledged nor explained within the film.

**violence:** in film and media texts this has been the subject of extensive debate throughout the history of the *moving image*. Along with sex and drug use, *screen* violence is one of the main factors governing film *classification* in the UK. Many narratives have depended on violence, and it is clear that violence in fictions gives pleasure to the audience. Some research, such as Bandura's experiments in the 1960s, suggests that violent media texts encourage violent behaviour in the audience, but this is by no means conclusive. It is equally possible that violent media images serve a valuable social function by providing audiences with a vicarious outlet for their violent impulses. Occasionally, media violence is the subject of a *moral panic* such as the *video nasties* scare of the early 1980s.

**viral:** *internet* slang for anything that suddenly achieves enormous interest from web users. Viral phenomena are so called because they behave like a virus, being copied and spreading at enormous speed. They also mutate as users adapt and alter them. A typical example was the so-called 'Star Wars Kid' in 2003. A two minute clip of a Canadian teenager awkwardly imitating the *Star Wars* character Darth Maul was posted to a file-sharing site by one of his peers. Within a short time it had become internationally famous, appearing on large numbers of websites in new forms, with added music, sound effects, altered by the addition of *CGI* or edited into scenes from famous films.

**viral marketing** is an advertising technique that attempts to create a viral effect. One of the earliest and most effective instances of viral marketing was the promotional campaign for the *low-budget* film *The Blair Witch Project* (Daniel Myrick/Eduardo Sánchez, USA, 1999). The film was promoted using a website (www.blairwitch.com) which claimed to document the 'true' story of three film makers mysteriously lost in the woods as they investigated the myth of the Blair Witch. By the time the film was released it had built up such massive interest that it made over $248 million worldwide.

**virtuality:** derived from *virtual reality*, the term is used to describe anything that 'exists' only inside a computer or other *digital* device. The console game *Nintendogs*, for example, is a *sim* in which the player owns a **virtual** dog. A friendship that takes place in chatrooms and/or over e-mail can be described as a 'virtual relationship'.

**virtual reality:** any computer-based system for creating an environment that has many of the characteristics of reality. The term came into popular use during the 1990s to describe three-dimensional environments that could be experienced using stereoscopic headpieces through which the viewer could 'move' using some kind of pointing device, such as a mouse or a specially designed glove. Virtual reality is the subject of various *science fiction* narratives, and may in the future become an important media technology, but is still at a relatively early stage in its development.

**visual discourse:** the transmission of messages through images. (See also *discourse.*)

**visual literacy:** the ability to *decode* or 'read' *visual discourse.*

**visual noise:** anything that we can see but are not interested in. For example, in city centres we are surrounded by a great deal of *visual* and *verbal discourse*, such as advertising hoardings, video screens, neon signs and so on. We experience most of this as 'noise': we are aware of it but do not give it much attention. The term suggests a lack of usefulness and a potential to cause irritation. Too much visual noise is considered a mark of bad design in websites.

**visual pleasure:** the enjoyment of looking. Most *moving image* media depend on visual pleasure to some extent. (See also *scopophilia*; *voyeurism*.)

**Vitaphone:** the first commercial system for delivering *synchronised sound* in a film, as used in *The Jazz Singer* (Alan Crossland, USA, 1927) and many other early *talkies*.

**VLS:** very long shot.

**VOD:** see *video on demand*

**voicer:** a short segment in a radio *news* broadcast that is written and read by a reporter rather than the newsreader. Voicers can be recorded on the spot or in the *studio*.

**voice-of-god narration:** any *voice-over* where the speaker is not connected to the *action* but seems to have complete knowledge of every element of the story. The approach may be very restrained and set out to appear objective, as in many *documentaries;* or it can be more *dramatic* in style, though this is now rather old-fashioned. The highly dramatic voice-of-god narration in TV crime series of the 1960s was *parodied* in the *Naked Gun* series of comedy films and its TV *spin-off* series, *Police Squad*.

**voice-over:** a type of *non-diegetic, asynchronous sound* in which the audience hear a voice that does not have a source either within the *frame* or within hearing distance, and which is not heard by the people on screen. Many documentaries make use of voice-over to clarify, explain or comment on the material on-screen. *Narrative* voice-over is used in *fictions* to make elements of *story* or *character* clear to the audience. These are almost never *voice-of-god* narrations. Typically, the *narration* is spoken by a character looking back on the events. An excellent example is the narration in *Stand By Me* (Rob Reiner, USA, 1986) performed by Richard Dreyfuss who, as the adult Gordie Lachance, is remembering the events of his boyhood. We sometimes hear characters' thoughts in voice-over. This is usually a *comic* technique.

**voice tracking:** a technique for pre-recording a radio *disc jockey's* links between songs and storing them digitally as an alternative to using a live DJ. Sometimes used so that a DJ can record a show in advance; sometimes so that the same show can be broadcast on several different stations. Very low-budget radio stations often buy in generic voice tracks so that they do not need to employ any DJs.

**vox pop:** a brief, unrehearsed interview with a member of the public. Often, news broadcasts will carry a *montage* of such interviews in order to give a flavour of public opinion on a *current affairs* topic. The term is short for the Latin phrase, vox populi, meaning 'voice of the people'.

**voyeurism:** literally means sexual *pleasure* gained from watching others, sometimes engaged in sexual activity. Metaphorically, it is used as a pejorative term to suggest that the *audience*'s interest in material presented by media texts is morally dubious. A good example is the tabloid press's coverage of celebrities' private lives, which can be said to appeal solely to the audience's voyeuristic interest. (See also *scopophilia*.)

**VPL:** the video equivalent of *PPL*, collecting royalties on behalf of the makers of music videos.

**VTR:** see *video tape recorder*

**Do you need revision help and advice?**

Go to pages 251–292 for a range of revision appendices that include exam advice and tips.

**walled garden:** A media environment, usually involving the *internet*, that restricts its users to a set of services controlled or selected by the provider. One example is the way in which many satellite and cable TV providers offer their users access to a limited range of internet sites through their TV sets, rather than the whole of the web. Walled gardens can be attractive, especially in the early days of a technology, because they reduce confusing choices and improve *user-friendliness*. Apple have been accused of operating a walled garden approach with their iPod hardware and iTunes software, which are very easy to use, but also integrate directly with the iTunes online music store rather than giving the user clear access to a range of services. As audiences become more confident, they often begin to feel frustrated with the limitations of the walled garden. *ISPs*, particularly *AOL*, began by providing walled gardens, but eventually had to expand their services to allow users free access to the whole of the web.

**war film:** an important film *genre* in which the subject or setting is an armed conflict. There are probably as many types of war film as there are types of film: most genres from period drama to fantasy epic can include elements of war. However, the core of the genre is a portrayal of a modern armed conflict, beginning with a series of films about the Second World War, made mainly between about 1940 and 1970. Some war films are straightforward *thrillers*, others are critical of warfare, perhaps using techniques of *satire* as in *Three Kings* (David O Russell, USA, 1999). Some, like *Saving Private Ryan* (Steven Spielberg, USA, 1998), celebrate the courage and sacrifice of soldiers. Many of America's most complex and self-searching films have been those dealing with the Vietnam War, such as *The Deer Hunter* (Michael Cimino, USA, 1978) and *Apocalypse Now!* (Francis Ford Coppola, USA, 1979).

**warm light:** light that creates an impression of high temperatures, typically using high proportions of red or orange.

**Warner Bros:** important *studio* during the era of the *Hollywood studio system*. Notable for the production of gritty *social problem films* and, later, short cartoons. Now part of *Time Warner.*

**watercooler phenomenon:** a media product, most often a TV programme, that is the subject of a great deal of discussion among people at work. The concept appeared first in the USA during the 1990s but is now in common use in the UK to describe the social effects of popular programmes such as *Lost* and *Big Brother.*

**watershed:** a fixed point of the evening in UK TV *scheduling*, before which it is not permitted to broadcast content which is deemed unsuitable for younger viewers, such as sex, violence or strong swearing. *Ofcom* sets the watershed at 9 pm. After this time, the later the hour, the stronger the material that can be shown. Films rated 18 cannot be shown before 10 pm unless they are *TV versions.*

**webcasting:** broadcasting over the *internet*. This may be in the form of *streaming content* or *podcasting*.

**webzine:** an online magazine. This may be an electronic version of a magazine published in print or, more properly, a magazine that is only available electronically. A webzine differs from other types of website in two ways: schedule of publication and issue structure. While most websites can be updated at any time, a webzine provides new issues on a periodic basis: weekly, monthly or quarterly. These issues are each presented as a distinct whole, often beginning with a cover page and contents list, in the manner of a traditional magazine. An archive of previous issues may be available. Publishing online overcomes many of the problems typically associated with the magazine industry (there are no print or distribution costs), but brings its own difficulties. Web magazines may find it difficult to build up a regular readership, and because there is an expectation that web content is free, it is especially difficult to make readers pay for a webzine. Many make their money by carrying banner advertising. A small number offer subscriptions. While some webzines are produced by big media businesses, the low costs and potential enormous audiences offered by the internet have encouraged many individuals and groups to set up *independent* publications, often with no intention of running at a profit. Many such webzines are similar to *underground press* and/or *fanzine* publications.

**weepie:** see *tear-jerker*

**Western:** an extremely important film *genre* and later a television genre during the twentieth century, also sometimes referred to as the 'Westerner'. Its basic template was established during the *silent* film period when it was successful because of its strong visual *codes* and emphasis on *action* rather than *dialogue* combined with a simple moral approach. The Western genre presented a *mythologised* version of nineteenth-century American history showing the taming of a wild land by 'civilising forces'. The white community was shown attempting to build an orderly life in the newly colonised western states, which usually meant setting up farms, towns or goldmines. These efforts would be threatened by forces of chaos: the 'enemies without' (savage 'Indians'; the harsh climate) or the 'enemies within' (drunkenness, prostitution and crime). The (male) hero would resolve the conflict by defeating the forces of chaos. As audiences became more sophisticated, and historically aware, the conventional Western became less acceptable. A particular problem of early Westerns was their representation of the 'Indians' or native peoples of the plains, such as the Sioux, the Apache and the Comanche, as little better than vermin, requiring extermination. Later Westerns, such as *Broken Arrow* (Delmer Daves, USA, 1950) and *Little Big Man* (Arthur Penn, USA, 1970) set out to show how the white settlers had victimised and oppressed the native population. Other Westerns, such as *Unforgiven* (Clint Eastwood, USA, 1992) challenged the idea of the 'hero' and the so-called *spaghetti Westerns* of the 1960s showed the west as a much more lawless and amoral place. After about 1955, the genre became less popular in the cinema, with occasional exceptions, but Western TV series such as *Rawhide*, *Bonanza*, and *The High Chaparral* continued to attract viewers. These died out during the 1980s, since when the only Western TV series of note have been HBO's *Deadwood*, which presented a more historically realistic version of life in a gold-prospecting town during the 1870s, and Steven Spielberg's *Into the West* (2006).

**whip pan:** a very fast *pan* creating strong *motion blur*. Also known as a 'whip shot', 'zip pan' or 'swish pan'. The latter probably refers to the type of swishing *sound effect* which often accompanies this camera movement on screen. A whip pan edit is a kind of 'cheat' *edit* in which a whip pan at the end of the first shot is *cross-faded* into another whip pan at the beginning of the second. The motion blur disguises the *cut* between the two shots, making it appear that they are part of the same *take.*

**white balance:** a feature of digital video and still cameras, designed to compensate for variations in the *colour temperature* produced by artificial lights and daylight. Without white balance, images shot under daylight look more blue, and under artificial lighting they look more yellow. It is particularly important to make sure that white balance is set correctly when moving from one to the other. A more professional lighting and camera *set-up* will involve the use of filters and gels to create a desired overall colour temperature.

**white-collar:** somewhat outmoded term referring to non-manual jobs. The term refers to the white shirt and tie traditionally worn by clerical employees. (See also *blue-collar.*)

**white paper:** an official report that sets out policy decisions. In British government, a white paper is often the final step in research and discussion before the creation of new *legislation.*

**white space:** any area of a page without print. The paper need not necessarily be white. White space is not simply unused paper; it contributes to the overall design and *layout.* For example, minimalist page designs using a great deal of white space are often associated with sophistication and elegance. Although originally a concept in print and graphic design, white space has become very important in web design, with overcrowding of the page often considered a key indicator of a badly constructed web page.

**wide angle:** see *cinematography*

**widescreen:** any screen wider than the 4:3 *academy ratio.* The American Widescreen (1.85:1) and *Cinemascope* (2.35:1) widescreen *ratios* are now in most common use, but there have been many experiments to create extreme widescreen experiences, such as using multiple cameras and multiple projectors. When shooting on film, there are two main ways to produce a widescreen image on standard 35 mm film *stock,* which has individual *frames* that are 4:3. The frame can be masked at the top and bottom, creating the widescreen image by using only the central area: this technique produces images in the American Widescreen ratio. Alternatively, an *anamorphic lens* can be used to squeeze the image horizontally into the 4:3 frame: this produces wider ratios, such as Cinemascope. Film makers and film audiences seem to prefer widescreen to 4:3, perhaps because it is well suited to highly dramatic images, or because it is closer in appearance to the normal human field of vision. Another possibility is that the widescreen image has become more conventionally *cinematic* in the minds of audiences than academy, which until recently was the ratio used for TV screens. 16:9 Widescreen TVs (a ratio almost identical to American Widescreen) are now in common use and, using digital technology, it is increasingly usual for TV programmes to be made in this ratio.

**wide shot (WS):** see *cinematography*

**wi-fi:** a wireless digital communication system covering a small area. Mainly used at present for home computer networks or internet 'hot-spots', but may eventually become a common way of distributing media content. A small number of systems now use wi-fi in order that MP3 players can be heard, and controlled, from anywhere in the home.

**wild sound:** any sound recorded during the filming process at a different time from the recording of the images. Examples can include ambient sound, off-camera dialogue or sound effects and lip-synched overdubs recorded on location so that the room tone is accurate. Also known as 'atmos', 'buzz track' or 'wild track'.

**willing suspension of disbelief:** the acceptance of obviously unreal or fictional *narrative*. Most fiction *genres* include elements that the audience know not to be true, but we are willing to accept them in order to be entertained. For example, you do not have to believe in ghosts to enjoy a ghost story such as *The Others* (Alejandro Amenábar, Sp/Fr/USA, 2001).

**wipe:** a shot transition in which the new image wipes over the previous one. A wipe-dissolve has a blurred edge. Wipes can suggest ellipsis or a significant change of location, as they do in the *Star Wars* films. Alternatively, wipes may be used for purely stylistic purposes, as in the opening sequence of Baz Luhrmann's *Romeo+Juliet* (USA, 1996). Horizontal wipes were favoured by the Japanese director Akira Kurosawa.

**wireless telephony:** a generic term for any mobile telephone system, such as cellphones and satellite phones. Also sometimes used to refer to wireless internet access.

**wire work:** a set of *stunt* techniques developed in Hong Kong martial arts films to create flying effects. Many sequences in *Crouching Tiger, Hidden Dragon* (Ang Lee, Taiwan/Hong Kong/USA/China, 2000) were designed to show off wire work techniques. Often combined with *chromakey* in *Hollywood* for action sequences, especially in superhero films such as *X-Men* (Bryan Singer, USA, 2000).

**WOB:** white text on a black background. Acronym of 'white-on-black' used in printing and web design.

**Women in Film and Television (WFT):** a UK association for women who work in the film and television industries. Established in 1990, it is open to anyone with at least a year's experience in the industries. 'WFTV exists to protect and enhance the status, interests and diversity of women working at all levels in both film, television and digital media industries.' (www.wftv.org.uk/home.asp)

**women's film/picture:** a term used during the era of the *Hollywood studio system* to indicate any film that was intended principally (but not exclusively) for a female audience. Mainly consisting of *melodramas* and *romances*, the category tended to refer to films with strong female *protagonists*, such as *The Nun's Story* (Fred Zinnemann, USA, 1959), *Imitation of Life* (Douglas Sirk, USA, 1959) and *Mrs Miniver* (William Wyler, USA, 1942) and had an emphasis on subject matter that related to the personal and relationships (as opposed to the universal, such as war). Arguably, some representatives of other genres, such as *screwball comedy* and *musicals*, may also be described as women's pictures. The women's film was largely superseded by the accessibility of television, which developed 'female' genres, such as the soap opera, which clearly had their roots in film melodrama. The term has been, and is often, used pejoratively by film executives and critics who are discussing a film's appeal, almost in a dismissive way, but the success of a number of more contemporary so-called woman's films made Hollywood take notice in the 1990s, when the action genre was floundering, with such unexpected hits as *Ghost* (Jerry Zucker, USA, 1990), *Pretty Woman* (Garry Marshall, USA, 1990) and *Thelma and Louise* (Ridley Scott, USA, 1991). The term is highly problematic now, as recent film successes as the *Saw* trilogy (James Wan, USA, 2004, 2005, 2006) have, perhaps unexpectedly in the film industry's terms, attracted large audiences of young women.

**women's magazines:** a segment of the magazine market that comes under the broader category of lifestyle magazines. The academics Angela McRobbie, Janet Winship and Margaret Ferguson have written extensively about women's magazines and their readers.

**word-of-mouth:** the informal social discussion and individual recommendations surrounding the release of a film. Also known as scuttlebutt. Although word-of-mouth can be shaped to some extent by media influences, such as *reviews* and *news stories*, it is acknowledged to be a force largely beyond the control of marketing. For most Hollywood films with *saturation releases*, the period between the opening weekend and the film being played out is so short that only very early word-of-mouth is of value. *Teaser trailers* and *press releases* long in advance of the film's completion are designed to start building expectation and word-of-mouth at the earliest opportunity. As much as good word-of-mouth can help a film to do well, if it is bad, the film's commercial chances are probably destroyed. Smaller budget films with a *platform release* can benefit from word-of-mouth, becoming surprise hits. For example, *My Big Fat Greek Wedding* (Joel Zwick, USA, 2002) became the fifth-highest grossing American film of its year and the highest grossing *independent film* up to that point, entirely as a result of good word-of-mouth. Scuttlebutt spread on the *internet* is increasingly important. For example, *Snakes on a Plane* (David R Ellis, USA, 2006) became one of the most eagerly anticipated films of the year because of this so-called 'word of mouse'.

**working class:** traditionally, referring to those who worked in chiefly manual trades and as unskilled workers, this is a difficult term to define these days as someone might choose to describe themselves as working class, although they might be well educated and on a high income. In this sense, the term refers chiefly to a culture and values inculcated when growing up.

**world cinema:** literally, film from anywhere other than the USA. In the UK, it means film from anywhere other than the USA or Britain. However, the term is arguably so broad as to be almost meaningless except as a means of organising the shelves in a DVD store. By definition, 'world cinema films' are the products of a vast array of cultures and film industries. The intention behind the classification, however, is to draw attention to the fact that many excellent films are made in countries other than America and in languages other than English.

**World Wide Web (www):** the body of interconnected material supplied via the *internet.*

**worm's-eye view shot:** see *cinematography*

**wrap:** the end of *shooting* on a film or TV production. The word can be used to mean that a director requires no more *takes* on a specific *shot* – 'It's a wrap!' – to indicate the end of filming for the day or that the entire production is now completely filmed.

**WS:** (wide shot) see *cinematography*

**WYSIWYG:** acronym of 'What you see is what you get'. The term refers to the way in which the image on a computer screen more or less exactly reproduces the output. WYSIWYG displays are the reason that it is possible to carry out desktop publishing and digital video editing.

**'X' rating:** was the *classification* used for films that were considered suitable only for adults by the *British Board of Film Censors* in the UK and by similar bodies in other countries. Some countries, such as France, still use the 'X' certificate, but Britain and the USA no longer do so on the grounds that age-specific certification (such as 18) is easier to understand and enforce. In the UK, the 'X' certificate was introduced in 1951, replacing the previous, purely advisory, H (for '*Horror*') certificate. Initially, X-rated films could be seen by anyone over 16, but this was raised to 18 in 1970 as a way of allowing stronger material to be certificated. The 'X' was awarded to films containing graphic violence, sexual content and/or drug-related material. In 1982, it was replaced by two new certificates: '18' for most material that could be shown in cinemas and *R18* for hard-core *pornography*. Although the 'X' certificate was given to many films that did not contain much, or any, sexual material, it has taken on an association with pornography, possibly because the letter 'X' appears at the end of the word sex. The terms 'X-rated' and the nonexistent 'XXX'-rated are therefore still commonly used in the marketing of pornography.

**youth culture:** a generic term for the behaviour, interests and fashions adopted by young people. Teenagers as a *demographic group* did not really exist until the 1950s, before which time people were considered either 'adults' or 'children'. For various reasons, a new social group emerged at that time, with four main characteristics:

- extensive free time and few responsibilities
- economic power – money to spend on entertainment
- a strong interest in media products, especially pop music, TV and film
- a desire to be markedly different from both children and adults in dress, language and behaviour.

These characteristics make youth culture very interesting (i.e. profitable) to the media industries. Initially, the idea of youth culture was confined to people more or less between the ages of 14 and 19 – hence the term teenager. It could also be clearly divided into *mainstream* youth culture and youth *subcultures*. The mainstream was defined by a largely conventional approach to fashion and social behaviour, along with the purchase of such mass media products as *top ten singles*. Youth subcultures were less conventional in dress, attitude and/or choice of media products. Over time, the definition of youth culture has become less clear. For example, the term 'middle youth' has been coined to identify a significant segment of the adult population who continue to be interested in the products of youth culture. The distinctions between youth subcultures are also much less clear than previously. Nevertheless, the youth market and youth culture continue to be massively important to the media industries.

**youth picture:** an older term for films dealing with the interests and problems of young people. Because they sometimes dealt with, and were often seen as encouraging, rebellious behaviour, youth pictures would often run into difficulties with the *censors*. For example, *The Wild One* (László Benedek, USA, 1953) starring Marlon Brando, was banned in the UK for thirteen years.

**zapping:** changing channel by use of the *remote control*. The term suggests a restless, semi-interested approach to watching TV, rather than commitment to a particular programme, and using the remote like a ray-gun to 'zap' any programme the viewer dislikes.

**zeitgeist:** German term, meaning 'spirit of the age/times'. The idea of zeitgeist is that in particular periods, a set of attitudes will dominate. For example, the 1960s are often seen as the era of peace and love, or the 1980s as a time of greed and selfishness. A zeitgeist may apply to a specific country or a specific social group.

**zip pan:** see *whip pan*

**zoetrope:** an early, simple form of *animation* using a cylinder into which vertical slits are cut at regular intervals. A series of images are drawn on the inside of the cylinder showing the progressive stages of a movement. When the cylinder is spun, the viewer sees a single *moving image.* The zoetrope is an early development in the history of the moving image. Francis Ford Coppola named his production company 'American Zoetrope' after the device.

**zombie film:** a film *subgenre* of *horror* in which reanimated dead people attack the living. Zombies (so-called 'living dead') have been appeared in films since the 1930s, but the template for the modern zombie film was created by *Night of the Living Dead* (George A Romero, USA, 1968). Romero's vision of ever-increasing hordes of mindless, decomposing creatures, staggering relentlessly forward in their desperation to eat living human flesh, has been repeated in innumerable zombie movies since then. Most zombie films depend on gruesome *horror* effects for their shock value, and can be considered as fitting into the *splatter* or gore film genres.

**zoo format:** an approach to entertainment programmes in which there are a two or more presenters and a deliberately chaotic, semi-improvised atmosphere is encouraged. The format was originally used for *radio* broadcasting, particularly in the morning. Banter between the presenters is interspersed with practical jokes, competitions and various silly or zany items. Attempts to transfer the zoo concept to *television* have often involved using personnel who have been successful with it on radio. The DJ Chris Evans, for example, has presented and produced a variety of zoo format programmes for TV.

**zoom lens:** a *lens* that can change its focal length while remaining in focus, creating an effect similar (though not identical) to moving closer to an object without actually moving the camera.

**zooming in** and **zooming out:** (also known as 'reverse zoom'). Used only infrequently in professional filming; film makers are more likely to *push in* or *pull out*, since these techniques draw less attention to the camera. In 1960s film-making, the crash zoom (a very fast zoom in or zoom out) was briefly fashionable, but it is rarely used now.

# MEDIA & FILM REVISION LISTS

The lists below have been provided so that you can go to a topic or concept that you are studying, then look up its definition in the main entries. You need to bear in mind that key film and media concepts can be applied to any topic of study and that there is frequent overlap between many terms, especially technical ones, but we have tried to make it quick and easy for you.

To avoid unnecessary repetition, since the same concepts will often apply to many media forms, some of the following lists cross-reference each other. The main headings are:

- 'Micro' textual analysis
- 'Macro' textual analysis
- Audience studies
- Media institutions
- Film studies
- Television studies
- News (broadcast, print and web)
- Magazines
- Radio
- Advertising
- New media
- Music

## Key concepts

The key concepts provide the framework which underpins all media study. The different awarding bodies refer to the key film/media concepts with slight variations. The following terms are those most commonly used (with the main variations given in brackets):

- Audience
- Genre (Categories)
- Ideology (Messages and Values)
- Industry/Institutions (Producers)
- Language (Forms and Conventions; Film Form; Micro and Macro Film Language)
- Narrative
- Representation

## Revision Lists

# 'Micro' textual analysis

(Close analysis of short sections of a media text)

### Analysis of all media forms

anchor
association
audience *(see separate list)*
binary opposition
cliché
code
commutation test
connotation/denotation
context
deconstruction
discourse
dominant ideology
encoding/decoding
exegesis
explicit meaning/implicit meaning
feminism
Freudian
gender
genre *(see separate list)*
ideology
index
intertextuality
juxtaposition
manipulation
meaning
message
messages and values
metaphor
mode of address
noise
norms
open sign/closed sign
pathos

patriarchy
perspective
phallic
pluralism
polysemic
production values
perspective
preferred meaning
presence and absence
primary audience
reception theory
representation *(see separate list)*
referent
register
salience
semiology
Shannon and Weaver's model
sign
signifier
staged/unstaged
subjective/objective
subliminal
subtext
subversion
symbol
synecdoche/metonymy
syntagm
syntax
tone
trope
typeage
visual discourse

# Analysis of print media (text and images)

advertorial

artwork

bagging/cover mount/lure

banner headline

bleed

byline

celebrity

colour saturation

comic strip/photostory

compact

composition

copy

cover price

cover shot

cover story

crop

digital image manipulation

editing

editorial

flat plan

four-colour printing

front cover

graphic design

graphic lines

headline

halftone

house style

IBC/IFC/OBC

icon/iconography

image

inverted pyramid

language

layout

leading

leading caps

lead story

masthead

mode of address

next matter

perspective

photographic truth

photo-journalism

photomontage

picture-driven/picture-led

plug

primary audience/target readership

problem page

production values

salience

sell lines/coverline

serif/sans serif

sidebar

special feature

special issue/edition

spine

splash

spread

staged/unstaged

standfirst

stereotype

TOT

typeface/font

upper/lower case

vignette

white space

## Analysis of cinematography (camera angle, shot, movement, position and focus)

Terms listed in **bold** below are defined under the general heading 'Cinematography' in this book.

180-degree rule

360-degree shot

ASA

**aerial shot**

**angle**

**big close-up**

**bird's-eye view shot**

camera

canted shot/frame

cinematography *(main entry)*

composite shot

composition

contra zoom

crab dolly

crab shot

crane shot

**CU/close-up**

deep focus

de-focus

depth of field

dolly

drive-by shot

Dutch angle

**ECU/extreme close-up**

**ELS/extreme long shot**

eye-level shot

film grammar

filter

fish-eye lens

fixed camera

fixed lens

fixed focus

flying cam

focus

frame

gauze shot

group shot

hand-held shot

headroom

high-angle shot

looking room/space

**LS/long shot**

**MCU/medium close-up**

mise en scène *(see separate list)*

**MLS/medium long shot**

**MS/medium shot**

o/s

overhead shot

OSS

pan

pedestal shot

pivot shot

POV/point-of-view shot

pull-back

pull out

push in

racking/pulling focus

reframe

reveal

reverse track

reverse zoom

selective focus

sequence shot

shallow focus

shot

**shot length**

soft focus

Steadicam

stock

subjective camera

telephoto

three-shot

tilt

tracking shot

travelling shot

two-shot

whip pan

worm's-eye shot

**WS/wide shot**

## Analysis of film/video editing

American Cinema Editors (ACE)
assemble editing
composite shot
continuity editing/system
cross-cutting
cross-fade
cut
cutaway
cut-in shot
discontinuity
dissolve
editing (main entry)
emblematic shot
establishing shot
ellipsis
eyeline match
eyeline shot
fade (in/out)
film grammar
final cut
freeze frame
graphic match
insert shot
intercutting
invisible editing/style
jump cut
lap dissolve
linear editing
long take
master shot
matte
match cut
match on action
montage
montage sequence

motivation
noddy-shot
non-linear editing
optical effect
o/s
overlapping sound
pace
parallel action
quick cut
reaction shot
re-establishing shot
reveal
reverse
reverse motion
rhythm
screen direction
segue
sequence
sequence shot
shot duration
shot-reverse-shot
slow motion
sound bridge
space and time
spatial and temporal contiguity
split screen
stills
subliminal
superimpose
tempo
temporal
time lapse
time splice/bullet time
transitional device
wipe

## Analysis of film/video lighting

ambient lighting

artificial light

available light

back lighting

chiaroscuro

cinematographer

colour temperature

diffused lighting

fill light

film grammar

filter

hard lighting

high-key lighting

key light

lighting *(main entry)*

low-key lighting

mise en scène *(see separate list)*

set-up

soft light

three-point lighting

top lighting

underlighting

## Analysis of mise en scène

blocking

cast

character

cinematography *(see separate list)*

costume

crowd scene

décor

diegesis

establishing shot

exterior

extra

film grammar

genre *(see separate list)*

interior

lighting *(see separate list)*

location

make-up

mise en scène *(main entry)*

motif

pathetic fallacy

performance *(see separate list)*

perspective

presence and absence

production values

profilmic/afilmic

props

realism

set

spatial relationships

special effects *(see separate list)*

studio

# Analysis of performance

accent

actor

address

ad lib

backstory

beat

body language

Brechtian

business

cameo

catchphrase

character

character actor

dialogue

diction

film grammar

gesture

improvisation

Kuleshov effect

lead actor

make-up

method acting

motivation

mugging

non-verbal communication/nvc

performance *(main entry)*

pitch

prop

screenplay

signature/trademark

star

star image

timbre

typecasting

## Analysis of sound

accent
ADR
ambience
ambient music/sound/noise
atmos/buzz track/wild track
call-to-view
canned laughter
connotation
contrapuntal sound
counterpoint
crescendo
dialect
dialogue
diegesis
diminuendo
direct sound
dissonance
dub/dubbing
dynamics
editing
film grammar
foley artist
interior monologue
laughter track
leitmotif

lip-synch
major key/minor key
Mickey-Mousing
mix
motif
narrator
non-diegetic
off-screen sound
o/s
overlapping sound
pitch
post-production
riff
signature tune
sound bridge
sound effects/fx
soundtrack
stab
surround sound
synchronous/asynchronous sound
tempo
theme music
timbre
voice-of-god narration
voice-over

## Analysis of special effects

animatronics
animation
back projection
Chromakey
CGI
double exposure
editing
green screen
make-up
matte
optical effect
photorealistic

post-production
prosthetics
pyrotechnics
rendering
special effects (SFX) *(main entry)*
sound effects
stunt
stunt double
surface realism
verisimilitude
wire work

# 'Macro' textual analysis

(Broader analysis of patterns within a whole media text)

## Analysis of narrative

allegory

arc

agent of change

backstory

character

character actor

circular narrative

cliffhanger

climax

closure

complication

controlling idea

crisis

diegesis

dénouement

dramatic device

dramatic irony

dramatic tension

dynamics

ellipsis

episode

episodic narrative

equilibrium/disequilibrium

excess

existential hero

exposition

fabula

faction

fiction

flashback/flashforward

foreshadowing

hermeneutic code

hero/heroine

image system

inciting incident

in medias res

jeopardy

linear narrative

major plot reversal

mid-act climax

multi-stranded narrative

narrative

narrative trajectory

Oedipal narrative

omniscient

o/s

pace

parallel narrative

plot

positioning

proairetic code

protagonist

quest

realism

resolution

restricted/unrestricted narration

seeker-hero

sequel

serial

series

setting

story

story arc

subplot

suspense

syuzhet

time code

timeline

trilogy

tragedy

turning point

twist

vignette

violation of expectation

## Genre: terms of use in analysis of all media

(also see specific media forms under separate headings below)

categorisation
cliché
codes/coding
codes and conventions
cross-generic
genre (main entry)
iconography
language
master genre
media triangle
mode
paradigm

parody
pastiche
repetition and difference
repertoire of elements
structure
style
subgenre
symbolism
target audience
taxonomy
theme
trope

## Analysis of representation

alternative
archetype
audience (see separate lists)
blue-collar
camp
celebrity
cultural capital
culture
dialect
dominant discourse
elaborated code/restricted code
elite
establishment
ethnicity
ethnic minority
ethnocentrism
exhibitionist
feminism
femininity
Freudian
gender
high culture/low culture
heterosexual
hegemony
homosexual
identity
ideology
left-wing/right-wing/political spectrum
Marxism
male gaze

masculinity
meaning systems
messages and values
middle class
minority
objectification
'other'
patriarchy
pluralism
political correctness/incorrectness
primary audience
queer
race
racism
realism
representation (main entry)
schema theory
sex
sexism
sexuality
social class
social construct
sociology
stereotype
subordinate culture
target audience/readership
tokenism
typeage
values
working class

# Audience studies

(also see lists below for individual media forms)

## Audience classification and targeting

ABC1C2DE

audience fragmentation

brief

certification

consumer profile

consumer research

crossover

cult film

demographics/demographic profile

downmarket

echo

ethnicity

fan/fandom

focus group

fog index

fragmentation

genre

geodemographics

heterogeneity/homogeneity

highbrow

high culture

inheritance factor

language

lowbrow

market research

mainstream audience/media

mass audience

mass communication

mass media

media plan

middle-brow

mid(dle) market

mode of address

narrowcasting

niche audience/marketing

peak time

penetration

producers and audiences studies

psychographics

public service broadcaster

race

scheduling

sexuality

social class

spot rating

subculture

tabloid

tabloidisation

youth culture

## Audience response/audience behaviour

abberant decoding

active audience, active reading

appropriation

association

audience expectations

catharsis

connotation/denotation

cultural capital

desensitisation

dominant hegemonic

dominant reading

effects model/theory

empathy

escapism

expectations

fourth wall

Frankfurt School

Freudian

gender/gendered reading/viewing

hegemony

hypodermic model/theory

identification

identity/identity politics

ideological state apparatus

immersion

inoculation effect/theory

interactive media

irony

manufacture of consent

Maslow's hierarchy of needs

meaning

meaning systems

media effects

mediation

medium is the message

message

messages and values

negotiated reading

omniscient

oppositional meaning

passive audience

pathos

perception

pleasure

pluralism

positioning

poststructuralism

preferred meaning

prejudice

primary level of attention

reception theory

schadenfreude

schema theory

scopophilia

secondary level of attention

sleeper/slow burner

socialisation

spectator

subject

subliminal

subtext

talkback

tertiary text

time-shifting

uses and gratifications model

willing suspension of disbelief

word-of-mouth

## Audience research, surveys and ratings

ABC (Audit Bureau of Circulation)

audience appreciation index

audience measurement

audience share

BARB

BRAD

brand positioning

field research

media research

NRS

opportunities to see/frequency

penetration

peoplemeter

pre-echo

quantitative/qualitative methods

RAJAR

ratings

reach

remote control

research methods

synchronising motifs

target group ratings (TGRs)

total survey area

tracking study

TVR

two-step flow

usage and attitude

values

violence

voyeurism

watercooler phenomenon

willing suspension of disbelief

zapping

## Other useful terminology relating to audiences

audience *(main entry)*

consumer/ism

interactive media

interpellation

intertextuality

opinion poll

representation *(see separate list)*

subject

user friendly

user interface

viewer

vox pop

# Media institutions

## General business terminology

(also see lists below for individual media forms)

anti-trust legislation

cartel

conglomerate

consumer

convergence

cross-media ownership

economies of scale

global village

globalisation

gross

industry

institution

institutional practices

low budget

remake

market economy

market penetration

market share

McDonaldisation

media imperialism

media magnate

media triangle

merger

multinational

ownership

power of the media

power elite

press baron

privatisation

profit

regulator

return on investment

self-regulation

synergy

transnational

vertical integration

walled garden

## Censorship, regulation and control

(also see lists below for individual media forms)

accountability

censorship

deregulation

gatekeeper

hegemony

Index on Censorship

media effects

ownership and control

pornography

power elite

self-regulation

sex

spectrum

subversion

taboo

violence

# Film studies

## Film genres, styles, modes and subgenres

(also see 'Macro' lists above)

abstract film
action
adventure
animation
anime
art film
auteur
biopic
black comedy
blaxploitation
Bollywood
buddy movie
caper film
chick flick
cinema of excess
cinéma vérité
comedy
costume drama
crime
detective/policier
disaster
documentary
documentary realism
essay film
epic
erotic thriller
experimental film
exploitation film
expressionism
fantasy
feminist film
film noir
formula film
frontier film
future-noir
gangster
ghost
gothic
gross-out
heritage
high-concept film
high-school movie
horror

literary adaptation
martial arts
melodrama
mockumentary
monster
musical
neo-noir
neo-realism
new queer cinema
occult horror
peplum movie
period drama
pornography
portmanteau film
propaganda film
psychological thriller
realism
road movie
rockumentary
romance
romantic comedy
samurai film
sexploitation
science fiction
screwball comedy
slasher/splatter/splatstick
social problem film
social realism
spaghetti Western
spy film
suburban gothic
swashbuckler
tear-jerker
teen movie
thriller
travelogue
urban gothic
vigilante
war
Western
women's picture
youth picture
zombie

## Film movements and new waves

black cinema
British new wave
counter cinema/film
Dogme 95
Free Cinema
French new wave
gay and lesbian film/queer
German expressionism
imperfect cinema
Italian neo-realism
New American Cinema

New German Cinema
New Hollywood
new waves
politique des auteurs
postcolonial film
post-heritage cinema
pure cinema
Soviet montage
Surrealism
third cinema

## Film cast and crew

actor(s)
'A' list
art director
assistant cameraman
assistant director
assistant producer
associate producer
best boy
body double
boom operator
cameo
camera, camera assistant, camera operator,
camera script
cast/casting
central casting
choreographer
cinematographer
clapper loader
co-producer
costume designer
crew
director
distribution; distributor

edit/editing/editor
extra
fight arranger/choreographer
film maker
floor runner
foley artist
gaffer
grip
lead actor
line producer
location manager
negative cutter
producer
production designer
production manager
screenwriter
second unit
sound crew
stand-in
star
stunt double
talent
unit

REVISION LISTINGS

# Film industry/institutions

(also see 'Media institutions' lists above)

above-/below-the-line costs
AMPAS
art-house cinema
back end
BFI (British Film Institute)
'Big Five'
'Big Six'
blockbuster
Bollywood
'B' picture/feature/movie
cult film
de Havilland decision
distribution
domestic box-office
event movie
exhibition
fan/fandom
film commission
film festival
franchise
Fordism
greenlight
high-concept
Hollywood
Hollywood studio system
horizontal integration
incentives
independent
international co-production
Little Three
major studio
mogul, movie

multiplex cinema
oligopoly
option
Oscar
package-unit system
Paramount Case
pay or play contract
pitching
player
post-production
premiere
pre-production
press junket
producer
production
release
release pattern
saturation release
script development
slate
sleeper
star bankability
star system
studio
subsidiary rights
synergy
tentpole movie
theatrical run
UK Film Council
unit
vertical integration
word-of-mouth

## Film audiences

(also see 'Audience studies' lists above)

avid

desensitisation

escapism

explicit meaning

fan/fandom

gender/gendered reading/viewing

immersion

implicit meaning

Kuleshov effect

male gaze/female gaze

object of the gaze

pleasure/visual pleasure

referential meaning

spectator

suture/reality effect

symptomatic meaning

willing suspension of disbelief

## Censorship, regulation and control: film/video industries

(also see 'Media institutions' lists above)

British Board of Film Classification

BBFC certificates (separate entries): U, Uc, R18

certification

censorship

Hays Code/Hays Office

hegemony

media effects

moral panic

MPAA (Motion Picture Association of America)

pornography

'R' rating

ratings system

self-regulation

sex

video nasties

violence

'X' rating

# Television studies

(also see 'Micro and 'Macro' textual analysis lists above)

## Television genres and modes

access/public access

bulletin

chat shows and talk shows

consumer-based

crime series

crossover

documentary

docu-drama

docu-soap

drama

drama-documentary

emergency drama

fly-on-the-wall

game shows and quiz shows

hospital drama

infomercial

issue-led drama

lifestyle programming

light entertainment

literary adaptation

made-for-tv

magazine format

murder mystery

music video

news

out-take

panel game

policier

reality television

reconstruction

rolling news

satire

situation comedy

sketch show

slice-of-life

soap opera

spin-off

suburban gothic

tabloid television

talent show

thriller

vox pop

Western

zoo format

## TV industry/institutions (analogue and digital)

(also see 'Media institutions' lists above)

access/public access/community broadcasting
acquisitions
advertising revenue
analogue switch-off
audience fragmentation
back catalogue
'Big Six'
Birtism
British Broadcasting Corporation (BBC)
broadcast flow
Broadcasting Acts
Channel 4
commercial broadcasting
commission
deregulation
franchise
free-to-air
Freeview
gatekeeper
independent
Independent Television (ITV)
Independent Television News (ITN)
licence
licence fee
market share
monopoly
multi-channel environment

narrowcasting
pay-per-view
pay TV
press kit
primetime
producer broadcaster
producer choice
Producer's Alliance for Film and Television (PACT)
public service broadcaster
publisher broadcaster
Reithian
repeat
satellite broadcasting
scheduling
spectrum
sponsorship
statutory regulation
subscription
syndication
talkback
target audience
terrestrial television
time shifting
TVR
video on demand
viewer

## Censorship, regulation and control: TV industry

(also see 'Media institutions' lists above)

Advertising Standards Authority
Broadcasting Acts
Department of Culture, Media and Sport
deregulation
Mediawatch UK

Ofcom
regulator
spectrum
watershed

## Television production

above-/below-the-line costs
budget
camera operator
commissioning editor
editing/editor
executive producer
floor manager
floor runner
gallery
introductory cue
lead-in
line producer
live
monitor
multi-camera production
music cue sheet
on air/off air
overlay
pilot
presenter
pre-title sequence
producer
production
prop

rolling credits
scanner
script/script writer
season
serial
series
set
set-up
shooting script
slot
soundtrack
strap titles
studio
stunt
superimpose
talent
talkback
teleplay
teleprompter
titles
trailing
unit
video tape recorder
wrap

## Television technologies

air
colour TV
digital
DVD
electronic programme guide
HDTV (high definition television)
home video
ident
interactive media
multi-channel environment
NTSC

PAL
remote control
set-top box
television
terrestrial television
time shifting
user interface
video on demand
widescreen
zapping

# News (broadcast, print and web)

## Selection of news: gatekeeping

(also see 'Media institutions' lists above)

accountability
agency
agenda
agenda-setting
background
balance
Campaign for Press and Broadcasting Freedom
celebrity
chequebook journalism
continuity
cool news/hot news
correspondent
current affairs
daybook
diary
doorstepping
editing
electronic press kit (EPK)
elite
ethics
ethnocentrism
exclusive
exposé
filler story
freelance
free press
frequency
Galtung and Ruge
gatekeeper
gonzo journalism
hard news/soft news
hegemony
hierarchy of discourse
human interest story
Hutton report
ideology
immediacy
institutional practices
interview
invasion of privacy
investigative journalism
journalism
kill
kiss-and-tell story
libel

meaningfulness
moral panic
negativity
news agency
news agenda
newsgathering
news values
obit/obituary
paparazzi
periodicity
personalisation
photo opportunity
photographic truth
photo-journalism
picture-driven
political interference
press agent
press conference
press junket
press office
press release
privacy
publicist
public interest
public relations
puff
regional press
repetition and difference
reporter
right of reply
right to know
running order
scoop
silly season
spike
spin
spoiler
staffer
star image
sting
stringer
taboo
target audience/readership
thesis

## News presentation: general

(also see 'Micro' and 'Macro' textual analysis lists above)

angle
balance
bias
bump
coverage
downmarket
dumb-down
house style
image
impartiality
lead-in
lead story
lowbrow
mainstream audience
mediation
media triangle
middlebrow
mode of address
news *(main entry)*

objectivity
ownership and control
power of the media
power elite
press
privileged access
register
report
reportage
representation
revelation
sensationalism
sound bite
story
structure
TOT
tragedy
values

## News presentation: print

(also see 'Micro' and 'Macro' textual analysis lists above)

| | |
|---|---|
| art editor | inverted pyramid |
| artwork | layout |
| banner headline | leader |
| Berliner | leading caps |
| body copy/text | masthead |
| broadsheet | MF/MFL |
| bulks | mid-market |
| byline | NAG |
| circulation | newspaper |
| column | NIB |
| compact | op-ed piece |
| context | patriotism |
| copy | press baron |
| cover story | Press Complaints Commission (PCC) |
| crop | readership |
| crosshead | sketch |
| edit/editing/editor | SOC |
| edition | splash |
| editorial | spread |
| feature | standfirst |
| fog index | strapline |
| freesheet | sub-editor |
| gutter | sub-head(line) |
| gutter press | tabloid |
| headline | title |
| house style | tone |
| image | TOT |
| indent | victim-hero |
| intro | WOB |

## News presentation: TV and Radio

(also see 'Micro' and 'Macro' textual analysis lists above)

| | |
|---|---|
| address | newsreel |
| archive footage | outside broadcast (ob) |
| autocue | overlay |
| breaking news | package |
| broadcast | packaging |
| broadcaster; broadcasting | producer |
| bulletin | public service broadcaster |
| caption | reporter |
| correspondent | running order |
| coverage (news) | scheduling |
| direct address | segue |
| direct broadcasting (dbs) | staged |
| headline | still-to-come |
| Independent Television News (ITN) | stock footage |
| infotainment | strap titles |
| lead-in | tabloidisation |
| live | talking head |
| live feed | unit |
| mode of address | voicer |
| news anchor | vox pop |

# Magazines

## Magazine genres/styles

(also see 'Macro' textual analysis lists above)

celebrity

compact

consumer magazines

fanzine

fashion

in-house

lad mag

lifestyle magazine

magazine (main entry)

market

mode of address

news (see separate lists)

human interest

paparazzi

photo-journalism

TOT

trade papers

underground press

webzine

women's magazines

## Elements of magazines

(also see 'Macro' textual analysis lists above)

advertising (see separate lists)

advertorial

artwork

classified advertising

comic strip

copy

cover mount/bagging/lure

cover shot

cover story

display advertising

editorial

feature

front cover

IBC/IFC

insert

layout

masthead

photo story

plug

problem page

sell lines

sidebar

spread

## Magazine audiences

(also see 'Audience studies' lists above)

consumer

consumerism

culture

interpellation

mainstream

Maslow's hierarchy of needs

niche audience

primary audience

publisher

readership

subscription

target readership

## Magazine industry/institutions

(also see 'Media institutions' lists above)

advertising revenue

Audit Bureau of Circulation (ABC)

Average Issue Readership (AIR)

'Big Six'

circulation

conglomerate

cover price

independent

media magnate

media triangle

NRS

Periodical Publishers Association

profit

sales revenue

syndication

## Magazine production

archive

art director

art editor

columnist

copy desk

desktop publishing

edit/editing/editor

flat plan

four colour printing

halftone

house style

issue

media pack

next matter

periodical

photo opportunity

picture editor

print run

print space

production values

rate card

special feature

special issue

spine

sub-editor

title

# Radio

## Radio programming

(also see 'Micro' and 'Macro' textual analysis lists above)

access/public access/community broadcasting
back catalogue
broadcast flow
crossover
current affairs
disc jockey
drama
interview
news *(see separate lists)*
peak time
playlist
programme
quiz show
radio genres
radio *(main entry)*

repeat
scheduling
serial/series
sketch
slot
soap opera
Sony Awards
talkback
talk radio
talk show
target audience
trailing
voicer
vox pop
zoo format

## Radio production

actuality
air
editor
fill
introductory cue
live
music cue sheet
off-air

on air
PPL
presenter
producer
scriptwriter
SOC
sound bite
sound image

## Radio technologies

analogue
AM/FM/Long Wave/Short Wave
analogue switch-off
digital audio broadcast (DAB)
Freeview
frequency

reception
signal
simulcasting
spectrum
streaming content
voice tracking

## Radio industry/institutions

(also see 'Media institutions' lists above)

advertising revenue

back catalogue

BBC (British Broadcasting Corporation)

'Big Six'

broadcast(er)

Broadcasting Acts

commercial broadcasting

franchise

licence

monopoly

Ofcom

penetration

pirate radio

public service broadcaster

Radio Academy

RadioCentre

RAJAR

ratings

reach

RSL

sponsorship

statutory regulation

syndication

total survey area

# Advertising

(also see 'Micro' and 'Macro' textual analysis lists above)

## Essential advertising terminology

advertisement

advertising

advertising revenue

brief

campaign

commercial

copywriter

corporate identity

creative

logo

marketing

pitching

plug

product

slogan

storyboard

strapline

unique selling point

## Types of advertising

above-the-line advertising
advertorial
banner advert
below-the-line advertising
billboard
celebrity endorsement
classified advertising
commercial
direct mail
display advertising
hard sell/soft sell
infomercial
insert
lifestyle advertising

lineage
niche marketing
point-of-sale advertising
poster
product placement
slice of life
sponsorship
subliminal advertising
teaser campaign
through-the-line advertising
trailer
vignette
viral marketing
word-of-mouth

## Advertising industry/institutions

(also see 'Media institutions' lists above)

advertising agency
Advertising Association
Advertising Standards Authority
Cinema Advertising Association (CAA )
commercial broadcasting
independent television

Institute of Practitioners in Advertising
ISBA
JICREG
media triangle
RadioCentre

## Buying and selling advertising space

media plan
media research
media sales
media schedule
payment by results
rate card

ratings
reach
solus position
spot
spot advertising
total survey area

REVISION LISTINGS

## Advertising and audiences

(also see 'Audience studies' lists above)

5 Ps

AIDA

brand image

consumerism

consumer profile

DRIP

frequency/opportunities to see

interpellation

Maslow's Hierarchy of Needs

materialism

penetration

perception

psychographics

recall

salience

spot rating

tracking study

TVR

usage and attitude

visual noise

# New media

## New media technologies

3-D film

analogue

animatronics

built-in obsolescence

cable

Chromakey

convergence

digital audio broadcast

digital camera

digital image manipulation

digitalisation

Dolby

DV

DVD

encryption

Firewire

future-proofing

FX

games console

games controller

HDTV (high definition television)

home cinema

internet

ISDN

JPEG

MPEG

new media *(main entry)*

plug and play

remote control

satellite

set-top box

surround sound

uplink

wi-fi

## Uses for new media technologies

additionality

avatar

blog

browser

CGI (computer generated imaging)

Easter egg

emoticon

game

hyperreality

manipulation

multi-media

pay per view

pay tv

photorealistic

podcasting

sim

special effects

THX

video on demand

virtuality

virtual reality

webcasting

webzine

## New media audiences

(also see 'Audience studies' lists above)

channel hopping/zapping

consumer

early adopter

electronic programme guide (EPG)

game environment

gameplay

gamer

global village

immersion

interactive media

interface

mainstream audience

Maslow's hierarchy of needs

mass communication

medium is the message, the

moral panic

niche audience

postmodernism

post-nationalism

primary medium

role-play

sticky content

surfing

technological determinism

user-friendly

viral

## New media industry/institutions

(also see 'Media institutions' lists above)

analogue switch-off

Apple

'Big Six'

BSkyB

Broadcasting Acts

channel

convergence

economies of scale

electronic press kit (EPK)

free to air

Freeview

globalisation

ISP

Microsoft

MTV

multi-channel environment

Napster

piracy

return on investment

Sony Corporation

surveillance society

synergy

viral marketing

walled garden

# Music

(also see 'Micro' and 'Macro' textual analysis lists above)

## Qualities and characteristics of music

accent

counterpoint

crescendo

diminuendo

dissonance

leitmotif

major key

minor key

music

pitch

riff

tempo

timbre

## Music industry/institutions

(also see 'Media institutions' lists above)

A&R (artists and repertoire)

agent

air

album

back catalogue

'Big Six'

Billboard

disc jockey

diversification

label

library

licensing

merger

MTV

music video/promo

Napster

packaging

Performing Right Society (PRS)

piracy

playlist

PPL

radio (see separate lists)

reissue

release

re-release

royalties

single

Sony Corporation

VPL

walled garden

## Music genres and audiences

(also see 'Audience studies' lists above)

ambient music

connotation

crossover

fan/fandom

fanzine

futurism

gothic

high culture

lip synch

mainstream audience/media

middlebrow

musical

music cue sheet

pop music

popular culture

popular music

punk

queercore

star

streaming content

style

subculture

target audience

theme music

youth culture

## Music recording

audio mixer

Dolby sound

dub

mix

multitrack

producer

sequencer

stereo

studio

take

talkback

# TOP 10 TIPS FOR EXAM SUCCESS

Have breakfast before a morning exam and lunch before an afternoon one. Make sure you are rested and hydrated (with water!). If you're tired, hungry and thirsty during your exam, your concentration will be severely compromised and you'll underperform. Take water with you and a mint or sweet for sugar.

Answer the exam question on the exam paper in front of you; not the one that was set last year, nor the one you got a grade A for in a timed test in class. The Examiner has a mark scheme that is closely geared to the precise wording of the question set. If you don't answer the question that is set, you won't get many marks, no matter how much you might know about a topic or text.

Read the question carefully and underline the key words; break the question down and be clear about what it is asking from you.

Make a very brief plan of what you are going to write in your introduction, in each paragraph and in your conclusion, together with the examples you are going to use.

Get straight to the point in your first paragraph, and address the question straightaway. Keep addressing the question throughout the essay. Refer back to the key words in the question regularly.

Don't waffle or try to impress with a grand, but empty, style; the Examiner will see through this in a second. Make every sentence you write have a point to it. Where possible, include an example.

Use a reliable pen in blue or black ink only (use a cartridge, rollerball or quality biro) and take a spare. Write neatly and legibly; develop a clear and quick style (even if only for exams). Cross out neatly – one line is enough. If the Examiner can't read your handwriting easily, they can't award marks.

Keep an eye on the clock. Leave some time to read through your answer to check your facts and watch for any important omissions.

Never leave a question unanswered as you will automatically get zero marks. Don't think that over-answering a question will compensate you for this, as there is a maximum mark for each question that you cannot exceed, no matter how long your answer is. Note-form answers, even if you are pushed for time, may be ignored by examiners, so get plenty of practice of writing to the time allowed.

Not answering the question is the main reason that good students underachieve unexpectedly in exams – so please, ANSWER THE QUESTION!

There are many film and media websites. The list that follows gives some that either we, or our students, have found useful in our studies.

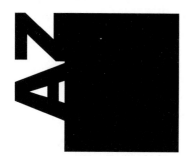

## WEBSITES

# Academic, fun or reference sites for students

Ain't it Cool News – **www.aintitcoolnews.com**

- Harry Knowles' 'word of mouse' US site of film reviews.

Barnes and Noble film glossary –
**http://video.barnesandnoble.com/search/glossary.asp**

- Lots of quick definitions of obscure film terms. Useful to search and fun to browse.

BBC Film and Media Studies – **www.bbc.co.uk/learning/subjects/media_studies.shtml**

- Online learning, support and advice on the BBC and media careers.

BBC Training – *The Good Shooting Guide: The Basic Principles* –
**www.bbctraining.com/television.asp**

- Select the title above at this link for a useful free online course on shooting for TV/film projects. BBC Training also has lots of advice on media careers, as well as style guides for journalists etc.

BFI Film Links Gateway – **www.bfi.org.uk/filmtvinfo/gateway/categories**

- A comprehensive list of links to useful sites for film and media study.

British Film Institute (BFI) – **www.bfi.org.uk**

- Become a member of the BFI for a whole range of discounts and members' offers.

BUBL Link (Strathclyde University, UK) – **http://bubl.ac.uk/link/f/filmstudies.htm**

- A list of useful links for film study.

Cultsock – **www.cultsock.ndirect.co.uk/index16.html**

- Mick Underwood's Communication, Cultural and Media Studies (CCMS) website, with a huge searchable 'infobase' on key terms and theories – undergraduate level.

Film Guardian – **http://film.guardian.co.uk/**

- Extensive film resource. The superb interview archive includes full transcripts of discussions with a wide range of film makers.

Film Programme Archive – **www.bbc.co.uk/radio4/arts/filmprogramme/index.shtml**

- BBC Radio 4 weekly film programme. The archive allows you to listen again to features and interviews going back to 2002.

Film Site – **www.filmsite.com**

- A website (from Massachusetts, USA) for film enthusiasts that provides information about films as well as independent short films and feature film trailers to download.

Hurtwood House Sixth Form College (Dorking, UK) – **www.hurtwoodmedia.com**

- A showcase of student media production for A level Media Studies, including short films, music videos and print projects, such as magazines.

Internet Movie Database – **http://uk.imdb.com**

- A comprehensive searchable database for information on all films, past, present and in production.

Jahsonic – **www.jahsonic.com**

- A personal, but fascinating, website for discussion of all aspects of popular culture.

Kamera film salon – **www.kamera.co.uk**

- An accessible online film magazine of reviews, interviews and features.

Long Road Sixth Form College (Cambridge, UK) – **www.longroadmedia.com**

- A showcase of student media production for A level Film and Media Studies, including short films, music videos and adverts.

Media Studies – **www.mediastudies.com**

- The site (based in Canada) serves as a hub, providing links to international news, media studies sites, and other resources for media educators, students, researchers, and the wider community.

Media and Communications Studies (MCS) – **www.aber.ac.uk/media**

- Daniel Chandler's undergraduate course web site hosted at the University of Wales, Aberystwyth, with a comprehensive collection of original and secondary articles on all aspects of film and media study: a virtual home-study media degree.

*MediaGuardian* – **www.media-guardian.co.uk**

- The media section of *The Guardian* newspaper, with an extensive searchable archive of past reports and articles on all aspects of the media, with added features, such as downloadable TV adverts.

Movie Theater Dictionary – **www.angelfire.com/film/alfredk39**

- A fun classification of types of film-goer.

A B C D E F G H I J K L M N O P Q R S T U V W X Y Z

*Scope* – **www.scope.nottingham.ac.uk**

- An online film journal, by students and staff at the Institute of Film Studies, University of Nottingham (UK).

Screenonline – **www.screenoline.org.uk**

- The BFI's definitive online guide to Britain's film and TV history, with interactive tours, video and sound clips from film and TV.

*Senses of Cinema* – **www.sensesofcinema.com**

- An online film journal (from Australia) devoted to the serious and eclectic discussion of cinema.

Shooting People – **http://shootingpeople.org/account/auth.php**

- A film community for US and UK indie film makers, with a jobsearch facility and much more.

*Sight & Sound* film magazine – **www.bfi.org.uk/sightandsound**

- 'Grown-up' commentary on films and DVDs – available at a reduced subscription price for students and BFI members.

Simply Scripts – **www.simplyscripts.com**

- A comprehensive site with downloadable scripts from thousands of films, past and present.

Skillset – **www.skillset.org**

- The sector skills council for the audio visual industries, with advice on work experience and media careers.

**www.theory.org.uk**

- David Gauntlett's website (University of Westminster, London, UK) for all aspects of popular cultural theory and **www.newmediastudies.com** which has extracts from his book, *Web.Studies* (Routledge, 2004), and the archived former site content.

Wikipedia – **http://en.wikipedia.org/wiki/main_page**

- The online encyclopedia that anyone can edit, this is an exhaustive resource, useful for contextual study as well as for film/media-specific topics. The information is of variable quality and reliability, so please double-check with other sources; also, be aware that some institutions may not consider it a valid research source.

Yale University Film Studies (USA) **http://classes.yale.edu/film-analysis/**

- The Film Analysis Guide has information on the vocabulary of film studies and the techniques of cinema, as well as definitions of terms, sample analyses and video clips of examples used.

# Websites of special interest to film and media teachers

*Auteur* – **www.auteur.co.uk**

- Publishes a wide range of well-regarded teaching resources for GCSE and A levels.

*Breaking the News* – **www.channel4.com/learning/breakingthenews/index.html**

- Channel 4's resources for students and teachers on TV news.

British Film Institute – **www.bfi.org.uk/education**

- The major player in UK-wide media education, the BFI publishes books, DVDs and learning resources, and provides teacher development projects, courses and conferences, as well as working with government agencies on the development of media education within the school curriculum and championing wider media literacy aims.
- The site is rather like the 'Tardis' in that it houses a huge amount of information; the library and research sections are well worth visiting, for example, for downloadable bibliographies to use to research teaching and student independent study topics.
- A range of membership discounts on books, DVDs, resources and events are available.
- Masters (MA) modules for film/media teachers: **www.bfi.org.uk/education/coursesevents/teachers/masters**

British Pathé Film Archive – **www.britishpathe.com**

- A digital news archive of free (for use in UK schools) recordings of film/TV news from 1896 to 1970.

Central School of Speech & Drama (CSSD) – **www.cssd.ac.uk**

- The CSSD, which is in London, offers the only specialist PGCE course in Media Studies as a single subject.

Children Youth and Media Centre (CYMC) – **www.childrenyouthandmediacentre.co.uk**

- A centre within the Institute of Education (London, UK), led by Professor David Buckingham, which holds events and provides post-graduate study and undertakes research into the relationships between young people and the media.

English and Media Centre – **www.englishandmedia.co.uk**

- A key organisation for learning resources and continuing professional development courses for English and Media teachers, and publishers of the *Media Magazine,* a quarterly magazine especially for A level Film and Media students.

Film Education – **www.filmeducation.org**

- An important website for free resources for the teaching of film, as well as the organisers of the National Schools' Film Week (which takes place annually in October).

Film Studies – **www.filmstudies.com.uk**

- The developing support website for WJEC Film Studies A level.

*Guardian/Observer* Newsroom – **www.guardian.co.uk/newsroom**

- Lots of details and resources on all aspects of news reporting and histories of *Guardian* newspapers.

*in the picture* magazine – **www.itpmag.demon.co.uk**

- The website for a termly magazine for film/media teachers which has news, book/resource reviews and many features on all aspects of classroom practice, with online resources.

MediaEd – **www.mediaed.org.uk**

- A website for film/media teachers, with an events calendar, news and learning resources as well as an online forum.

Media Education Association – **www.mediaedassociation.org.uk**

- A UK-wide professional association for those teaching film and media in both the formal and informal education sectors, with an annual conference and newsletter available by membership.

Media Education Wales – **www.mediaedwales.org.uk**

- Supports media and moving image education in Wales through resources, training, events, projects and more.

*Teaching Film & Media Studies* – **www.bfi.org.uk/tfms**

- The BFI's successful series of post-16 teaching resources, *Teaching Film & Media Studies*, has a webpage for each of the many titles, with sample downloadable photocopiable resources and useful links.

*Times Educational Supplement* Staffroom forum – **www.tes.co.uk/section/staffroom**

- An online forum for media/film teachers, useful for sharing queries, ideas and resources.

# Key media companies and organisations

It goes without saying that every media company has a website and there are far too many to list here. The *MediaGuardian Media Directory 2007: The Essential Handbook* (eds. Chris Alden, Jannine Gibson, Guardian Newspapers Ltd) is an annual publication that carries the contact details of all UK major media companies (except film). What follows is just a selection of the main ones:

AA (Advertising Association) – **www.adassoc.org.uk**

ABC (Audit Bureau of Circulation) – **www.abc.org.uk**

ASA (Advertising Standards Authority) – **www.asa.org.uk**

BAFTA (British Academy of Film & Television Arts) – **www.bafta.org**

BARB (Broadcasters' Audience Research Board Ltd) – **www.barb.co.uk**

BBC (British Broadcasting Corporation) – **www.bbc.co.uk**

BBC Training & Development – **www.bbctraining.co.uk**

BBFC (British Board of Film Classification) – **www.bbfc.co.uk**

Channel 4 – **www.channel4.co.uk**

Emap magazines – **www.emap.com**

FDA (Film Distributors' Association) – **www.launchingfilms.com/index.php**

Film Four – **www.filmfour.co.uk**

Five – **www.channel5.co.uk**

*The Guardian* – **www.guardian.co.uk** (also for *The Observer* newspaper)

*The Independent* – **www.independent.co.uk** (also for *The Independent on Sunday*)

IPC magazines – **www.ipcmedia.com**

ITV (Independent Television) – **www.itv.com**

Mediawatch-UK – **www.mediawatch.org.uk**

NRS (National Readership Survey) – **www.nrs.co.uk**

NUJ (National Union of Journalists) – **www.nuj.org.uk**

News Corporation – **www.newscorporation.com/index2.html**

Newspaper Society – **www.newspapersoc.org.uk**

Ofcom (Office of Communications) – **www.ofcom.org.uk**

PCC (Press Complaints Commission) – **www.pcc.org.uk**

RAJAR (Radio Joint Audience Research Ltd) – **www.rajar.co.uk**

RSGB (Radio Society of Great Britian) – **www.rsgb.org**

RTS (Royal Television Society) – **www.rts.org.uk**

*The Times* – **www.timesonline.co.uk/uk** (also for *The Sunday Times* newspaper)

Time Warner – **www.timewarner.com/corp**

# Selected bibliography

Arroyo, J (1999) *Action/Spectacle Cinema: a Sight & Sound Reader*, BFI

Blandford, S, Grant, B and Hillier, J (2001) *The Film Studies Dictionary*, Arnold

Bordwell, D (1989) *Making Meaning: inference and rhetoric in the interpretation of cinema*, Harvard University Press

Bordwell, D and Thompson, K (2004) *Film Art: An Introduction* (7th international edn), McGraw-Hill

Brierley, S (1995) *The Advertising Handbook*, Routledge

Burn, A and Parker, D (2003) *Analysing Media Texts*, Continuum

Clark, V, Baker, J and Lewis, E (2002) *Key Concepts and Skills for Media Studies*, Hodder & Stoughton

Cook, P and Bernink, M (1999) *The Cinema Book* (2nd edn), BFI

Gauntlett, D and Horsley, R (eds) (2004) *Web Studies* (2nd edn), Arnold

Hart, A (1991) *Understanding the Media: a practical guide*, Routledge

Hayward, S (2000) *Cinema Studies: the key concepts* (2nd edn), Routledge

Holland, P (1997) *The Television Handbook*, Routledge

Konigsberg, I (1987) *The Complete Film Dictionary*, Bloomsbury

McKay, J (2000) *Magazines Handbook*, Routledge

Masterman, L (1990) *Teaching the Media*, Routledge

Nelmes, J (ed.) (1996) *An Introduction to Film Studies* (2nd edn), Routledge

Orlebar, J (2003) *The Practical Media Dictionary*, Arnold

O'Sullivan, T, Dutton, B and Rayner, P (1994) *Studying the Media*, Hodder Arnold

Scott, J, Marshall G (2005) *A Dictionary of Sociology*, Oxford University Press

Watson, J and Hill (2003) A *Dictionary of Media and Communication Studies* (6th edn), Arnold